Evolving Security Dynamic in West Asia and India's Challenges

Add

EVOLVING SECURITY DYNAMIC IN WEST ASIA AND INDIA'S CHALLENGES

Edited by

Ambassador Anil Trigunayat (IFS Retd)

Vivekananda International Foundation
New Delhi

PENTAGON PRESS LLP

Evolving Security Dynamic in West Asia and India's Challenges
Edited by: Ambassador Anil Trigunayat

ISBN 978-93-90095-59-9

First Published in 2022

Published by
PENTAGON PRESS LLP
206, Peacock Lane, Shahpur Jat
New Delhi-110049
Phones: 011-64706243, 26491568
Telefax: 011-26490600
email: rajan@pentagonpress.in
website: www.pentagonpress.in

Printed at Aegean Offset Printers, Greater Noida, U.P.

To
Anu and Akankhsha

Contents

Foreword

West Asia, also known as the Middle East, has for long been central to global politics. The region, which has seen several wars in this century, the rise of terrorism with global reach, unprecedented anti-regime protests during the Arab Spring and several civil wars, continues to retain its global importance due to its geographic location at the intersection of three continents and as the most significant supplier of hydrocarbons to the world.

The region is in great flux. Even as the historical problems remain unresolved, new power equations are emerging. For the last decade and more, the USA, which is critical to the security of the region, has been struggling to find the right balance in its security commitment to the Middle East and the Indo-Pacific. US vacillation has created deep uncertainty in the minds of its regional allies. The Russian role in the regional security has grown greatly since its intervention in Syria in 2015. The Russian war in Ukraine will have a deep global and regional impact. Its outcome will influence the reshaping of the post-pandemic world order and the Middle East.

By concluding the Abraham Accords, Israel has initiated the process of transforming its relationships with core Arab countries. This has diluted the salience of the Palestinian question as several countries look towards improving relations with Israel. The Iranian nuclear question remains unresolved. Iranian-Israeli hostilities remain deep-rooted and unrelenting. Turkey is playing an increasingly assertive and ambitious role in the Middle East as it turns into an overtly Islamic country.

Oil prices are rising and, if President Putin is to be believed, they might even touch $ 300 a barrel, which will be disastrous for the emerging economies that are highly dependent on imports of oil and gas. Europe is facing the prospect of high energy prices if Russian supplies are discontinued. High energy prices could derail the fragile global economy, which is already reeling under the impact of COVID. It remains to be seen if this would propel the USA to conclude a nuclear deal with Iran so that Iranian oil and gas could flow to global markets.

China's deepening footprint in the region and acquisition of strategic assets in West Asia will have far-reaching consequences, especially for India with which it indulges in a zero-sum game. Both India and China are the biggest clients of oil- and gas-producing countries. Hence, at some point in time, at least in the medium term, their competition is likely to be accentuated as both of them race to greater economic prosperity. As China gains strategic access through various ports in Oman, Djibouti, Iran and even the UAE and Israel, it will be incumbent upon Indian policy makers to factor these into their Indo-Pacific strategy for which the western Indian ocean will acquire greater significance. Hence, time is of essence to convert the strategic partnerships with regional powers to a new level by enhancing and encouraging their stake holding in Indian development opportunity.

India has made determined efforts to reach out to all West Asian countries including Iran. The transformation of India's relations with key regional countries is a story worth telling. The West Asian countries have also changed their outlook and are today looking to harness the economic and technological potential of a rising India. They no longer see ties with India through the narrow prism of their ties with Pakistan. They see India as a rising power worth enormous potential. India's ties with the West Asian countries are driven by the expectations of economic and security benefits.

I am delighted that Ambassador Anil Trigunayat embarked on this edited volume on developments in West Asia and choices for India to which leading strategic thinkers and experts have contributed their wisdom and analysis of trends and likely outcomes in the region. Their projections on the evolving horizon and security implications make a compelling argument. As the regional countries come out of the impact of the pandemic, the major regional players are beginning to understand that rapprochement is better than rancour and conflict: a new collaborative matrix and a regional security architecture may emerge which will be beneficial for global peace. The authors have provided useful suggestions for consideration by Indian policy makers as they deal with the emerging challenges.

Dr. Arvind Gupta
Director
Vivekananda International Foundation

Preface

West Asia is in a flux. It has always been the arena of geo-politics, geo-economics, and geo-religious contestations. Internal dynamic among regional majors has been driven by wooing external actors and powers that further complicated the intra-regional contestations. Besides events like external interventions and Arab Spring, *sui generis* or engineered, not only removed the well-entrenched dictators but also created dangerous hotspots like Libya, Yemen, and Syria. These also spawned the ultra-terror groups like the ISIS (Daesh) that is far more sophisticated in its outreach and use of modern communication tools to propagate violence and Takfiri ideologies through a well-orchestrated recruitment spreading its tentacles far and wide, as most extremist and terror groups often work as a syndicate. The impact was also felt by the rich Gulf monarchies that had acted as a conduit and sometimes the accelerators for the external interventions that not only subsided the onslaught of public dissatisfaction through doles but also were forced to unleash socio-economic reforms in their respective countries. This was also activated by the impact of the pandemic, lower oil revenues and fungibility of these assets. Therefore, Vision 2030 became a marker of significant changes, diversifying the economies and society through some fundamental reforms in countries like Saudi Arabia and the UAE. Militarization of the foreign policies of the UAE, Qatar, Saudi Arabia, and Turkey is witnessing a hiatus. Hankering for some *modus vivendi* is visible as the reality of the withdrawal or inefficacy of US security cover hits their Arab allies post the Afghanistan exit and re-focus on the Indo-Pacific. The Abraham Accords and their likely expansion may become the new normal, especially in the Sunni world, if somehow, the Palestinian question is managed judiciously, and the historic wrongs are addressed on priority. But simultaneously, we are witnessing a new realignment of forces and ideologies concurrent with a regional and global outlook as the CRIPTAQ (China, Russia, Iran, Pakistan, Turkey, and Afghanistan with Qatar on the periphery) acquires salience. Doha, courtesy a blockade by the Quartet of Saudi Arabia, the UAE, Bahrain and Egypt for support to the Muslim Brotherhood and extremist groups, used the opportunity to exploit the fault lines with Iran and Turkey but eventually became a 'Go To' country for the West and others in the context of the Taliban and Afghanistan as well as between the USA and Iran as it enhanced their international profile. Again, indulging in smart diplomacy, it has become a country for gas supplies to Europe should the Russia-Ukraine conflict escalate to war. No wonder, having hosted the largest US airbase in the region, it has been designated as a non-NATO ally. Therefore, it may have better traction as a bridge or diplomatic conduit for many a conflictual situation in the region and elsewhere. It comprises a grouping of countries having an anti-US stance, despite their divergent approaches and undercurrents, to a great extent either in a geopolitical matrix or regional compulsions. This could create a potential two informal bloc grouping in West Asia.

The Middle East is India's extended neighbourhood and whatever happens there has a direct impact on India's wellbeing. The relationship with the region has been historic and civilizational but for several decades was driven by the Pakistani Islamic factor and transactional attitudes on both sides. India depends critically on the region for her energy security, maritime connectivity, food security, and Diaspora welfare. India, which has excellent bilateral relations with nearly all countries in the region, will have to contend with a new reality and not only the one she will face with the Chinese BRI wrapping around its neck. During the past decade, India has been successfully able to move the relationship to a much higher orbit than the strategic partnership that has begun to deliver dividends from defence and security in all its ramifications to focused economic enterprise and non-traditional areas with greater appreciation of mutual concerns. As such, extraneous factors like US sanctions, CAATSA, etc., adversely impacted on India's relations with Iran as well as its strategic connectivity aspirations through the Chabahar port. The revival of the Iran nuclear deal could be a positive development if the hardliner Raisi and the Khamenei regime and Biden's 'Back to Basics' and broadly equanimous outreach to the region are able to find a reasonable common ground. In the meantime, New Delhi has embarked on a sub-regional cooperation in the so-called 'New Quad or Quartet' with the UAE, Israel and the USA—all three of whom are her close strategic partners, which could provide a new techno-economic pedestal for harnessing mutual synergies and can have greater potential if leveraged with a vision. However, the major regional powers have their own security agendas and foreign policy priorities, which would have to be aligned in concert for optimum and durable outcomes.

It is with these trends in mind that this compendium was envisaged. Therefore, **Section I** explores the super power syndrome, rivalries and their own policies, limitations and outreaches; **Section II** examines the intra-regional dynamic and likely scenarios within the ambit of the big power rivalry apart from their own internal aches and pains; and **Section III** looks at the likely impact of these developments for India and a possible way forward as the region looks to India for playing a role commensurate with its status since hedging the bets may not be viable for too long.

I am indeed grateful for the excellent and in-depth analysis and contributions by a highly acclaimed set of distinguished West Asia experts and researchers who have made a name for themselves. Likewise, I am thankful to Dr. Arvind Gupta, Director, Vivekananda International Foundation—a leading foreign and security policy think tank in India, for supporting this venture. Hopefully, this compendium will provide a little more clarity on the intricate issues to policy makers and readers alike as every author has also suggested some options for India.

As West Asia, especially the oil-rich Gulf states are trying to cope with gradual US re-focus away from the region towards the Indo-Pacific and the Biden Administration's somewhat equanimous approach towards major players and quest for return to JCPOA, **James M. Dorsey** argues that it may not be bad for the region. The new thinking in Washington articulated in US President Joe Biden's *de facto* enunciation of a new doctrine that rejects wars involving large numbers of ground troops in favour of smaller more pinpointed and technologically cutting-edge operations has far-reaching consequences for the Gulf. The Gulf states are likely to discover that they are stuck with a less committed USA with few other options. Afghanistan has cemented Central Asia as opposed to the Middle East as Russia and China's primary security concern.

He further argues that reality will push the Gulf states to compensate for uncertainty about the USA with greater self-reliance and strengthening of formal and informal regional alliances, particularly with Israel and potentially with Europe. That may not be all bad news. Already, in anticipation of a Biden doctrine coupled with doubts about Russian and Chinese willingness to replace the USA as the region's security guarantor, the Gulf states have begun to dial back tensions with their Middle Eastern rivals. Reducing tensions would allow the Gulf states to contain threats in ways that would enable them to take greater responsibility more confidently for their own security.

China has been quietly expanding its BRI network and digital and health silk route initiatives in the region from Tehran to Tel Aviv. In Chapter II, **Dr. N. Janardhan** analyzes China's increasing footprint and its policy towards the region, which will have far-reaching consequences mentioning that China's Afghanistan strategy gives a peek into its proactive economic, diplomatic and security strategies in West Asia, which could potentially shape Beijing's global security policy in the future. Given its primary consideration for safeguarding and promoting its own economic interests, it is exploring tactics that include conflict 'management' instead of 'resolution' and promoting a 'non-conflictual' relationship between China's strategic partners in the region, especially in the Gulf, who are deeply divided and involved in proxy wars. This strategy is directly linked to the Belt and Road Initiative that links China's energy and trade ties with the rest of the world, including South Asia, and is assuming a security dynamic. This poses direct and indirect challenges—as well as opportunities—to India's thriving socio-economic-security relations with the region and its pre-eminent role in the Indian Ocean. He further explores China's multi-dimensional advances in the region, its implications for India and suggests potential policy options for New Delhi's consideration. He specifically advocates a Sino-Indian collaborative approach in the region to the extent possible.

In the next chapter on Russia's Growing Influence in the Middle East, I argue that the outcome of the Ukrainian conflict will possibly define the credibility and role of Russia in West Asia and North Africa.

In Chapter 4, Prof. K.P. Vijaylakshmi gives a historic tour d' horizon of US presence in West Asia and how its engagement has evolved. She argues that using the "twin pillar" strategy, it maintained close ties with both Saudi Arabia and Israel as the security-energy dynamics was at the core of its Middle East policy.

In **Section II**, presenting the Arab perspective and its historic rise from nationhood to statehood and the role of colonial and external powers in the West Asian security dynamic, **Dr. Waiel Awwad** underscores that the struggle for the control of the Arab world has been continuing for centuries because of its natural rich resources and strategic political geography that connects the East with the West through a natural corridor between three continents. Hence, it is for economic and political reasons that are the main attraction for colonial European powers. They ensured that this region remained weak, divided, and easy to ride. The USA continued the legacy of colonial European powers post World War II, when the whole world was held at ransom for the outcome of the US election to draw its own policy. This was more evident after the collapse of the Soviet Union and the US dominance of the world. The Arab world paid the price after the attack on the twin towers (11 September 2001) and remains at the receiving end of further division based on ethnic and religious lines and ensures that the Arab Gulf will continue to be the main dumping market for American goods and weapons. He further argues that Biden's Administration is trying to redraw its policy toward the region from Saudi Arabia to Iran, Afghanistan, Pakistan, and Turkey by including other countries into the Arab region, turning it into a laboratory to annihilate its unique identity of an Arabic and Islamic culture into a New Middle East and North Africa Order (MENA), the project for the New Middle East, floated by Israel and adopted blindly by the US administration. Hence, it makes the region more of a heterogeneous region by drawing a new common security order that serves US-Israel objectives and destroys any regime opposed to US interests.

Iran has seen transition from a moderate to a hardline more conservative regime under the presidency of Ebrahim Raisi, said to be close to the spiritual leader, Ayatollah Khamenei, and his possible successor. Many argue that for regional leaders there is a predictability in dealing with them. **Prof. Kingshuk Chatterjee** highlights the view from Tehran and how it will pan out with the withdrawal of the USA. The Islamic Republic of Iran is looking forward to an era (which indeed may never come) when Uncle Sam would stop casting his shadow on the region, leaving it to its own devices. They recognise that US withdrawal is almost certain to bring about a period of considerable uncertainty, and find themselves suitably placed for the political vacuum to gain a kind of leverage in the region's politics that Iran has not had for more than a century or two. There is, however, a recognition in certain circles that during such a period of transition, a lot of things can go wrong. Hence, many within the establishment have been advising caution to the revolutionary regime. How the regime responds is likely to be determined by a complicated interplay of domestic and foreign developments that are not very easy to anticipate accurately. He attempts to furnish a sense of the vista of the neighbourhood as it appears to the regime in Tehran, contextualising the prospect of the steady but seemingly irrevocable US withdrawal from the Middle East and then goes on to plot the consequent relative ascendancy of the Islamic Republic in the politics of the region. The essay then purports to assess the chances of this ascendancy being thwarted by the sanctions regime as much as the other powers of the region concerned with the steady rise of Tehran's profile in the regional politics. He then weighs in the China factor in the equation, and closes with the possible hand that India can play urging that if the nuclear talks fail, India, under pressure from USA disengaging further from Tehran, may yield the remainder of the space to China.

Israel, since 1948, as it celebrates its 75th anniversary, has remained the cornerstone of US foreign policy in the region. It is nuclear, hi-tech and a democracy at odds with the Arab and Islamic world on account of the nearly century old Palestinian conflict. But with the Trump Administration's efforts it has been able to wean away some key Arab countries, who themselves have developed some kind of a fatigue for the Palestinian cause. **Prof. Kumaraswamy** dwells on the changing Israeli landscape as Tehran and her nuclear ambitions remain the major cause of Israeli foreign and security policy. He says that now the Arab core is not only friendly towards Israel but also shares Israel's concerns vis-à-vis Iran. This enabled Israel to reverse the diplomacy of the periphery and join hands with key Arab neighbours against Iran, Bahrain and UAE directly and Saudi Arabia indirectly. Interestingly, Israel could do this without making any significant concessions to or accommodation with the Palestinians as manifested through the Abraham Accords and their aftermaths. Talking about the Mini QUAD in West Asia with the UAE, the USA, India and Israel, he avers that the continuing Israeli focus on Iran would undermine India's ability to pursue a robust policy towards Iran. This demands an India evolving and establishing a *modus vivendi*; Israeli inability to support India over China is not different from Indian inability to support Israel over Iran. If the Middle Eastern Quad had to succeed and flourish, an Indo-Israeli understanding and accommodation over China and Iran, respectively, will be inevitable.

Turkey has emerged as another pole in the region especially under President Erdogan who is said have the ambition of reviving 'neo-Ottomanism' and be a contestant for leadership of the Islamic world. It showed bold foreign policy moves from Libya to the Levant and from the Mediterranean to the Nagorno Karabakh. Its chequered relationship with the West, being a NATO member, and with Russia having made the country a force to reckon with. **Prof. Omair Anas** discusses the basic contours of Turkey's foreign policy in West Asia. The changing character of Turkey's economy, regional, and security roles and Turkey's domestic politics of new demographic ambitions are also shaping Turkish regional policy and politics. Neither the region is the same as it was a decade ago, nor is the international system the same in which Erdogan and his AK party had scripted the policy of Zero Problem and Strategic Depth. He argues that West Asian countries are looking at Turkey's troubled relations both as a problem and an opportunity. There are four fault lines in which Turkey is to craft its policy toward the region; first, the Arab uprisings as a continuity of anti-regime sentiments in the region; second, Israel's expansionist policies; third, Iran and Turkey as two non-Arab countries but increasingly involved in the region, and fourth, the world powers' changing perspectives towards the region.

Palestine has remained unresolved and it is a fact that peace in the region will remain precarious until the issue is resolved. But over time, the Arab world does not seem to be very sanguine in its support even as the Palestinian movement itself remains divided between Ramallah and Gaza. The Trump Administration's success in achieving the Abraham Accords has further distanced the dream. **Dr Sahar Am Al Majali** reiterates that the tender balance of peace in the Middle East hinges on the most heaviest and burdensome problem of the question of Palestine which has evaded a permanent solution for the past five-and-a-half decades mainly due to the intransigence of Israel to implement the relevant resolutions of the United Nations calling for recognition of the inalienable rights of the Arab Palestinians in peace, particularly in the West Bank. The Palestinians and their Arab compatriots have gone to the farthest end to accommodate Israel by recognizing it and establishing diplomatic relations with it with the hope that it would vacate the West Bank and allow the State of Palestine to thrive in peace. Despite the advisory opinion of the International Court of Justice (ICJ) for demolition of the wall in the West Bank, Israel has not heeded the call of the sane international opinion and continues to defy all ethical and legal norms to deny the Palestinians their inalienable rights to live in peace.

The economy is the crux and so is the geo-politics of oil in the region. How the post-pandemic recovery and equity in wealth distribution and socio-economic reforms will take place, as the regional majors are diversifying their economies from oil-driven to non-oil based spectrum, may have a much greater impact on the overall health of the region and elsewhere. **Dr. Jawad Anani** deals with the various dimensions of economic drivers and constraints as he underlines the main challenges and opportunities which western Asian countries will have to grapple with in their transition to more productive, equitable and sustainable states. All Arab countries which are members of the ESCNA (Economic and Social Council of Western Asia) are going through exogenously and endogenously imposed pressures to change and adopt reform measures. These measures are political, social, economic and cultural in nature.

The Red Sea has emerged a great deal more significant as the regional geo-economic contestations gain ground. Hence, it could easily turn into a major conflict zone. **Dr. Michael Barak** argues that the increase in the Red Sea's geostrategic, security and economic importance not only increases competition for influence and hegemony in the region but also strengthens the threshold of tension between the state actors. Moreover, Islamic terrorists, especially the Houthis in Yemen, identify the naval arena as another front of struggle against their rivals. The threat of terrorism and the proliferation of interests of countries in the region could turn the Red Sea region into a multi-system conflict arena. Regional cooperation between Israel, Egypt, Sudan, Saudi Arabia, and the United Arab Emirates is a guarantee for maintaining security and economic stability in the region. India's accession to this alliance will significantly contribute to its resilience and it will be able to deter terrorists and subversive players such as Iran and Turkey.

In **Section III,** effort has been made by the contributors to look at the security related challenges in the Indian context and specific references to collaboration with Israel and Turkey as well as India's defence and maritime security considerations that have been identified and suggestions for policy choices and next steps offered.

India-Israel relations in the past 25 years have moved from strength to strength becoming truly strategic in character and scope as India began her dehyphenated policy especially with regard to bilateral relations while following her principled stand on Palestinian issue and advocating for peace and dialogue in the region. **Nina Slama** argues that after more than four decades since the inception of the Jewish State in 1948, India and Israel established full diplomatic relations in 1992. Both countries are strategic partners and cooperate extensively in a wide range of sectors. Different dynamics in West Asia influence the scope of these relations. The eruption of the Arab Spring and the signing of the Abraham Accords allowed India and Israel to extend their relations by collaborating with other regional partners such as Bahrain and the United Arab Emirates. She also presents India-Israel relations during Prime Minister Narendra Modi's tenure and suggests ways to further expand them in the context of a challenging dynamic in West Asia.

Turkey and India's relations have often been seen through the Pakistani prism as the Turkish leadership did not show adequate sensitivity to India's concerns and its forays at international fora like the UNGA and OIC on the Kashmir issue that are considered inimical to India's strategic interests and sovereignty concerns and even as interference in internal affairs. It has resulted in non-optimal utilization of the full potential of the relationship despite obvious complementariness and historic connect. **Dr. Duygu Çağla Bayram and Prof. Dr. Hüseyin Bagci** argue that Turkey, which is the Westernmost Asian and the Easternmost European country, intends to maintain its role as the Asian in the West and the European in the East by keeping to participate in the European integration process as well as protecting its key position in the NATO on one side, and by reinventing its strong connection with Asia through the Asia Anew Initiative. They further reiterate in this quest that Turkey knows very well that it cannot afford an "either India or Pakistan" policy. Besides, Turkey never saw its close relations with Pakistan as well as India affecting each other ever. The Indo-Turkish relationship, therefore, should not be a prisoner of external issues that means India and Turkey should look directly at each other in their bilateral relations, as this relation is also a standalone relation.

Defence cooperation is an integral part of the strategic dimension of India's burgeoning ties with the countries in West Asia that have been taken to a higher orbit in recent years as the security landscape in the volatile region deteriorates and geo-political competition heightens with the US withdrawal. **Lt Gen Rakesh Sharma,** while delving deep into the current initiatives and historic context, maintains that though India's defence-related interactions with the Middle East date back to 1971, when Israel supplied mortars and ammunition to India during its war with Pakistan, formal memorandums of understanding (MoUs) on defence cooperation, with the region, were first signed only in 2001 (with Iran). Gradually, New Delhi signed agreements on defence and security cooperation with five other major countries in the region, such as the UAE (2003), Qatar (2008), Saudi Arabia (2014), Oman (2016) and Jordan (2018). Contextually, hence defence relationships stand elevated to credible levels, adding to strategic partnerships that include economy and trade, expatriates and energy. But, India's defence dialogues have yet to mature with the West Asian nations.

Maritime security is a major challenge especially as India's trading lanes and energy security are factors of regional stability and benign competition in West Asia. The emergence of the Indo-Pacific as a new theatre of competition predicates that India shores up its maritime assets and presence especially in the western Indian Ocean to secure her own strategic interests. **Vice Admiral Satish Soni** argues that the impending dilution of US military presence could trigger a power struggle amongst aspiring powers. Turkey, Iran, Russia, China, India, and the European countries amongst others, are jostling for influence to deepen existing partnerships with the littorals. Non-traditional challenges, economic dependencies and 'grey zone' warfare are the new-age challenges to the global arteries for energy and other resources. India's dependence on Gulf crude and the presence of more than eight million Diaspora in the region makes the area significant with regard to our national maritime interests. It may no longer be in India's interests to remain a mere bystander to the developments in our extended neighbourhood. It may be time for India to 'Act West'.

In the end, without sounding repetitive, I have suggested some next steps that India could consider in its quest for West Asia.

Anil Trigunayat

SECTION I

The Super Power Dynamic

1

New Biden Doctrine Not All Bad News for the Gulf

James M. Dorsey

ABSTRACT

The rise of the Biden Administration and, more recently, its chaotic withdrawal from Afghanistan has revived the debate about American foreign policy, particularly in the Middle East, and the assumptions that underlie it. New thinking in Washington articulated in Joe Biden's de facto enunciation of a new doctrine that rejects wars involving large numbers of ground troops in favour of smaller more pinpointed and technologically cutting-edge operations has far-reaching consequences for the Gulf. The Gulf States discovered that they were stuck with a less committed USA and few other options. They also recognized that the US withdrawal cemented Central Asia as opposed to the Middle East as Russia and China's primary security concern.

That reality pushed the Gulf States to compensate for uncertainty about the USA with greater self-reliance and strengthening of formal and informal regional alliances, particularly with Israel and potentially with India and Europe. That may not be all bad news. Already, in anticipation of a Biden doctrine coupled with doubts about Russian and Chinese willingness to replace the USA as the region's security guarantor, the Gulf States have begun to dial back tensions with their Middle Eastern rivals. Reducing tensions would allow the Gulf States to contain threats in ways that would enable them to take greater responsibility for their own security more confidently and forge alliances with regional powers such as Israel and India.

New Kid on the Block

A debate about the fundamentals of US foreign policy erupted just months after US President Joe Biden introduced a more multilateral approach that broke with the isolationist, "America First" strategy of his predecessor, Donald J. Trump. The debate was informed by the fact that Trump's black-and-white picture of the world had persuaded him to support US allies in the Middle East uncritically and unconditionally.

The debate was fuelled by the arrival in Washington of the latest kid on the block, the Quincy Institute for Responsible Statecraft, founded in 2019 with the goal of challenging the notion that the USA should serve as global policeman and that a failure to do so, as in Afghanistan, is a sign of weakness and decline. Quincy also sought to break the militarised mould in which US foreign policy had increasingly been cast.

The institute, funded by libertarian businessman Charles Koch and liberal philanthropist George Soros, and, headed by Andrew J. Bacevich, a conservative Catholic historian who served in the US Army and the 1991 Gulf war, promotes a "foreign policy that emphasises military restraint and diplomatic engagement and cooperation with other nations (that) will serve American interests and values better than policies that prioritise the maintenance of US global dominance through force."[1]

Prominent international relations scholars Daniel Deudney and G. John Ikenberry described the institute in a critical essay as an "odd alliance of domestic (US) libertarians, balance-of-power-realists and the anti-imperialist left",[2] schools of thought that have been adversaries for much of their history.

They nonetheless acknowledge the institute's impact on the policy debate in the Biden era. "Given its abundant resources in people, ideas and money, and the salience of its pledge to avoid another Iraq war, the Quincy coalition has appeared well-positioned to help shape US foreign policy and, by extension, the world order," the scholars wrote. They added, however, that the Quincy approach was "fatally flawed" because "its foreign-policy agenda is profoundly outmoded.... A critique of the Iraq blunder during the post-Cold War unipolar moment provides little guidance for conducting American foreign policy in response to cascading global interdependence, democratic backsliding, and a historic strategic challenge from an illiberal great power".[3]

Biden's staunch defence of the withdrawal from Afghanistan, despite the fact that it paved the way for the Taliban's return to power, appeared to reflect, in parallel with Quincy Institute thinking, his long-standing rejection of counter-insurgency as opposed to counter-terrorism notions that had nation-building at its core. The counter-insurgency approach was advocated by former President George W. Bush[4] as well as a class of big picture US military thinkers such as former generals, David Petraeus and Stanley McChrystal. "They wanted to try a large-scale counter-insurgency program in Afghanistan and suggested that (President Barak Obama) could then withdraw safely toward the end of his first term," noted Middle East scholar Juan Cole.[5] As vice-president, Biden, convinced that the generals were wrong and that "it was foolish to think we could do anything more than kill terrorists in Afghanistan," often sought advice beyond the military command that was requesting the despatch of additional combat troops, according to Ben Rhodes, who served at that time as the White House's deputy national security advisor.

In his withdrawal speech, Bush made that point. "Our mission in Afghanistan was never supposed to have been nation building. It was never supposed to be creating a unified, centralized democracy. Our only vital national interest in Afghanistan remains today what it has always been: preventing a terrorist attack on American homeland. I've argued for many years that our mission should be narrowly focused on counterterrorism—not counterinsurgency or nation building," Biden said.[6] He was referring to the initial purpose of the 2001 invasion of Afghanistan: the toppling of the Taliban government and destruction of the Al-Qaeda that was hosted by the Afghan group in response to the 9/11 attacks.[7]

Some veterans of US diplomacy suggest that the USA has been hampered in the Middle East by the fact that, for decades, it has reacted to events rather than developed a cohesive policy towards the region. "Despite having formally represented American foreign policy in the Middle East from 1963 through 1998, I cannot with any certainty remember that we ever had a defining overarching policy on the region. My country operated on a patchwork of ideas, interests, and assumptions developed at home and reactions (both considered and not) to whatever was happening anywhere else in the world that might have (or not) any consequences for the region," said Patrick Theros, a former counterterrorism official and ambassador to Qatar.[8]

In what could be part of a gradual paradigm shift in US policy, Middle East defence and security analyst and former Pentagon official, Bilal Y. Saab, argued that the Biden Administration will have to revamp the security aspects of its foreign policy if it wants to truly repair the damage done by the Trump Administration's unilateralism to relations with US allies. "Washington needs to overhaul how it conducts security cooperation. For too long, this enterprise, run mainly by the US Department of Defence since 9/11, has lacked vision, leadership, and organization. It is too narrowly focused on US military sales and tactical and operational support to partners, and (been) insufficiently attentive to the defence governance and institutional enabling mechanisms that allow for the proper employment and sustainment of US military assistance," Saab said.[9]

In Saab's mind, the USA should focus on long-term rather than short term goals such as building stronger, more sustainable ties to Middle Eastern militaries. That, in turn, would reduce the risk of the USA getting distracted from its overriding competition with China and Russia. "Key to this is a determination by US officials not just to train and equip the armed forces and security services of its regional friends, but also to assist them to the extent possible in developing the strategic, institutional, organizational and programmatic fabric of their defence and security sectors. Institutional capacity-building is integral to the success of US security cooperation and assistance programs because it helps partners improve their abilities to oversee, manage and employ human, materiel and financial resources," Saab said.

Former US Middle East peace negotiator Dennis Ross and one-time National Security Council director of Persian Gulf affairs Kenneth M. Pollack concluded from separate visits to US allies in the Middle East that they were seeking to understand what the USA was seeking to achieve in the region. The Middle East "still lacks a clear region-wide strategy that our friends and partners understand.... If Washington is going to overcome that confusion, it will have to articulate an overarching concept that integrates all of the country-specific strategies to accomplish a larger set of goals," Pollack and Ross wrote in a summary of their Middle East tours.[10]

"Absent such a comprehensive strategy, no Middle Eastern state will understand what the USA expects from them, what the USA intends to deliver for them, or what regional end state the USA seeks to create—and whether it is an end state that will meet their own needs. As one high-ranking Middle Eastern leader fretted to us, the USA is signalling to the region, 'Don't follow me, I'm lost'," the two former officials went on to say.

Is America Back?

The notion of a lack of a cohesive policy coupled with concern of the reliability of the USA as an ally was reinforced by the US negotiation with the Taliban and subsequent withdrawal from Afghanistan that allowed the militants to retake control of the country. The negotiations focused on getting the USA out of a two-decade-long forever war with little or no consideration of the consequences for Afghan forces and other US allies in Afghanistan as well as in the Central Asian country's neighbourhood.[11]

As a result, clarity may no longer be enough. The withdrawal sends US allies the same message that the Obama Administration sent in 2011 when it supported change at the expense of America's long-standing autocratic friends such as Egyptian President Hosni Mubarak. It was US support for the popular revolts that toppled Mubarak and three other Arab leaders that spurred countries like Saudi Arabia and the United Arab Emirates to greater assertiveness with at times disastrous consequences as with the Yemen war. That is not to say that support for the uprising was inherently wrong but suggests that it was ill-managed and implemented.

The effect of the withdrawal from Afghanistan was felt far beyond the Middle East, particularly in Asia where various nations have territorial disputes with China and were likely to question the value of their security cooperation with the USA. The withdrawal and collapse of the Afghan government called into question the meaning of Biden's assertion that the USA is back as a leader of the Western world after four years of rejection of multilateralism, isolationism, and a foreign policy driven in part by narcissism during the Trump Administration. The withdrawal, or at least the way it was executed, fed Russian and Chinese portrayals of the USA as a decaying power that cannot be relied upon.

The withdrawal further strengthened the positions articulated by the Quincy Institute and Democratic progressives. Quincy Institute president Andrew Bacevich, a historian and retired career US army officer, argued in a passionate and angry analysis entitled *After the Apocalypse: America's Role in the World Transformed*: "Regardless of whether our self-inflicted apocalypse leads to renewal or further, the USA will find itself obliged to revise the premises informing America's role in the world. Put simply, US policy must change."[12]

Biden's rejection of criticism of the way he withdrew US forces from Afghanistan appeared to acknowledge the need for change. His rejection constituted a rebuttal of the notion that the collapse of the Afghan government and military demonstrated the importance of US military support for its allies. The critics argued that 2,500–3,500 American troops backed by the US air force had stopped the Taliban from gaining ground beyond Afghanistan's rural areas until the President announced a final date for the withdrawal. The question the critics left unanswered was for how long and at what cost. The answer to the question potentially has as far-reaching consequences as the chaos that enveloped Kabul immediately after the collapse of the US-backed government.

Biden also left unaddressed the efficacy of privatization of various functions of the US military that contributed to the collapse of the Afghan security forces. "From the beginning, the USA and NATO partners struggled to develop efficacious training programs. Training concepts and doctrines changed often as different parts of the recruiting and training mission came under different contractors and national oversight," said South Asia scholar C. Christine Fair. Fair argued further that the reliance on defence contractors meant that at least 80 per cent of US$ 144.98 budgeted since 2002 for security training, reconstruction, development and humanitarian aid was boosted the US rather than the Afghan economy.[13] The flow towards the US rather than the Afghan economy meant that Afghan security forces were far too dependent on foreign defence contractors to ensure the creation of an independent police and military that would be able to sustain itself.[14]

A long-standing proponent of a more cohesive US policy in the Middle East, Senator Chris Murphy, the chair of the Senate Foreign Relations Subcommittee on the Near East, South Asia, Central Asia, and Counterterrorism, has laid out elements of a policy that would stroke with the thinking of the Quincy Institute thinking and Democratic progressives but raise ire among some of America's traditional allies.

"The Saudis and Emiratis cooperate with the USA on an awful lot, but they are acting very differently today than they were 30 years ago. They are acting contrary to our interest all over the region, and we should reorient our relationship with those countries so that we aren't empowering their bad behaviour.... What we want is to try to midwife a conversation about a regional security architecture, in which the Iranians and the Saudis and the Emiratis aren't constantly battling with each other through proxy fights," Murphy said.[15]

Much like the progressives, the senator based his proposed approach on the belief that Saudi Arabia and the UAE have nowhere else but the USA to go to when it comes to ensuring their security. "I just think it's time to play hardball with the Saudis. I don't believe this argument that the Saudis are going to walk away from a security alliance with the USA. They will never get from the Chinese nor the Russians what they get from the USA today. Yes, they want more. They want us to be tougher on Iran, but they don't have another potential partner like the USA," Murphy went on to say.

Perhaps, more fundamentally, the senator argued that a revamp of US foreign policy was needed because competition with China in the Middle East and elsewhere in the world was on economics rather than security. "We should learn from the success the Chinese have had, and we should empower (US) agencies...with the kind of economic assets that can be comparable to the Chinese, which right now we can't even imagine as a government. That's in part because no one was ever competing with us on that playing field.... It's not good enough to just offer some ships or some guns. You have to actually be able to offer real development in a way that we can't today," Murphy said.

Translating Murphy's approach into practical steps, the USA could build on the recognition by Arab governments of the need to diversify economies and ensure that they are competitive by helping them fine-tune grandiose plans for change and nudging them towards the judicial, educational and governance reforms that are a prerequisite. Plans like Saudi Arabia's Vision 2030[16] are sweeping but lack a roadmap for implementation that sets priorities and outlines steps for increased labour productivity, stepped-up innovation, and land reform.[17]

Murphy's suggestions may have become more immediately implementable in a Middle East that in response to Trump's fickleness and in a bid to please the former president and Biden's anticipated policy shifts has, by and large, sought to dial down tensions and shift towards a model of competition and cooperation. Four Arab countries—the UAE, Bahrain, Sudan and Morocco—established diplomatic relations with Israel while Trump was still in office. Egypt, Israel, the UAE and Saudi Arabia, countries that are at odds with Turkey, are since seeking to take the sting out of their difference. Saudi Arabia and Iran are holding talks on regional issues mediated by Iraq.

The Biden Administration is seeking to capitalize on its impact with mixed results. Before taking office this year, CIA Director Burns and National Security Advisor Jake Sullivan argued in a 2019 article about Iran that "diplomacy is the best way to test intentions and define the realm of the possible, repair the damage our unilateral turn has inflicted on our international partnerships, and invest in more effective coercion if and when it's needed to focus minds in Tehran."[18] Burns argued separately that year that a reduction of tensions would "depend on the prospects for Saudis and Iranians finding some basis for regional co-existence—built not on trust or the end of rivalry, but on the more cold-blooded assumption that they both have a stake in stable competition."[19] It's a message that most US allies in the Middle East have heard. Israel's covert war with Iran in Syria and on the high seas may be the exception.

Friends Versus Enemies

Debate in Washington about Iran implicitly tackles a key frame of US thinking: the frequent identification of one or more regimes, most notably Iran and more recently China, as *the* rather than *a* threat to regional security. In doing so, US policy is often shaped by the narrow lens of a demonised "enemy" or adversary. "We remain a 'friends versus enemies' society, which is perhaps the most important reason that we have never done balance of power well," said former State Department official and ex-US ambassador to NATO, Robert E. Hunter.[20]

Anatol Lieven, a Quincy Institute scholar who focuses on Russia, Europe, and South Asia, draws three lessons from the last two decades of US policy that were shaped by the 9/11 attacks and reinforced Washington's inclination to think of friends and enemies in black-and-white terms. "The first is not to become so obsessed with the enemy of the particular moment that this drowns out other important interests. Second, the USA should be careful not to allow a belief in the absolute evil of the enemy to justify its own evil actions and support for evil regimes. Third, it is absolutely essential not to lump a range of very different countries and forces in the world into one allegedly homogenous enemy camp," he said.[21]

He identified the 2003 invasion of Iraq, even though it had nothing to do with 9/11, as an example of the pitfalls of US inclinations.

In other words, Lieven was arguing that the problem with the "friends versus enemies" approach is that it encourages policies that are based on a distorted picture of reality. That was evident in conservative criticism of Biden's troop withdrawal from Afghanistan that was rooted in a perception of the Taliban as immutable. The criticism failed to take into account the fact that the current threat of attacks on US soil emanates from the Islamic State rather than Al-Qaeda and that the Taliban and the Islamic State are at odds with each other.[22] "Our enemies are ideologically opposed to Western civilization and will gladly stage another 9/11 if they have the opportunity and means. They are at war with us whether or not we are at war with them," said Republican House of Representatives member Dan Crenshaw.[23]

Pitfalls of US Policy

The pitfalls of US policy in the Middle East are exacerbated by structural problems associated with policy inputs, particularly US embassy cables from various capitals that report on the situation on the ground, which land ultimately in an upper echelon of the State Department that is populated by political appointees, rather than career diplomats.

Too often, cables are ignored by the higher echelons if they portray an on-the-ground picture that is at odds with the prism of a political appointee and/or the Administration. That was evident in reams of cables captured and published by Iranian militants who occupied the US embassy in Tehran in 1979 and held American diplomats hostage for 444 days.[24]

Similarly, Libya, a one-time international pariah in the view of the West, regained favour in the first decade of the 21st century as an ally in the war on terrorism and bulwark against illegal migration to Europe. The USA reverted, however, to its earlier description of Muammar Qaddafi as a 'madman' when he appeared determined to bloodily suppress a 2011 popular uprising with an assault on Benghazi, Libya's opposition-controlled second-largest city.

Diplomacy scholar Pablo de Orellana noted that US diplomats in Libya reported at the time on "vital nuances and warnings about the complex composition of the 'peaceful pro-democracy protesters' and how best to 'mitigate the potential for Islamic extremists and the Al-Qaeda to exploit the transition'. These reports were rarely pursued by the Secretary of State and were de-prioritised across US diplomatic knowledge production. Instead, Secretary (Hillary) Clinton relied on a small circle of informal advisors...who insisted on a simpler view featuring freedom-loving democrats rebelling against a tyrant."[25]

By the same token, US perceptions of Iran resulting as much from perception and politics as from reality on the ground and the ambitions of rival forces in the Islamic Republic have shaped attitudes towards the nuclear accord in both countries.

"The real question is why powerful political forces in the USA opposed the JCPOA from the start. The answer is that these forces do not want the USA to normalise relations with Iran. What they want is that pressure on Iran causes the exacerbation of the country's many problems, including its ethnic fault lines, and eventually leads to its disintegration.... Meanwhile, Iran's hardliners pay no attention to the country's national as opposed to revolutionary objectives and, by continuing to insist on untenable positions, they contribute to Iran's drift towards growing internal discord and, potentially, disintegration," said the Iran scholar and former Iranian diplomat Shireen Hunter.[26]

Her assertion is bolstered by the fact that the USA has not sought to engage Middle Eastern states in the creation of a regional security architecture which, in the words of her husband, Robert E. Hunter, a former State Department official, would "help to channel relationships, even adversarial relationships, in directions that could reduce the risk of conflict by increasing the capacity to predict the cost-benefit ratios of conflict.[27]

America's National Interest

At the core of the divergence between the analysis of the Quincy Institute on the one hand and Dr. Levitt and other proponents of a continued significant US military presence in the Middle East on the other lies a debate about what constitutes America's interest in the region. Political scientist Eugene Gholz argued in an earlier paper published by the Quincy Institute that US military objectives in the region should be limited to preventing the establishment of a regional hegemon and protecting the flow of oil through the Strait of Hormuz.[28]

Countering this definition, former US Defence Department official William F. Wechsler cautioned, in a paper published by the Atlantic Council, days after the release of the Quincy report against narrow definitions that underestimated the threat posed by Iran and failed to include US value-based interests.[29] Wechsler's paper did not mention Gholz or the Quincy Institute by name. Instead, it was framed as a response to a commentary[30] published by the Council on the same day as Wechsler's paper, in which two of his colleagues argued in favour of a US military drawdown in the Middle East along lines similar to Gholz's.

Wechsler insisted that US interests included "promoting democratic transitions, advancing human rights, combating corruption, providing humanitarian relief, and ending local military conflicts. These omissions are notable, as it would strain credulity to assert that the USA would be well-positioned to influence these interests after being seen as withdrawing from the region." Wechsler mirrored Deudney and Ikenberry's criticism that the Quincy approach would "diminish the prospects for liberal democracy and human rights globally."[31]

At the same time, Wechsler's rejection of the notion of a US withdrawal from the Middle East appeared to acknowledge that promotion of US value-based interests has more often than not served to pressure countries like Iran, which are defined by Washington as hostile, rather than as a yardstick that applies to all. "Rather than seek a near-total withdrawal from the region, which would once again upend the *status quo*, the USA should seek to return to the traditional US role of protecting and restoring that *status quo* while pushing for incremental improvements in regional security, prosperity, and general welfare," he cautioned.

The irony is that the facts on the ground suggest that US policy is to fortify rather than diminish America's presence in the Middle East. "When the USA chose to prioritise its limited defence assets towards the Indo-Pacific...the Gulf actually increased in importance. It was and remains one of the few areas where the USA has established bases to project power into the Indian Ocean...in recent years, the USA returned combat troops to Saudi Arabia for the first time since 2003. As the Afghan withdrawal winds down and the Biden Administration talks about 'over the horizon' support, ask yourself what bases exist 'over the horizon,'' said a prominent Gulf scholar.[32]

Former Trump national security and intelligence officials. Robert C. O'Brien and John Ratcliffe take the analysis of the Gulf scholar and Wechsler a step further. They argued that rather than reviewing US foreign policy wholesale, the Biden Administration will have to double down on a security-driven Indo-Pacific approach if it wants to repair the damage done by the Afghanistan withdrawal. The two men suggested that as the Afghanistan debacle unfolded the Biden Administration should expedite arms sales to Taiwan, redeploy to the Indo-Pacific troops withdrawn from the Central Asian state, revive the US naval base on American Samoa, and forward base in Australia and deploy the United States' only heavy icebreaker to shorten the distance it travels to Antarctica each year.[33]

Beyond defining the objectives of US policy, the truth in the differences between the Quincy Institute and Levitt's and Wechsler's analysis may lie in the middle. Their differences, for example, on the ultimate purpose of Iran's employment of proxies appear to constitute two sides of the same coin. Supporting proxies representing marginalised or disgruntled communities that have a popular base and are opposed to the *status quo* in countries where the state is weak or fragile is a pillar of Iranian foreign and defence policy. So is the opposite: supporting the *status quo* in those countries where Iranian proxies have emerged as powerful forces, like Lebanon and Iraq, even if the popular mood has turned against them.[34]

The Quincy Institute call for a paradigm shift in thinking about the Middle East and/or Iran takes on added significance in the light of debates about the sustainability of the Iranian clerical regime. Despite the resilience demonstrated by Iran over the decades, the country's detractors in the USA, as well as American allies in the Middle East, cling to the notion that the regime is teetering on the brink of collapse, and that continued pressure and sanctions will push it over the edge.

Several Iranian Americans sponsored by the Washington-based Institute for Voices of Liberty (iVOL) visited Israel in July 2021 in a manifestation of that hope, as part of the organisation's effort "to promote democracy, human rights, and freedom in Iran after the prospective collapse of the Islamist regime".[35] Erfan Fard, an activist and independent counterterrorism scholar, suggested that the visit "could lay the basis for a future relationship between Israel and Iran after the collapse of the ayatollahs' dictatorship".[36]

The hope was bolstered by protests in the Iranian province of

Khuzestan that were sparked by water shortages.[37] "Khamenei is on fire...the mullahs' regime is reeling," headlined Okaz, a Saudi newspaper that hews close to government thinking.[38]

Throwing cold water on the notion that the clerics' roots have been sufficiently uprooted to anticipate a change, widely respected Iran expert Karim Sadjadpour argues that the Iranian regime could have a shelf life of at least another generation.[39]

Sadjadpour drew a comparison with the Soviet Union. "Post-Soviet Russia...didn't transition from the Soviet Union to a democratic Russia, but it essentially became a new form of authoritarianism which took Communism and replaced it with grievance-driven Russia nationalism—led by someone from the ancient regime and a product of the KGB, Vladimir Putin," Sadjadpour argued.

"Likewise, if I had to make a prediction on Iran, I think that the next prominent leader is less likely to be an ageing cleric—like an Ayatollah Khamenei or Ebrahim Raisi—and more likely to be someone who is a product of either the Revolutionary Guards or Iran's intelligence services. Instead of espousing Shia nationalism, they will substitute that with Iranian nationalism—or Persian nationalism," he goes on to say.

Sadjadpour's prediction is shared by a growing number of Iran scholars. "A faction of right-wing leaders has the opportunity to reshape Iran's politics and society in ways that will expand the IRGC's control over the country's economy, further diminish political freedoms, and yet display limited tolerance on religious and social issues. It will champion Iranian nationalism to widen its popular base domestically, while relying on Shiite and anti-American ideologies to project power regionally," echoed international affairs analyst Mohammad Ayatollahi Tabaar.[40]

In that vein, Raisi's election campaign, as well as debates on social media, may be harbingers of a more nationalist, less religious, policy approach that is designed to create greater popular support for transition from Shia nationalism. Raisi promised to fight domestic violence and pledged to discourage the much-despised morality police from harassing ordinary people and to encourage them to instead go after economic and bureaucratic corruption. Images released by his campaign suggested that his supporters included women who did not follow the strict official dress code.

Other hardliners have struck a similar tone. Conservative activist Masoud Dehnamaki, known for his denunciation of reformists as 'un-Islamic,' declared in a recent debate on the Clubhouse chat app that compulsory veiling was no longer a serious concern for the regime.[41]

Opportunity Presents Itself

An Iranian nationalist regime could potentially contribute to regional stability. It would likely see groups like the Hezbollah, militias in Iraq, and the Houthi as liabilities rather than assets. That would reduce the threat of Iranian meddling in the domestic affairs of various Arab countries.

Already differences have emerged between Iran and some of its proxies in Iraq as well as among the militias themselves. At the same time, anti-Iranian public sentiment in Iraq is on the rise and Iran's ability to influence the Iraqi government is diminishing.

Iran's declining influence was evident during Quds Force commander Esmail Qaani's recent visit to Baghdad. He encountered unusual blowback when he asked pro-Iranian Iraqi militia leaders to refrain from attacking US targets until the nuclear talks were concluded. One militia commander insisted that they could not do so as long as the killing in January 2020 by the USA of Gen. Qaani's predecessor, Qassim Soleimani, and Abu Mahdi al-Muhandis, a senior Iraqi militia commander, remained unavenged.[42]

An official of the Kata'ib Hezbollah, the militia led by the late Al-Muhandis, warned in response to the announcement of a US combat troop withdrawal that an American failure to keep its promise would mean confrontation. "We may have a decision that is effectively independent of Iran, and this complicates things," the official said.[43]

The differences between Iran and some militia leaders speak to a more fundamental divergence that could open the door to the kind of relationship with Iran that the USA is seeking with China: strategic competition, coupled with cooperation in areas where the two countries' interests converge. That is if the USA does not repeat its mistake of two decades ago when it failed to exploit opportunities created by Iranian help in bringing Afghan President Hamid Karzai to office in the wake of the US invasion, and Syrian cooperation with the US war on terror in the immediate aftermath of 9/11.

A similar opportunity may be presenting itself in Iraq now. Iraqi Shiite leaders, including Ayatollah Ali Sistani, the country's most respected cleric, powerful nationalist political and religious leader Moqtada al-Sadr and Hadi al-Amiri, head of the Iran-backed Badr Organization, have embraced the fact that the USA will withdraw combat troops from Iraq by the end of this year but keep a sizeable force in the country to train their Iraqi counterparts, share intelligence, and provide other support.[44] Al-Amiri's support, in particular, appears to signal that Iran does not reject a continued US training and advisory role.

The divergence between Iran and some of the Iraqi groups fleshes out the notion of Middle East scholar Thomas Juneau that the widely-held belief in the USA that the concept of an Iranian proxy means absolute control and subservience to the interests of the Islamic Republic may be inaccurate. Dr. Juneau draws his conclusion from studying the relationship between Iran and the Houthi rebels in Yemen. The notion that "the Houthis are Iran's proxy, with the bigger power using the smaller actor to advance its own purposes...is, at best, only part of the story: the Houthis use their ties with Iran to advance their own interests as much as the reverse," he said.[45]

The shades of grey in the analysis of facts on the ground in Iraq and Yemen, coupled with Sadjadpour's prognosis, the Quincy Institute reports, and Postel's paper altogether suggest that the Biden Administration has an opportunity to gradually reframe Middle East policy in the long-term interests of the USA as well as the region and the international community. Granted, it would be an undertaking that would be the equivalent of turning a supertanker around in the Suez Canal, a gradual process at best, rather than an overnight change.

Potential Entry Points

The US withdrawals from Afghanistan and Iraq are potential entry points. So are the troubled nuclear talks.

A potential breakdown in the talks is already prompting calls for a Plan B. In the same vein, Ross, the former Middle East peace negotiator, and hardliners like Trump-era official Elliott Abrams are calling for a return to the policy of maximum pressure by invoking a snapback of United Nations sanctions that were lifted as part of the original accord.[46]

The policy failed then, and there is little reason to think that it would produce results now, which means that the time for a fundamental policy rethink is ripe, although US domestic politics is likely to foreclose that option. Plan B could involve the gradual exploitation of cracks, with the risk that from Iran's perspective, it would be too little too late.

One potential crack that the Biden Administration could spin as a more balanced approach is giving human rights greater weightage when it comes to US arms sales.[47] The policy under consideration by the Administration could affect Iran's foremost rivals, Saudi Arabia and the UAE—two primary clients of the US defence industry. Similarly, Egypt could constitute an imminent test of the shift, with Secretary of State Blinken deciding whether to withhold US$ 300 million from a US$ 1.3 billion annual military aid package. The US Congress has linked disbursement of the US$ 300 million to the release of political prisoners and respecting freedom of the press—conditions few would assert that Egypt has met.[48]

The problem from Iran's perspective is that the shift is likely to affect those arms and systems that would be used domestically in violation of human rights by police and paramilitary forces rather than the big-ticket, cutting-edge weapons that concern Iran the most. The shift, moreover, would constitute a double-edged sword for Iran. On the one hand, it signals US willingness to be more critical of its regional allies. On the other, this increases pressure on the Islamic Republic, whose human rights record is equally tarnished.

By the same token, concern in Beijing, Moscow, and Tehran about the fallout of the US withdrawals suggests that stabilising the greater Middle East in ways that conflicts can be sustainably managed, if not resolved, creates grounds for China, Russia, and the USA to cooperate on what should be a common interest: securing the free flow of oil and gas as well as trade. Iran, like China and Russia, is bracing itself for worst-case scenarios as the Taliban advance militarily, which enhances the potential for some form of cooperation.

Changes in the assumptions underlying US Middle East policy would facilitate the search for a more inclusive security architecture and potentially reduce the risk of conflicts spinning out of control and/or the USA being sucked into escalating tensions, such as the most recent shipping incidents. So may emerging alliances between regional players that could allow US allies to take greater responsibility and produce interesting results.

One such emerging relationship, dubbed the Indo-Abrahamic bloc by analyst Mohammed Soliman, would group India, the UAE and Israel, and could attract Saudi Arabia and others. Saudi Arabia held its first ever naval exercise with India in mid-August.[49] The burgeoning Indo-Abrahamic relationship raises the question of how it would deal with Iran given that India is the main backer of the Iranian Arabian Sea port of Chabahar, 70 kilometres down the coast from the Chinese-supported Pakistan port of Gwadar. "The size, power, and influence of the Indo-Abrahamic states—India, Israel, and the UAE—have the potential to transform the region's geopolitics and geoeconomics," Soliman said.[50]

Conclusion

Ironically, the reality in the Middle East is less likely to drive a fundamental change of US policy than domestic politics. That makes debate about the policy more important, even if its impact will not be immediate. Policy change is likely to be a gradual process resulting from the evolution of public opinion in key US domestic constituencies, including the Democratic Party and the evangelical and Jewish communities. The most recent debate reflected in a flurry of studies, reports, and analyses suggests that, ever so slowly, the guardrails of the discussion are shifting. The earlier US allies hear which way the wind is blowing, the better they will be able to accommodate inevitable change.

Biden appointees like CIA Director Burns, a former senior State Department official who headed the Carnegie Endowment for International Peace before returning to office this year, suggested in 2019 policy changes akin to the thinking of the Quincy Institute and others. In an essay in *The Atlantic* entitled 'An End to Magical Thinking in the Middle East,' Burns argued that "the temptations of magical thinking, the persistent tendency to assume too much about our influence and too little about the obstacles in our path and the agency of other actors, led to indiscipline and disappointments—steadily diminishing the appetite of most Americans for Middle East adventures. That leaves American policy at a crossroads. Our moment as the singular dominant outside player in the Middle East has faded, but we still have a solid hand to play. The key to playing it well will be neither restoration of the inflated ambition and over-militarization of much of the post-9/11 period nor sweeping disengagement."[51]

The earlier US allies listen to men like Burns and hear which way the wind is blowing, the better they will be able to accommodate inevitable change.

ENDNOTES

1. Quincy Institute for Responsible Statecraft, About QI, https://quincyinst.org/about/
2. Daniel Deudney and G. John Ikenberry, "Misplaced Restraint: The Quincy Coalition Versus Liberal Internationalism", *Survival*, vol. 63:4, 2021, https://www.tandfonline.com/doi/full/10.1080/00396338.2021.1956187
3. Ibid. Deudney and Ikenberry.
4. George W. Bush, *Decision Points*, New York: Crown, 2010, Kindle edition.
5. Juan Cole, 'The Biden Doctrine and Afghanistan: Lean Counter-Terrorism and the end of Bloated Nation-Building,' *Informed Comment*, 17 August 2021, https://www.juancole.com/2021/08/doctrine-afghanistan-terrorism.html
6. The White House, Remarks by President Biden on Afghanistan, 16 August 2021, https://www.whitehouse.gov/briefing-room/speeches-remarks/2021/08/16/remarks-by-president-biden-on-afghanistan/
7. Ben Rhodes, *The World as It Is: A Memoir of the Obama White House*, New York: Random House, Kindle edition
8. Email to the author, 4 August 2021.
9. Bilal Y. Saab, 'Enabling US Security Cooperation', *Survival*, vol. 63:4, July 2021, pp. 89-99.
10. Kenneth M. Pollack and Dennis Ross, 'Biden needs a Middle East strategy to avoid new crises', *The Hill*, 10 August 2021, https://thehill.com/opinion/international/567095-biden-needs-a-middle-east-strategy-to-avoid-new-crises
11. Vivian Salama, Nancy A. Youssef and Gordon Lubold, 'Speed of Taliban Advance Surprises Biden Administration, Dismays U.S. Allies', *The Wall Street Journal*, 11 August 2021, https://www.wsj.com/articles/speed-of-taliban-advance-surprises-biden-administration-dismays-u-s-allies-11628708393
12. Andrew Bahcevic, *After the Apocalypse: America's Role in the World Transformed*, New York: Metropolitan Books, 2021, p. 3.
13. C. Christine Fair, 'Pakistan and the United States Have Betrayed the Afghan People', *Foreign Policy*, 16 August, 2021, https://foreignpolicy.com/2021/08/16/pakistan-united-states-afghanistan-taliban/
14. Jack Detsch, 'Departure of Private Contractors Was a Turning Point in Afghan Military's Collapse', *Foreign Policy*, 16 August 2021, https://foreignpolicy.com/2021/08/16/afghanistan-military-collapse-private-contractors/
15. Jon Alterman, 'U.S. Restraint in the Middle East', Centre for Strategic and International Affairs, 10 August 2021, https://www.csis.org/analysis/us-restraint-middle-east
16. Vision 2030, https://www.vision2030.gov.sa/
17. Hani K. Findakly and Kevin A. Findakly, 'Whither the Arabs: The End of the Welfare State and the Start of a Journey into the Unknown', *Atlantic Council*, August 2021, https://www.atlanticcouncil.org/wp-content/uploads/2021/08/Whither-the-Arabs.pdf
18. William J. Burns and Jake Sullivan, 'We Led Successful Negotiations with Iran. Trump's Approach Isn't Working', *The Atlantic*, 16 May 2019, https://

www.theatlantic.com/ideas/archive/2019/05/trumps-iran-strategy-all-coercion-no-diplomacy/589558/
19. William J. Burns, 'An End to Magical Thinking in the Middle East', *The Atlantic*, 8 December 2019, https://www.theatlantic.com/ideas/archive/2019/12/end-magical-thinking-middle-east/602953/
20. Email to the author, 2 August 2021, Quincy Institute for Responsible Statecraft, 19 July 2021, https://quincyinst.org/report/no-clean-hands-the-interventions-of-middle-eastern-powers/
21. Michael Young, 'America Often Wrong', Malcolm H. Kerr Carnegie Middle East Centre, 2 August 2021, https://carnegie-mec.org/diwan/85059
22. James M. Dorsey, 'Taliban and Al Qaeda: Putting a fox in charge of the chicken coop?' The Turbulent World of Middle East Soccer, 19 August 2021, https://mideastsoccer.blogspot.com/2021/08/taliban-and-al-qaeda-putting-fox-in.html
23. Dan Crenshaw, 'The 'Endless Wars' Fallacy', *The Wall Street Journal*, 17 August 2021, https://www.wsj.com/articles/endless-wars-neocon-biden-afghanistan-withdrawal-kabul-taliban-terrorist-jihadist-11629209389
24. Malcolm Byrne, 'Iran's 1979 Revolution Revisited: Failures (and a Few Successes) of U.S. Intelligence and Diplomatic Reporting', National Security Archive, 11 February 2019, https://nsarchive.gwu.edu/briefing-book/iran/2019-02-11/irans-1979-revolution-revisited-failures-few-successes-us-intelligence-diplomatic-reporting
25. Pablo de Orellana, 'How Gaddafi went from friend to foe in US eyes', International Affairs Blog, 2 June 2021, https://medium.com/international-affairs-blog/how-gaddafi-went-from-friend-to-foe-in-us-eyes-e09cd4373b51
26. Email to the author, 31 July 2021.
27. Robert E. Hunter, *Building Security in the Persian Gulf*, Rand Corp, 2010, https://www.jstor.org/stable/10.7249/mg944.9?seq=1#metadata_info_tab_contents
28. Eugene Gholz, "Nothing Much to Do: Why America Can Bring All Troops Home From the Middle East, Quincy Institute for Responsible Statecraft", Quincy Institute, 24 June 2021¸ https://quincyinst.org/report/nothing-much-to-do-why-america-can-bring-all-troops-home-from-the-middle-east/
29. William F. Wechsler, 'No, the US shouldn't withdraw from the Middle East', *Atlantic Council*, 24 June 2021, https://www.atlanticcouncil.org/in-depth-research-reports/issue-brief/no-the-us-shouldnt-withdraw-from-the-middle-east/
30. Robert A. Manning and Christopher Preble, 'Reality Check #8: Rethinking US military policy in the Greater Middle East, *Atlantic Council*, 24 June 2021, https://www.atlanticcouncil.org/content-series/reality-check/reality-check-8-rethinking-us-military-policy-in-the-greater-middle-east/
31. Ibid. Deudney and Ikenberry.
32. Email on a private mailing list, 3 August 2021.
33. Robert C. O'Brien and John Ratcliffe, 'After the Debacle: Six Concrete Steps to Restore U.S. Credibility', *Foreign Policy*, 18 September 2021, https://foreignpolicy.com/2021/08/18/afghanistan-withdrawal-biden-indo-pacific-military-china-us-allies-credibility/
34. Thomas Juneau, 'How War in Yemen Transformed the Iran-Houth Partnership;, *Studies in Conflict and Terrorism*, 30 July 2021, https://www.tandfonline.com/doi/abs/10.1080/1057610X.2021.1954353?scroll=top&needAccess=true&journalCode=uter20

35. Institute for Voices of Liberty, Mission to Israel – Delegation, 19 July 2021, https://ivol.institute/2021/07/19/ivol-mission-to-israel-delegation/
36. Erfan Fard, 'Iranian Dissidents to Visit Israel', Begin-Sadat Centre for Strategic Studies, 26 July 2021, https://besacenter.org/iranian-dissidents-to-visit-israel/
37. Agencies, 'Iran accused of using unlawful force in water protest crackdown', *The Guardian*, 23 July 2021, https://www.theguardian.com/world/2021/jul/23/iran-accused-of-using-unlawful-force-in-water-protest-crackdown
38. Fahim Al-Hamid, "Khamenei is on fire...the mullahs' regime is reeling" (خامنئي يحترق..نظام الملالي يترنح), *Okaz*, 29 July 2021, https://www.okaz.com.sa/news/politics/2076929#.YQIRiB_HRWY.twitter
39. Jon Alterman, 'Iran's Future', *Babel*, 13 July 2021, https://www.csis.org/analysis/irans-future
40. Mohammad Ayatollahi Tabaar, 'Iran's War Within', *Foreign Affairs*, September/October 2021, https://www.foreignaffairs.com/articles/iran/2021-08-05/irans-war-within-ebrahim-raisi
41. Ibid. Tabaar.
42. Qassim Abdul-Zahra and Samya Kullab, 'Keeping up attacks, some Iraq militias challenge patron Iran', Associated Press, 9 July 2021, https://apnews.com/article/joe-biden-middle-east-religion-iran-lebanon-17a5d13c97f72e1992bb6254445e32f2
43. Mustafa Saadoon, "Exclusive: Kata'ib Hezbollah warns that US failure to withdraw 'means confrontation'," *Amwaj.media*, 28 July 2021, https://amwaj.media/article/the-mission-of-the-american-forces-in-iraq-is-not-over-will-it-return-under-the-n
44. David Ignatius, 'Biden seems to have found a sweet spot in Iraq', *The Washington Post*, 3 August 2021, https://www.washingtonpost.com/opinions/2021/08/03/bidens-careful-approach-iraq-is-built-all-thats-absent-afghanistan/
45. Ibid. Juneau.
46. Elliott Abrams, 'Biden Needs a Plan B for the Iran Talks', *National Review*, 4 August 2021, https://www.nationalreview.com/2021/08/biden-needs-a-plan-b-for-the-iran-talks/
47. Mike Stone and Patricia Zengerle, 'EXCLUSIVE-Biden plans shift in arms policy to add weight to human rights concerns', *Reuters*, 5 August 2021, https://www.reuters.com/world/us/exclusive-biden-plans-shift-arms-export-policy-favor-human-rights-sources-2021-08-04/
48. Editorial Board, 'Is Biden serious about fighting for democracy? Egypt will be a decisive test', *The Washington Post*, 4 August 2021, https://www.washingtonpost.com/opinions/2021/08/04/is-biden-serious-about-fighting-democracy-egypt-will-be-decisive-test/
49. *Middle East Monitor*, 'Saudi Arabia and India carry out first ever joint naval exercise', 11 August 2021, https://www.middleeastmonitor.com/20210811-saudi-arabia-and-india-carry-out-first-ever-joint-naval-exercise/
50. Mohammed Soliman, 'An Indo-Abrahamic alliance on the rise: How India, Israel, and the UAE are creating a new transregional order', Middle East Institute, 28 July 2021, https://mei.edu/publications/indo-abrahamic-alliance-rise-how-india-israel-and-uae-are-creating-new-transregional
51. Ibid. Burns, 'An End to Magical Thinking'.

2

India's Counter to China's West Asia Strategy: Cooperation, Competition or Confrontation?

N. Janardhan

Introduction

Driven by economic growth, China and India have consolidated their place in Asia and made their presence felt on the global stage. Recognizing their significance as economic allies, West Asian countries—particularly those in the Gulf—have pursued a 'Look East' policy since the turn of the century. This has intensified political cooperation with the Asian powers, along with Japan and South Korea, with noticeable intent of collaboration in the security realm too. Together with the USA, these countries are now crucial partners for West Asian countries.

While India has had historic ties and the USA has been the main security guarantor for decades, China has rapidly expanded its footprint in Wet Asia over the last two decades, becoming one of the region's top trade partners and foreign investors. China's announcement of the Belt and Road Initiative (BRI) in 2013, in particular, confirmed the strategic importance of West Asia in its global ambition.[1]

Other Chinese plans, including the 2015 'Vision and Actions on Jointly

Building Silk Road Economic Belt and 21st-Century Maritime Silk Road' and the 2016 'Arab Policy Paper', have also highlighted the centrality of economic cooperation to China's engagement with West Asia.[2]

A few trends in China's engagement with the regional countries are noteworthy. First, West Asia is a major supplier of China's energy needs. In 2017, China became the world's largest importer of oil, surpassing the USA. The region accounts for over 40 per cent of its oil imports and is a key liquefied natural gas source. Though China's energy suppliers are more diversified than India's, China's increasing energy consumption will lead to increased interdependence between Beijing and West Asian oil-exporting countries.[3]

Second, West Asian countries—particularly those in the Gulf—have been major sources of infrastructure contracts with Chinese firms, especially "projects that lend themselves to the BRI goal of connectivity...such as ports and industrial parks, as they create an economic chain that links China to the Gulf, the Arabian Sea, the Red Sea, and the Mediterranean".[4] In addition, Chinese investments in renewable energy, telecommunications, and space, have also increased exponentially recently.

Third, China's relationships with regional partners are moving beyond economic interests to incorporate strategic concerns as well. Over the past decade, China has forged a variety of 'strategic' partnerships with a host of countries in the region —'comprehensive strategic partnership' with Saudi Arabia, the UAE, Iran, Egypt and Algeria; 'strategic cooperation' with Turkey; and 'strategic partnerships' with Qatar, Kuwait, and Oman. Further, Saudi Arabia and the UAE are "pivot states" crucial to "China's global network politically and economically" and Turkey is a "node state"—a bridge to facilitate Chinese interests.[5]

Finally, as China's economic and diplomatic engagement in the region deepens, its security presence is also gradually expanding. In 2017, China opened its first overseas base in Djibouti, which has been described by Beijing as playing a crucial role in helping "fulfil its international responsibilities including anti-piracy work and to maintain the peace and stability of Africa and the world".[6] According to the Chinese Ambassador to the UAE, China has sent a "total of 31 fleets, 100 naval vessels and 26,000 officers and soldiers to the Gulf of Aden and waters off the coast of Somalia to carry out escort missions".[7]

Importantly, like India, China has managed to build friendly relationships with all states in West Asia, while keeping its distance from regional conflicts and rivalries. Contrary to the USA, it has promoted the idea of neutral engagement and mutual benefits with its regional partners. This has enabled China to maintain good relations with countries that are hostile to one another, such as Israel, Saudi Arabia, and Iran. Similarly, Beijing has been keen on expanding relations with the Gulf Cooperation Council (GCC) countries, in spite of enhanced ties with Iran—as illustrated by the 25-year strategic cooperation agreement signed in 2021.

There is no empirical evidence to suggest that China desires, at least in the short term, to replace the USA as the dominant external military power in the region, but there is no doubt that it will progressively become a major force shaping the stability and security of West Asia in the future.[8] While this has the potential to bring substantial benefits to the region—especially with regard to conflict management,[9] many countries, including India, are concerned that China becoming a key economic, political and security actor poses a serious challenge to US primacy in the region.

Thus, West Asian dynamics are increasingly being viewed through the lens of great power competition, which, in a context of intensifying USA-China rivalry, could impact regional developments and make it increasingly difficult for regional countries and India to manage their relations with other external powers, including the USA, and their traditional West Asian partners. This great power competition is already playing out in India's neighbourhood where China has warmed up to the Taliban regime, at the expense of the USA, by stepping up aid and diplomatic support for the extremist group's global recognition.

This chapter details China's multi-dimensional advances in West Asia and explores its implications for the USA, the principal security guarantor in the region. It also delves into the impact of China's expanding influence on India's thriving socio-economic-security relations with the region and its pre-eminent role in the Indian Ocean and suggests potential policy options for New Delhi's consideration.

Chinese Imports from West Asia

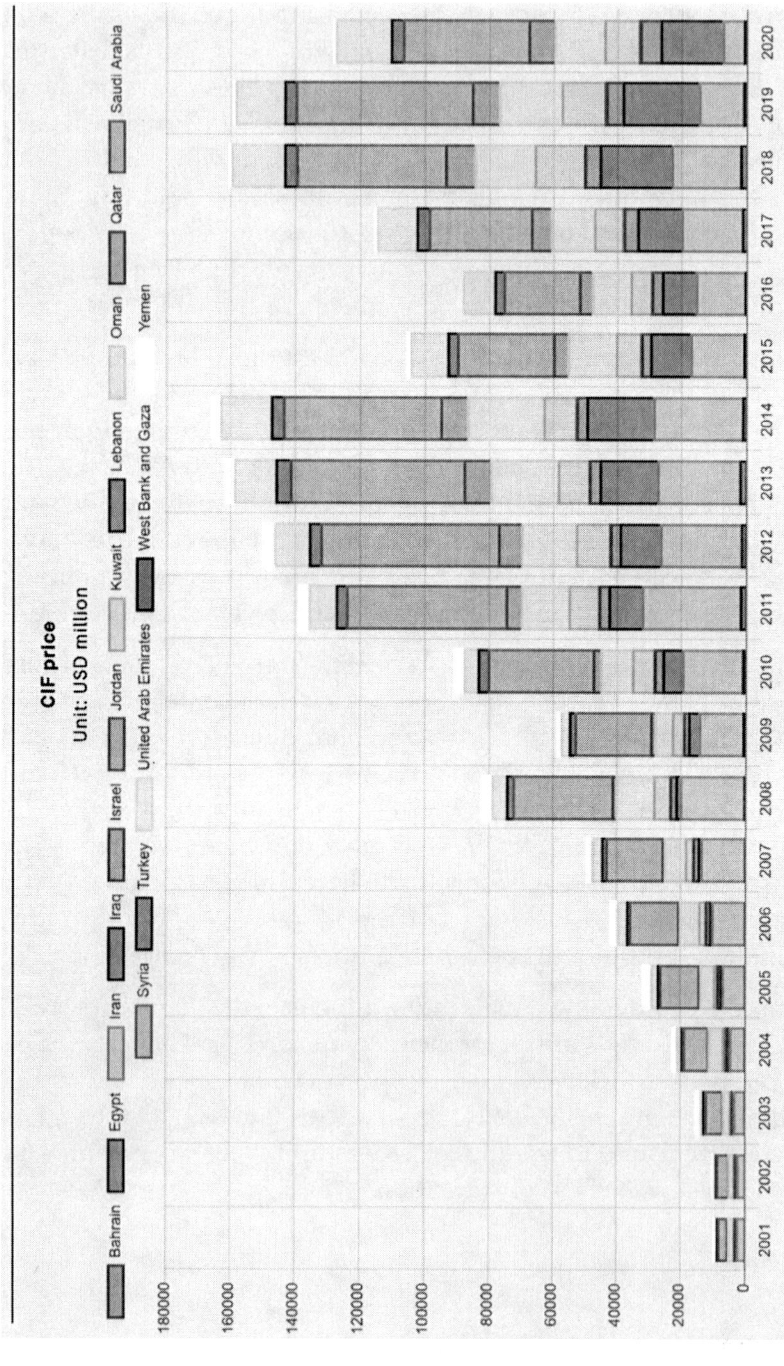

Chinese Exports from West Asia

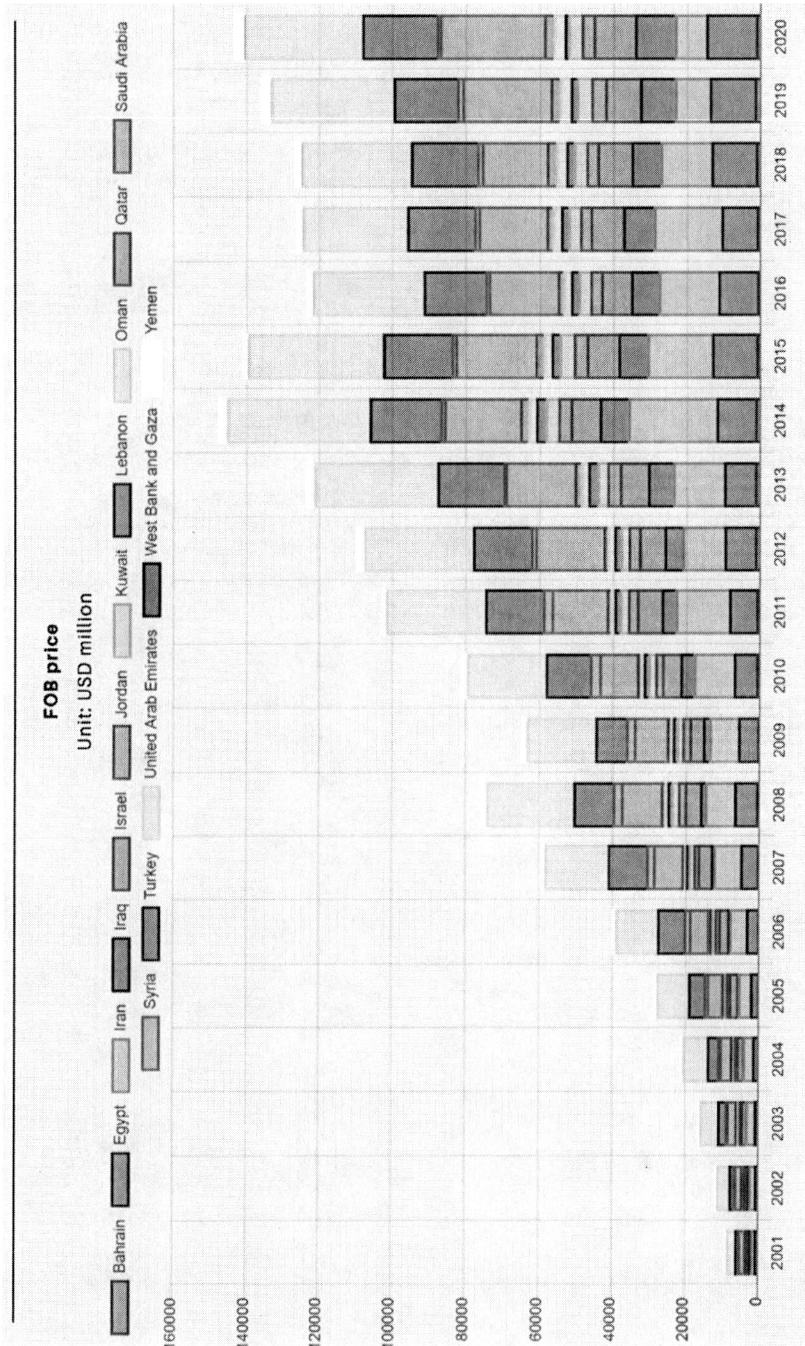

Value of Contracts Awarded to Chinese Companies in West Asia

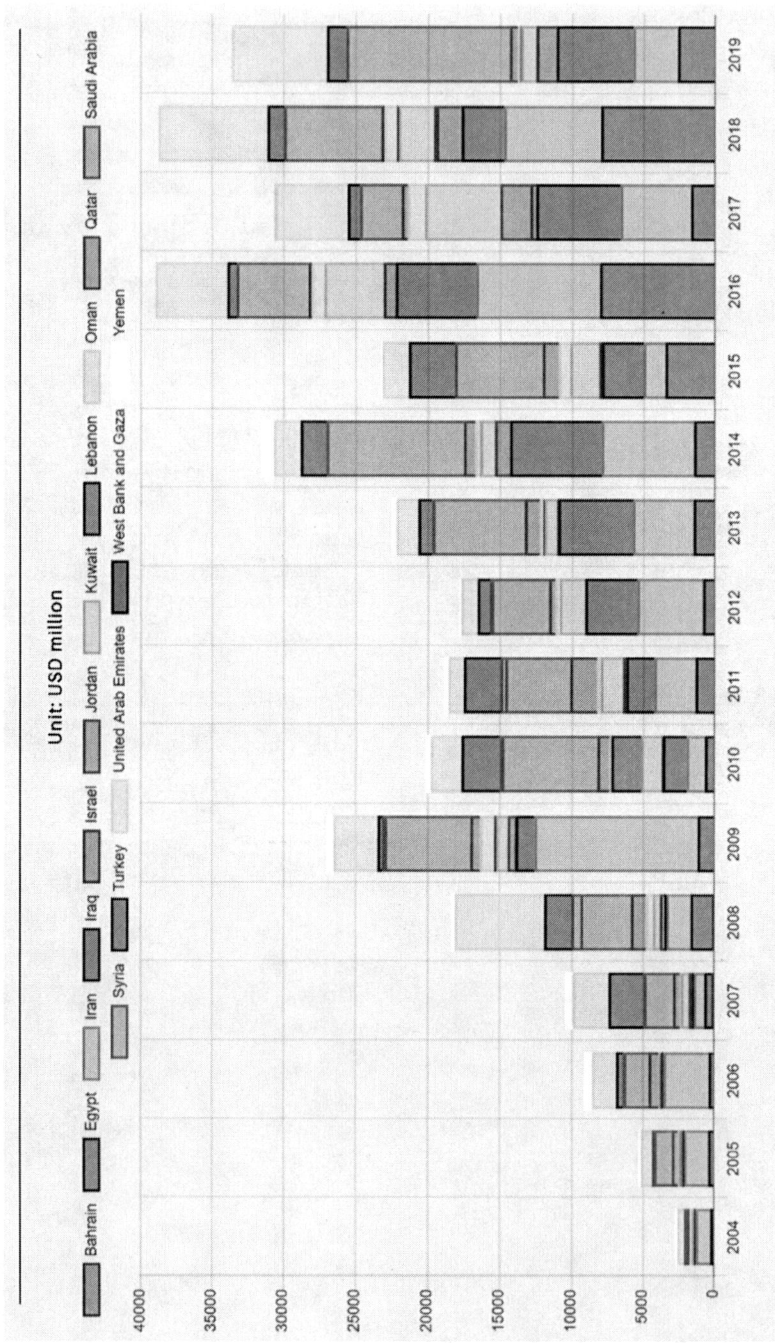

Chinese Dependence on Energy Imports from West Asia

Chinese FDI (Stock) in West Asia

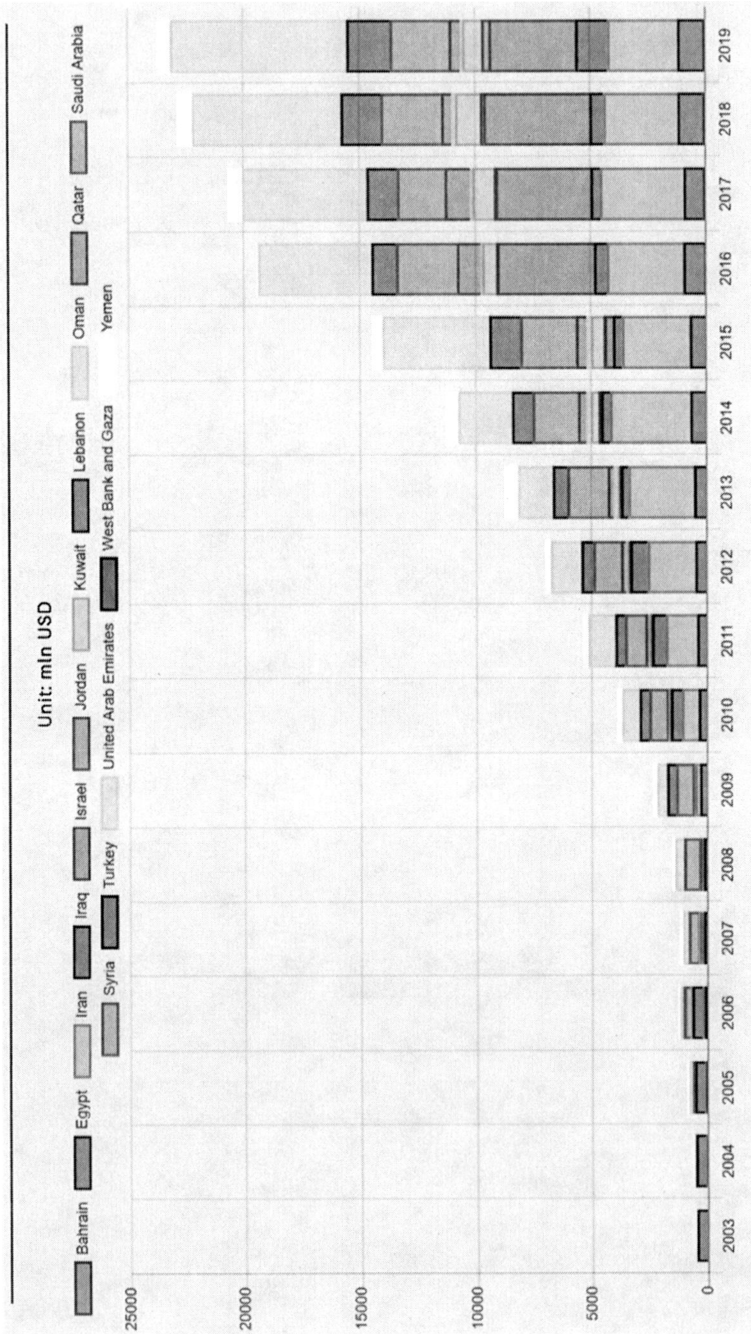

Source: ChinaMed Project, Torino World Affairs Institute, Italy.

BRI Stimulus

While the earlier statistical graphs attest to China's economic might in West Asia, a good way of explaining China's growing security imprint in the region is to link it to the BRI. The initiative was projected as a win-win economic plan for itself and its partners but is now assuming a political and security hue since it has coincided with diminishing Western influence in all the three spheres of global power—economic, political and security.

The BRI has served as a stimulus in West Asia-China ties in several ways. First, the progress is visible in the strengthening of policy coordination between the two sides. Together they have devised mechanisms of dialogue and communication such as the China-Arab Cooperation Forum and the Strategic Dialogue between China and the GCC countries.

China's first 'Arab Policy Paper' published in 2016 states that joint efforts will be made with Arab countries to promote the initiative under the principle of "wide consultation, joint contribution, and shared benefit".[10] It also states that China and Arab countries will adopt the '1+2+3 cooperation' pattern where 1 refers to energy cooperation as the core infrastructure, 2 pertains to construction and trade and investment facilitation, and 3 relates to innovative technologies in nuclear energy, space satellite, and renewable energy.

The BRI has facilitated frequent, high-level exchanges of visits between the leaders of China and West Asian countries. China has signed strategic partnerships with at least eight Arab countries and BRI-related construction agreements with six Arab countries. Further, seven Arab countries—including Oman, Qatar, Saudi Arabia, and the UAE from the GCC bloc—are founding members of the Asian Infrastructure Investment Bank (AIIB).[11]

Second, the progress is visible in infrastructure connectivity. Within the BRI framework, Chinese companies participated in the construction of several ports, including the Ain Sokhna Port, Egypt, and New Hamad Port, Qatar. Apart from increasing capacity and connectivity, these and other ports are expected to reduce transportation costs. China also established a logistics base in Djibouti, designed to enhance its capability to safeguard maritime transportation under the UN framework.

On land, the first freight train between China and Iran, via Central

Asia, completed its journey in just two weeks in 2016—30 days faster than the time taken previously.[12] Some Chinese experts have also proposed building a railway line linking China with Saudi Arabia via Afghanistan, Iran and other GCC countries. This might not be feasible given the political tension between the GCC countries and Iran, but cannot be ruled out completely either in light of the rapprochement bids taking shape in the region.[13]

Third, progress is visible in China's efforts to help regional countries improve their industrial capacities. The China-Egypt TEDA Suez Economic and Trade Cooperation Zone, which started in 2008, picked up speed after the BRI was announced.[14] Chinese President Xi Jinping inaugurated the second stage of the project during his visit to Egypt in 2016. Besides the China-Egypt TEDA, Chinese companies are also negotiating construction of an industrial zone in Tangiers, Morocco, which could help in connecting European and African markets. Further, China's plans to construct economic zones in Saudi Arabia and the UAE are taking shape.[15] The DP World and the Zhejiang China Commodity City Group Company agreed in 2019 to develop the 'Traders Market' in Jebel Ali Free Zone, Dubai.[16]

Fourth, the BRI's progress in West Asia is visible in financial cooperation through the establishment and activities of the AIIB. Among its 57 founding members, at least 10 are from the region, including four from the GCC bloc. China has also signed currency-swap agreements with a number of countries.[17]

As a result of these developments, Riyadh welcomed Beijing's "assiduous effort" to fulfil the BRI's potential and stressed that reviving such ancient trade routes complements its Vision 2030, based on their agendas' "common features and notions".[18] Kuwait has identified that the BRI has the potential to help it achieve the 2035 Vision for Development;[19] and Oman has indicated that it would be interested in investing in Gwadar's special economic zone, promoted by China in Pakistan.[20]

While none of the six BRI corridors formally includes the GCC countries, the five BRI connectivity themes—infrastructure, policy implementation, trade facilitation, financial facilitation, and people-to-people communication—keep the doors open for participation by the GCC countries. The scope for the GCC countries' involvement in the BRI can be linked to at least two factors: one, financial liquidity, which is evident in the bloc being home to some of the largest sovereign wealth funds, and their related investment interests; and two, their infrastructure capabilities, especially their reputation as air and maritime hubs, which have made them major trade and financial centres. After initial reservation to joining the BRI due to the benefits that Iran would accrue, the GCC countries are now participating in the China-Pakistan Economic Corridor and the China-Oman Industrial Project in Duqm, Oman. In fact, Beijing has underlined that "any type of bilateral cooperation (with China) can be considered part of the Belt and Road," which has enabled easier cooperation between the two sides.[21] (This, for example, enabled intense UAE-China cooperation in the health-tech sector after the outbreak of COVID-19 in 2020.)

Security Imprint

Following five years of achievements and controversies, Chinese President Xi Jinping used the Second BRI Forum of International Cooperation in 2019 to set the agenda for the next five years. While China has sought to tweak BRI 2.0 into a qualitatively different one than BRI 1.0 in terms of the economic processes, there are two other ways that the new version could be qualitatively different.

One, as much as it is identified as an economic initiative, the BRI is now a political instrument that China is using to challenge America's global hegemony. Just like the USA-China tariff war is not just about trade, the BRI too will assume a deeper political colouring in the future. In fact, a Chinese scholar has argued that the BRI is a "strategic necessity" because of the US pivot to Asia.[22] In addition, the Chinese Communist Party's Central Committee's official journal *Qiushi* referred to the BRI as a "strategy."[23]

Two, since a large part of the BRI routes are vulnerable to "political instability, religious and ethnic tensions, fragile legal environments, criminality, environmental degradation, social strains," and even transnational terrorism and anti-Chinese sentiments, it is likely that Beijing would enhance its security presence to protect its interests. This has "sparked the rise of a Chinese private security industry with Chinese characteristics"—recruiting retired People's Liberation Army (PLA) and police personnel, who operate with the knowledge of the Chinese government.[24]

Beyond the private security players, China's BRI projects in Pakistan, for example, have a military dimension. China's security dimension could also be linked to the establishment in 2017 of a naval base in Djibouti, astride the Bab-el-Mandeb—the key chokepoint connecting Asia and Europe. Beijing hopes this would serve as a practice ground to learn more about using foreign military facilities to protect its citizens and commercial interests abroad.

In one of its first acknowledgments, a year after the Djibouti base was established, the Ministry of National Defence said that the new facility would help Beijing "better fulfil China's international responsibilities, including anti-piracy work and maintaining peace and stability of Africa and the world".[25] Some reports suggest that China's Marine Corps could also become its primary rapid response force in the BRI countries that are part of the Indian Ocean littoral. One such Marine company is reportedly deployed in Djibouti, with another one expected in Gwadar, Pakistan.[26] According to China's *Global Times* "China has always adhered to the principle of non-interference in the internal affairs of other countries, but that doesn't mean Beijing can turn a deaf ear to the demands of Chinese enterprises in protecting their overseas investments."[27]

To meet its objectives, China is shifting from infantry to high-tech naval and aerial warfare.[28] Two examples denote its growing naval strength. One, in 2015, the PLA Navy (PLAN) evacuated 225 foreign nationals and almost 600 Chinese citizens from Aden in Yemen, amid fierce fighting. This was the second time that China used its armed forces to rescue its citizens and foreign nationals from a danger zone.[29] (The first was an air evacuation operation in 2011 in Libya.[30]) Two, it was also revealed that 31 Chinese naval fleets escorted 6,600 ships between 2008 and 2018 in the Gulf of Aden and waters off Somalia. Of these, 51.5 per cent was foreign vessels.[31]

Experts argue that the Chinese naval strength is already advancing steadily while that of the USA is declining. "In early 2017, the Chinese Navy had 328 ships. It now possesses nearly 350 ships and is already larger than the US Navy. China is the largest ship-producing country in the world and could soon operate 400 ships....In 2018, the US fleet consisted of 280 ships...in 12 years the active naval fleet will decline to 237 ships. As a result, the US allies' willingness to trust America to protect them will decline."[32] Apart from the quantity of PLAN ships, their quality has also improved with over 70 per cent of the fleet considered modern in 2017, up from under 50 per cent in 2010.[33]

Along with enhancing its physical naval prowess, China has worked hard to expand its naval infrastructure facilities in the BRI countries. A 2017 report pointed out that Chinese companies were involved in the building and maintenance of over 40 ports in about 35 countries, including West Asia and the Gulf.[34]

China has also increased security cooperation and military exercises with several regional countries, and its arms sales has soared in recent years—in particular for platforms and systems, such as drones, that the USA has been reluctant to sell to its regional partners.

China's security initiatives gel well with the security vacuum that is being felt around the world, including West Asia and the Gulf, where Washington's mixed signals under recent administrations have left regional governments confused. This has kept the region's choices open to the idea of exploring alternative security mechanisms that are no longer rooted only in the West.

Indian Ocean Region

Linking China's growing presence in West Asia to India's sphere of influence, it is becoming evident that the past 20 years have witnessed a profound increase in Chinese activities in the Indian Ocean Region (IOR). Almost all of China's trade with West Asia, Europe, and Africa transits through the IOR,[35] where the dominant power is the USA. While Washington maintains that its military presence in the region contributes to stability and guarantees safe passage for the world's cargo ships and oil tankers, Beijing takes a different view. It fears that in the event of any confrontation with the USA, the Chinese Sea Lanes of Communication in the IOR could be shut down by American warships.[36]

Recognising the regular presence of the PLAN in the IOR, Admiral Sunil Lamba, India's former chief of naval staff, pointed out that at any given time, the PLAN has between six to eight ships in the northern Indian Ocean.[37] In August 2017, the Indian Navy counted 14 PLAN surface warships in the Indian Ocean.[38]

In addition, since December 2008, the PLAN has been a regular contributor to the Gulf of Aden anti-piracy patrols. According to a US former naval attaché, the PLAN originally did not fully participate in the patrols. There was no coordination and "nobody knew what they were doing." However, after the second year of conducting patrols, the PLAN played a constructive role and even requested if it could chair some of the Shared Awareness and De-confliction meetings in Bahrain to showcase its capabilities.[39]

While the PLAN's anti-piracy patrols are confined to the region outside the Gulf, PLAN warships do make voyages to various GCC states. The UAE became the first country in the region in 2010 to host Chinese warships, with subsequent visits in 2014 and 2017.[40] These voyages fit into what the Chinese government, in its National Defence Strategy, called "frontier defence."

A Chinese expert describes frontier defence as "an offensive doctrinal-security guidance for projecting battles far away from China's homeland, most likely in the maritime regions. It relevantly factors in potential hostile scenarios against China's SLOCs through the Indian Ocean."[41]

Other related doctrines are the two "1.5 war scenarios." In the first scenario, a war in the South China Sea or East China Sea between the USA/Japan and China might cause India to take advantage of China's preoccupation by taking more land along their disputed land border. More relevant to this chapter is the second scenario where the Indian-US navies impede China's SLOCs in the IOR.[42]

In short, apart from the limited anti-piracy patrols in the Gulf of Aden, Beijing does not yet have the ability to play a significant military role in the IOR or the Gulf in the near future. However, as the BRI continues to unfold and Chinese economic interests rapidly expand, Beijing will increase its naval forays into the IOR.

China-USA Rivalry

In a sign of how the China-USA rivalry could impact small states in the region, and even put India in a spot in the future, the construction of a secret Chinese military facility near a port in Abu Dhabi was stopped in late 2021 after Washington's intervention. The USA had found evidence of the secret construction and the Biden Administration had warned the UAE government that the presence of Chinese military in its country could threaten USA-UAE ties.

The diplomatic adviser to the UAE leadership confirmed that the UAE stopped work at the port at Washington's behest. He added the UAE did not believe the facility was intended for military or security use. "You hear the concerns of your ally and it would be foolish" not to take them into account, he said of the Biden Administration.[43]

Washington has also been pressuring the GCC countries to limit their engagement with Beijing, particularly in the technology sector. In 2020, flagging Huawei's role in the UAE's 5G infrastructure projects, a US official said that it would make it "difficult" for the US and GCC forces to communicate. "These states have to weigh the value of their partnership with the USA."[44] Since there is no commensurate cost-quality alternative, the UAE has not altered its plans yet.

The USA-China economic-security rivalry has led to intense discussion about the future of the USA in the region. In 2016, the UAE said, "In today's world, the stability of the region cannot rest on American engagement alone. Other actors, including Russia, China, India, and the European Union also have an important role to play, which is why our foreign policy seeks to consolidate relations with these actors."[45]

Such and other assertions led US Secretary of Defence Lloyd Austin to say in 2021 that he had encountered from allies a "level of angst that the USA is not really committed to this region.... We remain committed to this region.... We have significant capability here...let me assure you that we are not going to abandon those interests going forward."[46]

Even India is waking up to the new realities. Despite its close partnership with the USA, External Affairs Minister S. Jaishankar said Washington is moving towards greater realism both about itself and the world and has shown a greater caution in power projection. "Since 2008, we have witnessed a greater caution in US power projection and an effort to correct its over-extension. It may have taken different forms and be articulated in very different ways. But there is a larger consistency over three administrations that they themselves may not readily recognize.... It is expressed in footprint and posture, terms of engagement, extent of involvement and nature of initiatives."[47]

In the same breath, Jaishankar addressed another trend—the rise of China. "The consequences of China's growing capabilities are profound because of the extrapolation of its domestic seamlessness to the world outside...whether it is connectivity, technology or trade, there is an ongoing debate on the changed nature of power.... Separately, we have also seen a sharpening of tensions on territorial issues across the breadth of Asia.... Agreements of yesteryears now have question marks."[48]

The above trends, combined with the ineffectiveness of the USA in defending the interests of the GCC countries during the 2019 and 2020 drone attacks on key energy installations, has pushed several West Asian countries to challenge Washington on various issues and look to Beijing as an alternative where possible. Two examples illustrate this. One, the UAE dared to suspend in late 2021 the $ 23 billion F-35s deal with the USA over unreasonable pricing and conditions.[49] And two, between 2016 and 2020, China's sale of arms to Saudi Arabia and the UAE increased by 386 per cent and 169 per cent, respectively, compared to 2011-2015.[50]

The region is extremely concerned about being caught in the middle of the USA-China rivalry. There is a "fine line" between competition, on the one hand, and a new Cold War on the other, the UAE underlined, adding that it does not want the rivalry "to slip into a second Cold War."[51]

Conflict Management Strategy

Along with increasing its economic and security influence in West Asia, Beijing has expanded its behind-the-scene role in regional diplomacy too. One such case is Beijing's role in helping negotiate the 2015 Iranian nuclear deal. After US President Barack Obama's re-election in 2012, Chinese President Xi began to openly lobby Tehran about his concerns over Iran's nuclear programme. In fact, Chinese Foreign Minister Wang Yi played the role of a mediator between Iran, Europe and the USA and asked the two countries to compromise. Beijing's attempts were motivated by concerns that Chinese economic interests in Iran would be threatened by Western sanctions. Some analysts argue that China played a "significant role" in bringing the 2015 agreement to fruition.[52]

To safeguard and promote China's economic interests, Chinese scholars are advocating diplomatic tactics, especially in West Asia, that could help strengthen Beijing's developing global security policy. These tactics include mediation to defend commercial rather than security interests; conflict 'management' instead of 'resolution'; and promoting a harmonious relationship among China's strategic partners, many of whom are deeply divided and involved in proxy wars.

These tactics serve two objectives. First, they dilute criticism about Beijing being uninterested and punching below its weight to stabilize West Asia. Second, they promote the Chinese notion of a balanced diplomatic approach that relies more on deft mediation rather than any form of aggressive intervention. Since West Asia is a key part of the BRI, stability is a concern for China amid friction involving Saudi Arabia, the UAE, Iran, and Turkey, among others.

One idea, "quasi-mediation diplomacy," promotes defending "commercial, political and diplomatic interests rather than core security and strategic interests." A state investing in this model "acts without seeking to dominate; to follow rather than to lead; to partake in the revision of the agenda rather than setting it; and to encourage conflict de-escalation in lieu of determinedly engaging in conflict resolution." Such an approach would involve "multifaceted intervention, proactive involvement, limited intercession and indirect participation," which would minimize China's risks amid the region's conflicts.[53] The stress is on China "seeking common ground while reserving differences," implying a tilt toward conflict management rather than resolution.[54]

Contrary to the popular perception that it has stayed away from intervention in West Asia conflicts, China has conducted "mediation diplomacy" by appointing special envoys for the West Asia peace process and the Syrian war. The task for these and other diplomats in Sudan and Afghanistan has been to 'contain' rather than 'resolve' conflicts. Though these efforts have yielded minimal results, it demonstrates Beijing's bid to deviate from non-interventionist policy.

China also played a quiet but significant role in the talks between the P5+1 and Iran that resulted in the 2015 Joint Comprehensive Plan of Action. President Obama thanked President Xi for Beijing's constructive role in securing the nuclear deal.[55]

The idea of working with competing countries to ensure that prevailing tensions do not escalate is now being extended to rivalries involving countries that could significantly impact the BRI. It focuses on conflict management with Saudi Arabia and the UAE on the one hand and Iran and Turkey on the other.

It is no coincidence that as the Turkey-Saudi rapprochement began in 2021 amid Foreign Minister Wang's visit to Turkey, Iran, Saudi Arabia, the

UAE, Bahrain, and Oman. Beijing announced a five-point proposal pertaining to conflicts in Syria, Libya and Yemen, where Turkey and different GCC countries back opposing groups.[56] Rather than focus only on the Palestinian-Israeli conflict, Beijing offered to host a "multilateral dialogue conference" to build trust among feuding Gulf States. While China maintained neutrality during the 2017-2021 Gulf dispute, some reports indicated that Beijing held mediatory meetings with UAE and Qatar diplomats.[57] This is consistent with a Chinese diplomat's view in 2014 that China is stepping away from its "passive and reactive diplomatic posture."[58]

Beijing's economic and political interests is likely to push it to constructively address regional rivalries rather than exploit them like the USA does, especially in the case of Iran-GCC ties. This assumes greater importance following the Iran-China 25-year 'Strategic Cooperation Pact,' spanning the energy, infrastructure, and defence sectors and Iran's formal membership to the Shanghai Cooperation Organization (SCO), both in 2021.[59]

Incidentally, these conflict management ideas are in line with the 2019 Russian endorsement of Iran's proposal for a "non-aggression pact" with the GCC countries that could significantly reduce the risk of disputes spinning out of control.[60] Some American scholars endorse these trends by pointing out that China's involvement is a mercantile-based and quasi-military approach that helps economies grow without threatening the political order, which is popular in West Asia.[61]

However, amid calls for active engagement in the diplomatic arena, there are Chinese voices of caution too. "If our side was to undertake escort operations in the Strait of Hormuz, it's very likely that a conflict would occur with one, or more, Gulf coastal state." China "should not rashly undertake a military intervention in this region."[62]

There is also a view that the Abraham Accords are Washington's way of checkmating Beijing's and Moscow's growing involvement in the region by promoting US ally, Israel, as an alternative economic, technological, and security partner in the region. This is seen as allowing the USA the luxury of continuing its phased disengagement, without ceding space to its strategic rivals.[63]

Overall, the discussions in China reflect Beijing's bid to re-balance from "politics among nations" to "politics among networks," focusing on "connectivity" (economic) rather than "control" (security). Such a nuanced approach, involving "maximum diplomacy" instead of "maximum pressure," may help calm tensions in the Gulf region, while also promoting the possibility of a non-US-centric security architecture in the region, which is discussed hereafter.[64]

Chindia Ties

The ugly China-India border row in 2020 has increased the decibel levels of jingoism on both sides, making middle ground a rare commodity. Over the decades, 'Chindia' has had a complex multi-layered relationship involving cooperation, competition and confrontation. As the economic power centre shifted from the West to the East during the last two decades, instead of greater cooperation, the Asian giants have assumed antagonistic positions. It would make sense if bilateral differences alone conditioned this environment. Unfortunately, other countries—notably the USA and Pakistan—are also influencing the Indo-Sino relationship. There is nothing wrong with China's desire to make a global impact. And there is nothing wrong in the USA pulling out all stops to protect its sphere of influence. The only problem is that India and some West Asian countries, among others globally, are caught in the crossfire.

It appears that while Washington desires a unipolar world and a multipolar Asia, China would prefer a multipolar world and a China-centric unipolar Asia. On the other hand, India—which is close to the USA—would like to see a multipolar world and a multipolar Asia, thereby intensifying Beijing-Washington and Beijing-New Delhi competition.

India is also reluctantly part of the Quadrilateral Security Dialogue (QUAD), involving the USA, Japan and Australia, to deal with challenges in the Indo-Pacific region. While there is a strategic rationale for this, there is also a political undertone to check Chinese domination. Despite India joining the SCO, this game of US-derived checks and balances has certainly hurt Chindia ties. Further, as a strategic defensive mechanism, Beijing is treating an 'enemy's enemy as a friend', which has adversely affected India-Pakistan ties. Ground realities suggest that while China's Pakistan-Nepal-Sri Lanka (and perhaps Bangladesh in the future) policies ring alarm bells in New Delhi, India's Japan-South Korea-Vietnam-Central Asia (and the US) policies are viewed as irritants in Beijing.

While Chindia have engaged in economic, political and even security dialogue, there is an inherent adversarial tinge surrounding it. Accompanied by rhetoric and tit-for-tat countermeasures, they have neutralized confidence-building measures. Chindia has oscillated among 'Hindi-Chini bhai-bhai' (Chindians are brothers) to bye-bye (due to differences) to buy-buy (economic complementarity) to returning again to bye-bye (change of the rules of engagement on the border and attempts at economic decoupling). Nearly a score meetings of the current leaders of the two countries since 2014, including the famous 'Wuhan Spirit' and 'Chennai Connect,' have done little to improve ties.

In the past, China implemented Mao Zedong's 1940s *'da da, tan tan'* (fight, talk talk) strategy. When Washington sought to influence Mao to stop the war against the Nationalist Army, he agreed for talks, but continued to make decisive gains, and eventually achieved victory on the battleground.[65] It has now tweaked and emerged out of another strategy, that of Deng Xiaoping's 'Hide your strength, bide your time, never take the lead' strategy. President Xi Jinping feels that it is China's time to lead (not necessarily the world). This means that Beijing's 'Wolf Warrior' diplomacy will pursue the *da, tan* strategy with its adversaries.

Conclusion and Recommendations

In such a milieu, India must recalibrate its strategy to achieve 'cold peace' with China or be 'frenemies' or 'rivalry partners'. The two countries with "oversized egos" must cooperate and compete, but avoid further confrontation. One way out is to consider de-hyphenating India-China ties from the USA, which would also address the India-Pakistan issue. Despite the recent events, this could help Chindia progress from "Inch (India and China) towards Miles (Millennium of Exceptional Synergy)".[66] It would be a decent strategy to make friends with the enemy next door rather than only remain close to a distant friend. This could help India's cause in West Asia as well, where China appears to be promoting the ideas of cold peace or frenemies or rivalry partners.[67]

It is equally important not to locate the GCC's or West Asia's 'Look East' policy as a replacement for its traditional ally, the USA. This means that any new alternatives that may materialize in future need not be viewed as competitors with the USA. Viewed in a cooperative spirit, a 'post-US world' is not necessarily an 'anti-US world', in which India would be fairly comfortable operating. New Delhi has already stressed that "the world is big enough for both countries and each is too big to be contained by the other."[68] This lends hope against confrontation.

The point is that China, India and other principal Asian players have to stop riding 'piggyback' on US naval presence in the region's waters at some point soon and find their own means of securing their sea lanes. Since this aligns with the security requirements of West Asia, it opens interesting and diversifying possibilities in the region's security arena. Against this backdrop, it is heartening that even US experts are propagating the idea of a collective security architecture for the region, which includes Chinese and Indian roles.[69] Amid these developments, India could consider the following policy options:

- Cooperate in BRI projects in a third country via a trilateral or plurilateral partnership, which would not only serve as an economic boost, but also mitigate tension and provide a diplomatic and security impetus.
- Host a Track II or Track 1.5 dialogue involving experts from West Asia (especially from the Gulf), China and India (and potentially Japan and South Korea too) to explore alternative security scenarios in the region.
- Promote Chinese and Indian leaders joining important West Asian regional summits to share thoughts on future cooperation (like Iranian and British leaders were invited to the GCC summits in December 2007 and 2016, respectively).
- Join China's conflict management strategies aimed at stabilizing hotspots in the region (since India also maintains equidistant ties with regional rivals).
- Begin a 2+2 or even a 3+3 (economy, foreign and defence ministers) meeting involving China and India and one or two other countries that have stakes in West Asia.
- Explore expanding joint exercises involving the armed forces of the West Asian countries, India and some of its allies (like the India-UAE-France joint naval activities), thus evolving a new collective security mechanism in the region.

ENDNOTES

1. Jonathan Fulton, 'China's Great Game in the Middle East', European Council on Foreign Relations, October 2019; Jin Liangxiang and N. Janardhan, "Belt and Road

Initiative: opportunities and obstacles for the Gulf", *EDA Insight*, Anwar Gargash Diplomatic Academy (AGDA), June 2018.

2. Fulton, "China's Great Game in the Middle East".
3. Michael Singh, 'China and the United States in the Middle East: Between Dependency and Rivalry', The Washington Institute for Near East Policy, September 2020.
4. Fulton, "China's Great Game in the Middle East".
5. Sinem Cengiz, 'China is quietly mending the Turkish-GCC split,' Gulf International Forum (Washington), 15 October 2021.
6. 'China builds new facility in Djibouti base for anti-piracy operations,' *Global Times*, 31 May 2018.
7. Ni Jian, 'Why China's relationship with the UAE is brotherly,' *The National*, 7 March 2021.
8. N. Janardhan, "Gulf Security in a 'Post-Free Riders' World," *EDA Insight* (AGDA), June 2020.
9. Poornima Balasubraminian, 'China's Approach to mediating Middle Eastern conflicts', *The Diplomat* (US), October 2020.
10. Full text of China's Arab Policy Paper available at Xinhua (China), 13 January 2016.
11. Turkey, Israel and Iran are the other Middle Eastern countries that have a stake in the BRI.
12. 'First train from China to Iran stimulates Silk Road revival,' www.usa.chinadaily.com, 16 February 2016.
13. "Proposed China-Saudi freight railway will promote Silk Road Economic Belt (*zhongsha huoyun tielu daidong silu jingjidai fazhan*)," available in Chinese language at http://www.chinadaily.com.cn/micro-reading/2016-04/07/content_24345519.htm
14. Eight years of China-Egypt TEDA Suez Economic and Trade Cooperation Zone: Development across civilizations', www.setc-zone.com, 27 April 2017.
15. "Ras Al Khaimah Free Trade Zone heads back to China to present the promising investment advantages in the UAE", www.rakez.com, 16 November 2015.
16. DP World, Chinese firm to develop region's first free zone market in Dubai', *Gulf News* (UAE), 26 August 2019.
17. 'UAE, China sign pact for bilateral currency swap,' *Gulf News*, 14 December 2015.
18. Ibid., Cafiero and Wagner.
19. "Kuwait, China share enthusiasm on 'Belt and Road' economic initiative", *Kuwait Times*, 13 May 2017.
20. 'Pakistan, Oman discuss opportunities offered by CPEC, Gwadar Port' *Times of Islamabad*, 8 May 2017. However, India has opposed the BRI in general, and the CPEC in particular, because it runs through the disputed territory of Kashmir, which it claims to undermine its sovereignty.
21. Jonathan Fulton, The GCC countries and China's Belt and Road Initiative: Curbing their enthusiasm?, Middle East Institute (MEI, Washington), 17 October 2017.
22. Wang Jisi, cited in Michael Clarke, 'Understanding China's Eurasian pivot'. *The Diplomat*, 10 September 2015.
23. 刘绍勇, "主动融入"一带一路"战略积极打造空中丝绸之路", 求是, Liu Shaoyong, "Actively Merge One Belt One Road and Positively Develop a Silk Road in the Air," *Qiushi*, 28 February 2017.

24. Alessandro Arduino and Xue Gong (eds.), *Securing the Belt and Road: Risk Assessment, Private Security and Special Insurances Along the New Wave of Chinese Outbound*, Palgrave, 2018.
25. Jeffrey Becker and Erica Downs, 'China's Djibouti military base the first of many', East Asia Forum, 27 June 2018.
26. "Reports of China using its 'Belt and Road' program for military purposes are 'no real surprise'," *CNBC*, 24 December 2014.
27. Ibid.
28. "China to extend offshore military reach to counter 'provocations'," *Reuters*, 26 May 2015.
29. 'Yemen crisis: China evacuates citizens and foreigners from Aden,' *BBC*, 3 April 2015.
30. David Brewster, 'The red flag follows trade: China's future as an Indian Ocean power,' in Ashley J. Tellis, Alison Szalwinski and Michael Wills (eds.), *Strategic Asia 2019. China's Expanding Strategic Ambitions*, The National Bureau of Asia Research. Washington D.C. 2019, p. 188.
31. 'Chinese naval fleets escort 3,400 foreign ships over past 10 years,' *Xinhua*, 1 January 2019; and 'Chinese naval fleets escort over 6,600 vessels in Gulf of Aden, Somalia over past 10 years,' *Xinhua*, 19 April 2019.
32. Robert Ross, 'The end of US naval dominance in Asia,' Lawfare Blog, 18 November 2018.
33. Ibid.
34. 'China invests in 42 overseas ports under Belt and Road project,' *Global Times*, 27 July 2018.
35. Erickson, Andrew S.; Denmark, Abraham M.; and Collins, Gabriel. "Beijing's 'Starter Carrier' and Future Steps." *Naval War College Review*. Winter 2012, vol. 65, no. 1, p. 39.
36. Zhang Wenmu, 'China's energy security and policy choices,' *Global Economics and Politics*, 14 May 2003, 11-16. 张文木. "中国能源安全与政策选择." 世界经济与政治 5.14.2003, 11-16.
37. Admiral Sunil Lamba's comments at the 2019 Raisina Dialogue. January 9, 2019. New Delhi.
38. Shaurya Karanbir Gurung. '14 Chinese navy ships spotted in Indian Ocean, Indian Navy monitoring locations.' *The Economic Times*, 27 January 2019.
39. N. Janardhan and Christopher Colley, 'Flag follows trade–China's security imprint in the Belt and Road Initiative, Indian Ocean and Gulf,' *EDA Insight* (AGDA), September 2019.
40. Fulton, 2019.
41. Janardhan and Colley, 2019.
42. Ibid.
43. 'UAE shut down China facility under US pressure, Emirates says,' *The Wall Street Journal*, 9 December 2021.
44. 'Gulf states should consider US ties when dealing with China—official,' Reuters, 7 May 2020.
45. 'US poll results have made global politics uncertain,' *The Gulf Today* (UAE), 14 November 2016.
46. "US defence chief reaffirms commitment to Middle East allies,' *Deutche Welle*, 20 November 2021.

47. 'US caution, rise of China: Jaishankar lists developments in geopolitics of Indian Ocean region,' *Livemint* (India), 4 December 2021.
48. "Jaishankar flags 'sharpening of tensions' across Asia amidst China's rise," Press Trust of India, 5 December 2021.
49, 'UAE suspends talks on F-35 deal with US,' *Al Arabiya* (Saudi Arabia), 14 December 2021.
50. 'China's surprising drone sales in the Middle East,' *Defence News* (US), 23 April 2021.
51. Ibid., 'UAE shut down China facility under US pressure.'
52. John Garver, 'China and the Iran nuclear negotiations: Beijing's mediation effort,' in James Reardon-Anderson (ed.), *The Red Star and the Crescent*. Oxford University Press, 2018, p. 124.
53. Degang Sun and Yahia Zoubir, 'China's participation in conflict resolution in the Middle East and North Africa: A case of quasi-mediation diplomacy?' *Journal of Contemporary China*, vol. 27, 2018, issue 110.
54. James Dorsey, 'Subtly, China pressures Gulf states to reduce regional tensions,' *Responsible Statecraft* (US), 20 November 2020.
55. 'Obama thanks Xi Jinping for China's role in Iran nuclear deal,' *CGTN America*, 21 July 2015.
56. 'Chinese FM reveals initiative to protect MidEast: Al Arabiya," *Arab News* (Saudi Arabia), 21 March 2021.
57. Rob Edens, 'The China wildcard in the Qatar crisis,' *The Diplomat* (Washington), 9 August 2017; and 'Qatar foreign minister in China after visit by UAE official,' *The National* (UAE), 20 July 2017.
58. Abdurrahim Sagir, 'China's mediation role between Israel and Palestine,' *Daily Sabah* (Turkey), 9 June 2021.
59. 'Iran and China sign 25-year cooperation agreement,' Reuters, 27 March 2021; Nazila Fathi, 'What will SCO membership mean for Iran?' MEI (Washington), 28 September 2021.
60. 'Lavrov: Russia ready to facilitate non-aggression pact between Iran and Persian Gulf states,' *Tehran Times*, 1 June 2019.
61. Jon Alterman, 'China's evolving strategy in the Middle East,' Youtube/*Atlantic Council*, 18 October 2019.
62. Lyle Goldstein, 'Should China police the Strait of Hormuz?' *The National Interest* (US), 9 November 2019.
63. Giorgio Cafiero and Daniel Wagner, 'China and the Abraham Accords peace agreement,' MEI (Washington), 22 September 2020.
64. Minghao Zhao, 'China's Middle East vision backs talks, not proxy,' *Khaleej Times*, 31 January 2016.
65. "Mao used his 'fight fight, talk talk' strategy on Chiang in 1945," *Today Online*, 6 November 2015.
66. "'Inch' towards 'Miles': PM Modi pushes for greater cooperation," *Hindustan Times*, 17 September 2017.
67. N. Janardhan, "India must learn China's 'da da, tan tan' strategy," *The Gulf Today* (UAE), 20 June 2020.
68. 'China, India can achieve win-win through cooperation,' *China Daily*, 24 April 2006.
69. Frederic Wehrey and Richard Sokolsky, 'Imagining a New Security Order in the Gulf', Carnegie Endowment, October 2015.

3

Russia's Growing Influence in the Middle East: The Ukrainian Context

Amb. Anil Trigunayat

The Ukraine crisis and conflict (2022) has created and displayed new alignments and equations emerging as a result of transitional global order or disorder in which countries in the Middle East are trying to find their anchor or multiple anchors as the US supremacy is being challenged by Russia and China. Ukraine has somehow become a sort of a litmus test as the diverse approaches, not necessarily in sync with the USA, have been witnessed in voting patterns by UAE and commentary by other regional powers which refused to decry the Russian invasion. The region was earlier, during Cold War 1.0, well contested by the two super powers and with the disintegration of the Soviet Union as well as the decline of erstwhile major regional powers like Iraq, Egypt and Syria with a corresponding rise of influence of the oil-rich Arab Gulf countries and their proximity and security dependence on Washington, Russia lost a great deal of its clout.

Moreover, as it was trying to find its feet and lost-dignity under President Vladimir Putin, Moscow began a concerted effort to regain its geostrategic influence by joining the fight against the Daesh (ISIL) by militarily intervening in Syria in 2015, at the invitation of President Bashar Al-Assad. Putin said concerning the Russian intervention in the Syrian civil war:

> "I decided that the positive effect from our active involvement in Syrian affairs for Russia and the interests of the Russian Federation would far outweigh non-interference and passive observation of how an international terrorist organization grows ever stronger near our borders.... We have managed to preserve Syrian statehood, no matter what, and we have prevented a Libya-style chaos there."[1]

U.S. President Donald Trump also thanked Putin for facilitating the operation to kill Abu Bakr al-Baghdadi, the leader of the Islamic State (ISIS).

In the wake of the Arab Spring in 2010-11, Moscow had learnt its lessons during NATO's Libyan intervention when, despite its diplomatic efforts, it felt short-changed by the West. Over the years, it acquired enough stakes and clout by cultivating General Khalifa Haftar in the eastern part of Libya where the UAE and other Gulf countries became its consort as the Russian Wagner group mercenaries or so-called military technical experts began to mark their presence. It expanded its collaboration with Turkey in the eastern part of Libya as it had done in Syria. The Mediterranean has become an arena of significant interest as Tartus and other ports in Libya provide it the requisite strategic heft. Russian presence and intervention in Syria saved President Assad, which provided them the respect and credibility of a dependable partner.

Russia has again emerged as a major power broker in the region. Iran, Israel, and Saudi Arabia are fighting a fierce proxy war in Syria, and the Kremlin has positioned itself as the power broker to whom all actors must talk. Russia can talk to everyone and is on good terms with everyone, so it is indispensable.[2] Rumer argues that Russia's new-found friends want something in exchange for their friendship. Israel wants Russia to restrain Iran and the Hezbollah in Syria, while Iran and the Hezbollah remain intent on waging their campaign against the Jewish state. The Saudis want Russia to take their side in their rivalry with Iran. But Russia has invested a great deal in its relationship with Iran and is not about to sacrifice it for the sake of better relations with Israel or Saudi Arabia. This has also given Russia new-found respect as it stands by its friends but finds a way to manage relationships. Its presence and say in both the OPEC+ (Organisation of Petroleum Exporting countries) partnership as well as in the GCEF (Coalition of Gas Exporting countries—Gas Exporting Countries Forum) have given Moscow an unusual dependency with regard to mutually sustaining negotiating leverage. Besides, Russia has also reached a deal with Egypt to create a Russian industrial zone in East Port Said and another with Sudan to establish a logistics support centre for its navy in Port Sudan. Russia also has indirect military involvement in Libya via the Wagner Group, a military contracting firm.[3]

Andre Kortunov of the Russian International Affairs Council (RIAC, 2019) emphasizes that Russian policy in the Middle East region can probably be considered one of the areas of most significant achievement for President Putin in recent years. With relatively small material investments and minimal combat losses, Moscow managed to transform itself from an almost imperceptible supernumerary on the Middle East scene into one of the region's main actors, without which not a single major issue of regional security can be resolved today. Russian successes are even more impressive if one compares the results of the Russian operation in Syria with those of the intervention of the USA and its allies in Iraq in 2003.

He further articulates that in contradistinction to other influential international players, Russia was able to maintain constructive relations with almost all sides of the Middle East conflicts—with the Israelis and Palestinians, with the Sunnis and Shiites, with the Turks and Kurds, and with Iran and the Arab monarchies of the Persian Gulf. In all likelihood, this peculiarity of Russia's positioning in the region is directly related to the country's initially marginal status in the Middle East (in the post-Soviet context): prior to the beginning of the 'Arab Spring,' Russia was, unlike the USA,, not burdened by rigid frameworks of close, allied relations with individual regional forces. Moscow is therefore now better suited to play the role of an 'honest broker' in the region than Washington.[4]

Russia has close relations with Iran, Turkey and Israel as well as Arab states. It has also been an interlocutor as well as a facilitator in the run-up to the JCPOA (Joint Comprehensive Plan of Action 2015) and is once again instrumental in getting them back to the table during the Biden Presidency while articulating the futility of the unjustified sanctions on Iran by subsequent US administrations. China and Russia have worked closely on this as they have supported Iran through the sanctions and projected its legitimate concerns to the West on every single occasion bilaterally, regionally and multilaterally while assuaging the concerns of other partners in the region who have fears, suspicion, and competing regional interests.

Moscow has waded successfully through the regional hotspots and cross-currents. Even as the revived JCPOA talks reach some conclusion, Russia's direct interests have an important dimension. Foreign Minister Lavrov has asked the USA and the West to ensure that the crippling sanctions imposed by them on it in the ongoing Ukrainian conflict will not impact and impinge on its trade and investments. Lavrov, following their own strategic interests, sought guarantees at least by his US counterpart, Anthony Blinken, stating, "We need a guarantee that these sanctions will not in any way touch the regime of trade-economic and investment relations which is laid down in the JCPOA" thereby creating yet another rider in the complex game.

Another major player is the UAE, which is currently in the UNSC as a non-permanent member (2022-23) and has been following its own style of a foreign policy both in the region and outside. While it wishes to follow a 'Zero Problem' policy that realises the changing power shift in the region as the USA takes a more equanimous approach under President Biden. It has been on the forefront to normalise relations with Israel under the ambit of the Abraham Accords and the relationship between Abu Dhabi and Tel Aviv has moved on at an unprecedented pace. Likewise, it is part of the newly founded Western Quad or Quartet with UAE, the USA, India, and Israel. It prefers dialogue and diplomacy to any overt conflict, including in Yemen, from where the Houthis have been launching drone and missile attacks on it. It maintains that the only way to overcome the current crisis is through concerted efforts to reach a Yemen-led, Yemeni-owned political solution under the auspices of the United Nations and in accordance with the three references, namely, the Gulf Summit, including its executive mechanism, the outcomes of the National Dialogue Conference, and the relevant Security Council resolutions, including resolution 2216. It however, worked for and welcomed the UN designating the Houthis as a terrorist group. This has also been its grudge against the USA, which removed the Houthis from terrorist designation post-Trump and suspended the sale of F-35s. It maintains closer relations with Tehran as well has mended its fences with Ankara. Its *de facto* ruler Sheikh Mohammed Zayed's visit to Turkey has closed a major gap and provided a $ 10 bn funding line. Russia-Turkey relations are also moving apace.

The UAE, along with India and China, abstained on the UNSC draft resolution by the USA and Albania which would have condemned the Russian aggression against Ukraine from where large quantities of wheat is imported by nearly all countries in the region. Wheat prices rose the highest in the past decade as a result of the ongoing conflict but correspondingly so did oil and gas prices compensating their bets. At the UNSC, it welcomes dialogue and diplomacy and explained that "We also welcome the second round of bilateral talks between Ukraine and Russia. The Security Council is responsible for maintaining international peace and security. And, as we know, nuclear threats are among the most devastating threats to humanity. The Council must make every possible effort to avoid any kind of nuclear disaster, whether from direct attack on a nuclear facility or as an unintended consequence of conflict. Such a disaster would have grave ramifications for generations to come. With regard to the conflict, we again reiterate our call for a cessation of hostilities, for de-escalation, and for dialogue mechanisms to be leveraged and to be supported by all of us. The risks of a failure in diplomacy are too grave to consider".[5]

During the Ukraine crisis, President Putin also spoke to Saudi Crown Prince Mohammad bin Salman (MBS) and Qatari Emir Sheikh Tamim, the two of its important partners in OPEC and GECF. Earlier, the Russian Foreign Minister made visits (March 2021) to the region and engaged leaders from Tehran to Turkey to identify similarities and synergies of cooperation outlines as it straddles across the conflictual and conflicting relationships. Saudi Crown Prince MBS who felt slighted by the Biden Administration apparently refused to talk to Biden when, in response to Russian threats, the latter wanted to talk to GCC leaders to increase oil production.

A tripartite meeting between the foreign ministers of Russia, Turkey, and Qatar in Doha on March 11 extended the Russian-Turkish "frenemy relationship" to yet another theatre in the Middle East. Besides the Arab world, especially UAE, Bahrain and Oman, is unable to comprehend the US sanctions policy like 'Caesar's act' that confronts their rapprochement and reconstruction efforts in Syria as the Arab League tries to bring the beleaguered country back into its fold.

Kuwait, recalling its own horrific invasion by Iraq in the 1990s, condemned the Russian invasion and had even joined the USA and 80 other countries in sponsoring the UNGA Resolution. However, Doha, which was most recently designated as a Non-NATO ally, preferred ambivalence to direct confrontation with Moscow which has been its partner on several fronts. Giorgio Cafiero, a leading expert, claims that it is important to note that while Qatar has stood up for Ukraine's sovereignty, Doha is not joining Western powers in advocating financial warfare against Russia. Having developed deeper ties with Russia in the spheres of investment, infrastructure, and tourism, Qatar wants to avoid burning its bridges with Moscow.[6]

Israel also has very good relations with Moscow despite its exceptional relationship with the USA and occasional tiffs with Russia, especially about Iran, the Hezbollah, Palestine and Syria on which both have differing viewpoints. But even in Syria they do cooperate within the context of counter-terrorism as Russia often looks the other way to Israeli airstrikes on the Hezbollah and Iranian targets in Syria. Israel also took a cautious position on the Russian-Western rupture following the 2014 annexation of Crimea. It neither actively condemned Russia nor joined sanctions against it and high-level meetings with Russian officials continued. President Putin highly appreciated then Prime Minister Benjamin Netanyahu's position, compared to sanctions and disengagement from most other pro-Western capitals. More than a million Russian Jews migrated to Israel creating a significant political constituency there. No wonder, Israeli PM Naftali Bennet tried to become a major initiator of peace and disengagement between Kiev and Moscow with the help of France and Germany.

Recognizing that Russia is in the Middle East for a long haul, many countries in the region are actively developing their relationships with Moscow: diversifying their arms supplies, increasing grain imports, and even cooperating in a grey area over the use of private armies and mercenaries. Since the US policy has essentially been to contain the Russian and Chinese influence, even if it is gradually extricating itself or becoming nonchalant in West Asia, the USA is unlikely to let the vacuum be filled by its adversaries. Most likely it will try and impose some direct and indirect costs through its bouquet of sanctions on very enthusiastic countries in the region. 'The USA will most likely resolve this contradiction by continuing to wind down its presence in the Middle East, while imposing sanctions on countries that try to use the situation to draw closer to Russia.'[7] Most of the regional powers feel more at home and comfortable with the Russian reluctance to do anything with their governance architecture or, for that matter, human rights, etc., which are major sticking points with the Americans and the West. Moreover, occasional arbitrary or a non-serious stance of the USA on issues of their concern makes the regional countries somewhat confused since for them the USA has been an arbiter of their security interests which appears to be not so reliable after-all. The ability of the Iran-backed Houthis to penetrate US equipment and air shields to attack their vital installations also sowed some seeds of doubt. Besides, during the Trump era, the Qatar blockade also opened new crevices where Turkey and Iran and Russia and China found an opening into the GCC fault lines. As such its military relationship with the region has continued to grow. Algeria remains its largest importer of arms and equipment.

Russia is also not looking to displace the US strategic orbit completely alone as it realizes its limitations to do so economically and militarily; hence filling up the partial vacuum with the rest by India and China would be acceptable to it. Having reasonably good relations with all aspirational leaders in the region, it can consider a 'whole-of-the-region' strategy which the USA and others have been missing as they have been seen siding with one or the other. Beijing and New Delhi follow similar positions in the region. However, being a super power, Russia has also not hesitated to evolve and suggest its security format for the region. It is comfortable in proposing an international peace conference or reviving the quartet on the Middle East; suggesting a joint security mechanism in the Gulf; and sponsoring dialogues among Libyan parties and bring on board opposing sides in Syria.

Russia's proposed 'Collective Security' for the Gulf and WANA region has not acquired salience as it is fraught with idealistic generalisations and is far too expansive in scope. The concept's core idea, which is to launch a multi-format dialogue between key regional players to discuss existing issues, is not something new. Since the late 1990s, and to varying extents over this period, the Kremlin has been promoting this concept on an international scale (usually recalling it during periods of diplomatic crises, such as periodical exacerbations of tensions in Israeli-Palestinian relations, the 2003 US invasion of Iraq, the 2006 International Atomic Energy Agency report on Iran's nuclear non-compliance to the United Nations Security Council, and others). Currently, Moscow tries to move slightly further; it talks about the necessity of applying its concept to the entire MENA region, in a format resembling the 1972–75 Helsinki process.[8] However, even to its close ally, Iran, the current format is not acceptable, and they promote their own Hormuz Peace Plan. Russian FM Lavrov, however, once again flagged it to his Middle Eastern counterparts during

March-April, 2021. Russian economic weakness is also a factor in its ability to play all actors for the collective security concept. Moscow's concept represents what can be called a 'Russian salad of ideas'—an eclectic mix of problems with little coherence or focus on practical steps to resolve them; the document touches on (without discussing in detail though) counter-terrorism, the supremacy of UN principles, the situation in Israel-Palestine, JCPOA, the crises in Iraq, Yemen and Syria, and even the idea of creating an equivalent to the Organization for Security and Co-operation in Europe (OSCE) for the Gulf.[9] Moreover, in view of the changing ground realities and effects of the pandemic, the regional powers themselves are working on a *modus vivendi* by creating dialogue mechanisms with their rivals to keep the differences below the threshold. To what extent the Russian proposal will fit into that matrix remains to be seen.

Even though many observers do not credit Russia with much of its soft power in the region, a noted Russia scholar, Samuel Ramani, while speaking at the Vivekananda International Foundation (April 2021) emphasized that Russia has optimally used its Islamic heritage and communal bonding to forge ties with West Asian states. Moreover, by establishing bureaucratic relations on institutional, ministerial, military, and personal levels, it has deepened sub-state relations. It has benefitted from regional polarisations by engaging with all sides and generally managing instability. In recent years, Russia's economic profile has been increasing, and private and public companies have acquired several construction and services contracts. Vaccine diplomacy has also added to its soft power approach in the region. However, the Ukraine conflict and crippling sanctions on Russia will limit its financial clout and capability to aggressively move to complete its geo-political and geo-economic objectives. It is quite possible that Russia may club with China in the region to the extent their common interests are subserved. The Ukraine conflict, if it turns in Moscow's favour, howsoever bloody it is, might give some clarity about Russian resolve to the West Asian countries who are keenly watching from the sidelines giving mixed signals. Perhaps, it will cement their belief that the USA had led Ukraine up the garden path of destruction and did not support Kiev to the fullest that was expected of them; hence alternatives have to be explored.

In a brilliant analysis, M.J. Akbar, a noted journalist and former State Minister of External Affairs, concludes (*Open* magazine, March 4, 2022), and is correct to a great extent, that "America sought the impossible, Russia the unattainable. Washington could never become the permanent guardian, guarantor, governor, philosopher, and global policeman of the 21st century. Putin wanted the virtual return of the Soviet Union's zone of influence. That was impossible, not because of American obstruction but because the zone had changed in a very fundamental sense. The nations of the old Soviet Union had discovered the meaning of independence". After Ukraine, America's allies are finding out the limits of their dependence. The crisis in Ukraine could initiate the restructuring of the present world order, for both the pillars of the 20th century have been undermined. THE BIGGEST CASUALTY of the Ukraine war has been trust in Washington. America's allies have got the message. If a crisis arrives with the speed and strength of a hurricane, Joe Biden, hiding behind the porous veil of "strategic ambiguity," will rush out statements rather than missiles. And this could be the outcome and narrative of the Ukrainian war."

Russia's quest for sharing leadership in the Middle East will have several riders and imponderables depending on the outcome of the Ukraine crisis and how soon it is able to strap up its boots and emerge as a dependable security guarantor and not only a provider of military equipment, whose efficacy will also be judged during this war.

ENDNOTES

1. Russia is Right on the Middle East (foreignpolicy.com).
2. Eugene Rumer in *Foreign Affairs* (October 13, 2019), Russia is the Middle East's Indispensable Nation, Foreign Affairs.
3. Russia in the Middle East: A source of stability or a pot-stirrer? - Atlantic Council.
4. RIAC: Russian Foreign Policy in the Middle East: Achievements and Limitations (russiancouncil.ru).
5. UAE statement at the UN Security Council Emergency Meeting on Ukraine—Permanent Mission of the United Arab Emirates to the United Nations (uaeun.org)
6. Analysis: Gulf states cautiously navigate war on Ukraine, Russia-Ukraine war News, Al Jazeera.
7. Biden, Russia, and the Middle East—Carnegie Moscow Centre—Carnegie Endowment for International Peace.
8. Russia and the Issue of a New Security Architecture for the Persian Gulf | Middle East Centre (lse.ac.uk).
9. Ibid.

4

US Policy towards the Middle East: Impact and Challenges

Prof. K.P. Vijayalakshmi

ABSTRACT

US involvement in the Middle East has been longstanding, and its role has grown during and beyond the Cold War. American foreign policy towards the Middle East, though, underwent various shifts starting with filling the vacuum left by the withdrawal of European powers to becoming the dominant external power focused on countering Soviet influence. Using the "twin pillar" strategy, it maintained close ties with both Saudi Arabia and Israel as security-energy dynamics was at the core of Middle East policy. However, developments like the Suez Canal crisis, Six-Day war, oil shock and the Iran Hostage crisis constrained the USA to review its policy. Israel's rise as a regional power and its improved position in US foreign policy, in contrast to the Arab countries despite the balancing strategy, became central to US diplomatic efforts in the region amidst failed attempts to broker peace between the two sides. In the post-Cold War era, the USA expanded its security presence in the region to contain Saddam Hussein's Iraq and the clerical regime in Iran. The 9/11 attacks, the Iraq and Afghanistan wars, and Arab Spring altered the US-led regional order. Since 2008, regional instability, deepening ideological rifts among its friends and partners plus violent outbreaks has constrained three administrations to make complex choices especially on ISIS, Syrian crisis and Iranian nuclear program. This chapter attempts to critically analyze the evolution of US foreign policy on the Middle East. It attempts an assessment of American interests, objectives, Presidential decisions, focusing particularly on presidents Obama, Trump and Biden. Evaluating policy practices amidst geopolitical shifts since the Cold War and its repercussion on US foreign policy would be central to the study.

Introduction

The USA, often referred to as an "immigrant" and "indispensable" nation, has viewed its purpose in the world as one of promoting democracy, prosperity, human rights and to fight totalitarianism and authoritarianism across the world through its security, strategic, diplomatic, and economic engagements. In the years since 1945, its foreign policy championed freedom and human rights, international security and order, economic stability and combating the aggression of "rogue nations".

As the Cold War ended, debates on the US role as "the world's policeman" reverberated with "America in Decline" prompting a reassessment of policy. After 9/11, the US-led Global War on Terror under Bush Jr., "leading from behind" under Obama and the "America First" policy of the Trump Administration represented a change in US foreign policy that impacted the Middle East as well. Yet, three factors remained important: the region acts as a bridge between Europe, Asia, and Africa; it remains a crucial economic hub beyond energy production that includes transit of people and cargo; and is a factor in the geopolitical competition with Russia and China. These have called for a deeper engagement by the USA as the challenge for the USA lay in protecting "its remaining and still important interests in that region in an era of austerity and fierce power competition, both in the region and globally."[1]

Context of US involvement

Until the mid-twentieth century, US involvement and engagement in the Middle East region was focused on commercial ties and oil supplies. Since Truman's recognition of Israel in 1948, US policy expanded from a narrow focus on shoring up oil supplies and energy security to one that included containment of the Soviet Union. As part of supporting anti-communist regimes, the USA backed Israel against Soviet-sponsored Arab countries. However, keeping in mind the vital need for oil and managing the consequences of the geopolitical competition with the Soviet Union, the USA adopted a "twin pillar" strategy that involved balancing options with both Arabs and Israel. Arguably, the USA acted "...like an offshore balancer from 1945 to about 1990: it wanted to prevent any state (including the Soviet Union) from controlling the Gulf as it had vital interests in the region.

It pursued this goal first by relying on Great Britain (until 1967) and then replaced Britain as the main security provider of the Persian Gulf states in the 1960s and 1970s, to ensure a stable flow of Gulf oil." It also began to rely on local allies like the Shah of Iran. After the fall of the Shah in 1979, the USA continued to pursue an off-shore balancing strategy that led to the creation of the Rapid Deployment Force (RDF) "...that could affect the balance of power swiftly and directly and thus deter a possible Soviet foray into the Gulf". However, "the RDF remained offshore and over the horizon and was not used until the Kuwait crisis of August 1990".[2] With the 1990s, this policy changed towards a more forward deployment and robust military presence due to the situation in Iraq and Iran. The Middle East also received a large portion of US military assistance annually (outpacing economic aid) with the major share given to Israel. Towards the end of the twentieth century, however, doubts over whether US reliance on military instruments were helping to achieve policy goals led to redefining the strategy.[3]

The USA has diplomatic relations with all the countries in the Middle East except Iran (whose 1979 revolution against the US-backed Shah Reza Pahlavi brought an anti-US government led by the Ayatollahs) and Syria whose relations have been suspended since 2012 due to the Syrian civil war. Its policy, though, has witnessed shifts in goals and objectives over the last fifty years. From a narrow objective of protecting US energy security, it expanded to becoming a security provider and guarantor for the region in the management of the Cold War. The resulting pursuit of an intense security alliance with Israel turned into a core interest that has remained. However, 9/11 and the Global War on Terror since 2001 placed combating terrorism as a primary objective along with managing rising regional threats from state and non-state actors, such as Iran and the ISIL. By 2008, US policy shifted again, as it faced domestic financial and economic crises, waning influence in the Middle East due to a variety of factors including winding down the wars in Afghanistan and Iraq, and Barack Obama's policy of military reticence with emphasis on diplomacy dialogue and sanctions on Iran and his "pivot to Asia" policy. American focus on the Indo-Pacific and developments in the region that involved changed equations among regional powers like Iran and Iraq and rivalry among the six Gulf States complicated US objectives that led to a recalibration of US strategy under Trump and Biden. Recently articulated priorities of the USA in the Middle East continue to include prevention of

Russian and Chinese influence, resolving the Arab–Israeli conflict, providing security for Israel, limiting the spread of weapons of mass destruction, promoting regional stability and countering terrorism. As stated by Resnik, the Deputy Secretary of State for Regional Security,

> "Our presence and our relationships with Middle East partners help prevent efforts by Russia and China to extend their influence into the region. Building and expanding security partnerships through security cooperation and defence trade enables our allies and partners to protect their sovereignty from malign influences, defend their borders, promote the rule of law in the air, on land, and at sea, respond to humanitarian crises, counter narcotics, transnational crime, and terrorism." Thus, US interests in the Middle East remain strong despite the reduced importance of the oil factor. However, the recognition that many of its allies and partners have become more capable and assertive has changed the USA' position as the primary external security provider despite continuing arms sales and counter-terrorism cooperation.

In this context, this study examines the developments in the Middle East since 2008 and US policy responses within the changing geopolitics that include the rise of China, resurgence of Russia, violence on the Gaza strip, Arab-Israeli relations, continuing tussle with Iran's nuclear aims, and resetting ties with Riyadh. This complex mosaic of issues has a deep historical context, but the US response to them remains dynamic as developments unfold.

This study contends that American interests, objectives and actions in the region are shaped by a mix of external (regional and global) and domestic factors that have exerted varied influence at different times. Security calculations have dominated the US approach, as evidenced in the various National Security Strategy documents[4] that include consistent support to Israel despite changes in administrations or different regional threat perceptions. This paper argues that by the time of the Trump presidency, recognition of a shift from a US-dominated regional security order to a US-led one has led to emphasis on countering the Chinese and Russian influence that altered the regional balance of power in the Middle East[5] and terrorist control of the region. Finally, it posits that changes wrought by the Trump Administration continue to be sustained in some part by a pragmatic Biden to sustain the main pillars of US policy that has some implications for India in the current context.

From Truman to George W. Bush Presidency

At the onset of the Cold War, the Truman Doctrine (1947) outlined an offensive US foreign policy that would support democratic countries via military and economic aid. As the Soviet Union pressurized Iran for oil concessions, supported communists in Greece, forced Turkey to grant a base to separatists from northern Iran, and Britain withdrew support to Greece, the USA reoriented its foreign policy.[6] The rationale for the US policy in the Middle East given by the CIA in 1948 was that, in case of war, "...denial to the Western powers of Near Eastern oil (by the Soviets) would seriously impair their war potential."[7]

The bipolar nature of the Cold War and the resulting security dilemma led to rapid militarization and the arms race. Apart from forming NATO with European allies, US defence expenditure grew from $ 11 to $ 50 billion.[8] Eventually, as part of resisting Soviet expansion in the Middle East, the USA successfully resolved the Greek crisis, and grew closer to Iran and Turkey. Subsequently, Eisenhower's response to the Suez Canal crisis of 1956 became a turning point that changed the internal dynamics of the Middle East. Egypt's Nasser aimed at developing a pan-Arab region by nationalizing the Suez Canal and drawing closer to the Soviet Union. Britain, France, and Israel formed an anti-Egypt coalition, even though the USA opposed any military moves. The eventual withdrawal of British and French troops from the region led to a power vacuum and expansion of Soviet influence. These developments critically shaped the Eisenhower Doctrine (1957) that responded by stating that a country could seek US aid if threatened by armed aggression "from any nation controlled by international communism".[9]

Kennedy inherited strained relations with Israel and Egypt. In order to regain lost ground, the USA focused on improving ties with Nasser to wean him away from the Soviets and eradicate the impression of being hostile to Arab nationalism. However, these attempts failed due to Egypt's involvement in Yemen and threats to Saudi Arabia, both close US allies in the region. These developments led to Saudi Arabia seeking supersonic fighter jets from the USA.[10] Similarly, his administration was in favour of lending sophisticated military hardware (missiles) to Israel, despite concern that Israel would take over parts of the West Bank to resist overall Arab control of the region. Iran, under the Shah, also received steady support. The Cold War, thus, allowed countries of the Middle East to wield influence over US policy.

The USA continued to nurture closer ties with Saudi Arabia, Iran and Israel during the Lyndon B. Johnson presidency. However, the Six-Day war between Israel, Egypt, Jordan, and Syria in 1967 altered US-Israel relations into a "special relationship",[11] with Israel seen as an asset in US efforts in the ongoing Cold War. The US objectives were to avoid a regional arms race, possibilities of nuclear proliferation, and resisting Soviet inroads. Furthermore, reserving strategic locations for US bases near areas of Soviet influence became a priority as much as denying the Soviets access to the resource-rich parts of the region.

As the containment strategy continued, US involvement in the Vietnam War, one of the bloodiest and most expensive US wars, faced strategic disappointment.[12] Nixon and his NSA, Kissinger, managing a range of foreign policy crises in Chile, southern Africa and other Cold War hot spots, focused the US policy in the Middle East towards mediated agreements between Egypt, Syria and Israel after the 1973 war. Kissinger, in particular, was credited with creating a "new political order" that allowed stable borders between the belligerents, reduced Soviet influence and affirmed the USA as a source of prodigious military aid to Israel and Egypt that continues till date. The Nixon Doctrine had already limited American commitments abroad but the "twin pillars strategy" centred on Iran and Saudi Arabia as two moderate and pro-USA states.[13] Yet, while Iran, under a unique agreement, was a recipient of the largest arms exports from the USA, the debates within the policy circle of Nixon reveal the strong bias of Secretary of State Kissinger towards Iran and against Saudi Arabia with Treasury Secretary Simon siding with Saudi Arabia. The energy crisis due to the oil embargo and the Saudi offer of lower prices with vast untapped oil reserves eventually saw the rise of the Saudis as allies.[14] By June 1974, the USA and Saudi Arabia signed a wideranging military and economic agreement that both said "heralded an era of increasingly close cooperation".

USA-Israel relations too strengthened in the Yom Kippur War of 1973 as the USA gave assistance in the form of air-to-air missiles.[15] Further, the 1970s saw a dramatic rise in US foreign assistance to the Middle East, more than any other region in the world, driven by packages to Israel and Egypt.[16] In essence, the US strategy perceived these regional heavyweights as "chosen instruments" that would "...spare the USA the cost of maintaining a security umbrella".[17] It seemed that developments in Soviet Middle Eastern policy and the need for capacity building in the military capabilities of the Arab states had a greater impact on US foreign policy than domestic factors.[18]

During the Ford presidency, Kissinger moved towards establishing closer ties with Egypt as it would enable the USA to receive support for its initiative on the Arab-Israeli dispute over the Golan Heights by acting as a direct intermediary between them. The main goals though, were to continue support of Israeli claims on Golan and decrease Soviet influence on the region. At the end of the decade, the Soviet invasion of Afghanistan (1979) led President Carter to respond with condemnation, announcement of sanctions, Olympic boycott, and support to the Afghan insurgents. Further, US policy included more lenient immigration laws as people fled political crises in Iran, Palestine, Lebanon, and Afghanistan in the 1970s. The Carter Doctrine also explicitly vowed that the USA would protect Middle Eastern oil supplies from Soviet encroachment.

However, the crisis in which 52 US citizens and diplomats were taken hostage by Iranian students in support of the Iranian Revolution posed the biggest foreign policy challenge to the Carter Administration. Carter's failed diplomatic endeavours and botched military rescue operation dramatically changed American perception of the Middle East and the future of USA-Iran relations. The crisis led the USA to rebuild its regional intelligence and military presence.[19] Israel emerged as the obvious choice for both goals, given its staunch support and technological capability. Carter support for Israel included solving the Israeli-Palestinian conflict with the signing of the Camp David Accord of 1978, (a peace treaty between Egypt and Israel), that continued the tradition of policy change through Presidential decisions vis-à-vis the region.

Reagan continued with Carter's objectives in the Middle East that placed significant importance on the Persian Gulf, in the "Reagan Corollary to Carter Doctrine".[20] To him, the Soviet Union's strengthened defence capabilities remained a core concern that was met with consistent growth in the defence budget, introduction of successive newer generation weapons and support systems and increase in tactical, aviation and ground forces.[21]

Defence spending rose to $ 456.5 billion in 1987, compared to $ 339.6 million in 1981.[22] The purpose of such a defensive build-up was to help America wage "the second Cold War" with the Soviets that played out forcefully in the Middle East. In an effort to rebuild American influence after the Iranian revolution, Reagan turned to cementing ties with Saudi Arabia. His proposed AIWACS sale to the Saudis caused a confrontation with the Congress (with both Democrats and Republicans opposing it on the grounds of promoting instability and being a direct threat to Israel), with the sale eventually being approved. Despite domestic criticism, American presidents have continued to cite national security interests for continuation of weapon sales. Domestic factors such as the Congress, pro-Israeli groups and oil companies nevertheless continue to influence policy.

George H. W. Bush's presidency and the First Gulf War in 1991 raised regional security as the primary responsibility of the USA. With "Operation Desert Storm" as a response to Saddam Hussein's occupation of Kuwait, expansion of American security and military presence began. Heralded as a success for both its multilateral diplomacy in building international coalition and conducting a land war, the American defeat of Iraq cemented its position as a guarantor of security for Arab states, particularly Saudi Arabia. US-Arab bonhomie also helped the USA initiate the Madrid Peace Conference in 1991 to further peace processes between Israel and Palestine. The legacy of the war resulted in US forces remaining in large numbers in the Gulf region that later proved to be detrimental with the rise of the Al-Qaeda.

The Clinton years were marked by deepening US efforts in furthering peace talks between Israel and her neighbours. Under American supervision and support, Israel and Palestine signed the historic Oslo Accord in 1993, followed by Israel and Jordan's peace deal in 1994. However, despite efforts, the peace process eventually deteriorated for a variety of reasons. Most importantly, US policy began to unravel as crisis escalated between Israeli expansion of West Bank settlements and Hamas bombings and the Israeli resistance in resuming the peace process. Netanyahu's closeness to the Republicans, who by then controlled the US Congress and their opposition to Clinton's policy, helped insulate Israel from any negative fallout. In addition, Clinton's "dual containment strategy" of Iran and Iraq that was expected to isolate Iran and Iraq from the world economy and encourage a change of regime did not succeed.[23] The criticism was that not only had Saddam emerged stronger by declaring himself as leader of the Arab world who would vanquish Israel, but there was also a dwindling of Arab and Muslim support for the containment of Iraq.[24] Thus, since the end of the Cold War, US policy decisions were inextricably linked with domestic and external developments.

The 9/11 attack on the USA, orchestrated by the Al-Qaeda as a response to US policy on Palestine, Somalia, Chechnya and Lebanon,[25] led to the Bush Doctrine that moved US foreign policy towards an assertive "pre-emptive response" to threats from terrorism and unilateral principles of conduct. With high public approval ratings and Congress authorizing the use of armed force,[26] Bush Jr. launched the Global War on Terror and with an attack on Afghanistan in 2001, successfully toppled the Taliban regime that was sheltering the Al-Qaeda, and later led an invasion on Iraq in 2003 with the stated aim of destroying WMDs developed by the Saddam Hussein regime. At this juncture, US policy focused on Iraq, Iran and North Korea as an "axis of evil" that threatened US interests by "seeking WMDs, funding terrorists and is a threat to allies".[27] While Iraq was not directly linked to the 9/11 attacks, "...decision to remove Saddam from power cannot be viewed in isolation from the attacks" as the White House clearly stated "...that after 9/11, we could not risk allowing a sworn enemy of America to have weapons of mass destruction, as intelligence agencies around the world believed Saddam did".[28] Thus, to the USA, the mantle of providing a security umbrella that covered non-proliferation objectives was part of Middle East policy.

The war on Iraq, however, severely impacted US credibility in the region. Saddam's collapse created a power vacuum by presenting opportunities for the rise of non-state actors like the ISIS, strengthened other Arab countries, facilitated Iran's rise, sectarian conflicts, ethnic divisions, and created regional instability. The USA's inability to eradicate terror and its use of unilateral force enraged the region and raised questions on the US ability to be a rational player guaranteeing the delicate balance of power in the region.

Obama, Trump, Biden and Middle East

Obama inherited the legacy of US involvement in the two wars and a worsening economic crisis both at home and abroad. His strategy focused on reinstating America's moral standing and leadership in world affairs and repairing the USA's tarnished image in the region. Describing Afghanistan as a "war of necessity"[29] and Iraq as "war of choice"[30] he announced the ending of the US combat mission in Iraq leaving a smaller force to assist "Iraqi forces during the transition period".[31] Obama approached the Arab world consciously "...by beginning a process of outreach towards the goal of disengagement from the region, reducing military presence, promoting peace among Palestinians and Israelis, appealing to the Iranian leadership, and adopting an iron fist approach in dismantling the Al-Qaeda".[32] Notably, his advocacy of democracy and political openness did not dictate his approach with countries like Egypt and Iran. Yet Obama too identified the Arab-Israel issue as a pivotal concern.

Obama's agenda of reducing the military footprint succeeded as the USA withdrew troops from Iraq by 2011. Rising sectarian conflicts gave way to the rise of the Islamic State in Iraq and Syria (ISIS) that conquered territories across the Iraq-Syria border. US-trained Iraqi troops unravelled, leaving Baghdad in chaos. The subsequent US air strikes[33] in the region did not thwart the ISIS's progress in the region. Eventually, in 2016, 600 more troops were provided in order to take Mosul back from the ISIS. The President's decision faced domestic criticism[34] that pointed to how the USA was unable to control the Iraqi political evolution or reconcile the Shia-Sunni differences that helped the ISIS.

Obama also supported the "Arab Spring" (civil unrest in countries like Libya, Tunisia, Iraq, Egypt, and Syria caused as a reaction to dictatorial regimes, monarchies, human rights violations, and growing political corruption). These protests, welcomed as a sign of the people's will to have more politically open societies, failed, creating further political instability and a growing threat from fundamentalists. For instance, in Egypt, the Arab Spring led to the Muslim Brotherhood establishing an Islamist state, an ardent critic of the West. This development led the USA and European allies to engage in saving democracy in Libya. However, partly due to American expectations from European partners, and its hesitation to have troops on the ground and increased violence after the fall of Hosni Mubarak, the efforts failed.

Domestically, Congressional criticism of the administration's response to brewing crises in the Middle East mounted especially after the attack on the US consulate at Benghazi that claimed the life of ambassador J. Christopher Stevens. The Libya fiasco impacted the administration's approach towards the unrest in Syria as well. Even though the President drew a "red line",[35] i.e., usage of chemical weapons by the Assad regime in Syria would call for an American response, he remained reluctant to intervene militarily and ultimately decided against it. This decision not only led to the escalation of the Syrian crisis but also became one of

Obama's most controversial decisions leading to doubts on American credibility. Both Republicans and some Democrats voiced opposition to "leading from behind" as an inappropriate strategy and that America must deliver on its promises.

Obama's rejection of the criticisms as part of the "missile playbook" mentality of Washington that did not accept the reality of an "unfixable Middle East" shaped his policy as did his "candid commentary on the intractable tribalism of the Middle East, saying that Saudi Arabia needs to "share" the neighbourhood with Iran; on the shortcomings of America's allies who act more like "free riders". And he is preserving and enhancing US power, not diminishing it, by refusing to wage unnecessary and unwinnable wars in the "fraying" states of the Middle East".[36]

For Obama, the most challenging aspect of the region was dealing with Iran's growing nuclear ambitions and their impact on the balance of power in the Middle East. Reports of Iran testing advanced centrifuges[37] led to the "dual track strategy"[38] that relied on diplomatic negotiations and sanctions to secure Iranian compliance. The US-led UN expanded proliferation-related sanctions on Iran and imposition of arms embargo continued the strategy.[39] Congress supportively passed the "Comprehensive Iran Sanctions, Accountability and Divestment Act" in the same year, expanding sanctions on investment in Iran's energy sector.[40]

Mounting international pressure finally led Iran to interact with P5+1[41] countries in 2012, and USA-Iran bilateral talks began in 2013.[42] The talks progressed as Rouhani (perceived as a moderate) became President of Iran and by November, an agreement between Iran and the P5+1 was reached with Iran agreeing to stop its nuclear activities for six months in lieu of lifting some of the sanctions.[43] By 2015, the "Iran nuclear deal" was achieved in the form of the Joint Comprehensive Plan of Action (JCPOA). In 2016, the IAEA declared that Iran had complied with all the measures required for the "JCPOA to enable implementation".[44]

Despite touting it as a success in Obama's foreign policy, the agreement invoked criticism from the Republicans in the USA, and by Israel and the Arab states in the Gulf region. Obama's insight was that a diplomatic agreement would mitigate fears of Iran's nuclear proliferation to Israel and others, mollify Iran and provide regional stability. It also addressed fears of regime change and encouraged the hope of reset US-Iranian relations. Further, sanctions relief would help Iran to rebuild its economy and reintegrate it into the global economy that would reduce the incentives for regional mischief.

Unfortunately, the fact that the deal left Iranian nuclear military sites off limits for inspection and Iran's intent to prove that it was not buckling under the pressure of the USA fuelled Israel's criticism as it disbelieved Iran's compliance, and rollback of the Iranian nuclear program. Republicans opposed it as being conciliatory with Mitch McConnell characterizing it as "flawed" that would not prevent, but delay Iran's quest for becoming a nuclear state and that it did not call out Iran's regional actions. Thus, a strong dissatisfaction to the policy was already underway in the USA that eventually culminated in the USA walking out of the deal under Trump who called it the "worst deal ever negotiated".

Donald Trump, campaigning on the slogans "America First" and "Making America Great Again", was already critical of past facets of US policy such as maintaining alliance networks and contributing to multilateral organizations. For instance, he argued against commitment to the NATO or the Paris Agreement. Guided by a transactional approach, he persisted with fierce criticism towards the liberal international order, free riding of allies, and failure to achieve burden-sharing and multilateralism. As for the objective of defeating terrorists, he turned his campaign rhetoric into policy by instituting the "Muslim ban" that effectively banned citizens of Muslim-majority countries like Iran, Syria, Libya, Yemen and Somalia, (as well as North Korea and Venezuela). While the administration argued that it was not against all Muslims, as evidenced by acceptance of Saudis and Afghans, the US Department of State's Bureau of Consular Affairs data showed that there was a significant decrease in the number of immigrant visas issued to Muslim countries affected by the travel ban. This harsh travel ban provided a glimpse of US counter-terrorism efforts to contain *jihadis*. Yet, his policy on the Middle East revealed a rejuvenated attempt at building an alliance system that unambiguously supported Israel and refined closer ties between Saudi Arabia, the UAE and Israel throughout his term. In 2017, contradicting the rhetoric of wariness to the idea of collective defence, the Middle East Strategic Alliance (MESA) likened by many as formation of an "Arab NATO" was drafted to counter the Iranian nuclear threat. The Riyadh Declaration of 2017 post the Arab-American-Islamic Summit in Saudi Arabia mentioned the principle of collective security. The aim for the six Gulf countries, Egypt, Jordan and the USA was to strengthen military cooperation and missile defence. The MESA was

Trump's attempt at reducing American security responsibility in the region and fashioning a new Middle East order that supported a greater role for Israel and Saudi Arabia.

However, this initiative lost momentum due to regional tensions. For example, Saudi Arabia economically blockaded Qatar in 2017, creating a diplomatic crisis. The spillover of the dispute impacted the Gulf countries and multilateral initiatives. Key administration officials like Jared Kushner, keen to de-escalate tensions and continue with cooperative initiatives in the Middle East, organized the Warsaw Summit in 2019 with European partners, Arab states and Israel. Unfortunately, ongoing regional and ideological conflicts dampened enthusiasm for the MESA.

The change in US-Saudi relations was evident throughout Trump's term when he sided with Saudi Arabia in the crisis with Qatar, despite the fact that the USA has its largest military base at Al-Udeid, Qatar.[45] In 2019, he defied the Congress (who opposed the sale of offensive weapons due to concerns over the Saudi involvement in the war in Yemen and the killing of journalist Khashoggi) by moving ahead with the sale of $ 8 billion worth of weapons to Saudi Arabia, the UAE and Jordan.[46] Closer ties by the USA with Saudi Arabia were accompanied by efforts to isolate Iran in the region. Believing that Iran would come back to negotiations under "maximum pressure" rather than incremental pressure as envisaged by the Obama deal, he withdrew from the JCPOA in 2018 and re-imposed "sanctions lifted under the deal" with a focus on the petrochemical, energy and financial sectors.[47] The search for a better deal did not yield dividends as Iran saw this as a breach of trust that masked US intent of a regime change and redoubled its efforts at nuclear development. It also continued to play a supportive role in conflicts in Yemen, Syria, and Iraq, with actions from Arabs, continuing regional instability.

While this move was viewed as a threat to the nuclear non-proliferation regime by countries like France, the UK and Germany,[48] countries like Israel, Saudi Arabia, the UAE, and Bahrain welcomed the decision. The international community perceived the move as a weakening of trust in international institutions, US commitments to multilateral deals and an obstacle to global attempts to bring accountability to the Iranian nuclear program. Additionally, questions of regional stability and war, if Iran were to nuclearize, were raised. One of the most tense moments in USA-Iran relations occurred after US drones successfully killed senior Iranian military leader Qassem Soleimani in 2020. This led Iran to abandon the limitations set by the nuclear deal on uranium enrichment and further developing the nuclear program.[49] Iran then launched a ballistic missile attack on the US base in Iraq in response to Soleimani's death. According to Iranian President Rouhani, the "final answer" to Soleimani's death would be to "kick all US forces out of the region".[50] These developments worsened tensions in the Middle East with many worrying about a possible war.

He also broke with tradition when the USA recognized Jerusalem as Israel's capital by moving the US embassy from Tel Aviv to the disputed city in 2018. Starkly reminiscent of Kissinger's policy, Trump also recognized Israel's sovereignty over Golan Heights. Syria viewed this as "a blatant attack on its sovereignty" and vowed to capture the area "through all available means".[51]

Conversely, the diplomatic initiative known as the Abraham Accords achieved a major political breakthrough wherein the UAE and Bahrain normalized relations with Israel in 2020[52] (later joined by Sudan and Morocco). Cited as bringing stability and peace to the region, this development was perceived as having initiated a new chapter in Arab-Israel relations that would pave the way for strong people-to-people interaction between member-states and the possibility of a two-state solution in the future.

In some ways, Trump continued the Obama policy on the issue of drawing down of troops since "terrorism was defeated" in Afghanistan and Iraq while Syria had some troop presence. The issue strategy of "maximum pressure" on Iran was a departure, but it was in search of a better deal. Democratic opposition to such a policy was that it set the USA up to a spiral of endless pressure from Iran and others invested in the JCPOA.

Biden took office in 2020 with the intent to reverse, restore, and rewrite many of Trump's policies. By placing democratic values, human rights, traditional diplomacy, restoring alliances and multilateral consensus at the core of foreign policy, Biden announced that "America was back" to take leadership of the world. The priority, however, remained in taming the COVID pandemic, rebooting the economy, battling the climate crisis, and tackling a domestically polarized USA. In foreign policy, managing the competition with China and the challenge of Russia was given precedence.

In the Middle East, Biden raised expectations that he would pursue a more muscular approach when he declared in his first foreign policy address in February 2021 that "war in Yemen must end". As a candidate, he criticized Trump's plan to withdraw American forces from Syria arguing that it would advantage the Assad regime and Iran while leaving the Israelis dependent on the others for their security. He had pledged that the Saudis would "pay the price" for the continuing crisis in Yemen.

As President, he preferred de-escalation to serve US interests and engaged Saudi Arabia, Egypt, Qatar, and the United Arab Emirates (UAE) along with Israel and Jordan to end the conflicts in Yemen and Syria. Special envoy Timothy Lenderking and other advisors have signalled that aiding the Lebanese or Syrians and blocking Iran and Russia are major objectives that would be based on a pragmatic approach. This has entailed Jordan and the UAE playing a larger role inviting stringent criticism from both hawks and human rights advocates in the Congress.

Biden's withdrawal from Afghanistan (part of the greater Middle East) changed US relationships with countries in the region, especially Saudi Arabia. However, Qatar, which during the Trump years, mediated between Washington and the Taliban in Doha for US withdrawal, is being viewed as an increasingly reliable partner with its institutional knowledge of the Taliban's views. American reliance on Qatar was evident when it assisted with the evacuation of approximately 57,000 Afghans during the withdrawal through Doha. Qatar's advocacy of dealing with the Taliban despite their non-adherence to promises made to stop other terror groups from gaining havens in Afghanistan has been influential with the USA.

Dealing with the Saudis who share a close relationship with Pakistan and were not enthusiastic about processing refugees from Afghanistan at the USA's behest was complicated. Saudi closeness to Russia as well as China (on a civilian nuclear program) has indicated that it is not dependant for its security on the USA alone. Concerned with the impact of the withdrawal, the Biden Administration outlined the US Middle East policy during November 2021 when top officials toured the region. Apart from Defence Secretary Austin, Brett McKurk, the White House Middle East Coordinator, signalled that the USA has a cautious approach with pragmatic goals that would allow "no more failed states" in the region. Acknowledging that "lessons have been learnt from the policies of the last three presidents", he stated that Washington had decided to adopt a strategy of "going back to basics" in foreign affairs, including giving up "regime change policies". He elaborated further by stating that the USA would stay in Syria providing troops and assisting with humanitarian aid, support the Iraqi government with assistance and advisory role and incentivize the Lebanese government to resolve its issues.

By its own admission, the Biden Administration was not interested in "transforming the region" but "...focused on the interests that impact Americans and our national security, and the national security of our friends".[53] It seemed a continuation of the policy of the past that essentially focused on US military dominance that aimed at protecting oil supplies, prevent control by adversaries, combat terrorists and regional proliferation of weapons of mass destruction, and encourage bilateral trade and economic prosperity. Both Saudi Arabia and Israel have benefitted from the *status quo* policy that was described as "going back to basics" in which the USA would pursue "the basics of building, maintaining and strengthening our partnerships and alliances".[54] Such a policy in some measure explains why Biden has not pressured the Saudis to call off the blockade of Yemen that has caused a humanitarian crisis as Yeminis starve for food, fuel, and other amenities. Further, the recent January 2022 Saudi air strikes on Yemen have not invited rebukes, but call for de-escalation. More importantly, in December 2021, the Senate rejected a bipartisan bid to stop a sale of weapons worth $ 650 million to Saudi Arabia despite its human rights record, supporting the Biden Administration's argument that such a move would "undermine the President's commitment to aid in our partner's defences at a time of increased missile and drone attacks against civilians in Saudi Arabia".[55] Interestingly, it is Biden's own party that is raising objections to his approach towards Saudi Arabia.

With Israel, Biden has not only continued with Trump's recognition of its claim to Syrian Golan Heights and the efforts to normalize relations between Israel and Arab states, and has not called for an end to the bombardment of the Gaza strip, preferring to work for a ceasefire through diplomacy. According to senior officials, "the security of Israel is first and foremost in his mind and ours". While Biden has restored a part of humanitarian aid to the Palestinians that was cut down by Trump, and supports a "two-state solution" to resolving the conflict, there has been no public admonition to Israel on the settlements issue, nor any move to establish a Palestinian consulate as promised earlier.

Another issue which the Biden Administration aimed to reverse and reset concerns the Iranian nuclear deal. The possibility of renewing the JCPOA faces headwinds following Iran's choice to not follow the key tenets of the JCPOA unless sanctions were lifted. Despite seven rounds of talks between Iran and P5+1 countries in Vienna in 2021, members noted Iran's lack of interest in negotiations and presenting viable proposals for future discussions. Congress too questioned the wisdom of negotiating to lift sanctions with an intransigent Iran on the nuclear issue, while adding the issue of Iran's ballistic missile program and regional agenda. Currently, talks are said to be on but Trump era sanctions are still in place and "Iran continues to use counter-measures such as seizing a South Korean ship in the Persian Gulf in January, to ramping up uranium enrichment to 60 per cent to show the invincibility of its nuclear program, to threatening to quit the Nuclear Non-Proliferation Treaty (NPT), and even hinting at assembling a nuclear bomb".[56]

Biden's policy on the Middle East is, thus, a work in progress that is defined by both continuity and shifts. The main pillars of the policy of alliance-based military cooperation, support for Israel, and combating regional non-proliferation and terrorism are intact. The shift is in the explicit underscoring of the US commitment to support its allies and partners without a regime change is a reflection of the tacit US acceptance of changing equations between countries of the region and Russia-China. It also betokens the US return to alliance strategy in foreign policy.

US Foreign Policy on Middle East and India

US policies since 9/11 greatly influenced Middle Eastern regional dynamics. The two wars in Afghanistan and Iraq rewired regional relations, gave rise to new phenomenon like the ISIS, spearheaded counter-insurgency efforts, and reshuffled power dynamics. American policy trajectory thus has significantly influenced policy choices of countries around the world. To India, the Middle East's importance in its strategic calculations rests on its growing multifaceted and socioeconomic engagements with Israel and the Gulf countries.

Estimates of over five million Indian Diaspora in the Gulf remitting nearly \$ 50 billion annually, merchandise trade of over \$ 150 billion and sourcing of nearly two-thirds of India's hydrocarbon imports and major investments has been the basis for India's "Look West" policy. India's political strategy in the region has emphasized balancing ties with Israel and the Arab states. Within this context, India's challenge to maintain strategic autonomy while finding means to converge with Washington DC remains critical. On the one hand, India has been engaging with countries like Saudi Arabia, the UAE, Israel, and Qatar; on the other, it has maintained ties with Iran.

Diplomatic balancing with the states in the region has become even more nuanced since 2014 as the Modi administration began proactive engagement abroad. India's diplomatic efforts with the 2021 virtual meet between the USA, Israel, the UAE and India, signalled a QUAD-like setup in the Middle East. Although it would be premature to conclude on India's successes, India's heightened cooperation in areas like defence, technology, and trade and investment with the Middle East over the years has prepared New Delhi to further bolster its regional relations. This mini-lateral mechanism has taken into account the ongoing geopolitical shifts in the region, as Iran gravitates towards China amidst stringent sanctions from the West. Post the Abraham Accords, Israel-Gulf relations have improved, creating an opportunity for India to mobilize efforts in countering China's growing connections with the region. Amidst these developments, India has been seeking like-minded countries to safeguard its critical interests. A possible "Quad of Middle East" presents a new opportunity for India to weave an ambitious foreign policy unlike those seen in the past.

ENDNOTES

1. Wittes, Tamara Cofman (2021), 'What to do and not to do in Middle East', Brookings, January 25, 2021, https://www.brookings.edu/research/what-to-do-and-what-not-to-do-in-the-middle-east/
2. Walt, Stephen M. (2016), 'Don't Knock Offshore Balancing Until You've Tried It', *Foreign Policy*, December 8, 2016, https://foreignpolicy.com/2016/12/08/dont-knock-offshore-balancing-youve-tried-it-obama-middle-east-realism-liberal-hegemony/
3. Kaye, Dalia Dassa, Linda Robinson, Jeffrey Martini, Nathan Vest, and Ashley L. Rhoades, (2021) *Reimagining U.S. Strategy in the Middle East: Sustainable Partnerships, Strategic Investments*, CA: RAND Corporation, https://www.rand.org/pubs/research_reports/RRA958-1.html.
4. US Department of Defence, Historical Sources, National Security Strategy, https://history.defense.gov/Historical-Sources/National-Security-Strategy/
5. The White House (2017), National Security Strategy, December 2017, https://trumpwhitehouse.archives.gov/wp-content/uploads/2017/12/NSS-Final-12-18-2017-0905.pdf
6. US Department of State (1947), Truman Doctrine, Milestones 1945-1952, https://

history.state.gov/milestones/1945-1952/truman-doctrine

7. Central Intelligence Agency (1948), Possibility of Direct Soviet Military Action during 1948, ORE-22-48, https://www.cia.gov/readingroom/docs/DOC_0000258340.pdf
8. Kennedy, Paul (1989), *The Rise and Fall of the Great Powers* (London: Unwin Hyman Limited), p. 383.
9. US Department of State (1957), The Eisenhower Doctrine, Milestones 1953-1960, https://history.state.gov/milestones/1953-1960/eisenhower-doctrine
10. US Department of State (1962), Memorandum of Conversation of President with Crown Prince Faisal, Foreign Relations of the United States, 1961-1963, vol. XVIII, Near East, October 5, 1962, https://history.state.gov/historicaldocuments/frus1961-63v18/d71
11. Lazarowitz, Arlene (2008), 'Different Approaches to a Regional Search for Balance: The Johnson Administration, the State Department and the Middle East 1964-1967', *Diplomatic History*, 32(1), p. 25.
12. CQ Almanac (1975), Vietnam Statistics War Costs: Complete Picture Possible, Library of Congress, https://library.cqpress.com/cqalmanac/document.php?id=cqal75-1213988
13. Smith, David O. (1991), 'The Postwar Gulf: Return to Twin Pillars', *Parameters*, 21(1), p. 51.
14. Mirzadegan, A 'Nixon's folly the White House and the 1970s oil price crisis' https://historicalreview.yale.edu/sites/default/files/files/mirzadegan.pdf
15. George Washington University National Security Archives (2003), Declassified Memorandum of Conversation between Henry Kissinger and Simcha Dinitz, RG 59, Records on Kissinger, October 7, 1973, https://nsarchive2.gwu.edu/NSAEBB/NSAEBB98/octwar-18.pdf
16. Sharp, Jeremy M. (2005), US Foreign Assistance to the Middle East: Historical Background, Recent Trends and the FY2006 Request, Congressional Research Service, RL32260, June 13, 2005, https://www.everycrsreport.com/files/20050613_RL32260_80f18159feba2f763c50e53d4ad80b1d8c9b86bf.pdf
17. See f.n. 2.
18. Quandt, William B. (1970), Domestic Influences on U.S. Foreign Policy in the Middle East: The View from Washington, https://www.rand.org/pubs/papers/P4309.html
19. US Department of State (1977-1980), Editorial, Foreign Relations of the United States, 1977-1980, vol. XVIII, Arabian Peninsula, https://history.state.gov/historicaldocuments/frus1977-80v18/d45
20. Kuniholm, Bruce R. (1986), 'The Carter Doctrine, the Reagan Corollary, and Prospects for United States Policy in Southwest Asia', *International Journal*, 41(2), p. 345.
21. US National Foreign Assessment Centre (1984), Soviet Spending for Defence: Trends Since 1965 and the Outlook for the 1980s, September 10, 1984, https://www.cia.gov/readingroom/docs/DOC_0000028136.pdf
22. Schneider, Greg (2004), 'Reagan's Defence Buildup Bridged Military Eras', *The Washington Post*, June 9, 2004, https://www.washingtonpost.com/archive/business/2004/06/09/reagans-defense-buildup-bridged-military-eras/ec621466-b78e-4a2e-9f8a-50654e3f95fa/
23. Gause III, F. Gregory, 'The Illogic of Dual Containment', *Foreign Affairs*, 73(2), p. 57.
24. James A. Phillips, 'How Clinton's policy has collapsed on two fronts, https://

www.heritage.org/middle-east/report/how-clintons-troubled-middle-east-policy-has-collapsed-twofronts

25. *The Guardian*, Full Text: Bin Laden's Letter to America, November 24, 2002, https://www.theguardian.com/world/2002/nov/24/theobserver
26. US Congress Joint Resolution, 107th Congress, Public Law 107-40, September 18, 2001, https://www.congress.gov/107/plaws/publ40/PLAW-107publ40.pdf
27. *The Washington Post* (2002), Text of President Bush's 2002 State of the Union Address, January 29, 2002, https://www.washingtonpost.com/wp-srv/onpolitics/transcripts/sou012902.htm
28. https://georgewbush-whitehouse.archives.gov/infocus/mideast/
29. Stolberg, Sheryl Gay (2009), 'Obama Defends Strategy in Afghanistan', *The New York Times*, August 17, 2009, https://www.nytimes.com/2009/08/18/us/politics/18vets.html
30. Kalb, Marvin, Obama's 'Oops' in Afghanistan, Brookings, January 23, 2012, https://www.brookings.edu/blog/up-front/2012/01/23/obamas-oops-in-afghanistan/
31. The White House, President Obama's Address on the End of the Combat Mission in Iraq, August 31, 2010, https://obamawhitehouse.archives.gov/blog/2010/08/31/president-obamas-address-end-combat-mission-iraq
32. Fawaz Gerges, 'The Obama Approach to the Middle East: The End of America's Moment?' *International Affairs (Royal Institute of International Affairs 1944-)* 89, no. 2 (2013): 299–323. http://www.jstor.org/stable/23473538
33. US Department of Defence, 'Operation Inherent Resolve: Targeted Operations to Defeat ISIS', https://dod.defense.gov/OIR/
34. Cooper, Helen (2016), 'US to Send 600 More Troops to Iraq to Help Retake Mosul from ISIS', *The New York Times*, https://www.nytimes.com/2016/09/29/world/middleeast/obama-troops-iraq.html
35. The White House (2012), Remarks by the President to the White House Press Corps, August 20, 2012, https://obamawhitehouse.archives.gov/the-press-office/2012/08/20/remarks-president-white-house-press-corps
36. 'The Obama Doctrine;: The Atlantic's Exclusive Report on the U.S. President's Hardest Foreign Policy Decisionshttps://www.theatlantic.com/press-releases/archive/2016/03/the-obama-doctrine-the-atlantics-exclusive-report-on-presidents-hardest-foreign-policy-decisions/473151/
37. Heinrich, Mark (2008), 'Iran Testing Advanced Centrifuges', *Reuters*, February 7, 2008, https://www.reuters.com/article/us-iran-nuclear-centrifuges-idUSL068392 8820080206
38. US Senate (2009), Testimony by James B. Steinberg, Deputy Secretary of State, Senate Committee on Banking, Housing and Urban Development, October 6, 2009, https://www.banking.senate.gov/imo/media/doc/Steinbergtestimony10609.pdf
39. United Nations Security Council (2010), S/RES/1929, June 9, 2010, https://www.un.org/securitycouncil/s/res/1929-%282010%29
40. US Congress (2010), 111th Congress, Comprehensive Iran Sanctions, Accountability and Divestment Act of 2010, Public Law 111-195, July 1, 2010, https://www.congress.gov/111/plaws/publ195/PLAW-111publ195.pdf
41. P5+1 countries are the USA, the UK, France, Russia, China and Germany.
42. Mohammed, Arshad and Parisa Hafezi (2013), 'US-Iran Held Secret Talks in March to Nuclear Deal', Reuters, November 24, 2013, https://www.reuters.com/article/us-iran-nuclear-bilateral-idUSBRE9AN0FB20131124

43. US Department of Treasury (2013), Joint Plan of Action, November 23, 2013, https://home.treasury.gov/system/files/126/jpoa.pdf
44. IAEA (2016), IAEA Director General's Statement on Iran, January 16, 2016, https://www.iaea.org/newscenter/statements/iaea-director-general%E2%80%99s-statement-iran
45. Frank Gardner (2021), 'Qatar Crisis: Saudi Arabia and Allies Restore Diplomatic Ties with Emirate', *BBC*, January 5, 2021, https://www.bbc.com/news/world-middle-east-55538792
46. Zengerle, Patricia (2019), 'Defying Congress, Trump sets $8 billion plus in weapons sales to Saudi Arabia, UAE', *Reuters*, May 24, 2019, https://www.reuters.com/article/us-usa-saudi-arms-idUSKCN1SU25R
47. The White House (2018), President Donald J. Trump is Ending United States Participation in an Unacceptable Deal, May 8, 2018, https://trumpwhitehouse.archives.gov/briefings-statements/president-donald-j-trump-ending-united-states-participation-unacceptable-iran-deal/
48. *Al Jazeera* (2018), 'World Leaders React to US Withdrawal from Iranian Nuclear Deal', May 9, 2018, https://www.aljazeera.com/news/2018/5/9/world-leaders-react-to-us-withdrawal-from-iranian-nuclear-deal
49. Wamsley, Laurel (2020), 'Iran Abandons Nuclear Deal Limitations In Wake of Soleimani Killing', NPR, January 5, 2020, https://www.npr.org/2020/01/05/793814276/iran-abandons-nuclear-deal-limitations-in-wake-of-soleimani-killing
50. Marcus, Jonathan (2020), 'Iran Attack: US Troops Targeted with Ballistic Missiles', *BBC*, January 8, 2020, https://www.bbc.com/news/world-middle-east-51028954
51. *BBC* (2019), 'Golan Heights: Trump Signs Order Recognizing Occupied Area as Israeli', March 25, 2019, https://www.bbc.com/news/world-middle-east-47697717
52. US Department of State (2020), The Abraham Accords Declaration, September 15, 2020, https://www.state.gov/the-abraham-accords/
53. Harb, Ali A. (2021), 'A year in, Biden's Middle East policy brings little change" *Al Jazeera*, December, 31, 2021, https://www.aljazeera.com/news/2021/12/31/a-year-in-biden-middle-east-policy-brings-little-change
54. Brett McGurk (2021), 'US 'going back to basics' with Middle East policy', *National News*, November, 25, 2021, https://www.thenationalnews.com/gulf-news/bahrain/2021/11/25/brett-mcgurk-us-going-back-to-basics-with-middle-east-policy/
55. Slodysko, Brian (2021), 'Senate rejects bipartisan bid to stop $650M Saudi arms sale', *Defence News*, December 8, 2012, https://www.defensenews.com/congress/2021/12/08/senate-rejects-bipartisan-bid-to-stop-650m-saudi-arms-sale/
56. 'The Biden administration and the Middle East: Reflecting on the first 100 days' https://www.mei.edu/publications/biden-administration-and-middle-east-reflecting-first-100-days

SECTION II

Intra-Regional Dynamic

5

West Asia and Security Implications: An Arab Perspective

Waiel Awwad

The Arab nation has changed over the last century from nationhood to statehood. The region extends from North Africa to West Asia and constitutes almost 450 million Arabs that share history, heritage, a common language, and a set of customs and traditions with common objectives and aspirations that have united them under a common goal and cause. The region was under Ottoman occupation for four centuries, and then under the reign of the victorious countries of the World War, i.e., France, Britain, Russia, and Italy. These countries decided to inherit the "Sick Man" Ottoman Empire and assigned the French and British diplomats, Francois Georges-Picot and Sir Mark Sykes (Sykes-Picot Accord in 1916), to divide the share among themselves. It was in 1917 that the Bolshevik communists, led by Vladimir Lenin, found a copy of the Sykes-Picot agreement in the government's archives, and Lenin called the treaty "The Agreement of Colonial Thieves" to ensure the birth of a "Jewish State" in the heart of Palestine by Britain which paved the way for achieving that mentioned in Balfour Declaration on 2 November 1917. The region's wealth, particularly oil resources, was looted and controlled by the colonial powers, and the original plan was erased and replaced by the San Remo agreement. The region was colonized and divided between France and Britain, which defined the shape and destiny of each Arab state.

Divide and Rule

The British and the French had a secret plan for the region to divide it into ethnic and religious lines. Thus, when the Ottoman Empire was falling, the British ditched the Arab leaders and promised them independence if they revolted against the Ottoman reign. The plight of the Arab people under Ottoman occupation forced many to flee their homes because they refused to join the World War with the Turkish Army, while those captured by the Turks were forced to fight and die cheaply for Ottoman glory. The Ottoman Empire distorted the fabric of the Arab societies, weakened their institutions, and ensured depriving them of all their natural resources and crops.

The Arab leaders were approached by the British and the French who promised them freedom from the reign of the Turk. They were deluded and fell prey to the plot. Against their will, the people were divided after the fall of the Ottoman Empire, drawing a bloody map that divided the Arab world into 19 small states (Sykes-Picot Accord, 1916-17) to keep it under Western influence and deny the Arab nation any future unity. While European nations ensured the birth of Israel State, the USA protected it and ensured its expansion and the annihilation of Palestine. The West created the Israel State in the heart of the Arab world in Palestine, after implementing the Balfour Declaration (1917). It served the political objective of the Zionist movement to establish a home for the Jews in Palestine. This plot led to the second Nakba in the Arab world and forced the Palestinians to flee their homes to save themselves from the genocide carried out by Zionist settlers supported by colonial Britain. The Sykes-Picot Accord drew the bloody borders and Britain supported the formation of the Muslim Brotherhood Organization in Egypt in 1918 to kill the secular Pan-Arab movement, create religious disputes, and introduce political Islam, while supporting minorities and secessionist movements, which turned into terrorist groups, in most of the Arab countries.

The division was deepening until the Second World War when the Arab countries started gaining independence and many leaders were installed against the will of the masses. Thousands of people lost their lives struggling for independence over the years. When the Arab countries started gaining independence post World War II, they were transferred into statehoods with different goals, sabotaging any attempt for unification among the Arab countries, ensuring limited nation nurturing. The political reforms in the Arab world were minimal. It was a transitional period from feudal societies to modern ones. Many political parties were barred, especially those with a Pan-Arabism slogan, and people's meetings were only allowed in mosques, which hardened the stands of those movements in the Arab world for any reconciliation with the ruling elite and led to the belief that all the sufferings are epitomized in one individual, the head of the state. Hence, they poured their anger on the regimes and called for a regime change. The youth in the Arab streets, fed up with the policy of puppet regimes that did not carry many reforms to meet the minimum requirements, decided to take the law and changes into their own hands and get rid of those regimes that suppressed them and denied them their basic rights.

With the emergence of the bipolar world, the interstate fight splits between the Eastern bloc and the America-Western bloc. The Arab League was created and supported by Britain to further prevent the Arab people from becoming a homogenous society extending from Mauritania to Qatar. This allowed each nation to link its domestic policy to its foreign policy and the bloc it belonged to, even if it was against the will of the people under preconceived notions. The Arab leaders never learned from their historical blunders, especially the unpopular leaders who resorted to the politics of the follies. They ultimately turned the region into a playing field for proxy wars among the great powers. This led to a tragic end of the security pact of the Arab world.

Pan Arabism Movement vs Political Islam

The Arab masses were up in arms following the attack on Egypt by the UK, France, and Israel, in 1956. The nationalization of the Suez Canal by President Gamal Abdul Nasser of Egypt threatened the interests of the colonial powers in the region. The post-colonial states of France and Britain continued to interfere in Arab affairs and sabotaged any attempt for Arab unity; this was supported by the USA and Israel. The old project of pipeline and rail connectivity continued to draw the attention of these countries to serve their interests and when required for the North-South Atlantic Corridor (Eurasia).

The struggle for the control of the Arab world continues for centuries because of its natural rich resources and strategic political geography that connects the East with the West through a natural corridor between three continents. Hence, it is for economic and political reasons that are the main attraction for colonial European powers. They ensured that this region remained weak, divided, and easy to ride. The USA continued the legacy of colonial European powers post World War II, where the whole world was held to ransom for the outcome of the US election to draw its own policy. This was more evident after the collapse of the Soviet Union and the US dominance of the world. The Arab world paid the price after the attack on the twin towers (11 September 2001) and remains at the receiving end of further division based on ethnic and religious lines and ensures that the Arab Gulf will continue to be the main dumping market for American goods and weapons.

The domestic policy of each Arab country evolved around the political system and foreign policy of these colonial powers that ensured that the Arab leaders would follow their dictates as long as they remained in power. To gain not only a legality but also rather legitimacy, the leaders engaged with their followers, and the process of decision making to avoid war, achieve security, stability, development, and ensure the welfare of the people, all together constitutes grounds for foreign policy conduct.

The global international political system changed to achieve the objectives of the big powers based on wars, security, peace, and transitional political-economic, cultural, and social systems that show interaction among the world political units. Hence, to understand international relations we need to learn how the international order operates.

The era of traditional wars and colonization ends up in an anarchical world order. The world is witnessing a scarcity of resources and collapsing of old systems of governance. A new era developed with traditional parameters and original state concepts equipped with new information technology and a modern war system, which requires no boots on the ground, and would shape the new world order in time to come.

It arises from the motivations of internal and external actors; ethnic-religious groups (the Kurds, and the Muslim Brotherhood Movement and their affiliate terrorist groups,) challenging the nationalist forces. The former aim to forge their own political and economic interests by armed struggle by regional and international actors (USA, EU, Israel, Turkey, Saudi Arabia, Qatar, and their allies and partners) in a bid to change governments by force in order to enhance the US hegemony on one hand. The later nationalist forces are backed by (Russia, China, Iran, and the nationalist forces) to maintain state sovereignty, and restore the role of international law and power balance to world order, on the other. What is happening in Mesopotamia is a clear indication of the intention of these forces to destroy this civilization, expel the natural inhabitants, and introduce political Islam, terrorism, radicalism, and fundamentalism into the region and hence make it a failed state to facilitate foreign intervention and further disintegration.

The systematic destruction of modern Arab states started with the invasion of Iraq and took a big leap during the Arab Spring. The COVID-19 pandemic exacerbated the crisis and led to an economic decline, more inflation, and unemployment coupled with bad governance and corruption.

Biden's Administration is trying to redraw its policy towards the region from Saudi Arabia to Iran, Afghanistan, Pakistan, and Turkey by including other countries in the Arab region, turning it into a laboratory to annihilate its unique identity of an Arabic and Islamic culture into a New Middle East and North Africa Order (MENA), the project for the New Middle East, floated by Israel and adopted blindly by the US Administration. This makes the region more of a heterogeneous one by drawing a new common security order that serves USA-Israel objectives and destroys any regime opposed to US interests.

This was a mere continuation of the policy of promoting and consolidating the idea of divergence in terms of ethnic, religious, interfaith, sectarian, and national identities. It became clear that this geographical expansion of the borders of the Middle East would include non-Arab countries and people of multiple nationalities, religions, cultures, and faiths, all of which have been combined with their aim of obliterating the unified nationalist identity of Arab countries and facilitating the integration of Israel into the region.

There are talks of ending the war in Yemen and checkmate the president of Turkey's expansion policy, his reluctance to be part of the US objective and his closeness to Russia, take on Iran by hyping its threat to Israel and the GCC while keeping a close eye on Israel's dominance and security of the region, since it is part of its own national security, and focus on China. The complexities of the burning issues in West Asia and the conflicting interests of each ally of the USA in the region will be a major challenge for President Biden and his team. The USA will ensure a sustainable flow of oil while remaining in total control of the Gulf countries, reduce the growing influence of China in the region, and contain China's dominance in the world.

New Players in the Region

The latest entry of China into the region has added a new dimension to the ongoing crisis. It will take time to shape this entry and whether it will be a military one after being an economic interest after the onset of the Belt Road Initiative (BRI), especially after the economic crisis in these countries because of the COVID-19 pandemic. The entry of China will lead to more confrontation with the USA and the West who consider this region as their own sphere of influence.

For its part, India has enjoyed a close cordial relationship with the Arab world for centuries. These relations were strengthened during the Cold War and India's pivotal role in the Non-Aligned Movement. After the dismantling of the Soviet Union and the emergence of a uni-polar world, India was in the process of economic reform and started using its soft powers to strengthen relations with the Gulf States. With 14 million Indians visiting the region annually, around 8 million Indian expats living there who contribute heavily to the growth and development of the GCC, and with more than 70 billion US dollars in revenue, India's energy security and geopolitical proximity make New Delhi a major stakeholder in ensuring peace and stability in the region. Hence, there is a great sense of urgency for India's proactive role in the region as a peace broker. The emergence of India as a big power creates global respect and a good reputation as the largest democracy in the world. It has given the ties between India and the region momentum and further cemented. It has been taken to a new level during Prime Minister Narendra Modi's leadership, which has been evident in the warm reception and repeated visits by the prime minister and top officials.

The emergence of President Recep Tayyib Erdoğan in Turkey, like other Turkish leaders with the obsession of reviving the Ottoman Empire, added the element of the Muslim Brotherhood organization to his advantage and to his supremacy over the Muslim world, setting up a clash with Arab nationalism and turned his Justice and Development Party into a symbol of Moderate Islam to be followed in many Arab capitals to fool the masses about the coexistence of political Islam and secularism which have taken the region by storm. President Erdoğan started amending the constitution in his country to cement his one-man party, availing the opportunity of his country's geopolitical strategic importance to his full advantage and strengthening his grip of power in Turkey, at the cost of gripping the economy under his leadership, and started directly interfering in the internal affairs of the Arab world with the onset of the "Arab Spring" turning himself into the New Ottoman Sultan, stating that "the Empire's properties lie in all the lands that the Ottomans reached, and that these properties belong to Turkey." He started unleashing his army of mercenaries (the Neo-Janissary) in different parts of the world and went on threatening the European nations with Islamophobia, facilitating the flux of migrants from Syria and Africa and blackmailing them by violating international maritime laws and started digging for exploration of natural resources in the Mediterranean Sea near Greece. He established military bases in Qatar, Djibouti, Somalia, and Niger and attempted to occupy North Syria and Iraq (eyeing Northern Iraq with its capital, Mosul) using terrorist organizations (ISIS). With his lust for power, he implemented his delusion of reviving the Ottoman Caliphate and drowning the Arab region again into an era of darkness. He took full advantage of the religious sentiment among the masses riding on their backs in the name of religion to let them bleed again and fight his wars, and further implement the Muslim Brotherhood project. The ultimate objective is to turn the region into one of communal wars, i.e., Sunni-Shia war with Iran. On the one hand, he threatened the Russian Federation and on the other hand incited the Muslim minorities there to achieve the USA's main objective of keeping Erdoğan's ambition unchecked. The border crossing between Turkey and Syria was under the control of foreign mercenaries with the help of intelligence agencies (USA, UK, France, Turkey, Israel, Qatar, Saudi, etc.) who ensured the flow of arms to reach anti-Syria militant groups under the pretext of supporting moderate rebels against Syrian government forces.

According to US and UN official documents, approximately 171,400 terrorists from 83 nationalities were smuggled into Syria through Turkey after training, brainwashing, and fully equipping them. Over 51,910 terrorists were eliminated by the Syrian Arab Army and 33,847 fled and more than 55,000 terrorists are still languishing in the northern city of Idlib in Syria under the protection of the Turkish army.

Terrorism has been used as a tool to achieve political objectives. It started with the *jihadi* culture in Afghanistan when the Saudi Intelligence, the CIA, and Pakistani Intelligence (ISI) formed the Al-Qaeda Terrorist

Organization to fight the Soviet occupation of Afghanistan. When the collapse of the Soviet Union happened after their withdrawal from Afghanistan, most of the Arab jihadists were sent to their respective countries to create small cells to destabilize the regimes. The USA went ahead and occupied Afghanistan under the pretext of fighting terrorist organizations and toppling the Taliban regime (Bad Taliban), then after two decades they brought back the same Taliban (Good Taliban) to power. After occupying Iraq in 2003, the USA activated terrorism in Mesopotamia and the Islamic State Terrorist Organization was created—19 of its founder-members were imprisoned earlier by US forces in Iraq. This became a global challenge to fight terrorism again and only Syria and Iraq were fighting terrorism, while the USA and its allies were promoting them. This revival of terrorism after the sudden American withdrawal from Afghanistan is a manifestation of the new phase of using terrorism as a tool to fight the Chinese against whom the USA is now more focussed with its Anti-China Policy, which is threatening the American dominance in the world.

The Arab Spring started as a revolution of change to meet the aspirations of the people for freedom and democracy. It was hijacked by the Muslim Brotherhood Organization and turned into one of total destruction and chaos in the Arab world, unlike other revolutions happening elsewhere that brought changes and improved the welfare of the people. Some people call the Arab Spring a conspiracy against the region and force those nations opposed to the American-Israeli hegemony to be replaced by a fanatic regime. The USA, the West, Israel, and certain Arab countries were openly supporting a forceful regime change policy, especially in Syria, Iraq, Libya, and Yemen. There was a total exodus of the elite group of society and the pillars of the state were destroyed.

The normalization of Israel with the Arab world was one of the main objectives of American foreign policy. Started with Egypt in 1979 during the Camp David Accord where Egypt was taken from the Arab-Israeli conflict followed by Jordan in 1994 after signing the agreement between the two countries followed by a step taken by the Palestinian organization in 1993 (Oslo Agreement). During the Trump Administration, many of the Arab countries were forced to normalize relations with Israel under the Abraham Accord, while ignoring the Palestinian cause and accepting Israel as a state in the Arab world, further denying the Palestinian people their right to return to their own country or the right to establish their own state and coexist with Israel. This is commencing a new era of the region and forming blocs to fight Iran as an enemy of the Arab world, and not Israel anymore. The Arab regional order has totally been replaced by more of a regional order to include non-Arab countries in the region. Arab integration became a far-reaching dream for the Arab masses. The imbalance of regional powers will lead to further fragmentation of the Arab world and disintegration. For the disintegration, weakening of the Arab states and ensuring the dominance of a powerful Israel—economically, politically, and militarily. This was the Israeli leaders' dream to normalize with the Arab world economically based on geographical cooperation and changing the geographical security border with an economic one. There is a redrawing of a greater Arab order with new regional states that will only achieve American interests and that of its allies. This will totally destroy all agreements and accords among the Arab nations and also the political-economical stability of each country and hence retain foreign intervention in Arab affairs.

After Russia and Iran stepped in to help Syria and Iraq defeat the terrorist organization, the ISIS, and had gained influence in both the countries, especially in Syria, this prompted the USA to use its NATO ally, Turkey, to intervene and change the balance of regional powers by playing the Muslim Brotherhood card, thus taking full advantage of the ruling party with President Erdoğan at the helm. There is a paradigm shift in the war against terrorism and inter-fighting among Arab nations.

President Erdoğan, for his part, is trying to convince the USA that he is the trusted ally in saving the American interests in the region. He was allowed to dig or to fish in the turbulent waters of the Mediterranean and extended his hand into Karabakh Enclave and sided with Azerbaijan in their fight with Armenia, expanding his influence in central Asia states with Turkish ethnicity, causing uneasiness in both Beijing and Moscow. This also caused more apprehension with Iran, especially with Azerbaijan minorities inside Iran trying to create havoc inside Iran. Therefore, the revival of terrorism in West Asia became a prime objective for the USA and its allies, using Turkish influence over the Muslim Brotherhood organization and other extremist organizations. So, countries falling along the Silk Route that the Chinese are trying to promote are becoming the main target of the USA that is leaving no stone unturned to stop the Chinese ambition. The mysterious Beirut port blast and frequent attacks by Israeli forces on Syrian ports are the trends of the future war in the region that will be fought between the USA, Russia, and Chinese allies. The political Islam phase is fading and being replaced by a more hard and dangerous phase, "violent face of Islam", which will be spread into the South and Southeast Asian nations.

Russia, for its part, under the leadership of President Vladimir Putin, started gaining its glory and influence in global affairs. The return of Russia into the international arena was more evident with its stand against the USA on its mission to change the government of Syria by force. This helped the Syrian government to gain most of its lost territories and Russia expanded its presence in Syria. There was also a closeness with Russia, Egypt, and Libya. This also gave more confidence to Moscow to play the alternative in the political affairs in West Asia and North Africa and fill the vacuum of US influence. The USA-EU Union prompted the Russian Federation closer to China and formed a strategic partnership to face the USA-NATO challenge, drawing a new security arrangement between two superpowers and their regional allies. Likewise, the USA, for its part, formed blocs like QUAD between the USA, Japan, India, and Australia, and AUKUS (Australia, the UK, the US), and the five fingers (New Zealand and Japan), all to counter the Chinese influence in the region. The Russians and the Chinese started playing proactive roles in Arab world affairs, securing strong bonds that prompted the USA to checkmate their influence in the Persian Gulf.

The Imbalance of Regional Powers

The contemporary West Asia and North Africa (WANA) Order is standing at an important juncture, led by regional players. Turkey's quest for the Neo-Ottoman policy is romancing the Muslim Brotherhood. Nuclear Power Israel, with an expansion policy and determination to annihilate Palestine and expand into Egypt, Syria, and Iraq to fulfil its dream of extending its borders from the Nile to the Euphrates. Future wars over water also are looming over Ethiopia, Egypt, Sudan, Turkey, Syria, and Iraq.

Iran with its nuclear ambition and anti-American policy is trying to expand its sphere of influence in the region by creating an access of resistance to USA-Israel hegemony. This has prompted the great powers to change their game plan. The USA will rally NATO allies to a new 'cold war' with Russia and China at a juncture of imbalance in the international world order. It is in the interests of the world to stabilize WANA due to its dependence on its natural resources and strategic importance. Prosperity and economic development will lead to improved socio-economic conditions of the people and reduce the chances of terrorism and radicalization. There has to be a new look in addressing issues facing the region by the people themselves and neighbouring countries as stabilizing WANA will benefit not only the people but the world.

While the USA and its allies are closing their eyes to the nuclear arsenal of Israel, they halt any Iranian ambition to go nuclear, if the 5+1 talks on Iran nuclear fails. This will add more security imbalance to the region, particularly when the USA is still keeping open the military option on the table to deal with Iran's refusal to bow to American and Western pressures. In addition, Tel Aviv is trying to convince Washington that its ballistic missiles and military action will end Iran's nuclear program while persuading the White House to accept Israel's military adventure, which will drag the USA into an all-out war in the Persian Gulf. The USA is not ready for it nor is Iran.

The multifaceted crisis facing the region has been exposed after the Arab Spring and the COVID-19 pandemic. There is a decline in human intolerance, low income, weakened national health system, and rise of radicalism and extremism in the Arab world, which is undergoing a multiplicity of political changes that will redefine its final outlook. The traditional wars and colonization era is over. A new generation and concept of dominance is drowned in the war rooms of sophisticated new technology and cyberspace. The impact will be global, and the region is not an exception.

The challenges from the Indo-Pacific region between the superpowers will have a direct impact on the future stability in the WANA region taking into consideration that WANA depends directly on the trade relationship with the Indo-Pacific region as a strategic cross-point between the South and North of the trade. The WANA region is no longer a priority for the USA, but it is for China. The political security is left to the Israelis and regional players to deal with it.

Redrawing Regional Maps

Some analysts believe that the presence of the US military in the region has kept regional powers at bay. However, as part of its strategy to remain a global hegemony, the USA has a sinister plot. Through this lens, we may be able to understand that the fading of US influence is part of its plan, and this is just a new phase of it where it relies on regional allies to protect its interests. The US choice to pull out their strategic arsenal and shutting down military bases will lead to security challenges and prompt regional powers to create havoc in the political affairs of each country. The absence of vision among Arab leaders and their alienation from the masses will lead to catastrophe led by their own self with only themselves to be blamed. There has to be a collective stand to redraw the new security arrangement in the region based on free from nuclear arms and ending of conflicts by allowing the Palestinians to have their own state coexist with Israel to end the Arab-Israel conflict. This will only be possible with the help of the regional and superpowers.

The new security agreement measures should take into consideration the interests and aspirations of the people and all decisions should be taken to meet them. Without the Arab masses' involvement in decision-making, there can be no future stability in the Arab world. It is also the responsibility of the United Nations to ensure peace, stability and support other international organizations to be involved in achieving them.

The highly volatile region is at the crossroads due to the poisonous environment surrounding it. There is no clear map or road for stability and tranquillity. The pandemic is spreading. Unemployment is rising and the economy is crashing. Mercenaries and terrorists are creating havoc in the region, and the inter-differences between the Arab nations are compounding the situation. The year 2022 may not carry much hope for the region; however, the upcoming Arab Leadership Summit in Algeria in March 2022, if it is held, may be the only hope of reconciliation among Arab nations to find a common ground and address the challenges facing the Arab world. The region that has given the world more than four civilizations, the oldest civilization of the world, and the cradle of all religions, may rise again if their leaders recognize the aspirations of their people and look to the future collectively. If not, the region will remain hostage while conflicts among global and regional powers continue; history will never forgive the leaders of the Arab world. It may be a wish that could drive away with the ever-present clouds of war.

6

ALL BETS ARE OFF: How Tehran Looks at the Impending Political Vacuum in the Middle East

Kingshuk Chatterjee

Most international observers looking at the geo-political landscape of the Middle East have been getting fidgety because the region is changing much too fast right before their eyes. The Arab Spring and its prolonged aftermath in Syria and Yemen have left behind resonances that disturb votaries of stability in the region. As American footfalls in the region reduce steadily over the years, the prospect of a political vacuum has begun to dawn on all the stakeholders in the extended neighbourhood. Almost all the regional players are preparing for a day when the global policeman might not be on the beat, and most do so with dread. The one capital where the prospect of American absence, and the geo-political unravelling that might follow it, is not keeping everyone awake (although not all are entirely at peace, either) is Tehran. The Islamic Republic of Iran is looking forward to an era (which indeed may never come) when Uncle Sam would stop casting his shadow on the region, leaving it to its own devices. They recognise that US withdrawal is almost certain to bring about a period of considerable uncertainty, and find themselves suitably placed for the political vacuum to gain a kind of leverage in the region's politics that Iran has not had in more than a century or two. There is however recognition in certain circles that during such a period of transition; a lot of things can go wrong. Hence, many within the establishment have been advising caution to the revolutionary regime. How the regime responds is likely to be determined by a complicated interplay of domestic and foreign developments that are not very easy to anticipate accurately.

This essay attempts to furnish a sense of the vista of the neighbourhood as it appears to the regime in Tehran. It would begin by contextualising the prospect of the steady but seemingly irrevocable US withdrawal from the Middle East and then go on to plot the consequent relative ascendancy of the Islamic Republic in the politics of the region. The essay then purports to assess the chances of this ascendancy being thwarted by the sanctions regime as much as the other powers of the region are concerned by the steady rise of Tehran's profile in the regional politics. The essay will then look at the China factor in the equation, and close with the possible hand that India can play.

The Reducing Shadow of the USA

There are many discernible differences in US foreign policy under the Barack Obama, Donald Trump and Joe Biden administrations. However, if there is one thing that is common to all three it is a determination to reduce American footfalls all across the globe in theatres that are (or, are no longer) central to the USA's strategic interests, and one of the earliest regions singled out for steady withdrawal from was the Middle East.[1] In the immediate wake of 9/11, the USA had gone on overdrive with its activism under the George Bush Administration. By 2003, as the neo-con adventurism began to go sour, the corridors of power in Washington DC had begun more sober deliberations on why 9/11 happened at all. A sort of a consensus seems to have emerged that maintained that through her policies of regime support extended to many authoritarian regimes in the region (viz., Egypt, Saudi Arabia, Bahrain, etc.), the USA had exposed herself to attacks from enemies of the regimes themselves (the Al-Qaeda being one).[2] While some segments of the American establishment favoured immediate removal of boots from the ground (from Iraq and Afghanistan, for instance),[3] others suggested caution against exit wounds and recommended a gradual drawdown,[4] while still others suggested (one-last-round-of) interventions (to the extent of even regime change) if need be to remove the potential sources of regional instability—but all agreed that the USA was overstretched, and needed to disengage from the region on an urgent basis. American foreign policy towards the region has since been characterised by one or more of these strands, by itself or in combination with the other two.[5]

From the time of the Obama Administration, Washington DC gradually, almost imperceptibly, but quite deliberately embarked on a steady drawdown of presence from the region. This drawdown was accelerated by the economic aftershocks of 2008-09, resulting in a complete pullout from Iraq (under Trump) and the extended neighbourhood (from Afghanistan, under Biden). Even though America maintains a substantial military presence in the region as of date, Washington DC's decision to effectively sit the conflicts out in Syria, Libya (Obama era)[6] and Yemen (Trump era)[7] is indicative of American determination to steer clear of any further entanglement. Even in taking out the Da'esh (Islamic State), the USA confined itself to providing logistical and other support for its allies (Kurds in Syria, the regime in Baghdad), allowing the Kurds of Iraq and the Shi'i militias to do much of the fighting along with the Iranians—the writing on the wall was for anyone who could read.[8]

American geostrategic interest and presence in the Middle East from after the Second World War was defined largely in terms of her need to ensure a steady supply of Middle Eastern oil to the global market, and, in particular, the American market. Hence, when the British Empire folded up after 1945, the USA stepped in as the muscle that guaranteed the smooth flow of oil from the Persian Gulf and on the high seas. However, with the emergence of new energy options like shale oil and fracking, and the growing capacity of other energy alternatives like wind, solar and nuclear power, America has begun to wean herself away from her dependence on oil, which has concomitantly begun to reduce her strategic interest in the Middle East.[9]

Countries in the region of course are fully aware that the American appetite for cheap energy was the single-most important factor behind her playing the role of the region's sheriff, and that US involvement would recede once her dependence on the region's energy exports diminishes. Fading of the only properly constituted security umbrella since the collapse of the British Empire is guaranteed to leave behind a major political vacuum. Fully cognisant of this impending vacuum, countries in the region have begun to consider building of a security architecture of their own, without relying much on Uncle Sam—the Abraham Accords (normalising the relationship between Israel and some of the Gulf Arab neighbours, and opening the way for the same with others), and even the new Quadrilateral Security Dialogues (New Quad, comprising the USA, India, Israel and the UAE) are expressions of engaging with the possibility of this vacuum.

However, not everyone is necessarily looking at the prospect with dread. For the Islamic Republic of Iran, America's role as the virtual arbitrator in regional politics was a great inhibitive factor in the politics in the neighbourhood for a very long time.

The Ascendancy of Iran and the Tremors that Come with It

From the standpoint of Tehran, the geo-political landscape of the Middle East has changed dramatically in the last twenty years to such an extent that perhaps for the first time since the end of the Iran-Iraq War, the threat perception of the Islamic Republic has actually reduced several notches. The Islamic Republic has been living in a hostile neighbourhood ever since it came into being, with most of its Arab neighbours along the Persian Gulf having chosen to support Baghdad. From the 1980s, the Baathist regime in Syria has been the only ally that Tehran has in the region. The regime's threat perception got more pronounced after the Gulf War of 1991, when Iraq's Weapons-of-Mass-Destruction Programme came to light in 1991. After 9/11, when the USA branded Iran as part of an Axis of Evil, and invaded, first Afghanistan and then Iraq, American military presence in the region historically reached its highest concentration. Tehran began to feel like a country under siege, but could do little about it.[10]

Tehran's initial response to this feeling of encirclement was to return to its tried-and-tested strategy of maintaining a second front—in Lebanon (with its support of the Hezbollah) and Palestine (with its support for the HAMAS). Tehran had been backing the Hezbollah right from the 1980s, providing it with crucial resources and logistical support (men, material and training) in its fight with Israeli forces during the Lebanese civil war. It began supporting the HAMAS from the 1990s, and particularly since its rejection of the Oslo Accords. The objective was to create (or retain the potential to create) some instability at will in the backyard of Israel (*Shaitan-e kochek*, the lesser evil), America's (*Shaitan-e Bozorg*, the greater evil) firmest ally in the region. This strategy proved extremely successful in 2006, when Tehran was able to deflect the massive pressure mounted on it over the nuclear issue by encouraging the Hezbollah to escalate a crisis against Israel, and bring about the prospect of a regional conflict.[11]

From 2005-06 onwards, the situation actually became somewhat more conducive for the Islamic Republic to push back. After a prolonged period of economic hardship, oil prices attained historically high levels, showering Tehran with an unexpected bounty. This was used fully by the Islamic Republic from the days of President Ahmadinejad to encourage opposition to US presence in the region, funding almost whichever segment of the Iraqi population was willing to join the good fight. Iran thus has had the occasion to side with most important Shi'i political figures in Iraq at different points of time in the last decade and a half—ranging from Moqtada al-Sadr and his Badr militia, Haidar al-Abadi—and also create its own proxy militias (such as Kataib Hizb al-Lah and Asaib Ahl al-Haq) in Iraq. The deeper the USA got stuck in the Iraqi quagmire, the more assertive Iran became, gaining leverage in Baghdad that it never enjoyed before.[12]

Ironically, for a regime that initially dreaded the disruptive potentials of the Arab Spring of 2011, Iran's influence in the region grew exponentially in its shadow. Iran dug in its heels behind the Baathist regime of Bashar al-Assad in Syria, her only proper ally in the diplomatic world of the neighbourhood, and along with Russia helped the regime prevail after a civil war that virtually tore the country asunder. Without the crucial military and logistical support provided by Tehran, the Assad regime was unlikely to have survived the challenge from its adversaries, in particular the Da'esh (Islamic State, or IS). In the process, Iran gained a physical presence in Syria, now having its own military bases in the country with the blessings and gratitude of the incumbent regime—a kind of stake that Tehran has never enjoyed before.[13] Even more importantly, when the Da'esh surfaced as a galvanising force for the Sunni component of the Iraqi population and began to pose virtually an existential threat for the Baghdad regime, with the USA wary of committing boots on the ground any more, Tehran mobilised the Shi'i militia to rally around the regime, and even coordinated the fight with the Kurdistan Regional Government. Tehran's dual intervention in the struggle against the Da'esh in Iraq and Syria was decisive in the defeat of the organisation, and left Iran with a kind of military and strategic presence in the neighbourhood that neither twentieth-century Iran nor Persia for several centuries before it had ever wielded. As Qassem Soleimani, one of the architects of this strategy of extension of Iran's influence, said sometime in 2017, it was possible for him to set out from Tehran and drive all the way to Damascus unmolested by anyone [even though not everyone could do the journey from Damascus to Tehran that easily].[14]

The success of the policy of threat projection by providing logistical support in Iraq and Syria seems to have encouraged trials elsewhere. It remains to be established whether the supporters of Houthi approached Tehran for logistical and other kinds of support, or whether Tehran approached the Houthi rebels to create trouble in the backyard of its regional rival, Saudi Arabia. Further, there is no intelligent estimate about the extent to which Iran has actually provided material and logistical support to the Houthi rebels. However, given the exponential increase in the combat capabilities of the Houthi rebels over the last seven-odd years, and the arsenal (especially the missiles and the drones) that the Houthis have deployed to destabilise the Yemeni government and even attack Saudi oil infrastructure, the possibility of Tehran's involvement is largely beyond dispute.[15]

Iran's increasing capacity of threat projection has for quite some time been spoken of in terms of the rise of a Shi'i axis. Not all of Iran's satellites happen to be Shi'i—HAMAS is a good example; the Houthis also are Zaidi Shi'i who are not looked at with favour by the Ithna 'Ashari Shi'i Iran. Nor indeed is it correct that Tehran seeks out only or even primarily the Shi'i forces wherever they go, as one would naturally assume from Tehran's own claims of export of its revolutionary ideology. A careful study of the trajectory of Tehran's projection of its influence abroad clearly shows that Tehran's choice of its regional allies and proxies is guided almost invariably by pragmatic political considerations—even when such outfits happen to be Shi'i.[16]

Iran's choice of its proxies and allies is almost invariably tactical, not necessarily driven by any ideology. After 9/11, Tehran had even tried to open the way for a rapprochement with the USA, and cooperated over Afghanistan. Tehran's adventurism in its immediate neighbourhood began only after being branded as the axis of evil. In the years that followed, while Iran's proxies and allies have held their ground, the USA has been steadily retreating. This has emboldened both Tehran and its allies and proxies to push for greater leverage in the prevailing background of instability, as more and more regional forces jockey for leverage in Iraq,

Syria and Afghanistan. Hence, what had originally began as a defensive strategy to neutralise America's strategic advantage on account of having virtually encircled Iran, has now evolved into quite an effective device of pushing for Tehran's own strategic advantage in what used to be an altogether hostile neighbourhood.[17]

From the standpoint of Tehran's critics, the problem is of course that in pushing for her own strategic advantage Tehran risks fracturing societies that are already quite unstable.[18] Lebanon has never quite healed from the civil war of the 1980s, and while the Hezbollah has, over the last two decades, steadily been trying to broaden its appeal across the sectarian divide, continuing to remain beholden to Tehran for continued logistical and military support has ensured that the organisation is not allowed to stand aside if Lebanon's interests are not directly affected. This was evident when the Hezbollah leapt to the defence of the Assad regime during the Syrian civil war. HAMAS is a good example of what may happen if any beneficiary of Tehran does not respond to do her bidding—HAMAS has seen its leverage in Tehran decline once it refused to be dragged into the Syrian conflict. The Iraqi militias aligned with Tehran are expected to show similar levels of allegiance to the Islamic Republic, which requires them to systematically push the Americans to such an extent that Washington DC would be forced to declare an end to the presence of its combat troops, which was finally accomplished in December 2021. The Houthis similarly pushed the entire region to the verge of a regional conflict in 2019 when they targeted (or claimed to having done so) Saudi oil installations—delivering what is now believed to be a message from Tehran that in the event of a conflict, no part of the kingdom is safe. The Saudis have since opened back-channel negotiations with Tehran, but it could easily have gone the other way.[19] It was largely this extended strategic capabilities of Tehran in its neighbourhood that made a section of the American establishment and the Israelis and the Saudis insist that the JCPOA allowed the Islamic Republic of Iran too much elbow room to operate in the neighbourhood when the sanctions regime on its nuclear programme was ended.

The Shadow of a Nuke: The Deal that Has Been and May Not Be Again

A major point of concern about the Islamic Republic that pervades the wider neighbourhood of the Gulf and the Levant pertains to its nuclear programme. Iran has been suspected of having a nuclear programme for a very long time, in particular since 2003 when the USA charged Tehran to be pursuing a covert nuclear weapons programme in violation of her NPT commitments. Tehran has of course persistently denied pursuing nuclear weapons capability.

In the aftermath of the first Gulf War, sobered by the discovery of Iraq's WMD programme, Tehran was poised over the dilemma whether it to seek nuclear weapons capability or not. Given the shortage of resources required for even its necessary economic reconstruction, the decision to embark on a nuclear journey was subjected to severe scrutiny, and split the establishment right down the middle—the security and para-military establishment of the *Sepah-e Pasdaran-e Enghelab-e Islami* (Islamic Revolutionary Guards Corps, or IRGC) and their political allies (mostly the conservatives of the *Motalefeh*, *Osulgiran* and like-minded factions) by and large favoured developing nuclear weapons capability as a kind of regime security; by contrast the reformist factions favoured developing nuclear threshold status, without actually fully going nuclear in violation of Tehran's NPT commitments.[20]

When international attention fell on Iran's nuclear programme in 2003, the reformists led by President Khatami persuaded the Iranian establishment to put its nuclear programme on hold, to the great chagrin of the IRGC and other components of the security and para-military establishment.[21] After Khatami left office, his successor Mahmoud Ahmadinejad, of the paramilitary reserve Basij forces, restarted and even accelerated Iran's nuclear programme. The progress made in the five or so years that followed was alarming enough for the USA to mobilise regional and international opinion (including specifically the European Union, generally a votary of constructive engagement with Tehran), and put in place the severest sanctions regime so far against Iran.[22] The Islamic Republic had lived with unilateral US sanctions against it right from 1979, but the 2010 sanctions regime was far more crippling than any other time in the past, and severely impaired almost every sector of the Iranian economy. Hence, even some sections of the conservative establishment that had previously favoured it, broke from the hardline and security establishment to open negotiations with the international community, with support from the Supreme Leader Ali Khomeini himself. Although the negotiations did not succeed, a political consensus grew in favour of a negotiated settlement on the nuclear issue. A crucial figure in Iran's nuclear negotiations team from the days of Khatami, Hassan Rouhani ran for the Presidency in 2013 on the issue, *inter alia*, of ending the sanctions regime and won. As President, he pulled off what he promised when he concluded the Joint Comprehensive Plan of Action (JCPOA) in 2015.[23]

The JCPOA—concluded between Iran and the P5+1 (the USA, the UK, France, Russia, China, and Germany) and the European Union in April 2015, and came into effect in January 2016—was designed to limit the scale of the Iranian nuclear programme for the next 10 years to levels where it could be not be deployed for military purposes. Under the treaty, Tehran pledged to not only confine its nuclear enrichment to only 3.5 per cent (80 per cent enrichment being necessary for nuclear weaponry), but also to dispose of its existing low and medium-enriched nuclear stockpile, and put a cap on its nuclear capacity building for the next decade. Crucially, Tehran further accepted the hitherto most intrusive verification regime for its nuclear installations, which would allow the international community to ensure that the nuclear programme remains limited to its stated purpose of civilian use of power generation. In return, subject to Iran's fulfilment of its obligations, the crippling nuclear-related sanctions regime imposed on Iran over the previous decade was to be dismantled by the USA, the EU and the UN.[24]

Critics of the deal, including Israel and many of Iran's neighbours, and, most importantly, many in the US defence establishment have maintained that the deal merely delays the Islamic Republic's attaining of nuclear weapons capability by ten years. Since the deal came into place, Iran's strategic footfall in the region has only increased (in Iraq, Syria and Yemen) to the great chagrin of Israel, Saudi Arabia and even the USA, who feel that Tehran has simply capitalised on the air of bonhomie generated by the deal to push its long-held revisionist agenda of regional domination. Hence, President Trump spoke for a quite a few of Iran's neighbours when he said that a deal that contained Iran's nuclear ambitions for the time without containing its larger geo-strategic ambitions was a bad deal, and pulled the USA out of the deal, and reinstated the sanctions regime unilaterally.[25]

Contrary to what often appears to the outside observer, the Islamic Republic does not actually have a house of like-minded, menacing people with an agenda of global domination. Indeed, there are people dominated by (but not limited to) the paramilitary Islamic Revolutionary Guards

Corps (IRGC), who have played at regional domination, and make up an extremely hawkish lot who aspire Tehran to become a nuclear power. There are others, such as President Rouhani and former President Khatami, who would prefer to reduce Tehran's regional footfall and concentrate on economic reform and ascendancy of Iran as a major economic power instead; they believe that Tehran should be a nuclear-threshold power, but never actually step across the threshold, lest it compromises Iran's economic potential due to international sanctions.[26]

Rouhani, like Khatami in 2003, had put much of his political capital on reconstruction of the sanctions-hit Iranian economy, and used the sanctions relief (courtesy the JCPOA) as a means to push for economic reforms. The EU's failure to counter-balance the damage caused to the treaty by the US withdrawal weakened Rouhani and the reformists irreparably, and propelled the hard-liner Ebrahimi Raisi to the presidency. Washington DC was alive to this possibility, and some sections of the US establishment thought that such a resurgence of the hard-liners would finally bring about a popular upheaval, which in turn could bring about the collapse of the Islamic Republic.[27]

Rouhani appeared to have convinced the establishment that the much-needed capital infusion in the Iranian economy would not materialise in the background of nuclear obduracy, and owed his ability to convince the Supreme Leader Khomeini on the political consensus he was able to forge, ranging from the reformists to the section of conservatives aligned with the *bazaar* (to whom Khomeini has always been personally very close). However, once the sanctions returned, the hardline element in the Islamic Republic that dominates the judiciary and the security establishment bayed for Rouhani's blood. The hardline Guardians Council (*Shoura-e Negahban*) debarred not only the reformists in the race for the President, but also those among the conservatives who had supported the nuclear deal (such as 'Ali Larijani).

Before leaving office, the Rouhani administration is believed to have almost agreed on a text in June 2021 after negotiations in Vienna for a return to the JCPOA,[28] but the Biden Administration was wary of concluding the deal with the outgoing administration. The newly-elected President Raisi personally has always been sceptical of Iran's interactions with the West; with a large number of people with IRGC/Basiji background in the cabinet, including Foreign Minister Hossein Amir Abdollahian, the present cabinet is virtually genetically programmed to drag its feet on the talks, if not to actually scupper it. Whether the Vienna Talks actually succeed or not would depend on how durable the consensus proves that Rouhani and Larijani had built with Khomeini's blessings in 2015.

The hardliners in the Tehran establishment, including the IRGC (who dominate the nuclear and missile development programmes)—as indicated—would prefer to develop nuclear capability as the only possible guarantee against regime change under foreign pressure. Many of them are equally unperturbed by the prospect of continuation of the sanctions regime because they are advocates of a "resistance economy", which (as the name suggests) is designed to be resistant to sanctions.[29] The support of the Sino-Iran treaty of 2020 under Rouhani received a ringing endorsement from the hardliners and IRGC members of the parliament (Majlis) largely because China is meant to play a crucial role in providing the capital and technology infusion into Iranian economy that the Rouhani administration was looking to the West for.

However, for most of the last decade (excepting 2015-18), the Iranian economy has been teetering on the brink of an economic debacle owing to the stringent sanctions regime imposed by the USA, which penalises not only those who do business with Iran, but also do business with those who do, thus affecting even banking and insurance companies. This has severely affected the Iranian consumer as prices have gone through the roof; items of daily use as simple as diapers have become exponentially expensive in the market. Far more significantly, the mercantile community (including the traditional *bazaaris*, aligned with the traditional conservatives and Khomeini himself) have been pushed with their backs to the wall as foreign trade and commerce have taken a major knock, somehow surviving by virtue of contraband commerce. Accordingly, the popular pressure for an end-to-sanctions regime is considerable, with which even members within the establishment are in sympathy.[30] Furthermore, as Tehran has already begun to understand, the full benefits of the China deal cannot fully materialise without an end to the sanctions regime.

Whether the Raisi administration caves in before these considerations or not would determine the outcome of the Vienna Talks. Given the composition of his government, and virtually total domination of the hardline conservative segment on every organ of the Iranian body-politik—the Presidency, the Majlis, the Guardians Council, the Assembly of Experts (*Majlis-e Khobregan*)—a return to the spirit of the JCPOA can be virtually ruled out, leave alone making the kind of changes that Iran's neighbours want (cap on Iran's extra-territorial adventures, restrictions on her missile development programme). There is even an outside possibility that the regime might decide to keep dilly-dallying, asking for terms such as a binding guarantee that no signatory could pull out of the deal as the USA did the last time—an assurance that cannot legally be given.

More importantly, the facts on the ground have changed much since Iran began retreating from its JCPOA commitments. Indeed, it claimed that the retreat was reversible, and Iran would return to its commitments once the sanctions regime was removed. However, in the time that followed—with Trump's last year in office and the Biden Administration assuming office and then waiting for the new Iranian administration take over—Iranian nuclear capabilities have gone way beyond what they used to be when the deal was negotiated. In 2015, Iran had enriched uranium till about 20 per cent; now it is known to have gone past 60 per cent and may be still closer to the crucial 80 per cent. Unverified sources reveal that Iran's break-out time as a nuclear weapons capable power has come down from 11 months in 2015 to about three months at present.[31] There are reports that the only thing that is holding Iran back is attaining capability of delivery, specifically putting on a nuclear device on a warhead.

Thus, even if an agreement were arrived at to revive the JCPOA, the changed circumstances have now ensured that the JCPOA is a dead horse, which cannot be flogged back to life. Even if the Raisi administration chooses to return to the old agreement owing to domestic economic compulsions, the effectiveness of the original deal has already been lost. Iran may choose to remain a nuclear threshold state (or a smart nuclear state) for the time being,[32] but that is not as if the genie has been put back into the bottle—just that the bottle is uncorked, and the genie is waiting for an opportune time to come out. Iran's neighbours know that the turmoil that has characterised the region's politics so far will begin to look like picnic if things go really bad.

The Shifting Sands of Middle Eastern Geo-politics

Iran's increasing leverage in the region has been causing great concern in the region. When Amman, Riyadh and Tel Aviv had been cautioning about a rising Shi'i crescent (Iran, Iraq, Syria and Lebanon, each with either a Shi'i or Shi'i-led government), they did not actually mean the spread of Shi'i political/religious ideology in a predominantly Sunni region.[33] Rather, they meant the growth of influence of the Islamic Republic of Iran through cultivation of satellites and proxy outfits in the neighbourhood, some of whom were not even Ithna 'Ashari Shi'i (the denomination predominant in Iran).[34] Rather, the legitimate fear is that in most of its neighbouring Arab states, where the Shi'i are mostly persecuted and discriminated against, Tehran has either tended to capitalise on the governance deficit to foment dissent, or have been courted by the dissident Shi'i for material and logistical support, which Tehran has happily provided for the strategic advantage to be gained by undermining its adversarial neighbours, regardless of the proxy's sectarian affiliations, Shi'i or Sunni.

Discomfort with increasing Iranian leverage began to grow when the various Middle Eastern states realised that the USA is now in a withdrawal mode, and short of some totally unforeseen development, unlikely to change. In the absence of the Americans, the region had no security architecture to speak of. The quickest to cotton on to this was Tel Aviv, which has been carrying out pre-emptive military strikes against Lebanon (2006) and Syria (against Iranian installations during the civil war); but Riyadh, Doha, and Abu Dhabi were close at its heel. Hence, when the USA stayed its hand (for all practical purposes in the Syrian civil war), Riyadh and Abu Dhabi stepped in supporting several of the belligerents against the Damascus regime, hitherto Tehran's staunchest ally in the neighbourhood. Similarly, in the case of the Yemeni civil war, the Saudi-led coalition entered into combat with Iran-backed Houthi rebels to save the government of the day. Riyadh and Abu Dhabi had also a hand in beefing up the Sunni resistance in Iraq before the rise of Da'esh and after its fall.

It is very tempting to see this as Iran's neighbours helping each other against the big bully in the neighbourhood—the reality is probably somewhat different. With the USA pulling out of the region, it is not only Tehran that is eyeing regional domination and extension of its influence; Riyadh, Abu Dhabi and Doha are doing the same, and may be joined by Cairo and Ankara before long. Riyadh always had regional ambitions, and was operating all along in Lebanon from the time of the Taif Accords, backing the Sunni movement of Solidarity led by Rafik Hariri and now his son, Saad. Saudi, Qatari and Emirati involvement in Syria and Iraq and of the former two in Yemen may overtly have begun at tandem, but they did not always back the same groups, and sometimes their proxies were also fighting each other.[35] It was largely Qatari success in gaining greater results in penetrating the 'Sunni' constituency in the Fertile Crescent that prompted the Saudis to mobilise all their diplomatic and political capital to impose a blockade against Qatar, accusing it overtly of befriending Tehran[36] (Iran, of course obliged Doha by helping it bypass the blockade) thereby undoing decades of hard work that went into the making of the GCC, which now is in a shambles.

Much more by way of a straight-forward response to the strategic threat posed by Tehran is the emergence of something resembling a security architecture, with Tel Aviv playing a pivotal role. Israel has been the strongest and the most unwavering opponent of Iran's nuclear programme. Israel has been routinely sponsoring Iran of spreading terrorism, and even having built a whole infrastructure of terror. It has repeatedly promised resorting to the military option to prevent Iran going nuclear (just as it had done against Iraq in 1982 and Syria)—although, given the dispersed and often underground nature of the installations it is doubtful how efficacious this could be.[37] It was also the harshest voice of denunciation of the JCPOA, arguing it was merely delaying the nuke by a period of 10 years if Iran actually played by the treaty. Exasperated with the JCPOA, Israel has been routinely resorting to elimination of scientists and other people associated with Iranian nuclear and missile development programmes, and is suspected of being behind the cyber attacks on Iran's nuclear and security.[38] Intelligence from Tel Aviv is believed to be crucial behind President Trump's withdrawal of the USA from the JCPOA. Israel has also repeatedly carried out military strikes against Iranian installations and military presence in Syria.

Tel Aviv has had an agenda of normalising its relationship with the Arab world for a very long time, partly to neutralise the popular support the Palestinian cause has historically enjoyed in the Arab world. Preparing for the eventuality of the disappearance of the American security umbrella, Tel Aviv quietly reached out to (or reciprocated to, depending on which version of the events one would go by) Gulf Arab states like the UAE and Bahrain, and concluded what have now come to be known as the Abraham Accords.[39] In all possibility, Riyadh would also have joined these by now, had it not been for the outbreak of unrelated disturbances in Jerusalem (over the proposed eviction of some Palestinians) which made the time very improper for a such a move by the vaunted leader of the Muslim world.[40] But a beginning has been made, and the alignment of Riyadh with Tel Aviv appears only a matter of time—for if there is one lesson

Riyadh has learned from the US response to attack on its oil installations by Iran's Yemeni proxy outfits, it is that America may no longer go for conflicts where its own interests are not directly affected. Israel is also a crucial component in the emerging formation of the QUAD—involving the USA, Israel, India and the UAE in a potentially strategic alliance that may become pivotal for the maritime security of the Indian Ocean where the USA refuses to do the heavy lifting by itself any more.[41]

In this chaotic regional landscape, all the various parties have so far balanced each other out, with no single actor emerging so strong as to become a regional hegemon. All the parties have also been taking very great precautions to avoid any open conflict, lest it degenerates into a much broader regional conflict. Every time Israel has carried out a military strike against the Iranians, the Israelis have taken good care that neither Russian or Syrian allies of the Iranians are affected in any way; even when Iran targeted US bases in Iraq in retaliation for the assassination of Qassem Soleimani in 2020, Tehran quietly alerted Baghdad some time ahead so that there would be no Iraqi (and presumably no American) casualties; when Saudi Arabian installations came under attack from Tehran-backed Yemeni proxies, after a while Riyadh opened back-channel talks with Tehran using the good offices of Pakistan.[42]

There is however no guarantee such composure would prevail all across the region at all times. As the global consensus begins to grow against fossil fuel and new alternatives such as shale oil and electric-cars become available and viable, the significance of petroleum in the world economy would steadily diminish. Dependent on rental income from the sale of the region's energy resources, and employment generated by the oil-rich economies among the population of their oil-poor countries, the prospect of the regional economy in the future is not very bright. Changing economic fortunes in the region is highly likely to trigger domestic unrest all across (including Iran)—as the last shock to the region's economy revealed during the global economic slowdown in 2008-09 by triggering off the region-wide turmoil of 2011. Any future unrest might spill over, or degenerate into a broader regional conflict, the possibilities of which are virtually built into the region. Hence, as the dependence of the Western economies on energy resources in the region begin to decline, countries of the region are looking at countries where such demand for fossil fuel is unlikely to reduce in the short run. For Tehran, for historical reasons, the two such favoured options are China and India.

Crouching Panda, Trailing Tiger

India has been a regular destination for Iranian crude exports, and had continued to be so right down to 2017, till which point of time nearly a fifth of all India's crude imports used to come from Iran (except for a brief decline during 2012-15). This was partly owing to the fact that Indian refinery capacity set up during the days of British rule were more suited to handling the type of crude that was found in the oilfields towards the north of the Persian Gulf. China entered late into the energy exports market (in only about the 1980s), and concluded an agreement with Tehran that began the course of China's engagement with the Middle East. In subsequent years, Chinese purchase of Iranian crude has steadily increased in volume to the point that Beijing imported nearly a fourth of all the oil exported by the Islamic Republic.[43]

The sanctions regime imposed by the USA and the EU in 2010 brought severe pressure to bear on India to cut her energy imports from Iran, and also refining of much of the crude for the Islamic Republic. Faced with the prospect of being debarred from the USA on account of having any trading connections with the Iranian oil sector, Indian petrochemical, banking and insurance companies proved reluctant to participate in the Iranian trade at the expense of a much more valuable relationship with the USA. India thus began to reduce its dependence on Iranian imports till 2015 with some difficulty in sourcing crudes from elsewhere.[44] Once the JCPOA was concluded, India resumed purchase of Iranian crude once again, but upon reinstatement of US sanctions, India per force had to reduce her imports from Tehran yet again after a period of grace exemption allowed by Washington DC. From Tehran's viewpoint, this was a clear statement of New Delhi's desire to climb on to the American bandwagon.

Beijing, by contrast, distinguished itself by standing by Iran in its hour of need. Even as India stopped refining Iranian crude and sending it back to the Iranian market, Beijing continued to do so right through the period of sanctions in the build-up to the JCPOA. Beijing's imports from China declined somewhat in 2020 because of sluggish demand presumably on account of COVID, but picked up yet again from November 2020, rising to the point of monthly imports of 3 million tonnes of crude.[45] China in fact began to negotiate a much closer relationship with Tehran, the Comprehensive Cooperation Programme, right from the time of Xi Jinping's visit to Tehran in 2016. The treaty was finally signed in Beijing on 24 March 2021, being the first of a series that was to follow.[46] It would seem that President Trump's trade war with China has become the undoing of his policy of "maximum pressure" towards Iran, because the talks on the 25-year Comprehensive Cooperation Programme between Tehran and Beijing, broached after the JCPOA, resumed only after the trade war started with Beijing. Till then, a section in the Beijing establishment argued that the US connection was more important, and made China go slow on cooperation with Tehran. However, once Sino-US relations began to deteriorate, such restraint towards Tehran no longer found favour.

Iran had tried to cosy up to China initially under the populist hardliner President Ahmadinejad (2005-13) to offset the tough sanctions regime then in place, but was thwarted by the reformist sections of the Tehran establishment (such as Hassan Rouhani) who wanted to reintegrate Iran with the global economy without being dependent on any one country. Rouhani favoured instead nuclear rapprochement with the West, and the JCPOA was a veritable coup that he pulled off. Trump's pulling the USA out of the deal was a major setback for Rouhani and the reformists. Thus, Rouhani turned to Beijing almost out of desperation, and hardliners endorsed the deal hoping that the alignment with Beijing would prevent any alignment with the West that the reformists had always sought.

As it happens, the Sino-Iran deal has the potential of hardening Iranian resistance to US pressure for renegotiation of the JCPOA, or even for a simple return to it. The proposed capital infusion by Beijing and guarantee of purchase of Iranian oil takes away much of the pressure that had mounted on Iran for a swift return to the deal. Tehran knows that the USA is on a withdrawal mode from the region, and they think time is on their side. With Beijing lending a hand, that confidence would only grow.

Iranian critics of the deal (hardliners, including Ahmadinejad) are saying that the agreement leases out an island in the Persian Gulf to China and allows deployment of Chinese troops around proposed transportation infrastructure—which the government denies.[47] If true, it could be bad news for New Delhi. With China gaining a foothold in the Gulf, she would gain ocean-denial capacity that Beijing did not hitherto have in the Arabian Sea. Further, last year, Tehran dropped New Delhi (because of Indian foot-dragging) from the railway project connecting Chabahar port with Zahedan, which was to connect with the Indian-built Delaram-Zaranj highway in Afghanistan. If it comes out that the Chabahar-Zahedan railway link (in which Beijing had previously expressed an interest) is among the transport infrastructure China is earmarked to build, it would reduce the strategic value of Chabahar for India. If India then starts to go slow on Chabahar as well, it could be a matter of time before she is pushed out of that too. China's shadow on the Indian Ocean appears set to grow.

India has already lost much leverage in Tehran, and Beijing has gained disproportionately at New Delhi's expense in the last decade. However, there are still forces within the Iranian body-politik—among the hardliners and reformists alike—who are not comfortable with the prospect of any one country gaining too much influence in the Islamic Republic, not even China. Prime Minister Modi's congratulating Ebrahim Raisi upon his elevation to the Presidency has been noted and appreciated in Tehran, and the National Iranian Oil Company has even been asking around the Indian oil sector whether India would resume its purchase of Iranian crude or not.[48] India's opportunities of a rapprochement have grown further with the political vacuum that has emerged in Afghanistan since the US pull-out from the country. Both Tehran and India have had misgivings in the past with the Taliban for different reasons. The atmosphere of uncertainty and instability in the country works against the grain of interests of both Tehran and New Delhi, and thus provides the kind of shared interests that may prove useful for New Delhi to regain its leverage in Tehran. However, if New Delhi proves reluctant to engage with Tehran in the event that the nuclear talks fail, as well they might, India would lose out to Beijing even further in the medium term.

Conclusion

The Islamic Republic of Iran is at a crucial conjuncture in the political landscape of the Middle East. As the USA retreats from the region, slowly but almost certainly, the political vacuum it leaves behind has begun to spark of regional rivalries, at the nerve centre of which stands the Islamic Republic. Sensing its moment, the incumbent regime in Tehran appears willing to engage in strategic brinkmanship to optimise its influence over the neighbourhood. This is, it would seem, primarily the reason behind Tehran playing hardball on the nuclear talks in Vienna before they eventually relent (as many observers seemed to think). It may indeed so transpire, but there is an equally strong possibility that it does not. Had the plug on the JCPOA not been pulled, Tehran may have continued on the path of reintegration with the world economy, and tensions might have been at a much lower level. By pushing Tehran away from the trajectory of reconciliation, the entire region has been made potentially more unstable than it would otherwise have been. As of now, all bets are off.

ENDNOTES

1. See, for instance, Doug Bandow, "A Blueprint for Getting Out of the Middle East", *the Cato Institute*, 8 July 2021. https://www.cato.org/commentary/blueprint-getting-out-middle-east [accessed on 12th August 2021].
2. Discussion at the Centre for Naval Analysis, Washington DC, under Chatham House Rules, October 2006.
3. See for instance *National Security Strategy 2010*, pp. 26-27. https://obamawhitehouse.archives.gov/sites/default/files/rss_viewer/national_security_strategy.pdf
4. Mike Sweeney, "A Plan for US Withdrawal from the Middle East", *Defense Priorities*, https://static1.squarespace.com/static/56a146abb204d5878d6f125a/t/5fdfef88f3f88b619f2fcccf/1608511372939/DEFP_A_plan_for_US_ withdrawal_from_the_Middle_East.pdf [accessed 13 January 2021].
5. Martin Indyk, "the Middle East isn't Worth it Anymore," *the Wall Street Journal*, January 17, 2020, https://www.wsj.com/articles/the-middle-east-isnt-worth-it-anymore-11579277317 [accessed 5 March 2020].
6. Jeffrey Goldberg, "the Obama Doctrine", *the Atlantic*, April 2016, https://www.theatlantic.com/magazine/archive/2016/04/the-obama-doctrine/471525/ [accessed on 5th March 2020].
7. Robert Malley, Stephen Pomper, "Accomplice to Carnage: How America Enables War in Yemen", *Foreign Affairs*, March/April 2021, https://www.foreignaffairs.com/articles/united-states/2021-02-09/how-america-enables-war-yemen [accessed 11 November 2021].
8. F. Gregory Gause III, *Beyond Sectarianism: the New Middle East Cold War*, Brookings Doha Center Analysis Paer, Number 11, July 2014, p. 23.
9. Mike Patton, "US dependence on Foreign Oil Hits a Thirty Year Low", *Forbes* 20 April 2016, https://www.forbes.com/sites/mikepatton/2016/04/20/u-s-dependence-on-foreign-oil-hits-30-year-low/?sh=40e89c61ff33 [accessed on 13 January 2017].
10. Kingshuk Chatterjee, "The 'Tehran' Factor in West Asia: Doomed to De-stabilise?", in Priya Singh, Susmita Bhattacharya (eds), *Perspectives on West Asia: the Evolving Geopolitical Discourse*, (New Delhi and Kolkata: Shipra Publications and MAKAIAS, pp. 127-28.
11. Ibid. pp. 120-23.
12. See RanjAlaaldin, *Containing Shia Militias: the Battle for Stability in Iraq*, Brookings Doha Center, Policy Briefing December 2017.
13. Amir Mohammad Haji-Yousefi, "Iran's Policy in the Syrian Civil War: from Liberal Pacifism to Liberal Interventionism", *International Journal of Economics and Politics*, 2(I), 2021, pp. 211-30.
14. Ali Asghar Gharedaghi, "Iran's Strategic Depth in Post-ISIS Syria", *Journal of International Relations and Foreign Policy*, December 2018, Vol. 6, No. 2, pp. 22-32.
15. Muhammad Hassan al-Qadhi, *The Iranian Role in Yemen and its Implications on Regional Security*, (Arabian Gulf Centre for Iranian Studies, 2017) pp. 43-49

16. Kingshuk Chatterjee, "Of Islam and Other Things: the Drivers and Rhetoric in Iranian Foreign Policy", in Priya Singh (ed) Re-envisaging West Asia: Looking Beyond the Arab Uprisings" (New Delhi and Kolkata: Shipra Publications and MAKAIAS, 2016), pp. 73-78.
17. See Said Golkar, Kasra Aarabi, *The View from Tehran: Iran's Militia Doctrine*, (Tony Blair Institute for Global Change, February 2021)
18. Seth Jones, 'War by Proxy: Iran's Growing Footprints in the Middle East', *CSIS Briefs*, https://csisprod.s3.amazonaws.com/s3fs-public/publication/190312_IranProxyWar_FINAL.pdf (accessed on 1 September 2019).
19. Kingshuk Chatterjee, "Brinkmanship in the Persian Gulf: What Drove American and Iranian Policy in the Summer of 2019?" *StosunkiMiędzynarodowe – International Relations*, nr 2 (t. 55) 2019, pp. 33-38.
20. Saideh Lotfian, "Nuclear Policy and International Relations", in Homa Katouzian, Hossein Shahidi, *Iran in the 21st Century: Politics, Economics and Conflict*, (London: Routledge, 2008, pp. 160-71.
21. Seyed Hossein Mousavian, *The Iranian Nuclear Crisis: A Memoir*, (New Delhi: KW Publishers, 2011), pp. 57-96.
22. Ibid. 259-81.
23. Kingshuk Chatterjee, "Iran: Scripting a New Era", *the Diplomatist*, February 2016, http://www.diplomatist.com/dipo201602/article001.html
24. https://www.documentcloud.org/documents/2165399-full-text-of-the-iran-nuclear-deal.
25. See: Kennneth M. Pollack, *Unthinkable: Iran, the Bomb, and the American Strategy*, (New York: Simon Schuster, 2013). See also, Peter Beinart, 'Why the Iran Deal Makes Obama's Critics So Angry', *the Atlantic*, 24 July 2015, https://www.theatlantic.com/international/archive/2015/07/iran-nuclear-deal-obama/398450/ (accessed on 5 September, 2019).
26. Chatterjee, "Brinkmanship in the Persian Gulf", pp. 31-32.
27. A Washington DC based US journalist, Robert R. Kaplan, in personal exchange with the author, May 2018.
28. "Iran Spokesman: New Committee Examining Text For Revived Nuclear Deal", *Iran International*, 21 June 2021, https://old.iranintl.com/en/world/iran-spokesman-new-committee-examining-text-revived-nuclear-deal [accessed 15 July 2021]
29. Ali Keshavarzi and Sarvoldin Fathi, "Resistance Economy, Turning the Sanction to Opportunity", *International Journal of Management, Accounting and Economics*, Vol. 1, No. 1, August, 2014, pp. 93-100.
30. Sanam Vakil, "Iran on the Brink: Challenges & Opportunities for Washington," a Hoover Institution Essay, 2018. https://www.hoover.org/sites/default/files/research/docs/vakil_iran_on_the_brink_updated_.pdf
31. Ariel (Eli) Levite, "Can a Credible Nuclear Breakout Time With Iran Be Restored?", Carnegie Endowment Commentary, June 2021, https://carnegieendowment.org/2021/06/24/can-credible-nuclear-breakout-time-with-iran-be-restored-pub-84833 [accessed 1st August 2021].
32. Mayumi Fukushima, "Why Iran May Be in No Hurry to Get Nuclear Weapons Even Without a Nuclear Deal", Rand Corporation, 28 June 2021, https://www.rand.org/blog/2021/06/why-iran-may-be-in-no-hurry-to-get-nuclear-weapons.html [accessed on 1st August 2021].

33. The Shi'i Arabs are the single largest component in Iraqi and population (as against the Sunni Arabs and Sunni Kurds); the Shi'i are the larger of the two Muslim denominations in Bahrain; they constitute the largest religious minority in Saudi Arabia, Kuwait, and Lebanon, and a reasonable-sized minority in Qatar and Syria. The Shi'i in the UAE are mostly expatriates.
34. Among its neighbours, only Bahrain, Saudi Arabia, Iraq and Lebanon have Ithna Ashari Shi'i as the dominant sect. Iran's closest all Bashar al-Assad is 'Alavi Shi'i; Yemenis Shi'is are Zaidi Shi'i, with some Islamilis and Ithna 'Ashari; Palestinians are Sunni in their confessional affiliation.
35. James Ottaway, "Saudi Arabia and the United Arab Emirates Turn Rival Allies", 20 July 2021, https://www.wilsoncenter.org/article/saudi-arabia-and-united-arab-emirates-turn-rival-allies
36. Anne-Marie Bissada, "Power struggle behind Saudi-led Qatar embargo", RFI, 3 July 2017, https://www.rfi.fr/en/middle-east/20170701-power-struggle-behind-saudi-led-qatar-embargo [accessed 1st August 2021].
37. Amos Harel, "An Israeli Strike on Iran Might Have Been Possible a Decade Ago. Not Today", *Haaretz*, 12 December 2021, https://www.haaretz.com/israel-news/.premium.HIGHLIGHT-israel-strike-iran-nuclear-not-so-fast-trump-biden-1.10454480 [accessed 13th December 2021].
38. Anchal Vohra, "Israel's Attacks on Iran Are Not Working" April 2021, https://foreignpolicy.com/2021/04/27/israels-attacks-on-iran-are-not-working/ [accessed on 1 May 2021].
39. *The Abraham Accords*, US Department of State, https://www.state.gov/the-abraham-accords/ [accessed 1 October 2021].
40. "Saudi Arabia Turns Its Back on the Abraham Accords" 27th July 2021, https://insidearabia.com/saudi-arabia-turns-its-back-on-the-abraham-accords/ [accessed on 29 July 2021].
41. Michael Kugelman, "Why is India Joining Another Quad", *Foreign Policy*, 21 October 2021, https://foreignpolicy.com/2021/10/21/why-india-is-joining-another-quad/ [accessed on 25 October 2021].
42. Chatterjee, "Brinkmanship in the Persian Gulf", pp. 33-36.
43. *Share of crude oil and condensates exports of Iran in 2017, by country*, https://www.statista.com/statistics/942332/iran-crude-oil-and-condensates-exports-by-country/ [accessed on 12 December 2021].
44. Chaitanya Mallapur, "How Iran's Nuke Deal Could Boost India" 14th August 2015. https://www.indiaspend.com/how-irans-nuke-deal-could-boost-india-94184/ [accessed on 16 August 2015].
45. Nidhi Verma, Shu Zeng, "Iran slips record volume of oil into China, reaches out to Asian clients for trade resumption", *Reuters*, 8th March 2021, https://www.reuters.com/article/us-oil-iran-asia-analysis-idUKKBN2B00OL [accessed on 12 December 2021]
46. The details of the agreement have not been disclosed yet even to the Iranian parliament, but the 18-page document leaked to the *New York Times* in July 2021 indicated that Iran and China are working towards a close strategic cooperation over a period of twenty-five years. According to the leaked document, China has undertaken to invest $400 billion over a 25-year period, of which $280 billion would go to refurbishing the infrastructure of Iran's oil, gas and petro-chemical sectors, and the remaining $120 billion would go into upgrading Iran's transport and

manufacturing infrastructure under the Belt-Road Initiative (BRI). In return China would be able to buy any amount of crude it chooses from Iran at a discounted rate of 12-20% on the market price.

47. Golnaz Esfandiari, "Explainer: Why Are Iranians Angry Over A Long-Term Deal With China?" Radio Free Europe, 13 July 2020, https://www.rferl.org/a/explainer-iranian-china-deal-anger-among-iranians/30724344.html [accessed on 15 July 2020]. Turkey's Foreign Policy in West Asia: Changing Determinants and Perspectives.
48. Verma, Zeng, "Iran slips record volume of oil into China, reaches out to Asian clients for trade resumption", 8 March 2021, https://www.reuters.com/article/us-oil-iran-asia-analysis-idUKKBN2B00OL [accessed on 10 March 2021].

7

Turkey's Foreign Policy in West Asia: Changing Determinants and Perspectives

Omair Anas

ABSTRACT

What determines Turkey's foreign policy under the AKG Party's long rule? There are many answers to this much-debated question. The simple answer may see the role of neo-Ottoman, pan-Islamic, or nationalist ambitions to explain Turkey's expanding influence in West Asia. However, the determinants of Turkish foreign policy are beyond the politics of ideology and identity. The basic assumptions of threats and security, that once considered Russia and China as the primary and unifying threat for the NATO and Western alliance, the lack of democracy in the Arab world as the reason for regional problems, the rise of Turkey as a role model for Islamic countries, Turkey's EU prospects, and Turkey's perceptions among West Asian rulers have entirely changed. Despite being deeply polarised on domestic affairs, anti-Westernism, and frustration against the EU's reluctance, the American support to anti-Turkey non-state actors in Syria, Libya, and Iraq has strengthened a sense of insecurity frustration against Turkey's Western allies. The changing character of Turkey's economy, regional, and security roles and Turkey's domestic politics of new demographic ambitions are also shaping the Turkish regional policy and politics. Neither is the region the same as it was a decade ago, nor does the international system remain the same in which Erdogan and his AK Party had scripted the policy of Zero Problem and Strategic Depth.

West Asian countries are looking at Turkey's troubled relations both as a problem and an opportunity. There are four fault lines in which Turkey is to craft its policy towards the region; first, the Arab uprisings as a continuity of anti-regime sentiments in the region; second, Israel's expansionist policies; third, Iran and Turkey as two non-Arab states but increasingly involved in the region, and fourth, the world powers' changing perspectives towards the region. On the other hand, Turkey's alliance with NATO and its strong relations with the European Union offer many opportunities and limit Turkey's response to how Turkey should react against its allies if their interests clash. This paper proposes to study the changing determinants of Turkey's foreign policy in general and its West Asia perspectives in particular within these limits and opportunities. The new approach, "active Middle East policy", is being crafted carefully to enhance Turkey's role within NATO, to become credible security and political actors of West Asia. Finally, this paper compares Turkey with other regional players to understand how Turkey has assumed the role of a key economic, political, and strategic player in the region.

Introduction

In the late nineteenth century, the Ottoman Empire was caught in competition between the Russian and the British empires, and the British Empire was favouring the Ottomans to push back the Russian's advance towards India. After the Russian revolution, the Bolsheviks wanted Pan-Islamists and Pan-Asianists to join hands against colonialism and the British rule in Asia. The Ottoman officials subscribed to the Pan-Islamist ideas offered by a host of Muslim nationalists. For most of the post-Ottoman period until the end of the Cold War, Turkey remained isolated in the Middle East, which it had once dominated for centuries. The Ottoman Empire's rise and decline, then the emergence and rise of a modern and Westernised Turkish Republic that would soon become part of the Western security alliance, has uneasy relations with its neighbours for many reasons. After decades of economic mismanagement and political instability in most of the Eighties and Nineties, strong and popular leaders of the post-Cold War era like Turgut Özal and Recep Tayyip Erdogan brought Turkey back to their region (Ataman, 2002), first for economic reasons and then to seek an ideological and security alliance. The post-Cold War Middle East was not the same that the Ottomans had left back in the 1920s. The Ottoman reformists and then revolutionaries led by Mustafa Kemal had revolted against *Pan-Islamic, Pan-Turanian*, and *Pan-Asian* projects that the late Ottoman politicians instrumentalised to seek an alliance against the British Empire. Many Persian Gulf countries that had gone under direct or indirect control of the British Empire would gain independence in the 1960s. As a modern nation-state, Turkey would find itself in the politics of the bipolar world in which it would make the most defining decision of joining the Western military alliance.

Turkey's membership of NATO, regardless of various ups and downs in Turkey-West relations, remains the most important determinant of modern Turkey's foreign policy. Even though the Cold War has ended long ago, Turkey finds it very difficult, if not impossible, to find a replacement of its West-oriented foreign policy to adjust with many geopolitical changes that did not exist at the time of joining the alliance. The Western nations are also no longer Western in the same sense as they used to be during the Cold War debates. Their relations with all non-Western powers, India, China, and Russia, have significantly transformed. Asian countries and their groupings, India, China, Russia, Indonesia, and Pakistan, are becoming increasingly influential in global and West Asian politics. In the new context, the Cold War fault lines are replaced by new fault lines, and the divide between the religious Gulf monarchies and secular military authoritarian states is no longer relevant. Turkey is no longer the favourite Western ally in the Middle East. Countries like Israel, the UAE, Saudi Arabia, and Egypt have assumed greater importance than the NATO ally, Turkey, in the Middle East perspective of Western countries. Turkey, nonetheless, has successfully returned to the Middle East by employing a combination of trade, soft power, and strategic cooperation. The presence of Turkey is visible from TV screens to market shelves to defence inventories. Turkey's overall trade volume, diplomatic exchanges, security, and strategic interactions with the Middle East have significantly increased. The rise of Turkey's strategic profile, mostly independent of the Western umbrella, has implicated the existing West Asian security architecture and challenged the *status quo*, as Turkey seeks an equal status. However, the return of Turkey to the Middle Eastern security architecture is also helped by certain conditions that have been coincidently progressing. Among these conditions is the process of "reimagination" of the region following the failed uprisings, the emergence of new fault lines, and a new political economy.

"Reimagination" of the Region

"Rethinking" has been an unending intellectual enterprise for scholars looking into the reasons of the problems in the Middle East since the departure of the colonial powers. One of the most prominent works was by Bernard Lewis, "*Rethinking the Middle East*" in 1992. Simon Brolmely

(1994) authored *Rethinking Middle East Politics: State Formation and Development*. *The Unmaking of the Middle East–A History of Western Disorder in Arab Lands* by Jeremy Salt came in 2008, and *The Rebirth of the Middle East* by Jerry Rosenberg came in 2009. The themes of "re-mapping", "reconfiguring," and "reshaping" have been dominating scholarly concerns and pursuits. These analyses have often defined the region as "the most troubled of regions" (Barry Rubin, 1980, *Foreign Affairs*) using different synonyms for turmoil and instability in the region. This association of the region with all destabilising narratives is perhaps more exclusive to the Middle East. The debate over terrorism, ideologies, and liberation remains polarised and intellectually contested as the regional order faces economic and technological globalisation and self-imposed political and cultural exclusion. The great debate over the stability of authoritarian rule in the Middle East has not yet settled. While instability is generally attached with the slogans of freedom and democracy raised by anti-regime forces, peace and stability appear on top of the agenda of authoritarian rulers of the region.

The violent phase of the Arab uprisings and the emergence of the Islamic State (*Da'esh*) has contradicted the peacefulness of the protest movements that began in 2010 and reached the height of violent rule in 2014 with the Da'esh in control of large swaths of Syria, Iraq, Libya, and Yemen. The Arab public sphere now is defined by angry yet controlled streets, vocal social media yet shrinking political space. Amid failing uprisings, disappointment, detachment, and disinterest in passionate slogans of change is the re-domination of the Arab public sphere. After the protests had spilled over from one country to another in the 2010s, the rulers have now successfully learned how to defend their regimes and suppress the pressure coming from the streets. The external intervention, apparently to prevent humanitarian disasters or counter-terrorism, have either helped the return of authoritarian rulers or the failure of democratic and peaceful transition.

However, it may be recalled that the region was already living with an incomplete process of post-Ottoman and post-colonial state-building and state-society relations. The Middle Eastern nation-states are neither modern, nor are their relations based on modern social contract. The Westphalian nation-states, elsewhere, have gradually assumed the features of industrial economy, territorial nationalism, people's sovereignty, and social contract—the four fundamental bases of a modern nation-state system. The "Arab Nation-State" still remains a questionable idea and susceptible to tribal, religious, sectarian, linguistic, and even ideological solidarities. The eruption and dramatic rise and fall of the Islamic States in Iraq and Syria exemplify how regional politics may easily fall to these imagined solidarities. As a result, every crisis and conflict in the region questions the viability and sustainability of the nation-state institution in the region. For decades, the region has not seen any credible political process and social reform in which the angry streets and disenchanted citizenry can engage in meaningful communication. The failure of the Arab uprisings, by violence or political failure has put the Middle East in a deep state of perplexity, to the extent that both state and non-state actors are revising the *status quo* and want to use the crisis to maximize their interests across the region. Nobody knows what shape the region will take in this process, but many of them are certain that the region is indeed moving from one order to another, uncertain and unpredictable, nonetheless.

The quest for change at this juncture of disruptive transition was mostly organic and technological. However, the changing global political economy, political communication and changing state-society relations have started a process affecting the regional *status quo*. The forces advocating change were neither aware of the upcoming storm nor prepared to make a political opportunity out of it. The failure of the uprisings has underlined the failure of state-society relations and the vulnerability of the regional order. With its strong state-society relations, its sliding democracy notwithstanding, Turkey, still, appears a more viable alternative for the military or monarchy-ruled, violent, and import-dependent failing Arab states. The process of uprisings has yet to complete its course, and the revolutionary tide may return any time. As a result, two parallel processes—the unfinished revolutions and unfinished counter-revolutions—are in serious competition against each other. The region is grappling with various forces that have emerged in this competition, and negotiation among all forces continues to define the Arab public sphere, the TV, newspapers and social media debates.

The New Fault Lines

The struggle between unfinished uprisings and counter-revolutions has also opened a prolonged cold war, not between the known rivals, Iran and Saudi Arabia, but rather between the two visions of the regional security architecture. The "expansionist" Iran and "assertive" Turkey on the one side where both countries have close alignments with revolutionary forces; and a rapidly changing and secularising Gulf monarchies, and stable authoritarianism in Egypt on the other side. This model of stability is being advanced by most GCC and Arab countries, Saudi Arabia, the UAE and Egypt more specifically, to return to the pre-uprising security architecture. In this architecture, Saudi Arabia would return as the main power broker in the region. Once a leading power in the region, Egypt does not have the resources to assert its regional leadership and has to rely on external resources, mainly the United Arab Emirates and Saudi Arabia. Since the military coup in Egypt in 2013, Egypt has lost much influence to Saudi Arabia and the UAE. Egypt-Turkey and Egypt-Qatar relations are examples that a country like Egypt had to lose its strategic autonomy.

At the same time, the differences between the United Arab Emirates and Saudi Arabia on managing regional security have also not been fully reconciled, particularly in Yemen, Libya, Palestine, and Syria. The UAE has successfully come out from the shadow of Saudi Arabia's big brotherliness. UAE-Israel relations have mostly advanced at the cost of Saudi Arabia's diplomatic prowess, which Saudi Arabia could have used as a precondition to normalize relations with Israel. While Saudi Arabia's regional ambitions need a regional and multilateral approach, the UAE's quest for greater autonomy is guided by unilateral activism. Since Saudi Arabia has been occupied by a massive re-engineering of its domestic politics, smaller Gulf nations like the United Arab Emirates and Qatar have successfully made strategic strides to increase their stakes in the future security architecture. At the same time, Egypt has also lost much of its regional influence, and so did Jordan, Lebanon, Sudan and Iraq. These fault lines, a competition between two different visions, and competition within countries' ambitions are advancing without a strong regional leader like King Abdullah bin Abdul Aziz or Gamal Abdul Nasser, or institutions like the Arab League, where differences would have been reconciled. In this context, the rise of Turkey, both as a military power and a trade hub outside the Western ambit, has offered new opportunities for individual countries. Turkey has successfully resisted an informal travel and trade ban imposed on it for supporting Qatar since 2017. The assassination of Saudi dissident Jamal Khashoggi was another example of how these fault lines can quickly turn into a global problem. Even though the top Turkish and Saudi leadership agreed to scale down the crisis (Anas, 2018), international stakeholders did not allow the crisis to die down easily. These fault lines have divided the region beyond repair, and the region's confidence in Saudi and Egyptian leadership in managing the region is on the decline (Cook, 2017). Turkey is gradually claiming this leadership vacuum.

Apart from state actors, there is also a steady rise of new and old non-state actors, such as Islamist and nationalist, liberal, and pro-uprising groups. The expansion of communication technology, mainly Internet-based communication and social media, have radically changed the hegemony of states on communication, and non-state actors have become much more active in producing anti-regime communication. Despite attempts by states to control communication tools and disseminate pro-state information, as Nasser's state machinery had artfully exercised during the 1967 war, it is now easily challenged by the widespread use of social media and the Internet in the Arab world. In recent years, frequent cases of information leaks from state institutions to Wikileaks, for example, and defiance of state control of information have been increasing. The number of social media users has drastically increased in the region to 93 million, with 47 per cent annual growth. The changing nature of socially mediated communication has also transformed the way states can control information. Instead of employing the Chinese model of restricting international social media, the Gulf countries have invested heavily in social media by establishing IT cells and intensifying online surveillance. This changing context of the Arab public sphere allows pro-uprising, reformist, and anti-regime narratives to directly compete with pro-regime and anti-uprising narratives. The presence of a vibrant social media, heavy state surveillance notwithstanding, keeps the risk of change and disruption in action. Turkish dramas, movies and social media activism mobilize public opinion in her interest within this context. More than one hundred Turkish dramas have been translated into Arabic (TRT, 2020). The popularity of Turkish dramas, not just historical dramas but also modern dramas has created a sense of discomfort among the pro-regime conservative forces of the Middle East. In 2020, several Arab governments, including the official Dar al-Ifta of Egypt, had banned the most popular Turkish drama *Ertugrul* (Amin, 2020). These dramas fill the gap that the Arab silence of regimes on Islamic history, Arab-Israeli conflict, Islamic ideology, and reforms has created.

Then there are humanitarian crises, emerging from civil wars of Syria, Yemen, Libya, Iraq and unresolved conflicts like the Arab-Israeli conflict,

Darfur, and Palestine sanctions-driven economic crisis in Iran that have contributed to the making of a public discourse that is essentially anti-Western and anti-regimes. Middle Eastern countries find it difficult to continue their public discourse without addressing these issues and without engaging with certain non-state actors. Each country is choosing a side to avoid any anti-regime sentiments in their own countries. Perhaps more disturbing for the region's autocratic rulers is maintaining four humanitarian crises at their neighbours without resolving them. Earlier, the Palestinian problem was the most significant source of emotional mobilisation against the "Zionist-Israeli enemy", but now there are Yemen, Syria, Libya and Iraq, where almost half of the population is severely affected by violence. The images of displaced, tortured and killed people become a challenge for the region's powerful rulers who need to justify their intervention, support either side of the conflict and their share in resolving the crisis and improving the humanitarian condition. The longer the humanitarian crises remain unresolved, the struggle between the forces of the *status quo* and change is more likely to continue.

On the economic front, the more the Arab States are forced to introduce neoliberal reforms, the reduced social spending and slashed subsidies will strengthen non-state actors' narratives against regimes. As Prof. Girjesh Pant argues, the Arab states are under pressure to undertake neoliberal reforms; however, the widespread unrest remains a challenge (Pant, 2012, pp. 335–336). The Saudi state is a typical case study of how the nature of the state has to transform, should the ruling family need to find alternative sources of income to compensate for the ever-dwindling oil revenues. The budget deficit, that shot up to 17 per cent of the GDP in 2016 and needs to come down to 1 per cent by 2022, has required Saudi capital going outside and earned instead by Saudi nationals, preferably by working women. The violent and non-violent non-state actors can seriously threaten the regime's stability and survival in case the economic mismanagement remains unresolved. Yet, any economic reform requires popular support and confidence-building, which most states cannot afford to do. As a result, violent reactions to economic woes loom large, as happened in the rapid expansion of Islamic States.

Turkish Foreign Policy

Turkey emerged as a new player in this context by favouring the state and non-state actors that supported the Turkish vision for the region. The post-

Ottoman republic led by Mostafa Kemal Ataturk sought a neutral policy and non-aggression pacts with its immediate neighbours in the eastern and western borders. In 1937, Turkey signed the Saadabad Pact with Iran, Afghanistan and Iraq, which helped Turkey to minimize military risks at its eastern border. Until then, the treaty was seen as neutral as Turkey-Soviet Russia had been maintaining their treaty of neutrality signed in 1940. However, with World War II looming large and the aftermath of the War, the security scenario started changing rapidly. Turkey joined the NATO and sought to repackage the Saadabad Pact with the Baghdad Pact (CENTO) by including non-NATO friends, namely, Pakistan, Iran, and Iraq, into it in 1955.

Meanwhile, Egypt and Syria observed a nationalist surge led by their military leaders who refused to join the pro-West alliance's Middle East Command (MEC) and Middle East Defence Organization (MEDO). Turkey's increasing isolation in the Arab world was mainly a two-way process. First, Turkey sought close cooperation with non-Arab Muslim states, Pakistan and Iran, then members of CENTO by forming the Regional Cooperation for Development (RCD) in 1964. Second, Turkey's non-NATO security cover started weakening with the rise of military nationalists in the Arab world, the Iranian revolution in 1979 and Pakistan's weakening relations with the West following the former's military conflicts with India between 1962 and 1971. In a post-Cold War world, where security alliances have weakened, and Turkey does not trust its traditional allies, a "multi-dimensional foreign policy" seems to be the most pragmatic way to advance its foreign relations.

Turkey's disenchantment is only growing and deepening with the West following the increased mistrust over the Syrian crisis. Turkish politicians are talking about the betrayal they have met with from their Western allies in their fight against Kurdish militants in Syria and Iraq. Turkey's Iran policy has also remained largely unaffected despite having a serious and troublesome difference over Syria. This can be said to be true in the case of Turkey-Israel relations, which derailed only after the killing of nine Turkish nationals by Israeli forces on board a flotilla in 2010. The deepening differences between Turkey and its Western allies have also made Turkey's waiting time for the EU membership frustratingly longer. All this has not come all of sudden, and the country's diversification of its strategic and international relations began quite a long time ago. Turkey is no longer West-centric; it is not completely a Middle Eastern country yet, either. The

Turkish ambitions, both official and political, are for a 'multi-dimensional, constructive, proactive, realistic and responsible foreign policy' to minimize its dependence on its Western allies, to access diverse and larger markets and to achieve the goal of what it calls 'expansion of the sphere of peace and prosperity in its region. As the determinants of Turkey's West Asia are defined by its overall security, trade, and political ambitions in the region, Turkey's changing foreign policy may not necessarily be anti-Western despite all disagreements. Ismail Numan Telci of Ankara-based think-tank ORSAM argues "the major players in the region have reached a new understanding of the post-pandemic political landscape in the Middle East. These actors do not desire further escalation of tensions as each has its own challenges to tackle. With its mature and responsible approach to foreign policy, Turkey has opened a new window of stability in the region (Telci Numan, 2021)."

Turkey's association with NATO and its aspiration to become a full member of the European Union remains one of the most sustained foreign policy objectives across the political spectrum in Turkey. Mustafa Aydin also argues that the key determinants of Turkey's foreign policy favours strong Turkey-West relations (Aydin, 1999). Turkey, under Erdogan or previous nationalist rules, has never discarded these two main objectives. If NATO is central to Turkey's security architecture in the Middle East, Eurasia, and Europe, EU membership is a social and cultural object of the Turkish public (TCCB, 2021). In one of the surveys, the Turkish people have disapproved of Turkey's EU membership, even at the high time of tensions in Cyprus. In the latest survey conducted by The German Marshall Fund of the USA (GMF), a majority of Turkish people favoured Turkey's EU membership bid (GMR, 2021). EU membership and NATO membership give Turkey both an economic and security cover that Turkey may not easily replace with any other region. Even though, sometimes, Turkish leaders send strong signals in favour of the Shanghai Cooperation Organization, the SCO community itself does not see Turkey as a potential membership candidate. Turkey's association with the NATO and the EU gives Turkey enough room for diplomacy in crises like the Syrian civil war, refugee crisis, and regional conflicts.

The problem, however, is an expanding sphere of competition among various NATO members for influence in the Middle East. France and Turkey have serious disagreements on Syria, Libya, Lebanon, and North Africa issues, while Turkey and the USA have differences over the Gulf,

Iran, and Syria. Turkey has failed to force the NATO states to evolve a common approach to violent conflicts on its borders, Syria, Iraq, Azerbaijan, and Libya. There is no NATO or unified Western view of the Middle Eastern problems (Dalay, 2021). The Arab-Israeli conflict, for example, remains one of the most serious challenges of Western diplomacy. Turkey successfully uses the growing frustration of Arab streets against the West's protection of Israel from accountability before international law, both against the authoritarian regimes and their Western backers. The Arab regimes are facing angry streets and social media, often fuelled by Turkish and Iranian anti-Israeli and anti-Western politics. The Trump Administration's famous Deal of the Century has been derailed largely because of Turkish, Iranian, and Jordanian opposition against it (Anadolu Agency, 2020). Saudi Arabia was left with no choice except to stay away from approving the Trump Administration's scheme. The Western countries' preoccupation with Chinese expansion and focus on Indo-Pacific realignments has left the Middle East temporarily out of focus. This Western withdrawal from the region has allowed countries like Russia and China to seek greater influence in the region, leading to a new competition between Turkey and Russia. As NATO sees no significant role in the region beyond counter-terrorism and refugee crisis, for Turkey, its threat perception must address the military presence of Russia at its immediate border and the presence of Russian-US supported groups in Northern Syria. For Turkey, the NATO alliance is indifferent to Turkish concerns (Anadolu Agency, 2016).

On the other hand, the political economy of Turkey needs an expansion of Turkish trade and investment relations beyond Europe, Turkey's largest trade partner. The transformation of the Turkish economy is still incomplete, and the Turkish economy cannot wait for EU membership. Despite an ongoing currency crisis, Turkey remains the fastest growing and the largest economy in the Middle East. Turkish exports to the region reached US$ 40 billion in 2020 (*Hurriyet Daily*, 2020). The export list now includes defence equipment, heavy and light arms, and, more importantly, unmanned aerial vehicles. At least Qatar, Oman, Iraq, Morocco, Tunisia, and Kuwait have either already acquired Turkish drones or have expressed interest. The use of Turkish drones in the Azerbaijan-Armenia conflict in 2020, Libya, and Syria has boosted the Turkish defence industry and has received significant international attention. The Arab States, depending so far on Western, Russian, and Chinese drones, may buy Turkish drones with little political and strategic strings attached. Turkish drones were decisive in expelling the Russian private militia, Wagner, from Western Libya, where the Russian militias were recruited to help the warlord Khalifa Haftar's failed march to the Libyan capital (Marson & Forrest, 2021). In Syria, Turkish drones had inflicted huge damage on the Syrian army after Syria-allied planes had bombed at least 33 Turkish soldiers in February 2020. Similarly, Turkish drones have forced the PKK terror groups hiding on the Iraqi and Syrian borders to revise their tactics to escape from killer drones. At the same time, Turkey's calculated confrontation in the East Mediterranean and the maritime delimitation agreement with Libya have brought more strategic fortunes to an otherwise isolated Turkey.

Turkey-Algeria, Turkey-Sudan, and Turkey-Nigeria relations have improved significantly in recent years, favouring Turkey's influence in the region. With these changes in Turkey's West Asian relations, Turkey aims to achieve some parity with regional powers like Egypt and Saudi Arabia. It may not be surprising if Turkey, at one stage, requests for Arab League membership, as the Arabic-speaking population in Turkey is steadily rising. Turkey-Iran coordination in Syria has paved the way for both countries to cooperate on many regional issues. By upgrading its overall strategic profile in the region, the traditional West Asian hegemons, Saudi Arabia, and Egypt, have to share regional leadership with a country that was kept aside for decades. Turkish and Saudi visions for a regional order have some fundamental differences and have often contradicted each other. The regional upheaval and countries' domestic problems in the region make the region more unpredictable. The forces of the *status quo* are becoming more repressive and hegemonic in their approach, eliminating all possible ways of moderation and reform in a peaceful way. While Turkey favours the change in the *status quo*, the change of ruling elites in the region, by-election, reforms, or revolution, Saudi Arabia strictly favours the *status quo* even by exercising military power. Both countries had serious disagreements on the military coup in Egypt in 2013, the War on Yemen, the Trump Administration's Abraham Accords, and, most importantly, the 2017 diplomatic blockade of Qatar (Anas & Telci, 2020, p. 8). Turkey firmly stood, by paying heavy trade and travel arrivals, with its position until both sought a thaw in their relations in 2021. Turkey still insists on carving out an independent role for itself and finding a new template for its regional policy. Turkish diplomacy plays with flexibility to win new allies, new friends, and convince rivals of no harm from Turkey.

Dialogue with its rivals has yet to start and qualify for a sustained normalisation of relations.

It is not just Turkey but the European countries also that are facing tough choices between morality and legality. As a Western nation, they have to express their adherence to democratic politics; with regard to the Middle East, they have to sit on a democratic agenda and tolerate authoritarian rules and military coups. Unlike European countries, Turkey maintains a more considered approach by adopting a more pro-democracy, pro-Palestine, pro-Muslim regional agenda so that regional governments find it difficult to adopt a pro-Western foreign policy. As Western governments put pressure on Turkey on many issues, Turkey finds itself in a tough balancing act to choose between direct trade and investment interests and ambitions for regional leadership. Turkey is in transit to a new phase of foreign policy to redefine its Middle East policy.

In the Persian Gulf, Iran and Turkey have competed in expanding their influence. Even in Afghanistan, Turkey's interests are not the same as Iran's or Pakistan's. All three countries have different approaches to Afghanistan's post-Taliban transition. Pakistan has been balancing between Iran and Saudi Arabia as it has to balance its relations with Turkey and the Emirates as well. Just like Pakistan has been balancing between the Gulf States and Iran, Turkey and Iran, too, have tried to balance their relations between India and Pakistan. A common political approach of Iran, Pakistan, and Turkey never fully materialised even with the help of the ECO or D8 until the Gulf and the Middle East politics have started looking beyond the sectarian alliance. Whether they can initiate a mini-OIC, as they attempted in 2019, through the much-hyped Malaysia Islamic Summit, depends on how Saudi Arabia and the UAE rewrite their engagement with Asian powers. Turkey is looking for increased engagements with Asian regional groups, the Shanghai Cooperation Organization, BRICS, SAARC, and ASEAN. It has recently upgraded the Turkic Council to Organization of Turkic States, with Turkish-speaking countries of Central Asia and Azerbaijan. With the Economic Cooperation Organisation (ECO), Turkey is closely connected with both Iran and Pakistan. With these engagements, Turkey has rebranded its Asia policy, as Asia Anew, to enhance its trade volume and Asian tourist arrivals.

Conclusion

This article concludes that the West Asian landscape is deeply divided into various fault lines; now, the unfinished Arab uprising currents are prominent among them. A combination of security, economic, and political challenges has put the region under tremendous pressure to make hard choices. As the West Asia region lags in introducing sustainable political and economic reforms, Turkey, despite its populist democracy, has a vibrant economic, political, and social space. Moreover, in the last decade, Turkey has upgraded its economic output and has advanced its defence industry, becoming the fastest growing defence exporter of the region. The Arab uprisings have left hard choices before the Arab regimes, between political reforms or violence. Turkey has carefully maintained an approach that supports political reforms in some countries and the *status quo* in some countries. In addition, Turkey has demonstrated her ability and willingness to assume greater security roles in her neighbourhood by protecting her allies and protecting her borders with her military and diplomatic prowess.

On the other hand, the Western countries face a serious policy conundrum in the region as they face a choice between moral vs. realist choice. In Libya, Syria, and Yemen, the Western powers have somehow maintained an ambiguous approach to protect their authoritarian allies. Turkey and Western policies have a direct clash in Syria, Libya, Azerbaijan, and Qatar. While Western nations have to adopt a rule-based position finally, Turkey exploits this policy conundrum in her favour. On the cultural front also, Turkey claims more soft power than any other West Asian regime in the region. By upgrading its soft power reach in the region, Turkey has indirectly challenged the moral basis of authoritarian regimes and Western support to their policies. However, by playing high-end games, Turkey has also faced severe economic backlash, export, and tourism boycotts. For economic reasons, Turkey has now started a rapprochement with all disgruntled neighbours. However, if successful, this round of rapprochement will offer Turkey new opportunities with the already gained ground. Turkish ambitions in the region are defined by the scope of her economic expansion, security roles, and diplomatic and ideational leadership. With the absence of the Western countries' unified and assertive approach to play an assertive and decisive role in the region, Turkey has found new cooperation opportunities, independent of the Western watch.

Turkey-West Asia Relations Level

	Change of regime since 2011	*Popular Islamism*	*Relations with Turkey*	*Relations with Saudi Arabia/UAE*
Algeria	Yes	Strong	Excellent	Good
Bahrain	No	Weak	Bad	Excellent
Egypt	Yes	Strong	Bad	Excellent
Iraq	Yes	Strong	Excellent	Improving
Jordan	No	Strong	Good	Improving
Kuwait	No	Strong	Excellent	Good
Lebanon	Yes	Weak	Excellent	Good
Libya	Yes	Strong	Excellent	Good
Mauritania	Yes	Strong	Good	Good
Morocco	Yes	Strong	Excellent	Good
Oman	Yes	Weak	Excellent	Good
Palestine	Yes	Strong	Excellent	Good
Qatar	No	Strong	Excellent	Improving
Saudi Arabia	No	Weak	Poor	
Sudan	Yes	Strong	Good	Excellent
Syria	Yes	Strong	Improving	Suspended
Tunisia	Yes	Strong	Excellent	Improving
United Arab Emirates (UAE)	No	Weak	Improving	Excellent
Yemen	Yes	Strong	Improving	Excellent
Iran	No	Strong	Excellent	Improving
Israel	No	Strong	Good	Improving

Turkey's Socio-Economic Status in the Middle East

	Per cent	*GDP*	*HDI Index*
Turkey	7.44	$ 852 billion	59
Brazil	0.98	$ 2.054 trillion	78
Iran	3.76	$ 454 billion	63
Africa	1.32	$ 349 billion	111
USA	2.27	$ 19.485 trillion	15
Russia	1.55	$ 1.578 trillion	49
Saudi Arabia	-0.86	$ 687 billion	36
Iraq	-2.07	$ 192 billion	120
Morocco			121
Egypt	4.18	$ 235 billion	116
Jordan	1.97	$ 40.07 billion	99
Israel	3.33	$ 353 billion	22
UAE	0.79	$ 383 billion	35
Algeria	1.60	$ 168 billion	81
Tunisia	1.96	$ 39.95 billion	91
Libya	26.68	$ 38.11 billion	111
Lebanon			93
Palestine			119
Qatar			40
Oman			47

Source: Compiled from Human Development Report 2019, http://hdr.undp.org/sites/default/files/hdr2019.pdf

REFERENCES

Amin, S. (2020, February 16). Dar al-Ifta joins in Egypt-Turkey culture war - *Al-Monitor:* The Pulse of the Middle East. Al-Monitor. https://www.al-monitor.com/originals/2020/02/dar-al-ifta-joins-in-turkish-egyptian-culture-war.html

Anadolu Agency. (2016, November 20). NATO allies should heed Turkey on Syria: Celik. https://www.aa.com.tr/en/americas/nato-allies-should-heed-turkey-on-syria-celik/689170

Anadolu Agency. (2020, February 9). Turkey won't allow 'Deal of Century' to threaten peace: President. https://www.aa.com.tr/en/jerusalem-red-line-for-muslims/turkey-wont-allow-deal-of-century-to-threaten-peace-president/1728582

Anas, O. (2018, October 15). Saudi Arabia's role in Jamal Khashoggi's disappearance—The Week. *The Week*. https://www.theweek.in/theweek/more/2018/10/12/saudi-arabias-role-in-jamal-khashoggis-disappearance.html

Anas, O., & Telci, I. (2020). *Towards a New Security Architecture in the Gulf.*

Ataman, M. (2002). Özal Leadership and Restructuring of Turkish Ethnic Policy in the

1980s. *Middle Eastern Studies*, 38(4), 123–142. JSTOR. https://www.jstor.org/stable/4284261

Aydin, M. (1999). Determinants of Turkish Foreign Policy: Historical Framework and Traditional Inputs. *Middle Eastern Studies*, 35(4), 152–186. JSTOR. https://www.jstor.org/stable/4284043

Cook, S. A. (2017, August 28). *The Tragic Tale of Egypt's Decline: Is It Also the Story of America's Future?* Council on Foreign Relations. https://www.cfr.org/blog/tragic-tale-egypts-decline-it-also-story-americas-future

Dalay, G. (2021, January 28). Turkey, Europe, and the Eastern Mediterranean: Charting a way out of the current deadlock. *Brookings*. https://www.brookings.edu/research/turkey-europe-and-the-eastern-mediterranean-charting-a-way-out-of-the-current-deadlock/

GMR. (2021, April 29). Turkish Perceptions of the European Union. The German Marshall Fund of the United States (GMF). https://www.gmfus.org/news/turkish-perceptions-european-union

Hurriyet Daily. (2020, April 15). Turkey's trade with the Middle East surpasses $40 billion—Latest News. *Hürriyet Daily News*. https://www.hurriyetdailynews.com/turkeys-trade-with-middle-east-surpasses-40-billion-142666

Marson, J., & Forrest, B. (2021, June 3). Armed Low-Cost Drones, Made by Turkey, Reshape Battlefields and Geopolitics. *Wall Street Journal*. https://www.wsj.com/articles/armed-low-cost-drones-made-by-turkey-reshape-battlefields-and-geopolitics-11622727370

Pant, G. (2012). From the Vantage Point of Tahrir Square: Popular Uprising in the Arab World. *International Studies*, 49(3–4), 331–350. https://doi.org/10.1177/0020881714534031

TCCB. (2021, November 17). Presidency Of The Republic Of Turkey: "The European Union should approach its relations with Turkey from a strategic perspective." Presidency of the Republic of Turkey. https://www.tccb.gov.tr/en/news/542/133545/-the-european-union-should-approach-its-relations-with-turkey-from-a-strategic-perspective-

Telci Numan, I. (2021, May 27). ORSAM-Centre for Middle Eastern Studies. ORSAM-Centre for Middle Eastern Studies. https://www.orsam.org.tr/en/turkeys-reorientations-and-new-era-in-the-middle-east/

TRT. (2020, August 27). The young Syrian who translates Turkish dramas for the Arab world. TRT. https://www.trtworld.com/life/the-young-syrian-who-translates-turkish-dramas-for-the-arab-world-39251

8

Israel and Emerging Strategic Dynamics in MENA

P.R. Kumaraswamy

ABSTRACT

The turbulent Trump Administration has facilitated Israel's legitimacy and acceptance in the Arab-Islamic world and delinked the Palestinian question from the larger issue of Arab-Israeli normalisation. Despite its reservations over the marginalisation of the Palestinians by its predecessors, the Biden Administration seeks to shore up Israel's interests by strengthening Arab-Israeli relations, and the mini-Quad is a clear manifestation of this strategy. The continuing Israeli focus on Iran would undermine India's ability to pursue a robust policy towards Iran. This demands of India evolving and establishing a modus vivendi; Israeli inability to support India over China is not different from Indian inability to support Israel over Iran. If the Middle Eastern Quad has to succeed and flourish, an Indo-Israeli understanding and accommodation over China and Iran, respectively, will be inevitable.

The new government headed by Naftali Bennett and Yair Lapid formed in June 2021 coincided with a host of regional and international developments that offer immense opportunities to Israel to build and expand recent diplomatic gains. Some of these shifts and challenges facing Israel would benefit India, while on others, both have to minimise and accommodate their differences. One could identify six broad issues that would dominate Israel's strategic worldview and which have a direct bearing on India.

End of Netanyahu Era: Israel is slowly coming to terms with the post-Netanyahu era and all that it entails. Netanyahu, whose tenure as prime minister was longer than David Ben-Gurion's, dominated the Israeli political landscape for over three decades. Ever since he succeeded Yitzhak Shamir as the leader of the Likud after the 1992 Knesset election, he oscillated between ruling and opposition benches. Since 1993, he emerged as a staunch opponent of the Oslo process and played a significant role in the eventual failure of the Israeli-Palestinian peace negotiations. Even though he came around to accepting the possibility of an independent Palestinian State, Netanyahu was not enamoured by the idea of the internationally recognised two-state solution to the Israeli-Palestinian conflict.

Netanyahu was first elected prime minister in May 1996 and was in office until 1999 and his second innings lasted for 12 continuous years (2009-2021). He did not hesitate to disagree and even confront the Obama Administration (2009-2017), with nuclear Iran being his prime agenda. The arrival of the Trump Administration greatly enhanced his influence, and Netanyahu succeeded in leapfrogging the Palestinian question and forge closer ties or working relations with a host of Arab countries. Corruption charges and four rounds of Knesset elections between 2019 and 2021 did not diminish his hold on the Likud. Known for his shrewd political instincts, he did not hesitate to reach out to the Islamist Ra'am party towards forming a government, only to be vetoed by his more hard-line supporters. Eventually, the Bennett-Lapid team, not Netanyahu, formed the coalition government in June 2021. Netanyahu's hopes for the government's premature end were dashed when the Knesset passed the budget in November, the first one in two-and-a half years.

The Bennett-Lapid government is the narrowest in Israeli history and has the support of only 61 out of 120 members in the Knesset. The ruling coalition comprises inherently conflicting parties, and hence, its long-term survival is far from certain. Not radically moving away from Netanyahu's policy on other issues, the Bennett-Lapid government is more sensitive to the Palestinian question and the need to mend fences with Jordan. More importantly, Israel had to repair some of the damages done by Netanyahu to the larger issue of relations with the USA.

Under Netanyahu (interestingly, coinciding with Narendra Modi), Indo-Israeli relations progressed significantly. There were a host of political visits, official engagements and military engagements. Strategic relations moved away from the narrow military-security arena and encompassed human security issues such as water and agriculture. Both leaders frequently hosted, met, congratulated, greeted and tweeted regularly.[1] Netanyahu even used Prime Minister Modi's montage in his election campaign.[2] India, however, was quick to engage with the Bennett-Lapid government, and during his visit to Israel in October 2021, External Affairs Minister S. Jaishankar conveyed an invitation to Prime Minister Bennett to visit India at the earliest convenient date.[3]

Gains and fallouts of the Trump Administration: The surprising election of Donald Trump in November 2016 started a turbulent four years not only for the people of the USA but also for most of the Middle Easterners. Internal schisms, support for conservatism and embracing of intolerance exposed deep internal divisions within the USA that culminated in the riots of the Capitol on 6 January 2021, seen by many as an insurrection. Likewise, since his campaign days, Trump has been demonstrating his opposition to the Iran nuclear deal, one of the hallmarks of the previous Obama Administration. Moreover, his anti-Islamic remarks during the election campaign became virulent after he assumed office in January 2017, leading to a series of measures that angered and alienated vast sections of the Middle East.[4]

However, Israel remained an exception to the otherwise bleak foreign policy outlook of the Trump Administration. No American president has been more supportive of, some might say biased, towards Israel than President Trump, since the days of Harry Truman, who granted diplomatic recognition within minutes after Israel was proclaimed on 14 May 1948.[5] Trump broke away from traditional American positions on several occasions and embraced unconventional and hence controversial policies vis-à-vis Israel. Coming after the Obama Administration, which was cool and even 'unfriendly' towards Netanyahu, the Trump Administration was manna from heaven. Traditionally, US presidents never made demands on the peace process in excess of what Israel was prepared to concede. Whether the occupant was Republican or Democrat, arm-twisting of Israel, hopes of several Arab countries since the Suez crisis, was never the policy option of the White House. Yet, even by that generous definition, President

Trump was an exception. Some of the most notable moves of the Trump Administration vis-à-vis Israel include:

- **Jerusalem as Israel's capital**: The Declaration of Independence, which announced the formation of the State of Israel on the Sabbath eve of 14 May 1948, was silent on the capital. Israeli leaders were not prepared to declare Jerusalem as the capital lest they antagonise the international community, especially when the UN partition plan declared Jerusalem to be an international city. At the same time, declaring Tel Aviv as the capital would mean accepting a Zionist state without Zion, another name for Jerusalem. Hence, the silence of the Declaration of Independence regarding a capital was prudent. The following year, once Israel became a member of the newly-formed United Nations, Jerusalem was declared Israel's capital, and all the symbols of sovereignty—office of the president, government offices, parliament and supreme court—were established in or moved to Jerusalem. Meanwhile, Israel and Jordan signed the armistice agreement on 3 April 1949, dividing the city into East and West Jerusalem. As a result, between 1948 and 1967, western Jerusalem was under Israeli control and sovereignty, and Israel captured the eastern part of the city in the June 1967 War.
- However, much of the international community did not recognise even west Jerusalem as Israel's capital, let alone Israeli sovereignty over the east. Since 1967, various American administrations have considered the Greenline (armistice lines of 1949) as Israel's borders in Jerusalem. However, in November 1995, the US Congress overwhelmingly adopted the Jerusalem Embassy Act, which demanded the shifting of the American embassy from Tel Aviv to Jerusalem; but using executive prerogative, successive presidents deferred its implementation. Finally, President Trump changed that with the least warning on 6 December 2017 when he recognised Jerusalem as Israel's capital. Overriding a near-unanimous UN General Assembly resolution against this shift,[6] the American embassy was moved to the city in May next year.
- **Golan Heights**: On 25 March 2019, Trump recognised Israel's sovereignty over the Golan Heights through a presidential proclamation. The sovereignty over the Heights captured from Syria during the June War was not in doubt until then. On that

premise, in the 1990s, Israel conducted peace negotiations with President Hafiz al-Assad with the active participation of the Clinton Administration. By declaring Golan as Israeli territory, the Trump Administration also legalised the Israeli settlements on the Heights.

- **Settlements**: On 18 November 2019, the Trump Administration declared that it no longer considered Israeli settlements in the West Bank (since Israel had pulled out of the Gaza Strip in September 2005) a violation of international law, that is, the settlements are not illegal. This once again went against the established norms and interpretations of the Fourth Geneva Convention of 1950, which proscribes the demographic transformation or exploitation of resources of the occupied territories. In the past, various US administrations had voted in favour of UNSC resolutions that declared Israeli settlements in the occupied territories to be illegal and contrary to international law. The Trump Administration moved away from this.

Interestingly, some of these moves came amidst election campaigns in Israel and were seen as Trump's efforts to shore up support for Prime Minister Netanyahu, whose efforts briefly succeeded when he formed a unity government in 2010 with the Blue and White party headed by Benny Gantz.[7]

Despite the controversial nature of these moves and their international disapproval, the Biden Administration's ability to reverse them is slim. Tensions between Israel and the USA have already started over the Biden Administration's efforts to reopen the US consulate in East Jerusalem, shut down by the Trump Administration. Finding a political compromise without exposing the fragile Bennett-Lapid government to criticism from the right will not be easy for the US President. Hence, at least in the medium term, the Biden Administration would have to live with and continue the policies of the Trump Administration concerning Jerusalem, Golan Heights and the settlements, thereby diminishing the prospects of Israeli-Palestinian peace.

Abraham Accords: Hailed by his supporters as the 'Deal of the Century', President Trump unveiled his peace plan in January 2020, right amidst his impeachment trial.[8] It expressed conditional American support for an emasculated, diminutive and fractured Palestinian state surrounded by large swaths of the Israel-controlled West Bank and hence was dismissed by the international community as unfair and unviable.[9]

Not intimidated by the near-universal rejection of his peace plan, President Trump pushed for Abraham Accords between Israel and the wider Arab world. Beginning with the UAE (13 August 2020), the process was joined by Bahrain (15 September), Sudan (23 October) and Morocco (10 December) towards normalising relations with Israel. Despite the absence of formal ties, Oman and Qatar have hosted Israeli leaders in the past. In the last days of the Trump Administration, countries like Saudi Arabia, Pakistan[10] and Kuwait were mentioned as possible candidates. Though the diplomatic march did not happen, it is safe to conclude that Bahrain and UAE would not have forged ties with Israel without Riyadh's strong but tacit endorsement. Saudi Arabia seems to be waiting for a more opportune moment to maximise its advantages by recognising Israel. Towards this end, Prime Minister Netanyahu flew to the Kingdom and met Crown Prince Mohammed bin Salman in November 2020.[11] The Abraham Accords were followed by normalisation of relations, opening resident diplomatic missions, high-profile political visits, robust economic engagements and even participation in military exercises involving Israel and Arab countries.

The Abraham Accords and their aftermath had two key consequences. First, they are part of the Israeli search for recognition and normalisation of relations towards greater acceptance and legitimacy and contribute to Israel's 'normalisation' among the Arab-Islamic countries. Furthermore, the willingness of these countries to forge diplomatic relations also signals the delink between the Palestinian question and the Israeli-Palestinian conflict. At least some Arab countries are prepared to establish relations with Israel even without resolving the Palestinian question or an end to the Palestinian stateless. By gaining Arab-Islamic acceptance and the delink, Israel seeks to marginalise the Palestinian question in the international arena. While the Palestinian statelessness invokes popular sentiments in the Middle East and beyond, its priority in inter-state relations has fallen in recent years.

The expansion of the circle of friends has one long-term advantage for Israel. In the initial years of the Oslo Accords, Egypt and Jordan were the principal mediators between Israel and the Palestine National Authority (PNA) during periods of turbulence and disagreements. When the Fatah-Hamas internal schism intensified, countries like Saudi Arabia and Qatar stepped in, especially during violent clashes. If Saudi Arabia organised the Mecca Agreement in February 2007, Qatar sought to mediate the Israel-Gaza violence in the 2014 Gaza War. Normalisation of relations has brought the UAE into the picture, and there are indications that the Emirates could narrow down the political differences between Israel and Jordan.[12]

Iran and the Diplomacy of the Periphery: Iran continues to be Israel's major foreign policy preoccupation, but its strategic approach has changed.[13] In the 1950s, to circumvent its regional isolation, Israeli Prime Minister David Ben-Gurion developed the polity of peripheral diplomacy whereby Israel would leapfrog the immediate and hostile Arab core and befriend countries and groups that share a common animosity or unfriendliness towards the Arabs.[14] Not an anti-Muslim alliance in its approach, this policy brought Israel closer to Turkey, Iran, the Kurds of Iraq and Maronite Christians in Lebanon. Though Iran pulled out of this equation after the Islamic revolution, peripheral diplomacy contributed to Israel-Turkey relations and, for a while, kindled hopes of a Maronite ally in neighbouring Lebanon.

Recent years saw a reversal of Israeli priorities. If Erdogan's Turkey has been less dependable and even unfriendly, Iran has emerged as its prime threat. The Shia Crescent in the region cannot be dismissed merely as a Western construct aimed at containing Iran. Objectively speaking, with the help of a host of proxies and non-state actors like Hezbollah (Lebanon), Hamas (Palestine), Houthis (Yemen) and Popular Mobilisation Forces (Iraq), Iran has expanded its reach and regional influence that, in turn, contributed to the fears of Iranian hegemony in the Persian Gulf. The Obama Administration's willingness to override Arab concerns and conclude the nuclear deal with Iran brought countries like Saudi Arabia and others closer to Israel.

Now the Arab core is not only friendly towards Israel but also shares Israel's concerns vis-à-vis Iran. This enabled Israel to reverse the diplomacy of the periphery and join hands with key Arab neighbours against Iran; Bahrain and the UAE directly and Saudi Arabia indirectly. Interestingly, Israel could do this without making any significant concessions to or accommodation with the Palestinians as manifested through the Abraham Accords and their aftermaths.

Managing China: Since its formation, Israel has had a complex relationship with China. In January 1950, Israel became the first Middle Eastern and the seventh Western-bloc country to recognise the People's Republic of China but was also the last country in the region to be recognised by Beijing.[15] To entice China and reducing its rhetoric, in the late 1970s, Israel opened a military-diplomatic route[16] that fructified on 24 January 1992 when China recognised the Jewish state. However, the end of the Cold War and the emergence of China as a future threat resulted in the USA reversing its erstwhile position and exerting pressure on Israel to cease military ties with China. As a result, the cancellation of the Phalcon deal in 2000 and subsequent Israeli withdrawal from upgrading Chinese military inventories in the following years largely ended the Sino-Israeli military ties.

At the same time, Israel could not ignore China's economic ascendance, political clout and regional preponderance. Under the decade-long premiership of Netanyahu, both countries entered into strategic economic partnerships, and Chinese companies began to participate in Israeli infrastructure projects like ports, tunnels and railroads. In addition, Chinese companies began to invest in sensitive Israeli hi-tech companies. Both these developments increased American concerns over Chinese footprints in Israel.[17] These concerns were conveyed to Israel by also the Trump Administration, which was otherwise friendly towards Israel and Netanyahu.[18]

As the US pressures greatly influenced, slowed down and shifted the strategic nature of the relations, Israel's relations with China did not evoke sufficient attention in India. From the information currently available in the public domain, despite cautions,[19] the Sino-Israeli military relations did not figure in official Indian discussions with Israel. Moreover, despite Israel raising Iran in its engagements with India, the latter never broached China in its conversations with Israel. Indeed, the Indian foreign policy establishment took serious note of the challenge only after the cancellation of the Phalcon deal.

At the same time, Israel's ability to accommodate India's concerns over China is extremely limited. China's importance to the global economy and strategy means that Israel would be sensitive to Beijing on all major issues. Though watchful of the recent Sino-Indian border tensions, Israel would continue to stay neutral and indifferent. Any Israeli military-security assistance that would directly affect the balance of power along the Himalayas would be limited; if Israel were to change the military balance in India's favour, China might retaliate by encouraging the power capabilities of its adversaries, mainly Iran.

Formation of Mini-Quad: The formation of a mini-Quad during the Israel visit of External Affairs Minister Jaishankar is an interesting development at two levels; one, India has increased the visibility of Israel in its foreign policy; and two, it is upgrading its relations with Israel to a multilateral level. This is largely an outcome of the Abraham Accords, which facilitated Israel-Gulf normalisation. Three out of four members—Israel, UAE and the USA—are eager to shore up support for and consolidate the gains of the Abraham Accords. Taking India, which seeks closer relations with all the three countries, sounds logical and even inevitable. It also signals a major step in the Gulf towards Indo-US interest convergence and political cooperation. Moreover, logically it would pave the way for India's greater strategic involvement in the Persian Gulf region when the USA is shifting its attention to the Indo-Pacific theatre. For its part, India should be prepared to shoulder a greater burden on softer issues like maritime security.

Though its association with the mini-Quad adds to India's position and leverage in the region, there is a flip side to it. When it comes to implementing promises and commitments, India is not known for walking the talk. Even well-intended projects tend to suffer from time and hence cost elasticity. The other three Quad members, for example, have a long list of unfulfilled Indian promises; the August 2015 Emirati pledge to Prime Minister Modi to invest up to US$ 75 billion in India made no significant progress; Israel has been negotiating a free-trade agreement with India for over two decades; and the USA has a long laundry list over Indian inactions. Thus, the Quad membership and the desire of Israel and the UAE to fast-forward their bilateral relations should increase the Indian efficiency and, prioritisation and, hence, its influence.

Some caution is needed concerning the future prospects of the mini-Quad. The framers have emphasised the economic focus of the group. In the words of Israel's Alternative Prime Minister and Foreign Minister Yair Lapid, "Synergy is what we are going to create, starting from this meeting.... Synergy is what will help us work together on infrastructure, digital infrastructure, transportation, ports, trains and maritime security."[20] There are already suggestions that countries like Bahrain, Cyprus, Egypt, France and Greece might join the forum[21] and this might necessitate a formal nomenclature such as *Abu Dhabi Dialogue* or *Emirati Conclave*. While expansion is a good idea, more membership would come with the prospect of the forum being another talk shop without much clout. A delicate balance is needed if the Quad were to be effective.

Moreover, concerns have been raised within India over the political motives and calculations of the mini-Quad. Unfamiliarity with the regional dynamics and ideological blinkers resulted in several otherwise informed persons viewing the Quad as an anti-Chinese or anti-Iranian exercise. For some, it is a new anti-China exercise plotted by the Biden Administration.[22] For others, it lacks a cohesive focus, unlike the older Quad, which is largely China-centric.[23] The former Indian ambassador to the UAE and Saudi Arabia went a step further and argued: "The US' only concern is now containment of China. This group (mini-Quad) is aimed at that."[24] Making a pun over the virtual meeting of the Quad members, one seasoned journalist identified China as the "elephant in the zoom room".[25]

The media editorials also flagged China. According to the *Times of India*, the new forum "ties India into another alliance with the USA, which is imperative to counter China's belligerence."[26] Flagging 'many conflicts' in the Middle East, *The Hindu* felt: "The USA is clearly seeking to lessen its footprint here as part of its pivot to East Asia to tackle China's rise, which is redrawing West Asia's traditional equations."[27]

Most, however, did not ask some elementary questions. Can Israel and the UAE, the two key regional players, view China as an adversary? Can they afford to take an explicitly anti-China stand? Do they have the desire or stomach to antagonise an economically powerful and politically important country? Or what would they achieve by making the mini-Quad an anti-China forum?

Despite their disagreements regarding Sino-Iranian relations, neither Israel nor the UAE views China as an adversary. A confrontational approach towards China would bring both countries more misery than gain. In short, neither Israel nor the UAE would project the Middle Eastern Quad as an anti-China exercise.[28]

How about Iran? There are sufficient reasons to argue that if mishandled, the mini-Quad could take an anti-Iran character. Since the

Oslo accords, Iran has emerged as the prime regional adversary of Israel, and the nuclear controversy only increased the anti-Iranian rhetoric by Israel. While there are strong disagreements over the strategies, the current regime in Iran is depicted as the most severe security challenge facing Israel. Anti-Israeli and anti-Jewish rhetoric of the Iranian leaders, including Ali Khomeini, did not help the matter. The Iranian refusal to accept Israeli existence and the two-state solution to the Israeli-Palestinian conflict continues and is unlikely to change. Iranian leaders have even been critical of India and others for their closer ties with Israel and often draw parallels between the situation in Palestine and Kashmir.[29] Iran has continued to occupy the three Emirati islands since 1971 with no diplomatic solution in sight.[30] Thus, the concerns of Israel and the UAE are legitimate and both might prefer a regional forum that would express support for their respective positions and concerns. Hence, some have warned New Delhi to avoid making Quad an anti-Iran platform.[31]

What's the stand of the third party, the USA? Unlike the Trump presidency, the Biden Administration does not view Iran in hostile terms. The USA-Iran rapprochement would not be easy and will be painstaking. Both sides have a long list of grievances and complaints, and if the nuclear deal took over a decade to materialise, the wounds of the hostage crisis of 1979 would take even longer to heal. Yet, the Biden Administration's ability to return to the nuclear deal would require a moderate policy towards Tehran. Thus, transforming the mini-Quad into an anti-Iran forum does not serve larger American interests or agenda.

Where does India stand? India views Iran as a strategic partner for a host of political and economic reasons. Its desire for an active role in the Afghan peace process can only be accomplished through a robust cooperation with Tehran. With prudence and foresight, India should leverage the mini-Quad to gain greater Iranian attention and inclusion to engage with the Taliban-ruled landlocked country. Despite the numerous players and forums, Iran remains the pivot for an Indian role in Afghanistan.

Furthermore, India still considers Iran a friend despite disagreement over remarks on Kashmir, stalled gas pipeline, not getting exploration deals, and uncharitable remarks over the 2003 vote in the IAEA. Besides a role in Afghanistan, India needs Iran for a transport corridor to Central Asia, countering Pakistan, energy security, a bourgeoning Iranian market and its ability to play a constructive role in the maritime security of the Persian Gulf region. Hence, ganging up against Iran through the mini-Quad is not a viable strategy for New Delhi. On the contrary, India should use the new forum to seek greater Iranian attention and enhance its importance vis-à-vis Afghanistan.

In short, the mini-Quad acquiring an anti-China posture might serve India at present, making it a forum against Iran that suits Israel; but other countries do not view the Quad through such narrow prisms. Hence, leaving political and strategic issues aside, the mini-Quad should focus on economic and developmental issues. Otherwise, its efficacy, relevance, and long-term survival would become questionable.

Conclusion

The turbulent Trump Administration brought several benefits to Israel and India, but Israel's gains transformed its strategic contours and foreign policy gains. It has facilitated Israel's legitimacy and acceptance in the Arab-Islamic world and delinked the Palestinian question from the larger issue of Arab-Israeli normalisation. Despite its reservations over the marginalisation of the Palestinians by its predecessors, the Biden Administration seeks to shore up Israel's interests by strengthening Arab-Israeli relations, and the mini-Quad is a clear manifestation of this strategy.

The continuing Israeli focus on Iran would undermine India's ability to pursue a robust policy towards Iran. This demands that India evolve and establish a modus vivendi; Israeli inability to support India over China is not different from the Indian inability to support Israel over Iran. If the Middle Eastern Quad has to succeed and flourish, an Indo-Israeli understanding and accommodation over China and Iran, respectively, will be inevitable.

ENDNOTES

1. P.R. Kumaraswamy, 'Reading Modi's Visit to Israel,' *India Quarterly: A Journal of International Affairs*, 74, no. 1 (2018): 1–16, https://doi.org/10.1177/09749284177 49644.
2. "PM Modi Features in Netanyahu's Election Campaign in Israel," *The Hindu*, July 29, 2019, sec. International, https://www.thehindu.com/news/international/pm-modi-features-in-netanyahus-election-campaign-in-israel/article28744105.ece.
3. When he visits India, Naftali Bennett would become the third Israeli Prime Minister to visit India after Ariel Sharon (September 2003) and Benjamin Netanyahu (January 2018).

4. Talmis Ahmad, "Trump's Toxic Legacy In West Asia", *Outlook India*, November 27, 2020, https://www.outlookindia.com/website/story/world-news-trumps-toxic-legacy-in-west-asia/365509.
5. For example, see Uri Pilichowski, "100 Times President Trump Supported Israel," *The Times of Israel*, October 27, 2020, https://blogs.timesofisrael.com/100-times-president-trump-supported-israel/.
6. On 21 December 2017, the UNGA adopted a resolution declaring the Trump Administration's decision as 'null and void' by 128 to 9 votes, with 35 abstentions and 21 absentees.
7. Between 2019 and 2021, Israel held four Knesset elections in April and September 2019, March 2020 and March 2021.
8. The White House, "Peace to Prosperity: A Vision to Improve the Lives of the Palestinian and Israeli People", (The White House, January 28, 2020).
9. P.R. Kumaraswamy, "Trump Peace Plan: A Good Diagnosis but Medication," *CLAWS Journal*, 13, no. 1 (2000): 48–64.
10. Lahav Harkov, "Pakistan's PM Imran Khan Pressured to Recognise Israel", *The Jerusalem Post*, November 16, 2020, https://www.jpost.com/international/pakistans-pm-imran-khan-pressured-to-recognise-israel-649154; Anadolu, "PM Imran Claims He Is 'under a Lot of Pressure to Recognise Israel,'" *The Nation*, November 13, 2020, sec. Top Stories, https://nation.com.pk/13-Nov-2020/pm-imran-claims-he-is-under-a-lot-of-pressure-to-recognise-israel.
11. Oliver Holmes, "Netanyahu Holds Secret Meeting with Saudi Crown Prince", *The Guardian*, November 23, 2020, sec. World news, http://www.theguardian.com/world/2020/nov/23/benjamin-netanyahu-secret-meeting-saudi-crown-prince-mohammed-bin-salman.
12. AP and TOI Staff, "National Security Adviser Confirms Solar, Water Swap Deal with Jordan," *The Times of Israel*, November 21, 2021, https://www.timesofisrael.com/national-security-adviser-confirms-solar-water-swap-deal-to-be-inked-with-jordan/
13. P.R. Kumaraswamy, *Israel Confronts Iran: Rationales, Responses and Fallouts*, IDSA Monograph Series 8 (New Delhi: IDSA, 2012).
14. Yossi Alpher, *Periphery: Israel's Search for Middle East Allies* (New York, NY: Rowman & Littlefield, 2015); Jean-Loup Samaan, *Israel's Foreign Policy beyond the Arab World: Engaging the Periphery* (Routledge, 2018).
15. Yitzhak Shichor, "Hide and Seek: Sino-Israeli Relations in Perspective," *Israel Affairs*, 1, no. 2 (Winter 1994): 188–208.
16. Yitzhak Shichor, *Proxy: Unlocking the Origins of Israel's Military Sales to China*, CIRS (Doha: CIRS, 2020).
17. Shira Efron et al., *The Evolving Israel-China Relationship* (RAND Corporation, 2019), https://doi.org/10.7249/RR2641; Shira Efron, Karen Schwindt, and Emily Haskel, *Chinese Investment in Israeli Technology and Infrastructure: Security Implications for Israel and the United States* (Santa Monica, CA: RAND Corporation, 2020), https://doi.org/10.7249/RR3176
18. Natalie Liu, "Contract Decision Raises Doubts About Israel-China Tech Ties," *VOA News*, June 5, 2020, sec. VOA News on China, USA, https://www.voanews.com/east-asia-pacific/voa-news-china/contract-decision-raises-doubts-about-israel-china-tech-ties
19. P.R. Kumaraswamy, "Israel-China Military Relations: India's Red Lines," *Strategic*

Analysis, 18, no. 6 (September 1995): 781–92.

20. Lahav Harkov, "Israel, US, UAE, India Agree to Launch Joint Economic Forum," *The Jerusalem Post*, October 19, 2021, https://www.jpost.com/breaking-news/yair-lapid-speaks-with-blinken-uae-and-indian-foreign-ministers-682422?utm_source=jpost.app.apple&utm_medium=share
21. Seth J. Frantzman, "The Israel-UAE-India-US Partnership Is a Quiet Revolution - Analysis," *The Jerusalem Post*, October 19, 2021, https://www.jpost.com/international/the-israel-uae-india-us-partnership-is-a-quiet-revolution-analysis-682452?utm_source=jpost.app.apple&utm_medium=share
22. Desk, "EXPLAINED: Is 'New Quad' of India, US, UAE, Israel Aimed At Addressing The Dragon At The Table?," *News18*, October 20, 2021, https://www.news18.com/news/explainers/explained-is-new-quad-of-india-us-uae-israel-aimed-at-addressing-the-dragon-at-the-table-4344041.html
23. Rudroneel Ghosh, "Second Quad: Nomenclature and Posture Matter, India Shouldn't Be Sleepwalking into the Platform," *The Times of India*, October 21, 2021, https://timesofindia.indiatimes.com/blogs/talkingturkey/second-quad-nomenclature-and-posture-matter-india-shouldnt-be-sleepwalking-into-the-platform/
24. Nayanima Basu, "India-Israel-US-UAE Grouping 'Not against China', Can't Rule out Trade Deal, Israeli Envoy Says," *The Print*, October 20, 2021, https://theprint.in/diplomacy/india-israel-us-uae-grouping-not-against-china-cant-rule-out-trade-deal-israeli-envoy-says/753811/
25. Jyoti Malhotra, "Why US and India Are Taking on China with a 'Middle Eastern Quad'," *The Print*, October 19, 2021, https://theprint.in/opinion/global-print/why-us-and-india-are-taking-on-china-with-a-middle-eastern-quad/752775/
26. TOI. Editorial, "Second Quad? Exciting Opportunities Await India in Middle East, but Not without Risks," *The Times of India*, October 18, 2021, https://timesofindia.indiatimes.com/blogs/toi-editorials/second-quad-exciting-opportunities-await-india-in-middle-east-but-not-without-risks/
27. Editorial, "The Other Quad: On Virtual Meet of Foreign Ministers of India, US, Israel and UAE," *The Hindu*, October 20, 2021, sec. Editorial, https://www.thehindu.com/opinion/editorial/the-other-quad-on-virtual-meet-of-foreign-ministers-of-india-us-israel-and-uae/article37079666.ece
28. Guy Burton, "No, the 'Middle East Quad' Is Not Anti-China", *The Diplomat*, October 29, 2021, https://thediplomat.com/2021/10/no-the-middle-east-quad-is-not-anti-china/.
29. Santosh Chaubey, "Iran's Supreme Leader Khamenei Rakes up Kashmir Bogey Twice in Two Weeks," *India Today*, July 5, 2017, http://indiatoday.intoday.in/story/irans-supreme-leader-khamenei-rakes-up-kashmir-bogey-twice-in-two-weeks/1/994600.html.
30. Richard A. Mobley, "The Tunbs and Abu Musa Islands: Britain's Perspective," *Middle East Journal*, 57, no. 4 (2003): 627–45.
31. Suhasini Haidar, "Worldview with Suhasini Haidar: A New Chapter in India-Iran Ties?," *The Hindu*, August 6, 2021, sec. National, https://www.thehindu.com/news/national/worldview-with-suhasini-haidar-a-new-chapter-in-india-iran-ties/article35775560.ece; Ghosh, "Second Quad."

9

The Economics of Western Asia

Dr. Jawad Anani

The purpose of this concise and straightforward paper is to shed light on some of the main challenges and opportunities, which Western Asian countries will have to grapple with in their efforts to transition their societies into more equitable and sustainable states. Every Arab country that is a member of the Economic and Social Council of Western Asia (ESCNA), is dealing with external and internal pressures for change, which require them to adopt new measures for reform. These reformations are economic, cultural, political, and social in nature and various combinations of these four facets are necessary for each state's successful progress. Before elaborating on these required changes, it is imperative to clear up some ambiguities from the onset: A) The definition of the term "West Asia" can be limited to countries that occupy the specific geographical region on the map, whether it be fully or partially through proximity. If this narrow interpretation is accepted, then the term is limited to the Gulf Cooperation Council (GCC), the Greater Levantine countries (Syria, Palestine, Lebanon, and Jordan), as well as Iraq, Yemen, and Egypt. B) The wider definition of the term "West Asia", which is more inclusive, involves all of the aforementioned countries, in addition to the remaining Arab League members, with the exceptions of Djibouti, and the Comoros Islands. It is my contention that the latter definition of the term is the more accurate and inclusive one, as it represents all the members of the ESCWA.

Prince Hassan of Jordan, in his role as the chairman of the Arab Thought Forum (ATF), has been an advocate for the renaming of the "Middle Eastern" region as the "Western Asian, North African" (WANA) region. In his elaborations on the matter, this reframing would confer a more accurate and recognizable continental identity than the one currently used as a label in global discourse. It is imperative to state that the WANA label is not strictly confined to the Arabic speaking countries of the geographical location, but rather includes other non-Arab states such as Iran, Turkey, and, in a peaceful futuristic hypothetical, even Israel. In order for this renewed continental partnership and grouping to be successful, the four main demographics within the region: Arabs, Turks, Persians, and Kurds, must coexist harmoniously and peacefully. Although these four large demographics do not include all the varying and nuanced identities that live in the area, it does cover a very large percentage of the inhabitants of the region.

Now that this caveat in definition has been asserted, we can employ the initial and limited interpretation of "West Asia", for the analytical purposes of this text. In other words, the focus will be on the ESCWA members who are located in the Western Asiatic region geographically. Although it is difficult to address the complex transformations contemporarily taking place within the Arab countries, the following powerful quote by the late M.K. Gandhi can help simplify them eloquently: "Your beliefs become your thoughts, your thoughts become your words, your words become your actions, your actions become your habits, your habits become your values, and your values become your world."

After the drastic defeats suffered by the Arab world at the hands of Israel in 1948, and in 1967, the region has been going through a process similar to the one aptly described in the aforementioned quote by M. K. Gandhi. The train of sequential improvement has been constantly derailed by many factors. This can, in part, be attributed to the rigidity of religious beliefs, which in turn stifle the potential of Arab minds. In his book *'The Formations of the Arabic Mind'* Mohammed Al-Jabiri addresses the various factors, including the rigidity of faith, which have stunted the development of Arabic ingenuity within the last century. The path to change begins by changing thoughts, so that values, actions, and ultimately behaviours can change.

The internal process of changing minds is not alone sufficient for real and concrete change. The marriage between demagoguery and political institutions has led to hegemonic structures that do not allow for self-criticism and/or positive change. The structures of power, fuelled by bad ideas and malignant actors, have allowed for control systems that can be calibrated and modified to fit the needs of the powerful elite. The need for internal change, which translates into meaningful action, can be summarized in Morocco's fight for independence from France, during which Allal Al-Fasi, who founded the Istklal Party and authored the book *'Al Naqd Al-Thati'*, discusses the need for active reflection in faith. He became a major reference for many burgeoning political parties in the Arab World during his time. Unfortunately, after this attempt to restructure Arab thought, and, in turn, political structures, many external effects impacted the region negatively. The two wars with Iran led to coup d'etats and revolutions that changed long-established regimes, and in Iraq, Syria, Egypt, Tunisia, Sudan and Libya, cardinal changes occurred. There were also attempts to overthrow the monarchy in Jordan (1957, 1970), but which never materialized. Many of these changes and new regimes transformed their nations into dystopian dictatorships that further derailed the path to progress. In his book *'Thief and Dogs'*, the Egyptian Nobel Laureate for Literature, Nagib Mahfouz, highlights the hypocrisy of many of the revolutionaries who betrayed the principles they espoused after attaining seats of power.

Enter the Oil Boom era, which came at the heels of another Arab-Israeli war in 1973, and which changed the region drastically. Consumerism, globalism, and a new affluent ruling class emerged. These new wealth profiles in the GCC and neighbouring countries would soon become indoctrinated with a nightmarish interpretation of the "American Dream", but during the early days of this boom (1974-1985), big governments replaced the big scary stick with a delicious carrot, and the masses responded accordingly. In this initial period of the oil boom, the Arabs of West Asia enjoyed a very good standard of living, as new infrastructural development and construction began to take place. The region soon became a hub for international speakers and intellectual discourse, and Arab economic prosperity reached new heights. The Arab economic prosperity during the early days of the oil boom directly contrasted with the economies of non-oil producing countries, which suffered a period of stagflation: a vicious hybrid cycle that combined stagnation or unemployment with inflation. Money was being spent just as quickly as it was being made.

Interestingly, President Anwar Sadat decided to give a speech in 1977 at the Israeli Knesset, where he pledged that Egypt would not continue fighting on behalf of the Arabs, and incurring massive costs, while rich Arab countries remained oblivious to Egypt's economic woes. When he, Sadat, eventually signed the Camp David treaty with Israel in 1979, other Arab leaders convened in Baghdad and voted to terminate Egypt's membership in the Arab League. The League's headquarters were subsequently relocated from Cairo to Tunis, and the Egyptian secretary was replaced by a Tunisian one.

In 1979, the Shah of Iran was deposed and the country was subsequently renamed the 'Islamic Republic of Iran.' It was then governed by a tripartite political structure composed of: 1) The Shiite clergy, 2) The civil government, 3) and the Army. The supreme ruler who reigned over the country was the Imam, Ayatollah Al Khomeini, and his governing council known as the 'Ulama', which was composed of the religiously educated elite. This new ruling regime began to zealously express its desire to export the Islamic revolution elsewhere. To gain political legitimacy within the Arab and Islamic worlds, the new government of Iran immediately severed its political and economic relationship with Israel, including the termination of their oil exports to them. Israel substituted that oil supply with oil from the Signori Peninsula. The first country to be targeted by Iranian proselytization was Iraq, which at that time was under the rule of the powerful and secular Baathist regime, led by Saddam Hussein. A few months after the Iranian revolution, the war between Iraq and Iran began, and it lasted until August 1988, making it one of the longest battles in modern history. This was ideal for American foreign policy, which sought to maintain control of the two nations through what Henry Kissinger labelled "dual containment".

During the first five years of the war, the price of oil continued to rise until it peaked at 40 dollar per barrel by the end of 1984. However, this was followed by a sharp decline in oil prices, and by mid-1986, the price of oil had plummeted to 6 dollars a barrel. Both Iraq and Iran became desperate to sell their oil and fund their troops, so they began to distribute their reserves in the open and black markets at much reduced prices. This resulted in other OPEC members being forced to sell their own oil at a much lower rate in order to keep their share of the market. The state of affairs decimated not only the economies of oil-producing countries in the Arab world, but also all the economies of the region as a whole. 1986 also witnessed a decline in the price for raw materials, particularly in Iran, as cement, zinc, and vegetable oil values collapsed.

It was at this point that countries like Malaysia began to express their disapproval of the Arab world, because the latter had squandered a golden opportunity to improve the terms of trade with the industrial powers of the world. This sentiment of disapproval was made public by the Malaysian Prime Minister at the time, Dr. Mahatir Mohammad, who vocalized his disapproval chiefly due to the losses that his country's economy had endured. Malaysia had lost a great deal of its foreign exchange receipts due to the drop in prices of palm oil—because it was deemed a carcinogen—as well as the drop in prices of tin, and, most importantly, the collapse in prices of crude oil. I met Dr. Mohammed in 1986 during a conference about the world economy, which was organized by the Malaysian Institute of Strategic Studies (MISS), and he reiterated the same sentiment of disapproval. By the year 1988, after the war had ended, the price of crude oil had experienced a surge and the cost per barrel had gone up to 24-26 dollars. Also, the claims that palm oil was causing cancer had been scientifically refuted, and the tin mines in the UK had been closed. These three factors gave Malaysia's economy the boost it needed, and it retrieved the glory it once lost.

Unfortunately, the same could not be said about the economies of the Arab nations. Saudi Arabia's attempts to host peace negotiations between Kuwait and Iraq had failed to bring any resolution to the disputes about oil prices and other debt-related issues in 1990, and Saddam Hussein sent his troops to Kuwait without any prior warning. This ploy jeopardized Iraq's stature and reputation within the Arab world. At that time, the Allied Forces also refused to abide by the Security Council Resolutions (661-773), and neglected many other measures, which were adopted in accordance to chapter 7 of the UN Charter. This alliance of more than 35 countries then commenced an attack on Iraqi troops in Kuwait, which resulted in the humiliating defeat of Saddam's army. Following these events, many Jordanians and Palestinians were evicted from Kuwait and other GCC nations, and forced to return to Jordan. Subsequently, at least one million third-country nationals were crowded in hastily assembled camps in Jordan's desert. The Arab world had shunned Jordan, and the Palestinian Liberation Organization (PLO) for choosing not to be involved in the fight, and had placed them in a dire economic situation. Other countries like Egypt, on the other hand, who supported the Allied Forces in their mission to liberate Kuwait, had gained a lot in terms of employment, trade, and investments in one-way financial transfers.

Jordan, during the early years after that war, saw its formidably fortified and stable Dinar lose approximately 50 per cent of its dollar value. It, along with many other Arab countries, went into a painful debt overhang as well as economic adjustments through the IMF. At that point, it became clear that the mirage of the oil bonanza was fading, and what had been previously considered a win-win situation during the early days of the boom was slowly transforming into a hostile alternative of zero-option modalities. In 1991, Jordan and the PLO had received a golden opportunity to vindicate their standing in the form of an invitation to attend the Madrid Conference for Peace in the Middle East. Mr. James Baker, who designed the peace negotiations architecture, and formulated the invitations to Madrid, had conducted eight rounds of negotiations in the concerned Arab capitals before his initiative. Relations among Arab countries began to improve, but this was happening at a slow and cautious rate. Iraq, which had launched rockets into Israel during the Gulf war in 1991, was marginalized in these negotiations, and the pressures of extremely well monitored economic sanctions dug deep into its abilities to sustain basic life necessities for its people. Iraq was seen by America's unipolar foreign policy in the region as a renegade country, and was being gradually prepped for an ultimate TKO, which arrived more than a decade later in 2003.

During the time after the first Gulf War, Iran and Turkey began experiencing an economic and political resurgence. Both Turkey—especially during Erdogan's premiership and presidency—and to a lesser degree Iran, were challenging Israel, and jousting for Palestinian rights for independence and self-determination. The sentiments of aggrievement towards Israel helped offset the sense of loss of both nations in prestige regionally. At this point, the Lebanese borders and the Gaza Strip were war zones. The Hezbollah, an Iranian-backed Shiite organization, and Hamas, a Sunni breakout movement that was disenchanted by the PLO's peace treaty with Israel, broke out in war with the Zionist nation. Both Hamas and Hezbollah were non-governmental organizations, that despite their religious differences and inferior militaristic capacities, caused embarrassing losses to the Israeli army and reasserted the belief that Israel could be defeated. Also, the economic progress that Turkey experienced, along with the developments in the heavily sanctioned Iran, gave the Arab populations a modicum of hope.

In 2008, following the global economic recession, and the rise of China from its isolationist standing to become a giant economic player on the global stage, the USA' unipolar privileges in the West Asian economies were beginning to erode. China's trade deals with Arab states made them the biggest trade partner in the region. For example, the Road and Ring Project of China, as well as the Asian Development Bank, became viable alternatives for Arab nations to not surrender to the unfair terms of trade posed by Western countries. The non-oil producing countries of the region saw rates of unemployment skyrocket, especially amongst the youth, and the prospects of hope and change began to dwindle. This was a sign for opinion makers in the region that an invisible metamorphosis was taking place. Arab ruling regimes were accused of being dictatorships, and charges of corruption were beginning to surface. This *modus operandi* presented all the symptoms of unsustainability and instability. Reports about Arab failures in IT and other technologies, as well as their failed attempts at democratic experimentation, further cemented the notion that a serious malfunction existed and needed to be addressed. It was a foolish waiting game to depend on those who were enjoying the *status quo* to bring about the necessary reforms for addressing these malfunctions. Hence, a popular, peaceful movement was necessary. One that took lessons from the experience of M.K. Gandhi and his brand of sustained non-violent resistance.

The necessary elements for the Arab Spring were all in place, except for the official spark that would ignite the despair, and manifest it into action. Who was going to hang the bell on the unwilling cat's neck? This spark came in the form of a youthful street vendor, who sold apples in the streets of Tunisia to make ends meet, and was stripped of his scales for selling without a permit. He attempted to retrieve his scales, but was denied a meeting with the police commissioner. In an act of desperation and protest, Mohammed Bouazizi set himself ablaze. This young fruit vendor has gone down in history books as the challenger of authoritative governments, and as the man who took his own life in defiance of the dictator Zain Al Abiden Bin Ali, the dictator-in-chief at the time. Interestingly, the economic data from Tunisia then suggested that the country was doing well financially, but the hidden figures concealed the skewed nature of the distribution of that wealth and income. An astute reading of the events that took place is that the economy could not afford a feasible job opportunity for the young man, whose family had spent its entire life savings to see him through college. In his attempts to make a living for himself, Muhammed began operating in the unofficial economy, where his labour was untaxed, and licences non-existent; hence, no fees were paid to the government. When the unofficial economy begins to bustle, tax-paying merchants who operate within the official market are threatened. This tension resulted in the government defending its tax-paying clients through the use of law enforcement. Azizi became a symbol for the unrepresented, and despairing demographic segment of society that was trapped at the bottom of the bottle, and far from its neck.

The popular uprising that took place in Tunisia was overpowering and overwhelming. It took only a few days for the ex-President, Ibn Ali and his influential wife, to escape on a private plane. The religiously-inclined residents of Tunisia, who reside in the non-coastal areas of the country, found their alternative in the Islamic party Al Nahda. The secular and pro-Western regimes, and their supporters, were revealed to be corrupt and undemocratic to the core. After a short interim, the Al Nahda party won the new elections, and began its rule. These events spawned a domino effect in the region, and within the following year (2012) four Arab regimes had been toppled. Hosni Mubarak in Egypt, Ali Abdullah Saleh in Yemen, Muamer Al Qadhafi in Libya, in addition to the previously mentioned events that took place in Tunisia. In 2019, Omar Al Bashir of Sudan was also deposed. The Arab popular movement, or Arab Spring, was not only confined to the countries that underwent regime change, but sentiments had also spread to other places within the region, such as: Syria (2011), Jordan (2011-2012), Oman (2011), Bahrain (2011-2013), the occupied Palestinian territories, and even Iraq, which had been under occupation for over a decade. Even countries such as Mauritania and Algeria had experienced a similar fate. Changes in leadership occurred in some of the Arab countries due to other reasons as well. For instance, King Abdulla Bin Saud's passing meant that King Salman Ibn Saud would become king. Through various political manoeuvres, the latter managed to install his son, Mohammad Bin Salman (MBS), as the heir-apparent, despite the disapproval of many members of the royal family there. The young prince, emboldened by his father, began to put in place sweeping reforms, which aimed at rebranding Saudi Arabia from a religiously conservative society into a seemingly open and global one. The Western-educated youth of the country were on board with these proposed changes and shifts in paradigm. Diversifying the Saudi economy away from its dependence on oil became the focal point of this proposed radical shift. It is naive, however, to assume that these changes were welcomed by all the members of Saudi society, nor is it safe to say that the Saudi economy is completely liberated from the impact of its oil reserves. The race against time, and the tides, is something that MBS fully recognizes.

MBS tried to grasp hegemonic control of his society by reining in all of his opponents, real and potential, and had successfully managed to excise large amounts of their assets from them in order to fund his overly ambitious NEOM project. Through his radical actions, the liberation of his country from some of its arcane laws, especially as they pertained to women, became associated with these socially liberated transformations, for better and for worse. Another example of the unholy alliance between progress and autocracy is the murder of Adnan Khashoggi in the Saudi embassy in Istanbul. This event brought with it a huge amount of negative press for the Kingdom, and its new ruler, which was propelled to more negative media attention after he imposed sanctions against the Emirate of Qatar. This had signalled that a new approach, namely one of reconciliation amongst members of the GCC, was needed. In its role as the "big brother", Saudi Arabia was expected to initiate and maintain these efforts of reconciliation, so that the GCC itself did not collapse. In 2021, MBS succeeded in his attempts to avoid the seemingly imminent collapse.

A major challenge facing Saudi Arabia, and which threatens the stability of the region as a whole, is the proxy war with Iran in Yemen. This war has been devastating in terms of its impact on the well-being of the Yemeni population, as well as the cause of financial ruin for the country. If Iranian-Saudi relations improve, and both nations are to reach a resolution, particularly from the Iranian side, then the chances of MBS and his brand of rulership to succeed will improve, and with it the reform paradigm will prevail. If this costly war and confrontation continues unabated then it undoubtedly threatens the stability of both the Islamic Republic of Iran, and the Kingdom of Saudi Arabia.

Despite many attempts, the Arab Spring had failed to bring about regime change in Syria. Many reasons can be attributed to this, but three main factors can be stated: 1) Russia and its leader, Putin, would have never squandered the opportunity to get a foothold in the warm waters of the Mediterranean, 2) The presence of Iranian troops, as well as the Hezbollah's support from Lebanon offered unlimited militaristic support for Bashar Al Assad, the president of Syria. 3) The Syrian Army is dominated by the minority group of Alawites, to which Assad belongs. The major civil war that ensued in the country has displaced 8 million Syrians at home and 4.5 million Syrians abroad. Many refugees fled to the borders of Lebanon, Turkey, Jordan and many trekked on a perilous journey towards Europe. Prior to the war, Syria's economy was one of the region's most promising. It is a country endowed with many skilled labourers, as well as natural resources such as crude oil and gas, industrial output, agricultural land, and water. Its foreign debt was under control prior to the war, and it was self-sufficient in food production. The promise of Syria has now been dealt a major blow, and the country needs urgent revival.

Iraq, until 1984, had the biggest promise of growth. Since then, Iraq has experienced two Gulf wars—in 1991 and 2003—where the second led to its occupation. These major events downsized the country's immense potential. In the wake of Iraq's past spring elections, many new complexities emerged. The presence of American troops had been reduced to 2,000 non-combative trainers, but the Shiite factions were unable to reach common ground with the new government that had been formed. Dr. Mustafa Al Kazime, Iraq's appointed President, had exerted great efforts to mend broken fences with neighbouring countries and encouraged GCC investments. He also hosted talks between Saudi and Iranian security top officials in Baghdad, reopened the borders with Jordan and Syria, and extended a hand to Turkey. In addition, he forged a tripartite arrangement with both Jordan and Egypt. Dr. Kazime always reiterated Iraq's independence, and reasserted that it is a free Arab, and Muslim state. In terms of military, he is trying to demilitarize the militias, particularly the Iranian-backed mobilization forces, as well Al Aqsa brigades, and is attempting to integrate them into the country's armed forces. The Government budgetary allocations earmarked for the popular forces were over 10 billion dollars a year, without any commitment of allegiance to the official government of Iraq. Iraq is a wealthy country, but its capacities after 41 years of internal demographic hostilities and external battles has reduced quite significantly. The political system that had been installed proved to be quite dysfunctional, but nonetheless, Iraq could be the closest among the war-torn Arab countries to cross the reform threshold and recuperate.

Jordan is unique in the fact that it has weathered all the economic storms after 2008, such as the receding relationships with the Gulf states, and the decline of the economies of neighbouring countries, and of course the impact of COVID-19 on the global economy. Jordan is now dabbling with an all-encompassing reform package, which was initially met with cynicism in the courts of public opinion, and is now the national preoccupation. Lebanon is a country, which has seen its potential completely stifled by proxy wars and lethal sectarianism. The various sects within the country had their own set of inherent leadership roles, which were rationed among them. However, at this moment in time, the Maronites, Sunnis, Shiites, and Druz populations have been segmented into warring tribes and militias lead by chieftains. The Hezbollah streamlined the other Shiite wing known as the Amal Party, which is headed by Nabih Birri, who is the parliament speaker. The Maronite sect, which is the wealthiest Catholic demographic in the country, has many leaders such as President Michel Awn, the Maradah headed by Subiman Franjieh, and Al Kataeb, who are headed by the Shamoun family, and last but not least, there is also the leadership of Sameer Jaaja, who leads the militia. The Sunni population has a more volatile divisiveness, but ostensibly, the main leaders are part of the Al Mustaqbal coalition founded by the Late Rafiq Al Hariri, Najib Miqtali, and the current Prime Minister of Lebanon, along with other smaller splinter groups like the Miri'bi class in Akar. With all these divisions, Lebanon's political scene is so messy and complex, which makes it immune to reconciliation efforts. As a result of these divisions, the Lebanese economy is in a shambles, and the Lebanese Lira dropped to (30,000) per dollar. More than 70 per cent of the Lebanese population lives in poverty, and there are major shortages in food, drugs, and fuel. Beirut, previously known as the "Paris of the Middle East" is living in its darkest days, and in a dystopian state of affairs.

A 2021 ESCWA report issued in June estimated that the Arab economic growth in 2020 was negative. With the exceptions of Egypt and Qatar, all the other members of ESCWA showed negative GDP growth rates. However, the numbers for June of 2021, as reported by ESCWA, the IMF, and the World Bank, show a growth of (4.3%) regionally. This is an impressive rebound. The countries with the best results were Egypt, whose growth rate rose from 3 per cent in 2020 to 7.3 per cent in 2021, as well as Morocco, which made a quantum leap in GDP from negative (-3.4%), to an estimated growth rate of (6.3%) in 2021. The various international ratings for the two nations are very good, and regional as well as international investors have been showing great interest in both countries. Jordan has made a modest rebound from (-2.02%) in 2020, to (2.0%) growth in 2021. This growth enables the economy to lessen the rate of unemployment by

3-5 per cent annually. The economy of Jordan reveals a paradoxical nature within the labour market. While the country suffers from a 23.5 per cent unemployment rate among job-seeking Jordanians, (this equates to 500,000 people), the economy is accommodating more than a million jobs for Egyptian, Syrian, Iraqi, Yemeni, Libyan, and Asian refugees. The unemployment rate amongst Jordanians is composed mainly of college graduates, while jobs occupied by non-Jordanian labourers are in agriculture, construction, and tertiary services. Similar trends have also been observed in all GCC countries, especially in Saudi Arabia, Oman, and, to a lesser degree, Kuwait. Yet, the economies there are creating millions of job opportunities for residents from other countries.

The 2022 estimates are based on the basic assumption that the highest growth rates occurred in 2021, following the COVID driven slump of 2020. These estimates will be subject to change if the new OMICRON strain is more lasting than had been predicted. Even if that does not prove to be the case, it would not change the fact that most Arab countries would grow slower next year (2022), than they had in 2021. Of course, this assumption would not stand if inter-Arab and Arab-Iranian relations stabilize. If the wars should stop, and the Iranian nuclear deal is signed, and if the Palestinian-Israeli peace negotiation resume, then 2022 may be a surprising year. If these conditions are met, then the various permutations of reform, which are currently being prepared and implemented, will begin to take root. Infrastructural reconstruction of torn down cities and homes will initiate inter-regional collaborative projects, to build roads, railroads, pipelines (water, gas, and oil), and joint border projects will be in full swing. The countries of West Asia are not poor, and they have the necessary means to undertake such massive "Marshall-ian" reconstruction. Just as John Stuart Mill observed, countries that are coming out of destructive wars show a great stamina for reconstruction.

If the years 2022 and 2023 witness the formation of coherent Arab governments, if fighting factions replace their swords with ploughs, and if overall peace is restored, then a massive economic rebound will ensue. An important line of questioning to ask is: "If and how India can benefit from this bonanza?", and "Would the current Arab-Indian exchange of modalities sustain a higher level of cooperation?" The answer is simple: India needs to improve its image in the Arab world as a non-Muslim nation. The Hindu-Muslim relations under Modi are not as rosy as they had been under Nehru and Gandhi. Then there is the proclivity to tolerate Israel's mistreatment of occupied Palestinians, in order to strengthen relations with them, which is unacceptable in the context of historical Arab-Indian relations. India must play a more constructive role in the conflict before any projected future negotiations between Israel and Palestine kick off. Another important point to address relates to the possible loss of many Indian jobs in the UAE, Qatar, and Bahrain, once the thriving construction boom slows down, although India is a huge market for Arab oil and minerals (potash and phosphates). In return, India can send more goods and services to the Arab world. The reshaped international division of labour gives India more room to sell more goods in Arab markets. India can also reveal its competitiveness in executing infrastructural projects.

The Indian agenda, or strategy, in dealing with the Western Asia region is unknown. Dialogue in think tanks about this topic is very rare and produces no impact. Such endeavours should be encouraged and supported. The technology sector in India can also work on bridging the deficit in IT and technology in the Arab world. The government of India should encourage Indian institutions of learning to partner with their Arab counterparts and address this trade in knowledge. Having an esteemed Indian university in the region would bring excellent results. These suggestions are meant to provoke more cooperation between the two regions, in the economical, political and social domains.

The misery that the Arab world had endured requires a massive economic recovery, in order to restore this robust region to its international role as a vehicle for global economic revival. Arab countries, and Western Asia generally, may look unruly, but digging deeper than the surface reveals a major regional metamorphosis on the horizon. If the world powers stop their meddling and allow this wealthy region of the world to take a sustained course towards reform, the whole world stands to benefit. If peace becomes the norm in the region, then its endowments will extend far beyond its borders, and India in particular stands to benefit a great deal. Invoking positive relations through think-tanks, enhancing cultural and educational relations, and addressing local political shifts in attitude towards Arabs and Muslims will give India a massive advantage in the region. Arabs need India in the next 30 years as a big market, and India should take the opportunity to benefit from the imminent shifts within the Arab world, and position to benefit greatly.

10

Maritime Security in the Red Sea and Implications for Israel, Egypt and Saudi Arabia

Dr. Michael Barak

In recent years, there has been a growing interest in the Red Sea region by the states along it, state players in distant circles, and the superpowers. The increase in its geostrategic, security and economic importance not only increases competition for influence and hegemony in the region but also strengthens the threshold of tension among the state actors. Moreover, Islamic terrorists, especially the Houthis in Yemen, identify the naval arena as another front of struggle against their rivals. The threat of terrorism and the proliferation of the interests of the countries in the region could turn the Red Sea region into a multi-system conflict arena. Regional cooperation between Israel, Egypt, Sudan, Saudi Arabia, and the United Arab Emirates is a guarantee for maintaining security and economic stability in the region. India's accession to this alliance will significantly contribute to its resilience and will be able to deter terrorists and subversive players such as Iran and Turkey.

The Red Sea is a continuation of the Indian Ocean and is connected to the Mediterranean Sea by the Suez Canal. Its area is 438,000 square kilometres, and its maximum depth reaches 2,221 metres. Ten countries are located along it—Israel, Jordan, Egypt, Sudan, Saudi Arabia, Eritrea,

Yemen, Djibouti, Somalia and Somaliland. The population along it is estimated at 620 million and is expected to grow by about 1.3 billion people by early 2050.[1]

The geopolitical importance of the Red Sea lies in being a major axis of movement that connects international trade (about 10%) between the three continents of Asia, Africa, and Europe. Every year, about 30,000 merchant ships pass through it, including oil tankers that make their way to Europe.[2] The Bab al-Mandab Straits, located at the southern entrance of the Red Sea, are considered a very important strategic junction through which merchant ships enter the Suez Canal and from there sail to the Mediterranean and international markets. In 2020, about 19,000 ships reached the Suez Canal after crossing the Red Sea. Impairing the safety of commercial traffic in the Red Sea could severely damage the global economy. In March 2021, a Panamanian ship got stuck in the Suez Canal and blocked maritime traffic for several days. As a result, oil prices in international markets have risen sharply.[3]

In addition to its commercial importance, there are large oil and gas reserves in the Red Sea basin. An American geological survey estimates that this region has an average volume of 5 billion barrels of undiscovered oil and 112 trillion cubic feet of recoverable gas.[4] Hence, it is understandable why many countries are trying to get a foothold in the economic waters of the Red Sea.

The Threat of Terrorism on the Red Sea's Maritime Traffic

The Red Sea region has been under threat from Somali piracy for years. Many merchant ships were hijacked along with their crew. This threat has been almost completely eliminated thanks to successful international counterterrorism activity in which an international maritime policing force has taken part in which India, China and other countries have joined. Since 2017, the pirates have failed to hijack any vessel, except for a single successful pirating case that occurred in 2020 when Somali pirates hijacked a Panamanian cargo ship.[6] Nevertheless, the IMB PRC warns that Somali pirate groups continue to possess offensive capabilities in the Somali Basin in the Indian Ocean and that they possess advanced automatic weapons.[7] Pirates in the Red Sea are now being replaced by local terrorists, led mainly by the Houthis.

The Red Sea[5]

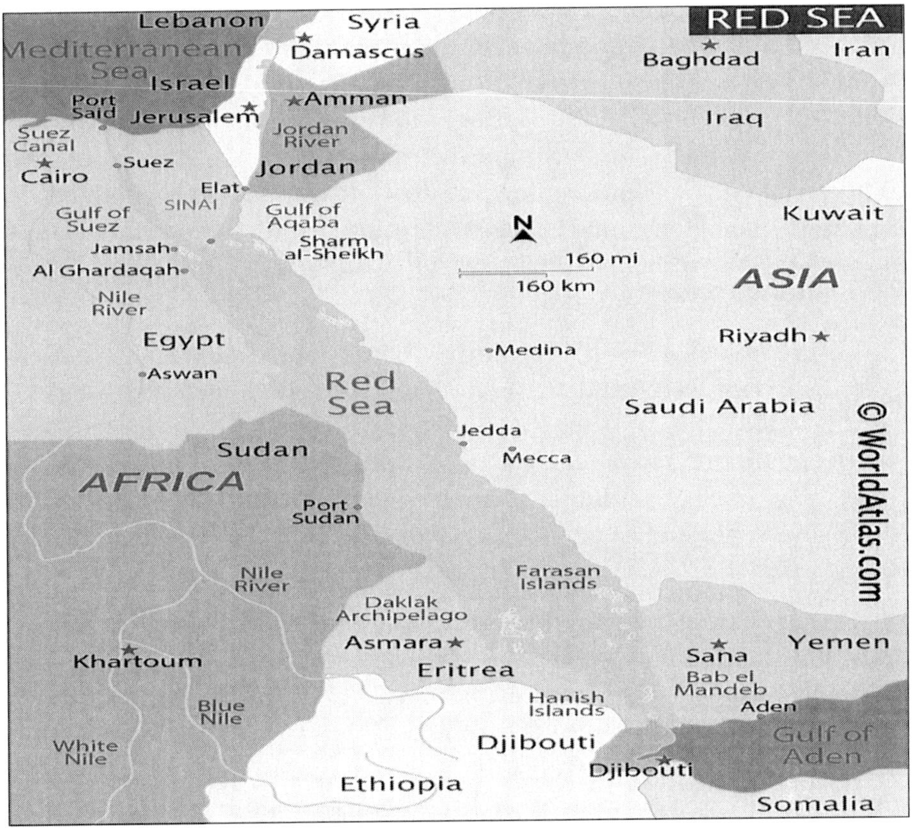

The Houthis who belong to the Zaydi Shiite community in Yemen are considered a rather acute threat to the stability of the Indian Ocean and the Red Sea due to widespread Iranian support articulated in armaments, funding, training and guidance. Yemen's deterioration to civil war after the Arab Spring, the absence of a strong central government and the severe humanitarian crisis plaguing Yemen have been identified as a fit time for Iran and the Houthis to seize territories in the country and establish Iranian influence in them. Fears of the Houthi takeover of the Bab al-Mandab Straits, considered one of the most important strategic sea crossings in the world and at the mouth of Yemen, led Egypt in May 2015 to send four Egyptian ships to protect the Gulf of Eden and deter the Houthis from realizing their intention.[8]

The Houthis have exploited the naval theatre as an area of action against Saudi Arabia by deploying naval mines, using remote-controlled bomb-laden boats, gliders and firing missiles.[9] For example, in the period between January 2017 and June 2021, they carried out 24 attacks against Saudi targets at sea using aerial drones.[10] In March 2021, the US Treasury Department blamed Houthi leaders Mansour al-Saadi and Ahmad al-Hamzi for the attacks "impacting Yemeni civilians, bordering nations, and commercial vessels in international waters". It alleged that al-Saadi heads the Houthi naval forces and is the mastermind behind the attacks on ships in the Red Sea, while al-Hamzi supervised missile and explosive-laden-drone attacks in Yemen and on Saudi Arabia.[11]

US President Joe Biden's decision of February 16 to remove the Houthis from the list of designated terrorist organizations[12] only strengthens the Houthi's motivation and morale to continue their naval terrorist activities and deepen their grip on Yemen. In November 2021, the Saudi-led Arab coalition accused the Houthis of continuing to use explosive-laden boats in the southern Red Sea against Saudi destinations and warned that the Houthis posed a threat to international shipping.[13]

The **al-Shabab al-Mujahideen** organization, which is the official branch of the al-Qaeda in Somalia, has been able to strengthen its forces in recent years in Somalia and even in nearby territories such as Kenya. Several factors contribute to this trend: Withdrawal of Ethiopian army forces from Somalia in the wake of the expanding uprising in the Tigray region; political rivalries and disputes over the presidential and parliamentary elections in Somalia; and strengthening its ties with local tribes. The decline in regional and international aid to the Somali government and the expected withdrawal of AMISOM forces from Somalia may increase the threat to national security not only towards Somalia but also towards stability in the African and Red Sea region. The al-Shabab's possible takeover of Somali ports in the Red Sea and the possibility that it would set up a logistical assistance network in cooperation with the Houthis in Yemen could threaten maritime traffic and threaten the strategic interests of the countries holding logistical and military bases in the region.[14]

In the absence of security stability in Yemen and the Horn of Africa, especially in Somalia and Ethiopia, the ability to monitor and maintain the security of maritime borders, including the Red Sea, may be weakened. Terrorist operatives including members of the **Islamic State** may take advantage of this situation to cross the maritime space and build terrorist nests in various areas. It should be noted that in recent years there has been a trend of illegal immigration from the Horn of Africa countries to Yemen and the Gulf countries, especially to Saudi Arabia, to find better life. In 2019 alone, 138,000 migrants from the Horn of Africa crossed the Gulf of Eden to reach Yemen. About 90 per cent of them intended to continue to Saudi Arabia.[15] Terrorist activists may take advantage of these waves of immigration and assimilate themselves among them and reach remote districts.

The Red Sea as a Theatre of Rivalry between State Actors

The Red Sea region has become a hot theatre in which there is international competition between regional and international state players for influence, protection and promotion of economic and security interests. **Djibouti** in this aspect symbolizes more than anything else this trend due to the high number of foreign military bases that are on its soil. It currently has six military bases designed to fight US naval piracy (founded 2002); EU (founded 2008); Japan (founded 2011); France (founded 2012); Italy (founded 2013); and China (founded 2017). Military forces from Germany, Spain and Britain are also present on Djibouti soil, and Saudi Arabia appears to have laid the groundwork for a military base in Djibouti. Military forces from Germany, Spain and Britain are also present on Djibouti soil.[16] The strategic location of Djibouti on the Red Sea and the Horn of Africa and its governmental stability are among the main reasons why it has been courted by many countries.

Somalia has also become a courted player since 2018 mainly by China and the USA due to its strategic location in the Gulf of Eden and the Indian Ocean and due to the improvement in its international status following the peace agreement between Eritrea and Ethiopia. In August 2018, Somalia joined the "Belt and Road" initiative out of a desire to encourage Chinese financial investments in Somalia.[17] In May 2019, the two agreed that China would invest in the construction of a new port in the Red Sea town of Eyl in Nugal. This is in exchange for exclusive rights off the coast of Somalia and temporary ownership of part of the port until the loan is repaid. In July 2020, they even agreed on joint naval patrols in the Red Sea in order to prevent naval piracy.[18] On the other hand, the USA reopened its embassy in Somalia in October 2019. In addition, US military experts continue to train Somali soldiers against the al-Shabab al-Majhadin terrorists despite the withdrawal of 700 American soldiers from Somalia in 2020.[19]

The father of modern maritime strategy, Alfred Thier, emphasized the importance of geographical components such as the country's coastal structure, port availability, the importance of rivers for sailing, land fertility, proximity to shipping lanes (SLOC—Sea Lines of Communication), ease of access to the open sea and so on, in the state's maritime power.[20] Geographic considerations of such sort still shape the attitudes of countries in relation to the sea and its strategic agenda.

Iran

Iran aspires to achieve a hegemony on the Middle East arena. Therefore, it has been thriving to develop its maritime navy and to expand its influence in the naval zones outside the Arabic Gulf such as the Aden Gulf and the Red Sea. Iranian Chief of Staff Muhammad Bakri noted that Iran aims to build a valuable naval force that will include a military fleet in the Amman Sea, another fleet in the Indian Ocean and naval bases along the coasts or islands near Yemen and Syria.[21] Iranian support for the Houthis can be seen as an articulation of Iran's efforts to expand its influence in the Red Sea. According to reports, which have no verification, Iran is assisting the Houthis through a naval base it has established in northern Eritrea.[22]

Iran's penetration into the Red Sea began in 2011 with the sending of Iranian warships and submarines on the ground that they were designed to protect Iranian merchant and oil ships that sailed through the Red Sea to the Mediterranean.[23] However, Iran's intention was to form a deterrence against the KSA and Israel and to strengthen its levers of influence in the region. In November 2021, the naval force, air force and the Iranian Revolutionary Guards, conducted a military manoeuvre called "Zulfikar-1,400" in the Indian Ocean and the Red Sea. The manoeuvre was intended to convey a threatening message to the USA, Israel, and its allies that Iran has an offensive capability against any factor that threatens its national security, even in the maritime arena.[24]

Israel and the Gulf states are not interested in an Iranian consolidation in this area and take various countermeasures. In April 2021, Arab media reported that an Iranian ship moored in the Red Sea was hit as a result of mines attached to it. The Iranians alleged that it was an Iranian cargo ship that was hit, but in reality, this ship was tasked to gather intelligence and on commando activity of the Iranian Revolutionary Guards. The identity of the attackers is unknown, but some attribute to Israel the responsibility for the attack against the background of dozens of attacks it has carried out against Iranian ships in the Red Sea and the Mediterranean in the past three years. The attacks were aimed at two types of targets, mainly oil tankers engaged in smuggling to Syria and ships smuggling Iranian weapons into Syria and Lebanon.[25] Continuation of this trend could deteriorate the Red Sea into a clash between Israel and Iran and threaten world trade.

KSA

The **Kingdom of Saudi Arabia (KSA)** perceives the Red Sea as an important pillar in its national security, in part because of its coastal strip which stretched to at least 1,020 km. This area has historical, economic and symbolic importance in the eyes of the Saudis, especially the city of Jeddah, which is considered an important port used as a arrival station for pilgrims to Mecca.[26]

In view of this, the KSA aims to cultivate security cooperation with the Red Sea countries. In January 2020, it established the Council of Arab and African Coastal States of the Red Sea and Gulf of Aden, which serves as the highest level of coordination between the Council's eight members: the KSA, Jordan, Egypt, Eritrea, Yemen, Sudan, Djibouti and Somalia. The purposes of the Council:

I. Increasing the level of cooperation between member-states, coordinating policy positions, strengthening security cooperation in the face of threats and dangers in the Red Sea, increasing the security and safety of maritime navigation and preventing any threat to it or its exposure to any risks;
II. Development of economic and trade relations, increasing investment between member-countries;
III. Increasing maritime transport, free movement of goods and services between council members;
IV. Strengthening cooperation between seaports along the Red Sea coast and coordinating cooperation between them, in addition to opening channels of communication with countries not bordering the Red Sea and the Gulf of Aden and regional and international organizations.[27]

The KSA is also engaging in conflicts between African countries to maintain the region's stability. In 2018, the KSA, in cooperation with the Emirates, led a historic reconciliation between Ethiopia and Eritrea in a peace agreement signed in Jeddah. It is also involved in attempts to bring peace between Egypt and Ethiopia against the background of the conflict that is erupting between them following the construction of the Al-Nahda Dam in Ethiopia, which is perceived by Egypt as a threat to its national and existential security.[28]

Aside from the security aspect, Saudi Arabia has grandiose plans for economic development of the Red Sea. In 2016, the KSA published a document called "Saudi Vision 2030" that articulated a desire to bring about a series of reforms and economic and social ventures that would generate additional revenue for the state coffers and reduce its dependence on oil. In line with the 2030 vision, the KSA plans to develop tourism along the Red Sea coastline, to establish a new city called Neom that will include a bridge over the Red Sea, which will connect the city to Egypt and from there to the rest of Africa.[29]

The UAE

The UAE strives to fortify its regional status, protect its national security and strengthen its influence in the Middle East including the Red Sea and East Africa. The upheavals that have befallen the Middle East since the Arab Spring in 2011, the crisis between Qatar and the Gulf states in 2017, the gradual shifting interests of the USA from the Middle East to the Chinese Sea and fears of increasing Iranian subversion in the region were among the factors that led the Emirates to cultivate its security ties beyond its economic ties with the Horn of Africa countries. Thus, it has established security agreements with some of the Horn of Africa countries that give it the right to lease their ports such as the port of Berbera in Somaliland, the port of Assab in Eritrea, the port of Djibouti, and the ports of Bosaso and Mogadishu in Somalia.[30]

Fears of Iranian intensification in the Red Sea region have led to cooperation between the Emirates, the KSA and even Egypt to act in various ways to thwart this trend. Under pressure from all three, Djibouti, Somalia and Sudan severed ties with Iran. The Sudanese regime even closed the Iranian bases in the country and prevented Turkey from establishing a military base on the Sudanese island of Suakin. The UAE along with Saudi Arabia led to a reconciliation agreement between Eritrea and Ethiopia. Moreover, the UAE and the KSA continue to support Yemeni forces loyal to them on Yemeni soil in the war against the pro-Iranian Houthis.

Despite leading a joint front against Iran's consolidation in the Red Sea, there is competition between the KSA and the UAE for influence in the Red Sea. This trend is articulated in deepening the diplomatic ties and economic relations between the KSA and Sudan following the military coup in Sudan two years ago. In 2020, the KSA invested $ 35 billion in Sudan, of which $ 25 billion was earmarked for agricultural development alone to maintain food security in the country. In strengthening its ties with Sudan, the KSA also strives to develop the field of tourism on the shores of the Red Sea within the framework of Saudi Arabia's 2030 vision. The KSA also intends to build a new port in Sudan that could challenge the economic power of the UAE's Jabal Ali port located between the Indian Ocean and the Red Sea. Beyond that, the KSA seeks to reach an agreement with Sudan on the development of an extensive industrial zone around the port of Sudan. Analysts allege that the trend indicates a weakening of the UAE's influence in Sudan.[31]

Egypt

Egypt's national security is significantly affected by the stability of the Red Sea and the Bab al-Mandab Strait due to being an important sea route connecting to the Suez Canal, which is considered a major artery in Egypt's economy and international maritime transport. In April 2015, al-Sisi stressed that "the protection of maritime traffic in the Red Sea and the protection of the Bab al-Mandab Straits are considered the highest priority in Egypt's national security".[32]

The Egyptian fear that the southern part of the Red Sea would become a crime-ridden environment characterized with illegal arms trade, drug trafficking, human trafficking and the consolidation of terrorists, led the Egyptian government to establish a new Egyptian naval base on January 15, 2020 named "Berenice" at the eastern Red Sea entrance.[33]

In general, in recent years, Egypt has invested a lot of resources in developing its navy both in quality and in number due to its desire to achieve regional hegemony and to build a deterrence. In this context, Ethiopia is perceived as an immediate threat due to its determination to fill the Renaissance Dam with Blue Nile water in a way that could endanger Egypt's water security. The rising tensions between the two countries could lead to an armed confrontation between them and undermine the security of the Red Sea. Although Ethiopia does not have direct access to the Red

Sea, the peace agreement it signed with Eritrea in 2018 and the agreement with France to establish an Ethiopian navy (2019) reinforced the fear that Ethiopia would be able to act against Egypt in the naval arena as well. Although France suspended the military co-operation with Ethiopia in July 2021 due to the Tigray conflict in Ethiopia,[34] it does not conceal the fact that Ethiopia has intentions to build its own navy in the Red Sea. Turkey is also seen as a threat due to its support for the Muslim Brotherhood, its attempts to stir discontent in conflict areas close to Egypt including Libya, and its efforts to consolidate in the Horn of Africa and the Red Sea.

In addition, Egypt considers the Red Sea as an area with potential for economic development in the field of tourism and international investment due to the growing international interest in it. Egypt has also granted three international companies oil and gas exploration concessions off the Red Sea coast.[35]

Against the background of changes in the Red Sea basin and competition between the powers, Egypt is working to strengthen its position in this region through cooperation in joint naval manoeuvres, security agreements with countries in the region such as Saudi Arabia, investments in the region and more. Iman Rajab of the Egyptian Al-Ahram Research Institute has argued that the changes in the Red Sea have made Egypt a key player in the set of international and regional considerations and calculations in maintaining its security, stability and growth.[36]

Turkey

The doctrine of the "blue homeland" is a strategic Turkish military doctrine that seeks to transform Turkey under Erdogan's leadership into a regional maritime power by establishing its control over two maritime spaces: 1) the seas that surround it—the Mediterranean, the Aegean and the Black Sea; 2) The Red Sea, the Caspian Sea, and the Arabian Sea including the Persian Gulf. According to the doctrine, Turkey also seeks to control oil and gas reserves in the above-mentioned maritime space, to assist the countries of the region, to establish military bases and to train military forces to stand by its side.[37]

Turkey's efforts to consolidate in the Red Sea and the Indian Ocean are reflected in its attempts to form alliances with some of the East African countries. In Somalia, Turkey has invested several tens of millions of dollars in building a military base in Mogadishu that is considered to be the largest outside Turkey in order to train 10,000 Somali military personnel. In 2010-2009, 2012 and 2015, Turkey signed a series of military agreements with Somalia.[38] In Sudan, Turkey has sought to establish a seaport after signing with Sudan in 2018 an agreement to establish a naval base on the Sudanese island of Sukan that was in the distant past under Ottoman control. Egypt interpreted this as a threat to its national security and in response sent hundreds of troops to the UAE base in Eritrea for fear of Turkish provocation. Eritrean President Isaias Afwerki, for his part, accused Turkey of trying to strengthen the Muslim Brotherhood in the Red Sea region and warned of violating security stability in the region. Finally, the agreement was shelved due to the military coup in Sudan against Omar Bashir and the rise of a pro-Egyptian and pro-Emirati Sudanese regime that signed a peace agreement with Israel.[39]

Israel

Israel attaches importance to maintaining security in the Red Sea for two main reasons: a) Being a major maritime trade route for Israeli goods coming from India and the Far East; b) Israel's unwillingness to allow terrorist actors, especially Iran, to consolidate in the Red Sea using it as a platform to threaten Israel's national security. In 2018, former Israeli Chief of Staff Gadi Izenkot stated in an interview with the Saudi newspaper *Elaf* that "Tehran plans to take over the Middle East in two axes: One axis passes through Iraq to Syria and from there to Lebanon, and a second axis passes through the Gulf from Bahrain to Yemen to the Red Sea". A senior Israeli navy official explained that "Iran's establishment in Yemen and the transfer of advanced weapons to the Houthi forces in the region are a threat to merchant ships making their way in the Red Sea".[40]

Israel faces these challenges in several ways:

I. Marine patrols in the Red Sea to protect Israeli cargo ships and prevent the smuggling of Iranian weapons.

II. Strengthening alliances with the UAE. According to unconfirmed reports, there is an Israeli-Emirate plan to jointly establish a base on the island of Socotra, 350 kilometres off the coast of Yemen, to gather intelligence on maritime traffic in the Gulf of Aden, the Horn of Africa, and Bab al-Mandab, and to monitor Iran's maritime and the Houthis in Yemen.

III. Military manoeuvres with Israel's allies in the Red Sea. On November 11, 2021, for the first time, the IDF and US Navy held a joint training with the KSA, the UAE, Bahrain and Egypt in the Red Sea. The cooperation is intended to strengthen security and maritime trade routes and to warn Iran against subversion in the Red Sea region.[41]

Since the establishment of the Abrahamic Agreements between Israel and the UAE, Bahrain and Sudan, security cooperation between the two countries has improved in a way that can help effectively protect the security of the Red Sea. The addition of India to this axis can significantly fortify the Red Sea's deterrence and security capabilities.

The European Union

In July 2021, the EU defined the Red Sea as an area with "geo-strategic priority" against the background of increasing competition of state actors for influence in the region. In 2018, the Council of the EU adopted the conclusion that "there was renewed geopolitical competition on both shores of the Red Sea." The EU further stressed that "at stake are the preservation of the security of the Bab el Mandeb maritime route through which a significant proportion of trade to and from Europe passes; the harnessing of irregular migration flows; the containment of terrorist threats; and the prevention of instability in the EU's wider neighbourhood".[42]

European research institutes point to the importance of the EU's integration into regional strategic partnerships in the Indian Ocean and the Red Sea and in strengthening alliances with state players such as Japan while aiding NATO, mainly to secure the naval trade routes.[43]

The Super Powers

China

China aspires to become a global land and sea power as evidenced by a long-term strategic plan published by President Xi Jinping in 2013 under the name "Belt and Road Initiative. It seeks to establish Chinese bases by land and sea by forming alliances with various countries that will allow it to build and develop infrastructure, develop existing ports, and establish new ports from China to East Africa and the Red Sea. The land route is called the "Economic Silk Belt" and the sea route is called the "Maritime

Silk Road", named after the historic Silk Road. The USA calls the network of seaports built by China the "pearl chain".

In December 2008, China first sent Chinese warships to the Indian Ocean to eradicate the threat of Somali piracy. In 2013, China's maritime presence in the Indian Ocean increased in the wake of its ambition to protect its maritime trade routes but also to advance the "Belt and Road" program. In August 2017, China inaugurated a new port in Djibouti designed to serve as a logistics centre. China has also been able to strengthen its economic ties with many countries bordering the Red Sea, such as the KSA and Egypt, and even with Israel, and to develop the infrastructure in some of them.[44]

It seems that China is seeking to secure its economic growth through control of distant waters. However, US analysts warn that the grandiose initiative is characterized by China's military intensification indicating China's possible long-term use of military force to advance its agenda or threaten its rivals not to take any action against it. The increase in the arms race between China and the USA in the maritime arena from the South China Sea to the Indian Ocean, as well as the increase in competition between China and India seeking to expand their influence in the Indian Ocean region, reinforce this assessment.[45]

China Belt and Road Initiative[46]

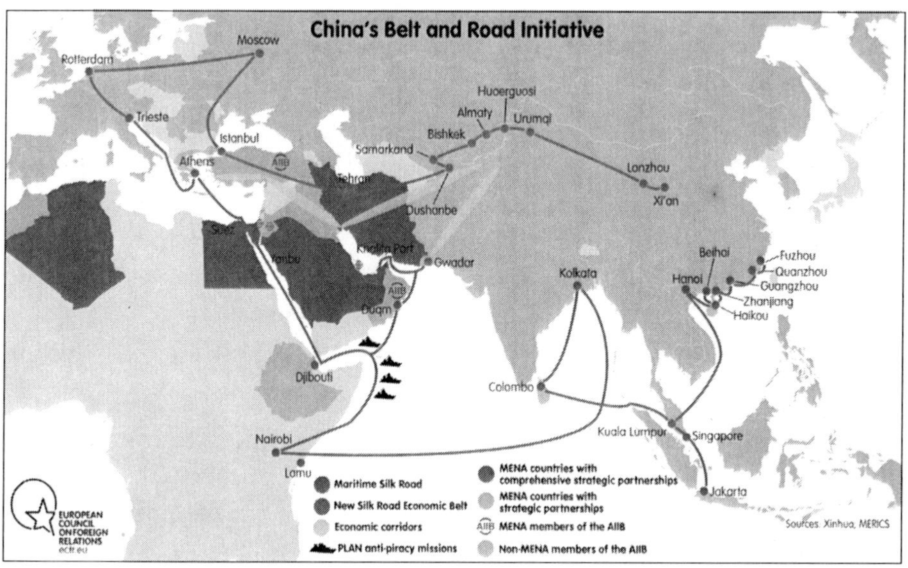

India

Until 2007, the Red Sea was of secondary importance in the strategy of the Indian Navy, but with the growing threat of terrorism and the increasing penetration of many state players, especially China, to this theatre, the Red Sea has gained primary importance. Moreover, India's consolidation in the Red Sea aims to not only protect its maritime trade routes in the Indian Ocean but also curb China's efforts to achieve hegemony over the region.

Since 2007, India has been working on consolidation of a network of military facilities along the Indian Ocean and the leasing of local ports under economic and security agreements designed to achieve the above two objectives. It signed a logistical military agreement with the USA and France allowing India to use its military bases in the Indian Ocean. In February 2018, India and Oman signed an agreement providing the Indian Navy with logistical assistance from Dokam Port. This agreement increases India's ability to operate in the western Indian Ocean.[47] In September 2020, India signed an agreement with Japan allowing it to use the Japanese base in Djibouti and the Japanese navy to use the Indian military bases.[48] A year later, in September 2021, the Indian Navy for the first time held a joint military manoeuvre with the Sudanese Navy in the Red Sea. It should be noted that the future opening of a Russian port in Port Sudan will allow for cooperation between the Indian Navy and the Russian Navy in the Red Sea. Cooperation with Taiwan, which is based in Somaliland, and the UAE's outposts along the shores of the Red Sea and the Gulf of Aden can help India prevent China's efforts for hegemony in the Red Sea.[49]

The deepening of security cooperation between India and Israel in the Red Sea Basin can significantly contribute to the security of the region and the strengthening of the regional alliance in which Israel, the UAE, the KSA and Egypt are members. Through partnerships with India-friendly allies, it will be possible to deter subversive factors and use the economic waters of the Red Sea in a wise and agreed-upon manner.

The USA

The focus of US interest in the Red Sea region is mainly to fight against the consolidation of terrorist elements in the region, to prevent naval piracy, to curb Iran's intrusion into the region, to prevent Chinese and Russian influence in the region and to protect submarine communication cable infrastructure in the Red Sea region, specially the Bab al-Mandab Straits.[50] To this end, the USA seeks to maintain a military presence through the maintenance of military bases along the Indian Ocean, the Gulf and the Red Sea as in Djibouti.

US analysts warn that China's growing influence on the African continent threatens American interests and assets in the region. Therefore, it would be better for the USA to have a naval presence in the Red Sea if any conflict with China develops, as its strategic importance is on the rise. They thus emphasize that the Biden Administration is committed to formulating a strategic plan in the African continent that will compete with China for influence in the region and have warned that if it avoids this it will have to give up Africa in favour of China.[51]

Russia

Russia attaches strategic importance to the Red Sea especially to Bab al-Mandab due to economic and security reasons. It seeks to ensure safe maritime passage for its oil barrels in the region but at the same time is interested in challenging the power of the USA and Europe in the region. However, its scope of influence and involvement in the region is quite limited.[52]

Russia's growing interest in the Red Sea began in November 2017 when Vladimir Putin met Omar Bashir in Sochi in November 2017. The two agreed on the establishment of a Russian naval military base in Sudan that would host up to four Russian ships with 300 soldiers on board and provide them with logistical support in exchange for the supply of weapons and military equipment. However, this agreement was frozen following the military coup in Sudan with the rise of Burhan to power. In December 2021, the latter expressed a desire to honour the agreement and allow a foothold for the Russians in Sudan.[53] In recent years, Russia has signed more than a dozen security cooperation agreements in Africa to protecting its access to ports and maritime bases, particularly the port of Barbara in Somalind, Massawa and Assab in Eritrea and Port Sudan in Sudan.[54]

Some analysts argue that Russia's growing interest in the Red Sea is related to Russia's aspiration to strengthen its hold on the Indian Ocean. In the maritime doctrine published by Russia in 2015, it gave a regional priority for the Indian Ocean as well as how to expand its influence in the region by increasing the volume of maritime transport, cooperating with other countries searching for gas fields and building underwater pipelines, ensuring Russia's maritime presence in the Indian Ocean and more.[55] In July 2021, Russia updated its national security strategy and emphasized that cultivating relations with India and China are a priority of its foreign policy.[56]

Conclusion

The strategic importance of the Red Sea is, without a doubt, on the rise. Although the maritime piracy plague in the Red Sea basin is almost completely eradicated, thanks to the military intervention of foreign countries, at the same time it has provided them with a golden opportunity to establish their grip on the region for strategic, security and economic motives.

The security of the Red Sea is no longer only affected by the dynamics between the traditional players such as the Horn of Africa states, but is also affected by the rivalry, tension and competition between new players who exploit the weakness of the Horn to consolidate their influence and power. Increasing tensions in the Red Sea basin between the USA and China and Russia, between China and India, between Japan and Thailand, between Israel and Iran, between Turkey and the KSA and the UAE, between Egypt and Ethiopia and the like can weaken state capacity to protect Red Sea security and even lead to regional conflict. This could play in favour of terrorist players such as the ISIS and the Houthis.

Maintaining Red Sea security requires monitoring the development of the crisis in Yemen, maintaining the stability of the Somali government from collapse, maintaining the stability of the Sudanese regime, and lowering the threshold of tension between Ethiopia and Egypt and Sudan. Deepening cooperation and cultivating a coordination mechanism between Israel, India and the USA and the moderate Sunni states axis that includes the KSA, the UAE, Egypt and Sudan will help protect its stability and economic development.

ENDNOTES

1. Fahd al-Rasheed, "Red Sea artery of global trade", *Arab News*, February 12, 2016. https://www.arabnews.com/columns/news/879221
2. Fahd al-Rasheed, "Red Sea artery of global trade", *Arab News*, February 12, 2016. https://www.arabnews.com/columns/news/879221
3. Miriam Berger and others, "How did a ship get stuck in the Suez Canal, and what

happened afterward?" *Washington Post*, March 31, 2021. https://www.washingtonpost.com/world/2021/03/25/faq-suez-canal-ever-given/

4. Assessment of Undiscovered Oil and Gas Resources of the Red Sea Basin Province", USGS, 2010. https://pubs.usgs.gov/fs/2010/3119/pdf/FS10-3119.pdf
5. https://www.worldatlas.com/seas/red-sea.html
6. "Somali pirates capture Panama-flagged cargo ship", *BBC*, August 2, 2010. https://www.bbc.com/news/world-africa-10838226
7. "ICC-IMB Piracy and Armed Robbery Against Ships, Report - 01 January - 31 December 2020", *ICC International Maritime Bureau*, January 30, 2021. https://www.icc-ccs.org/reports/2020_Annual_Piracy_Report.pdf
8. "An Egyptian move to secure the Gulf of Aden and Bab al-Mandab" (in Arabic), *al-Jazeera*, May 26, 2015. 26.5.15. https://www.aljazeera.net/news/arabic/2015/3/26/تحرك-مصري-لتأمين-خليج-عدن-وباب-المندب
9. Caleb Weiss, "Analysis: Houthi naval attacks in the Red Sea", *Long War Journal*, August 17, 2019. https://www.longwarjournal.org/archives/2019/08/analysis-houthi-naval-attacks-in-the-red-sea.php;
   The Houthis pose a major threat to Saudi national security. On February 15, 2021, the Houthis used UAVs to attack two airports in Saudi Arabia, one in Jeddah and the other in Abha. On March 7, they attacked oil rigs and on March 19, a refinery using UAVs. The attacks led to a rise in oil prices.
10. Håvard Haugstvedt, "Red Sea Drones: How to Counter Houthi Maritime Tactics", *War on Rocks*, September 3, 2021. https://warontherocks.com/2021/09/red-sea-drones-how-to-counter-houthi-maritime-tactics/
11. "US sanctions 2 Yemeni rebels for cross-border, sea attacks", *AP News*, March 3, 2021. https://apnews.com/article/yemen-us-news-red-sea-saudi-arabia-702523e8b0d5bdf51a163f0c63e77275
12. "Biden administration to lift blacklisting of Yemen's Houthis", *al-Jazeera*, February 12, 2021. https://www.aljazeera.com/news/2021/2/12/biden-administration-to-lift-blacklisting-of-yemens-houthis
13. 22.11.21. https://www.bloomberg.com/news/articles/2021-11-22/saudi-warns-iran-backed-rebels-using-bomb-laden-boats-in-red-sea
14. Shayma al-Baksh, "Red Sea security in a Changing Strategic Environment" (in Arabic), *al-Marsad al-Masry*, July 3, 2021. https://marsad.ecss.com.eg/58499/
15. Journey from Africa to Yemen Remains World's Busiest Maritime Migration Route", *IOM*, February 14, 2020. https://www.iom.int/news/journey-africa-yemen-remains-worlds-busiest-maritime-migration-route
   Today there is a reverse trend: a return of immigrants from Yemen back to the Horn of Africa countries. This is due to three main reasons: the inability to find work; Human rights violations in Yemen; Closure of the Saudi-Yemen border.
16. Michael Tanchum, "China's new military base in Africa: What it means for Europe and America", *ECFR*, December 14, 2021.https://ecfr.eu/article/chinas-new-military-base-in-africa-what-it-means-for-europe-and-america/
17. Zach Vertin, "Red Sea Rivalries: The Gulf, the Horn, & the New Geopolitics of the Red Sea", *Brookings Doha Centre*, June 2019. https://www.brookings.edu/wp-content/uploads/2019/06/Red-Sea-Rivalries.-The-Gulf-The-Horn-and-the-New-Geopolitics-of-the-Red-Sea-English-pdf.pdf
18. Dipanjan Roy Chaudhury, "China sails unhindered in Somali waters", *The Economic Times*, August 20, 2021.https://economictimes.indiatimes.com/news/defence/

china-sails-unhindered-in-somali-waters/articleshow/85478300.cms

19. Meghann Myers, "US troops now 'commuting to work' to help Somalia fight al-Shabab", *Military Times*, April 27, 2021.
20. Geoffrey Till, *Seapower: a guide for the twenty-first century*. Routledge, London, 2018.
21. Ahmad Majidyar, "Iran's Expansionist Naval Plans Threaten Gulf Stability", *The Middle East Institute*, November 28, 2016. https://www.mei.edu/publications/irans-expansionist-naval-plans-threaten-gulf-stability
22. Anna Ahronheim, "Rebel spokesman: Houthi missiles can hit covert Israeli bases in Eritrea", *The Jerusalem Post*, October 2, 2017. https://www.jpost.com/israel-news/rebel-spokesman-houthi-missiles-can-hit-covert-israeli-bases-in-eriteria-506376
23. Ibid.
24. "Admiral says Iran achieved expected goals in Zulfiqar 1400 exercise", *Tehran Times*, November 10, 2021. https://www.tehrantimes.com/news/466924/Admiral-says-Iran-achieved-expected-goals-in-Zulfiqar-1400-exercise
25. Amos Harel, "An Iranian ship linked to the Revolutionary Guards was hit by naval mines attached to it" (in Hebrew), *Haaretz*, April 6, 2021. https://www.haaretz.co.il/news/politics/.premium.HIGHLIGHT-1.9689076
26. "The Red Sea's Security" (in Arabic), *Masarat*, Oct-November 2018. https://www.kfcris.com/pdf/fbcffa4e306812289c75e071d8bdc45a5bffdc95598a8.pdf
27. Ayman Rajab, "Why the Importance of the Red Sea in Egyptian Strategic Planning Has Increased" (in Arabic), *Al-Ahram Centre for al-Dirasat al-Siasiyya and al-Istritajiyya*, December 13, 2020. https://acpss.ahram.org.eg/News/17005.aspx
28. "Red Sea Peace Initiatives: The Role of the Saudi Kingdom in Bringing Eritrea and Ethiopia Closer" (in Arabic), *King Faisal Centre for Research and Islamic Studies*, April 2020.
29. "The Red Sea project", https://www.vision2030.gov.sa/ar/v2030/v2030-projects/مشروع-البحر-الأحمر/
30. The United Arab Emirates in the Horn of Africa", *Crisis Group*, November 6, 2018. https://www.crisisgroup.org/middle-east-north-africa/gulf-and-arabian-peninsula/united-arab-emirates/b65-united-arab-emirates-horn-africa
31. Jihad Mashamoun, "Winners and Losers of Red Sea", *Africa Argument*, August 6, 2021. https://africanarguments.org/2021/08/winners-and-losers-of-red-sea-politics-in-sudan/
32. "Sisi: Bab al-Mandab is an Egyptian national security, and we will not abandon the Gulf states" (in Arabic), *DW*, April 4, 2015. https://www.dw.com/ar/%D8%A7%D9%84%D8%B3%D9%8A%D8%B3%D9%8A-%D8%A8%D8% A7%D8%A8-%D8%A7%D9% 84%D9%85% D9%86%D8%AF%D8%A8-%D8%A3%D9%85%D9%86-%D9%82%D9%88%D9%85%D9%8A-%D9%85%D8%B5%D8%B1% D9%8A-%D9%88%D9%84%D9%86-%D9%86%D8%AA%D8%AE%D9%84%D9%89-%D8%B9%D9%86-%D8%A7%D9%84%D8%AE%D9%84%D9%8A%D8%AC%D9%8A%D9%8A%D9%86/a-18361884
33. "The Seven Mistakes of Egyptian Policy towards Africa, Especially the Nile Basin Countries from 1995 to 2013" (in Arabic), *Democratic Arabic Centre*, 12 May 2020. https://democraticac.de/?p=66249
34. "France Suspends Military Cooperation with Ethiopia as Tigray Conflict Intensifies", *al-Arabiyya*, August 13, 2021. https://english.alarabiya.net/News/world/2021/08/13/France-suspends-military-cooperation-with-Ethiopia-as-Tigray-conflict-intensifies

35. Hassan Abdel Zaher, "New naval base boosts Egypt's presence in the Red Sea", *The Arab Weekly*, January 19, 2020.https://thearabweekly.com/new-naval-base-boosts-egypts-presence-red-sea
    For more details on the scope of Egyptian investments along the Red Sea, see Ali al-Tiri, "Airports, ports and major projects. Countless achievements during the era of President Sisi in the Red Sea" (in Arabic), *al-Ahram*, November 18, 2021. https://gate.ahram.org.eg/News/3140155.aspx
36. Ayman Rajab, "Why the importance of the Red Sea in the Egyptian Strategy Increased" (in Arabic), *Markaz al-Ahram lil-Dirasat al-Siyassiyyawal-Istritajiyya*, December 13, 2020. https://acpss.ahram.org.eg/News/17005.aspx
37. Aurélien Denizeau, "Mavi Vatan, The Blue Homeland: The Origins, Influences and Limits of an Ambitious Doctrine for Turkey", *Études de l'Ifri*, April 2021. https://www.ifri.org/sites/default/files/atoms/files/denizeau_mavi_ vatan_turkey_2021.pdf
38. Guled Ahmed, "Far from a benefactor, the Turkish government is exploiting Somalia's fragility", *MEI*, October 21, 2021. https://www.mei.edu/publications/far-benefactor-turkish-government-exploiting-somalias-fragility
39. Michaël Tanchum, "The Geopolitics of The Eastern Mediterranean Crisis: A Regional System Perspective on the Mediterranean's New Great Game" in Michaël Tanchum (ed.), "Eastern Mediterranean in Uncharted Waters: Perspectives on Emerging Geopolitical", *Konrad Adenauer Stiftung*, December 2020, pp. 11-26. "Turkey's Presence in the Red Sea: Forms, Objectives and Prospects", EPC, March 22, 2020.
40. Pazit Rabina, "Israel, the UAE and Yemen: Cooperation that will change the region" (in Hebrew), *Makor Rishon*, September 3, 2020. https://www.makorrishon.co.il/news/261211/
41. Anna Ahronheim, "Naval war drill: Israel, US, UAE, Bahrain hold first joint sea exercise", *The Jerusalem Post*, November 11, 2021.https://www.jpost.com/israel-news/israel-uae-bahrain-and-us-hold-joint-drill-in-red-sea-684697
42. Fabrizio Tassinari & Mehari Taddele Maru, "Global rivalry in the Red Sea", *DIIS*, October 5, 2021. https://www.diis.dk/en/research/global-rivalry-in-the-red-sea
43. Luis Simón and Tomohiko Satake, "Rules-based connectivity, maritime security and EU-Japan cooperation in the Indian Ocean", Real Institute Elcano, May 14, 2020. https://bit.ly/3q9Eg6Y; Fabrizio Tassinari & Mehari Taddele Maru, "Global rivalry in the Red Sea", *DIIS*, October 5, 2021. https://www.diis.dk/en/research/global-rivalry-in-the-red-sea
44. The Djibouti regime, for its part, believes that strengthening its ties with China will lead to economic prosperity in a way that will make Djibouti "Singapore of Africa". Zach Vertin, "Great power rivalry in the Red Sea China's experiment in Djibouti and implications for the United States", *Brookings*, June 2020. https://www.brookings.edu/wp-content/uploads/2020/06/FP_20200615_ china_djibouti_vertin.pdf ; David H. Shinn, "China's Maritime Silk Road and Security in the Red Sea Region", *Middle East Institute*, May 18, 2021 https://www.mei.edu/publications/chinas-maritime-silk-road-and-security-red-sea-region ; China's Impact on Conflict Dynamics in the Red Sea Arena", *USIP*, April 28, 2020. https://www.usip.org/events/chinas-impact-conflict-dynamics-red-sea-arena
45. Ibid.
46. Camille Lons and others, China's Great Game in the Middle East", *ECFR*, October 2019. https://ecfr.eu/wp-content/uploads/china_great_game_middle_east.pdf

47. Neil Melvin, "The Foreign Military Presence in the Horn of Africa Region", *SIPRI*, April 2019. https://sipri.org/sites/default/files/2019-04/sipribp1904.pdf
48. Rajesh Basrur & Sumitha Narayanan Kutty, "Modi's India and Japan: nested strategic partnerships", *International Politics*, February 2021. For further information on Japan's activities in the Horn of Africa, see Ahmad Askar, "Countering Chinese influence is Japan's primary challenge in the Horn of Africa", *Trends*, May 26, 2021. https://trendsresearch.org/insight/countering-chinese-influence-is-japans-primary-challenge-in-the-horn-of-africa/
49. "Indian Navy holds exercises in the Red Sea, not far from the Suez Canal", *WION*, September 15, 20021. https://www.wionews.com/india-news/indian-navy-holds-exercises-in-the-red-sea-not-far-from-the-suez-canal-413202
50. Paul Cochrane, "Red Sea cables: How UK and US spy agencies listen to the Middle East", *Middle East Eye*, March 4, 2021.https://www.middleeasteye.net/news/red-sea-cables-how-us-uk-spy-agencies-listen-middle-east
51. Allison Schwartz, "The US does not have an Africa strategy, but China does", *Georgetown Security Studies Review*, November 30, 2021.https://georgetownsecuritystudiesreview.org/2021/11/30/the-us-does-not-have-an-africa-strategy-but-china-does/; "Red Sea Rivalries: A Conflict of Interests - Narrated by David Strathairn - Full Episode", YouTube, March 20, 2020. https://www.youtube.com/watch?v=Srso7hFm4m4
52. Samuel Ramani, "Russia's Growing Ambitions in the Red Sea Region", *RUSI*, September 2021. https://static.rusi.org/pb-russia-red-sea-final-web-version.pdf
53. "Sudan's Burhan hopes Red Sea base consolidate relations with Russia", *Sudan Tribune*, December 4, 2021. https://sudantribune.com/article226546/
54. Joseph Siegle, "Russia and Africa: Expanding Influence and Instability," in *Russia's Global Reach: A Security and Statecraft Assessment*, (ed.) Graeme P. Herd (Garmisch-Partenkirchen: George C. Marshall European Centre for Security Studies, 2021), https://marshallcenter.org/en/publications/marshall-center-books/russias-global-reach/chapter-10-russia-and-africa-expanding-influence-and-instability, pp. 80-90.
55. "The 2015 Maritime Doctrine of the Russian Federation", (trans. Anna Davis), *U.S. Naval War College*, 2015. https://digital-commons.usnwc.edu/cgi/viewcontent.cgi?article=1002&context=rmsi_research
56. Anurag Bisen, "India–Russia Cooperation in Indian Ocean Region, Arctic and Russian Far East", IDSA, December 6, 2021.https://idsa.in/policybrief/india%E2%80%93russia-cooperation-in-indian-ocean-region-arctic-anuragbisen-061221

11

Middle East and Palestine

Dr. Sahar Al Majali

Introduction

The tender balance of peace in the Middle East hinges on the most heaviest and burdensome problem of the question of Palestine that has evaded a permanent solution for the past five-and-half decades mainly due to the intransigence of Israel to implement the relevant resolutions of the United Nations, calling for the recognition of the inalienable rights of the Arab Palestinians in peace, particularly in the West Bank. The Palestinians and their Arab compatriots have gone to the farthest end to accommodate Israel by recognizing it and establishing diplomatic relations with it with the hope that it would vacate the West Bank and allow the State of Palestine thrive in peace. Despite the advisory opinion of the International Court of Justice (ICJ) for demolition of the wall in the West Bank, Israel has not heeded the call of sane international opinion and continues to defy all ethical and legal norms to deny the Palestinians their inalienable right to live in peace. It is against this backdrop that this paper attempts to appraise the peace process in the Middle East with special focus on Palestine.

Historical Setting

Palestine is one of the ancient states whose history dates back to more than five millennia. Scientific and archaeological studies have established that "the indigenous and ancestral inhabitants of Jerusalem and Palestine were the Canaanite Semitic Arabs who had migrated to Palestine from the Arabian Peninsula more than 5,000 years ago." Geographically, lying between the Mediterranean in the west, Lebanon in the north, Syria and Jordan in the east and Sinai in the south and south-west bordering with Egypt, Palestine territory had been subjected to constant military forays since ancient times that affected its demographic spectrum. The territory remained part of the Roman Empire from 63 AD to 400 AD. The subsequent Arab conquest of Palestine was the most remarkable event because the conquerors brought with them their "government, language as well as religion" and a vast majority of the inhabitants accepted all the three, to what Professor Rodinson calls "the invaded melted with the invaders". The Arab rule saw the construction of the mosque of Aqsa, the Dome of the Rock and the Haram-esh-Sherif was reconstructed. For a considerable period, Palestine remained under Arab domination despite the military expeditions of the Crusaders and the series of intermittent invasions from Christian Europe. The advent and subsequent expansion of the Ottomans during the fifteenth century and in the beginning of the sixteenth century culminated in the expansion of the Turkish Empire in far-flung areas. In 1517, Palestine also became a part of the Ottoman Empire and the Turkish domination lasted until the end of the First World War. The Jewish immigration into Palestine during the 1880s under the Ottoman rule, though in a small number, entailed the potential of sowing the seeds of ethnic conflict between the Arab Palestinians and the Jews inhabiting Palestine in the embryonic form that could sprout later.

Jewish Immigration

The conclusion of the First World War saw the collapse of the Ottoman Empire and its erstwhile Arab territories including Palestine were placed under the control of the victorious European Powers. Britain was awarded the Mandate for Palestine by the League of Nations in 1920, and its terms came into effect by 1923. The terms of the Mandate echoed the Balfour Declaration and Britain was to be responsible for its implementation until the subject region could become a self-governing sovereign country. Following the creation of Trans-Jordan, later renamed as the Hashemite Kingdom of Jordan, under Amir Abdullah, comprising all land east of the Jordan River, Jewish immigration, and Jewish land ownership were forbidden in Trans-Jordan. The Arabs opposed not only the Balfour

Declaration but also any move to establish any Jewish homeland in Palestine.

Under the British Mandate in Palestine, the Jewish immigration continued to pour into Palestine unabatedly. Between 1920 and 1939, the Jewish population in Palestine reached 445,000, thereby recording an increase of 452 per cent as compared to the total population increase by 128 per cent during the same period. The continued Jewish influx hardened the attitude of the Palestinian Arabs towards the Jews and the lines of conflict between them seemed to have been drawn. By the second half of the 1930s, the Arabs, being convinced that their demands were not going to be conceded by the British, launched violent agitations throughout Palestine directed both at the Mandated Administration and the Jews. The British by then realised the inevitability of the partition of Palestine but shelved the idea temporarily. Following the conclusion of the Second World War in 1945 and the emergence of the United Nations, the Palestine problem was passed on to the UNO.

United Nations Resolutions

The issue of Palestine came before the United Nations in early April 1947 when Britain urged the holding of a special session of the UN General Assembly for the purpose of appointing a special committee "to make recommendations...concerning the future government of Palestine." The Arab countries made concerted endeavours to obtain a substantive debate on the Palestine issue and urged the General Assembly to place an additional item on its agenda regarding "the termination of the mandate over Palestine and the declaration of its independence". Subsequently, the UN appointed an 11-member United Nations Special Committee on Palestine (UNSCOP). The majority of the members of the UNSCOP recommended the partition of Palestine into a Jewish and an Arab state with an economic union and a UN Trusteeship for Jerusalem and other holy places. The minority proposal envisaged an independent Palestine as a federated state with Jerusalem as its capital.

After deliberating on the UNSCOP's recommendations, the General Assembly adopted Resolution 181 on 29 November 1947 envisaging the partition of Palestine into a Jewish state and an Arab state and Jerusalem to be administered by the UN Trusteeship Council. The British mandate over Palestine was to be terminated by 15 May 1948. In the meantime, the partition resolution had evoked great resentment among the Arab countries and the Arab Palestinians. Eruption of violence had made the situation inside Palestine unmanageable. Making use of the fluid situation, the Jews declared a unilateral 'establishment of the State of Israel' on 14 May 1948 with the tacit approval of the USA, which accorded recognition to Israel the same day. Apprehending Jewish hegemony in their neighbourhood, the Arab countries invaded Israel. However, the United Nations ordered a ceasefire on 29 May 1948 but could succeed in bringing about a temporary truce only on 11 June 1948.

The efforts of the Arab countries to undo the formation of the Israel State did not succeed mainly because of the support of Western countries to Israel. However, Jordan had succeeded in annexing the West Bank. The Israeli authorities unleashed a reign of terror on the Arab Palestinians living in their territories in order to force them to flee. The Arab Palestinians became refugees in millions, most of them seeking refuge in the West Bank and many thousands in other neighbouring Arab countries. In November 1949, the number of Palestinian refugees was estimated at around 726,000. The UN General Assembly, vide its resolution 302(IV) on 2 December 1949, established the United Nations Relief and Works Agency for Palestine Refugees (UNRWA) to look after the Palestinian refugees. The bitterness that had developed between Israel and the Arab countries culminated in another Arab-Israel war in June 1967 in which Israel succeeded in annexing the West Bank, Gaza Strip, Sinai Peninsula and some territory of Syria.

Subsequently, the UN Security Council vide its resolution 242 of 1967 called for the vacation of occupied Arab territories and a just settlement of the refugee problem, but Israel did not bother about the resolution and continued its oppressive policies in the occupied Arab territories thereby forcing the native population to flee. By 1972, the number of registered refugees with UNRWA stood at 1.51 million. The Palestine Liberation Organisation (PLO) had emerged as the legitimate organisation of the Palestine refugees and some of its front organs adopted militant means for the realisation of their objective of returning to 'their homeland.' In the meantime, there broke out another Arab-Israel war in October 1973, which further escalated the hostilities between Israel and the Arab countries. The Security Council's resolution 332 calling upon Israel to vacate the occupied Arab territories as per resolution 267 of 1967 was not heeded by Israel.

Though the PLO had gained wide recognition as the legitimate representative of the Palestinians and was represented in the UN as an observer along with many Arab countries, including Jordan, rendering support to it, yet Israeli intransigence not to abide by the UN resolutions as well as not to recognise that the PLO kept the Arab-Israel stalemate alive. The Camp David agreement between Israel and Egypt in 1978 was decried by the PLO and many Arab countries. The Palestinians living in the West Bank were least hopeful of outside help in their struggle against Israeli oppression and they devised the method of Intifada as the potent weapon to deal with Israel on their own.

The Effect of Intifada on the Peace Process

The Intifada that began in late 1987 was a massive uprising by the Palestinians directed against Israeli occupation of the West Bank and Gaza Strip. It was an uprising against 40 years of Israeli policies and had its roots as far as 1948 when Israel was formed "as an exclusionary Jewish state on the land of Palestine". What distinguished the Intifada from past resistance efforts was popular participation, its long duration, and the prominent part played by Islamic groups. Stone-throwing, blocked roads and tyre burning was common. Another feature of the Intifada was commercial strikes, which adversely affected the Israeli economy. The Arab uprising brought immense pressure upon Israel from the USA and other nations to make concessions to the Arabs in order to stop the violence.

The Intifada's primary effect was to convince Israel and the USA that something had to be done. In view of PLO leader Yasser Arafat's announcement of renunciation of terrorism and recognition of Israel's right to exist in 1988 the Shamir government of Israel had to formulate a response in the form of the May 1989 peace initiative. While the Intifada had a key role, the primary impetus was provided by international events like the disintegration of the Soviet Union and the Gulf War in the beginning of the 1990s. These developments brought a change in the Arab world's attitude towards Israel just enough to enter into negotiations aimed at resolving the old conflict. The 1991 Madrid Peace Conference, facilitated by the USA, was a watershed event because, for the first time, Israel entered into direct, face-to-face negotiations with Syria, Lebanon, Jordan, and the Palestinians.

The Second Gulf War and the Peace Process: Jordan Case Study

Jordan has consistently followed a pro-Palestine and pro-Arab policy despite its close relations with the Western countries because of its national interests. Palestinians constitute a sizeable part of Jordan's population and it is a determinant factor in Jordan's Palestine policy. Jordan's support for Iraq during the first Gulf War worsened its relations with the West. Although the Government of Jordan stated its opposition to the Iraqi occupation of Kuwait, popular support for Iraq was driven by Jordan's Palestinian community, which favoured Saddam as a champion against Western supporters of Israel. Undoubtedly, the first Gulf War considerably impaired Jordan's economy but it weathered that loss while protecting its national interests. Following the first Gulf War, Jordan largely restored its relations with Western countries through its participation in the Middle East peace process and enforcement of UN sanctions against Iraq. Following the fall of the Iraqi regime of Saddam Hussein, Jordan has played a pivotal role in supporting the restoration of stability and security to Iraq. The Government of Jordan signed a memorandum of understanding with the Coalition Provisional Authority in Iraq to facilitate the training of up to 30,000 Iraqi police cadets at a Jordanian facility.

Jordan signed a non-belligerency agreement with Israel on July 25, 1994. Jordan and Israel signed a historic peace treaty on October 26, 1994. The USA has participated with Jordan and Israel in trilateral development discussions in which key issues have been water-sharing and security; cooperation on Jordan Rift Valley development; infrastructure projects; and trade, finance, and banking issues. Jordan has proved to be the closest thing to an ally that Israel could claim in the peace process, mainly for geographic and demographic reasons and because the two countries share fresh water resources. Since the outbreak of the Intifada in September 2000, Jordan has worked hard, in a variety of fora, to maintain lines of communication between the Israelis and the Palestinians to counsel moderation and to return the parties to negotiations of outstanding permanent status issues.

Jordan is a key player in the Middle East peace process. No lasting permanent peace in the region can be established without Jordan's participation. The survival of a Palestinian entity is critically dependent on Jordan for economic and strategic reasons. Besides, Jordan's tremendous goodwill in the Gulf countries, its cordial and sound diplomatic, political, and economic relations with Israel can serve as a channel for other Arab countries not on good terms with Israel to open a window for them for trade and diplomatic interaction.

Separation Wall and its Impact on Peace Process

Israel has been trying to complete the 673-km long 'security wall' in the Occupied Palestinian territories, encroaching upon large tracts of Palestinian land in the West Bank. The wall, on which the Israelis are working at a frenetic speed, is at present 183-km long. Its construction has separated thousands of Palestinians from their lands, schools, or medical services. The UN General Assembly had adopted a resolution on 8 December 2003, asking the International Court of Justice (ICJ) for a legal opinion on the Israeli wall being built in the Occupied Palestinian Areas. The ICJ in its opinion called upon the General Assembly and the Security Council to see to it that the construction of the wall was halted. The court ruled that the construction of the wall and its associated regime were contrary to international law.

Israel and the USA were quick to criticise the ICJ ruling. Israeli Prime Minister Ariel Sharon rejected the ICJ ruling. Similarly, the White House spokesman said that the court was not the 'appropriate forum' to decide on the legality of the wall. Some US senators also supported the hard-line stance of Israel. On the other hand, Palestinian leader, Yasser Arafat, described the ICJ's decision as a 'pronunciation from the world' that it was standing beside the Palestinian people 'against the apartheid wall.' Ahmed Qureia expressed the hope that the USA would 'not sabotage' the endeavours of the international community to make Israel dismantle the 'apartheid wall.'

The Israeli move of erecting the wall is a big setback to the ongoing process of peace in the Middle East. Like its past behaviour, Israel continues to be defiant of world bodies like the UN, ICJ and other fora and has least concern for international public opinion. Israel, which has entered the international arena through the route of peace process, should honour the sane advice of the same community before it is too late and the doors of peace are slammed against it.

International Legitimacy and its Implementation in the Middle East

The ongoing peace process has given a fresh lease of life and legitimacy to the Palestinians as well. The acts of terrorism on either side are uncalled for at this juncture because deterioration of the situation in the region will breed religious fundamentalism, which thrives on poverty. Terrorism in any form is a serious threat to most of the regimes in the region. It goes without saying that economic development has become more important to Arab governments than traditional strategic considerations. Peace and domestic stability are two conditions *sine qua non* for attracting serious economic investment and technology from Western Europe and the USA. The peace process holds bright prospects for all the parties involved to attract foreign investment provided peace and not confrontation is given a chance.

Both the Israelis and the Palestinians have traversed a long road of mutual hostility for over half a century to reach the negotiating table. Revival of hostilities is not in the interest of either side because this is one of the oldest conflicts of the twentieth century that has already seen an ocean of human blood flowing without any gain. Both sides should give peace another chance by accommodating each other for their people's sake and at the stance of outside powers.

Conclusion

Making his debut at the United Nations General Assembly of 1974, Arafat had told delegates that he had come, "bearing an olive branch and a freedom fighter's gun". He asked them, "Do not let the olive branch fall from my hand". These words are more relevant now and it is for the Palestinians as well for the Israelis to work in unison to strengthen the forces of peace. It devolves on Israel to stop all provocations including the ongoing work on the so-called apartheid wall to show its genuine appreciation and regard for the international community in general and Palestinians in particular that it is equally interested in the peace process. At the same time, the Palestinian leadership should also stop the militant Islamic groups from running the show at their free will. Militancy will breed militancy with greater vengeance.

The moderate leadership on either side should be encouraged to be at the helm of affairs, thereby relegating the militant elements to remain in low key. The spread of nuclear and other WMDs portend a great threat to the very existence of humankind. Any fragile situation in the Middle East is likely to accelerate such a process and pave the way for non-state actors to call the shots. The USA owns a greater responsibility in this entire scenario as it has vital stakes in the Middle East. As Washington has got a strong hold on Israel, it should play its role responsibly in persuading Israel to adopt a moderate approach towards the Palestine people and not push them to the wall. At the same time, the Arab countries should also restrain the militant elements from 'sabotaging' the process of dialogue for peace. Genuine and sincere endeavours on the part of all parties to the Middle East peace process are essential at this juncture to break the deadlock and forge ahead towards establishing lasting peace in the region and make the region an oasis of peace and prosperity.

SECTION III

India's West Asian Quest

12

Next Steps for India-Israel Relations in the Context of West Asia

Nina Slama

After more than four decades since the inception of the Jewish State in 1948, India and Israel established full diplomatic relations in 1992. Both countries are strategic partners and cooperate extensively in a wide range of sectors. Different dynamics in West Asia influence the scope of these relations. The eruption of the Arab Spring and the signing of the Abraham Accords allowed India and Israel to extend their relations by collaborating with other regional partners such as Bahrain and the United Arab Emirates. This chapter presents India-Israel relations during Prime Minister Narendra Modi tenure and suggests ways to further expand them in the context of different dynamics in West Asia.

Gradual Changes in India's Israel Policy during Modi's First Term in Office

Since Prime Minister Narendra Modi came to power in May 2014, he wanted to pay an official visit to Israel. He had visited Israel when he was the Chief Minister (CM) of Gujarat in 2006. Israeli Prime Minister Benjamin Netanyahu officially invited him to Israel during their meeting at the United Nations General Assembly (UNGA) in September 2014. Prime Minister Modi wanted to gradually develop a strong relationship with the Jewish state, without alienating the Arab states and the Palestinian Authority (PA). This is why he decided to pay state visits to the United Arab Emirates (UAE), Saudi Arabia, Iran, and Qatar in the beginning of his first term. The main objective of these visits was to strengthen India's political, economic and security relations with strategic partners in West Asia. Nevertheless, Prime Minister Modi did not neglect Israel. He aspired to extend the relations with Israel by promoting high-level visits of Indian politicians and diplomats to the Jewish state. During these visits, leaders of India and Israel focused on a wide range of sectors such as security, agriculture, and trade. In November 2014, Indian Home Minister Rajnath Singh paid an official visit to Israel. During his visit, he encouraged Israel to be part of the 'Make in India' initiative, which Prime Minister Modi promoted in order to extend the development and production of the industrial sector in India. Prime Minister Netanyahu was in favour of this policy. He believed it would diversify Israel's manufacturing opportunities. In October 2015, Indian President Pranab Mukherjee paid an official visit to Israel. He was the first Indian President to visit the Jewish state. Before going to Israel, he paid an official visit to Jordan and the West Bank in order to show India's commitment to the Palestinian cause. In January 2016, Indian External Affairs Minister (EAM) Sushma Swaraj paid an official visit to Israel. Like President Mukherjee, she also paid an official visit to the PA in order to assert India's support to the Palestinian cause and maintain a balanced approach between Israel and the PA. This balanced approach characterized India's Israel policy since the normalization of relations between both countries on 29 January 1992 (Kumaraswamy, 2010; Rajiv, 2012; Keinon, 2015; Kumaraswamy, 2015; Pillalamarri, 2014; Wootliff, 2015; Keinon, 2016; Cowshish, 2017; Kaura, 2017; Kumaraswamy, 2017; Kaura, 2019; Ningthoujam, 2021b).

Israeli politicians also paid official visits to India. Israeli Defence Minister Moshe Ya'alon visited India in 2015. He was the first Israeli Defence Minister to do so since the establishment of full diplomatic relations between both countries in 1992. Minister Ya'alon expressed his willingness to help Prime Minister Modi to promote his 'Make in India' initiative by providing Israeli technologies to India. Israel is India's second-largest defence supplier after Russia and India is Israel's third-largest trade partner in Asia (Roy Chaudhury, 2015; Kumaraswamy, 2022; Prasad, 2022; Singh, 2022a). Both countries extended their defence relations and enhanced their cooperation in the fight against terrorism and radicalization not only on the bilateral level but also on the multilateral level together with the USA and the Gulf countries. India and Israel are located in challenging geopolitical regions and have to deal with Islamist extremism (Quamar, 2016; Haidar, 2017; *The Indian Express*, 2017, *The Jerusalem Post*, 2018; Ramesh and Ruttner, 2019). By cooperating together, they will be able to address these common security challenges.

In November 2016, Israeli President Reuven Rivlin paid an official visit to India. He was the second sitting Israeli head of state to do so, following President Ezer Weizman's visit in December 1996. During his visit, India and Israel signed agreements in the field of agriculture, water management, defence and aerospace. President Rivlin also declared that he was not only ready to 'Make in India' but also to 'make with India' (Pant, 2016; Quamar, 2016; Kaura, 2017), thus, emphasizing the need of mutual cooperation between both countries in order to promote their respective interests.

These official visits prepared the ground for the much-anticipated state visit of Prime Minister Modi to Israel in July 2017. It was considered an historic visit since Modi was the first sitting Indian premier to pay an official visit to the Jewish state. During his visit, India and Israel signed seven agreements in different areas such as agriculture, energy, space, and water management. Modi and Netanyahu also signed a Memorandum of Understanding (MoU) for the establishment of the India-Israel Industrial Research and Development (R&D) and the foundation of a Technical Innovation Fund. Both leaders also declared they would establish an Indo-Israel cyber security partnership in order to address common threats in cyberspace. Prime Minister Modi also met the Indian community in Israel and declared that Israeli citizens of Indian origin will receive Overseas Citizen of India (OCI) cards. The Indian Diaspora around the world is an important component of India's foreign policy since it enables India to maintain good relations with different countries in the world (Khalid, 2017; *The Indian Express*, 2017; Srikumar, 2017). Modi's visit to Israel enabled India to have a more open and public relation with the Jewish state. It also permitted India to decouple its relations with Israel from its relations with the PA, which is known as the de-hyphenation policy. The main objective of this policy is to treat Israel and the PA separately without being compelled to balance the relations between both entities. This policy was first manifested when Prime Minister Modi paid an official visit to Israel without immediately paying an official visit to the PA, as it was done before and during his first term in office (Kumaraswamy, 2010; Kumaraswamy, 2015; Cowshish, 2017; Kumaraswamy, 2018; Rasgon, 2018; Kaura, 2019; Pate, 2020; Keinon, 2021; Ningthoujam, 2021b).

Prime Minister Netanyahu paid a reciprocal state visit to India in January 2018. He came along with a business delegation of 130 members and signed economic, science, high-tech, agriculture and defence agreements with India. Netanyahu emphasized the importance of expanding the cooperation between both countries in the areas of innovation, business, trade, higher education, science, technology, tourism, and culture. His objective was to change the perception of the Indian people about Israel and strengthen the people-to-people relations of both countries through cinema and tourism. Netanyahu was the second Israeli Prime Minister to pay a state visit to India, as Prime Minister Ariel Sharon had been the first Israeli premier to do so in September 2003 (BBC, 2018; Pant, 2018; Roy, 2019).

During Modi's first term in office, Modi and Netanyahu were able to extend the relations between their respective countries and upgrade them to a strategic level. Both countries cooperated extensively in a wide range of areas such as defence, trade, agriculture, innovation and space. The close and personal relations between both leaders enabled them to introduce a more open and visible relation between both countries (*India Today*, 2017; Khalid, 2017; Keinon, 2019; Berman, 2021), without being concerned about possible negative implications on the national, regional and international levels.

Strengthening Relations during Modi's Second Term in Office

During Prime Minister's Modi second term in office since May 2019, the relations between India and Israel continue to thrive. Both Modi and Netanyahu proved time and again that they can rely on each other in time of distress and need. The eruption of the COVID-19 virus took the entire international community by surprise. Many countries decided to close their borders and reduce the export of medicines and medical equipment in order to assure their domestic needs. During this period, there were no official visits taking place in India and Israel because of nationwide lockdowns and closure of international borders. Nevertheless, India and Israel cooperated very closely during the COVID-19 pandemic. In March 2020, India decided to ban the export of masks and raw material for the production of medicines in order to assure its domestic needs. Prime

Minister Netanyahu called Prime Minister Modi and personally asked him to lift export bans on Israel, as Israel depended heavily on India's raw materials for medicines. Israel also suffered from a shortage of protective masks and was afraid it could not provide appropriate equipment for its medical personnel treating COVID-19 patients. Prime Minister Modi agreed to exempt Israel from the export ban on masks and raw materials, and help the repatriation of Israeli citizens after imposing a national lockdown in March 2020. Both countries also conducted joint research, field trials and vaccine development for COVID-19 (Hebbar, 2020; Jeffay, 2020; Ningthoujam, 2020; PTI, 2020a; *The Times of Israel*, 2020; Harkov, 2021a). Israel also came to India's assistance in time of distress. When India was experiencing a sharp rise of COVID-19 cases and high rates of death in April 2021, Israel decided to send medical equipment and assistance to India. Many Israelis from the public and private sectors sent oxygen generators, medication, respirators and other medical equipment to India (Harkov, 2021a; Jeffay, 2021). It exemplifies how the close and personal relations between both prime ministers have benefited both countries greatly in time of need and despair.

The first high-level visit to Israel, which took place since the eruption of the COVID-19 pandemic, occurred in October 2021. India's External Affairs Minister, Dr. Subramanyam Jaishankar, paid an official visit to Israel. The main purpose of his visit was to extend the strategic relations of India and Israel, and meet the new Israeli government led by Prime Minister Naftali Bennet since June 2021. Prime Minister Bennet considered India to be an important friend of Israel. He expressed his willingness to extend the relations between both countries in different areas. During Dr. Jaishankar's visit to Israel, Prime Minister Modi invited his Israeli counterpart to pay a state visit to India. Both countries also resumed talks on a Free Trade Agreement (FTA), in order to expand their economic and trade relations, and decided to mutually recognize COVID-19 vaccination certificates to enable Indian travellers vaccinated with Covishield to travel to Israel (Gaurav, 2021; Haidar, 2021; Harkov, 2021b; Lis, 2021; Ningthoujam, 2021b; Wootliff, 2021).

During his visit to Israel, Dr. Jaishankar also met Israeli Minister of Energy and Water Resources Karin Elharar, who signed an agreement of Israel's accession to the International Solar Alliance (ISA). The ISA was established by India and France in November 2015 at the United Nations Climate Change Conference (UNCCC) in Paris. The main objective of the

UNCCC is to reduce the dependency of countries on fossil fuels. By being part of the ISA, Israel will be able to share its knowledge on solar power and cooperate closely with other members of the alliance (PTI, 2020b; Haidar, 2021; Ningthoujam, 2021b; Sibal, 2021). On 2 November 2021, Prime Minister Bennet and Prime Minister Modi met on the sidelines of the UNCCC in Glasgow. The Israeli premier expressed his commitment to strengthen the relations and the cooperation of both countries in the areas of security, agriculture, technology, space, innovation, and climate change. Prime Minister Bennett also informed his Indian counterpart about his popularity in Israel and facetiously invited him to join his party (Keinon, 2021; PTI, 2021).

On 29 January 2022, India and Israel celebrated 30 years of full diplomatic relations. Prime Minister Modi asserted the importance of the bilateral relations with Israel over the course of significant changes the world has been witnessing. He expressed his confidence that the relations between both countries will continue to thrive and said it was the right time to set new goals which would enable them to take the relations between both countries forward (*Hindustan Times*, 2022; *The Indian Express*, 2022).

Regional Dynamics which led to the Strengthening of Relations between the Countries

What enabled Prime Minister Modi to change India's Israel policy and conduct a more pragmatic approach towards the Jewish state was the eruption of the Arab Spring in December 2010, the signing of the Joint Comprehensive Plan of Action (JCPOA) in July 2015 and the signing of the Abraham Accords in September 2020. The Arab Spring destabilized many countries in West Asia and put aside the Palestinian issue from the regional and international agendas. Many countries in West Asia changed their attitude towards Israel and considered the Jewish state to be a source of stability in a combustible region. The hegemonic aspirations of Iran in West Asia and the signing of the JCPOA, known as the Iran nuclear deal, were another reason for Arab states to get closer to Israel. The unwillingness of the USA to be involved in regional issues also alarmed many Arab States in West Asia and led to the signing of the Abraham Accords between Israel, Bahrain, the UAE and the USA (Gharekhan, 2017; Kaura, 2019; Puthan Purayil, 2020; Quamar, 2020; Quamar, 2021b).

The Abraham Accords enable India to explore new opportunities of cooperation with Israel, Bahrain and the UAE in trade, innovation, technology, food security and healthcare. Each country will be able to promote its comparative advantage in order to bring progress and prosperity to the region of West Asia (Laskar, 2020; Roy Chaudhury, 2021; Quamar, 2021a; Quamar, 2021b). Following the signing of the Abraham Accords, India and Israel extended their relations from the bilateral level to the multilateral level by conducting a virtual quadrilateral meeting between the foreign ministers of India, Israel, the UAE and the USA in October 2021. This multilateral engagement, known as the Quad of West Asia, will allow these countries to extend their security, economic and political engagements by addressing common threats and opportunities in West Asia (Malka, 2020; Blarel, 2021; Ningthoujam, 2021b; Rajagopalan, 2021). Some commentators compared the Quad of West Asia to the quadrilateral alliance which was formed in the Pacific between India, Australia, Japan and the USA, known as the Quad. These commentators also believed that the main purpose of the Quad of West Asia is to counter China's aspirations in the region with the Belt and Road Initiative (BRI). The main objective of the BRI is to enhance the connectivity and trade relations between different countries by building terrestrial and marine routes across the world. The Abraham Accords will allow India to have better connectivity and access to the Israeli and European markets by shipping goods through the UAE, Saudi Arabia and Jordan (Berman, 2021; Keinon, 2021; Rajagopalan, 2021).

India and China were able to forge economic and strategic relations with different countries in West Asia. The disengagement of the USA from the region could lead both India and China to promote a more proactive policy in the region. However, India will apparently continue to balance its relations with its strategic partners in West Asia. The question is whether India will be able to maintain this policy towards Israel, Iran, Saudi Arabia and the Gulf States following the withdrawal of the USA from the JCPOA in May 2018 and the signing of the Abraham Accords. These developments led India to get closer to Israel and the Gulf countries at the expense of Iran (Ganguly, 2017; Blarel, 2021; Zeeshan, 2021).

Prior to this, Iran was India's main supplier of oil. After withdrawing from the JCPOA, the USA imposed sanctions on Iran. However, India was exempted from these sanctions until May 2019. In order to assure its oil supplies, India decided to get closer to Saudi Arabia, Iraq, Kuwait,

Qatar, the UAE and Israel (Burton, 2019; Erlanger, 2019; Blarel, 2021; Ningthoujam, 2021b). India and Israel began to explore possibilities of extending their relations in the energy sector. In January 2018, both countries signed a Memorandum of Understanding (MoU) which allows them to engage in the oil and gas sectors. Israel became an important exporter of gas since the discovery of the field Liviathan in December 2010. It is in India's interest to diversify its energy sources (Ningthoujam, 2021a). The fact that Israel is a stable and reliable partner will allow India to pursue the procurement of regular gas supply from the Jewish state.

The abrupt withdrawal of the USA from Afghanistan in August 2021 led to the return of the militant Taliban to power. This withdrawal and the willingness of the USA to revive the Iran nuclear deal raised many concerns among the Gulf countries. Following these developments, the UAE understood that in order to maintain regional stability it should cooperate not only within the newly formed Quad of West Asia but also explore possible areas of cooperation with Iran. This is why the senior national security adviser of the UAE, Sheikh Tahnoon bin Zayed Al Nahyan, paid an official visit to Iran and met his Iranian counterpart, Ali Shamkhani, and Iranian President Ebrahim Raisi (Hafezi, 2021; Reuters, 2021; Singh, 2022b). This policy is quite similar to the balancing approach India is promoting with different countries in the world.

Conclusion

Regional dynamics have an impact on bilateral and multilateral relations of different countries in the world. Old foes can put aside their differences and cooperate on a wide range of sectors. Regional developments in West Asia enabled the Modi-led government in India to gradually transform India's Israel policy and make it more open and visible. The relations between India and Israel became strategic and include a wide range of areas such as security, trade, agriculture and space. The eruption of the Arab Spring, the US withdrawal from the JCPOA and the signing of the Abraham Accords changed the position of Israel in West Asia. Israel, which was considered to be a source of regional unrest, became a source of stability in a combustible region. It enabled both India and Israel to develop multilateral engagements with West Asian countries in order to address common security, economic, climate, health and other challenges. These engagements are important since each and every country can share its comparative advantage and lead to mutual developments. However, it is also necessary to understand that multilateral engagements bring the countries to compromise on essential issues in order to maintain a fruitful dialogue and promote practical actions. Moreover, regional and international dynamics could change policy orientations and form new alliances between countries that did not have diplomatic relations before. Therefore, India and Israel should continue to extend their bilateral relations while developing multilateral engagements with stable countries in West Asia. It seems that both countries will continue to have strategic relations regardless of the leaders who will sit in the head of their respective governments. The only difference will be manifested in the level of openness and visibility of these relations.

REFERENCES

BBC (January 15, 2018), Netanyahu and Modi praise 'new era' in India-Israel ties.

Berman, Lazar (October 23, 2021), Expanded Israel-India ties start taking shape, after the Netanyahu-Modi bromance, *The Times of Israel*. Retrieved from https://www.timesofisrael.com/expanded-israel-india-ties-start-taking-shape-after-the-netanyahu-modi-bromance/

Blarel, Nicolas (2021), Modi looks West? Assessing change and continuity in India's Middle East policy since 2014, *International Politics*. https://doi-org.ezprimo1.idc.ac.il/10.1057/s41311-021-00314-3

Burton, Guy (August 6, 2019), India's "Look West" Policy in the Middle East under Modi, *Middle East Institute Policy Analysis*. Retrieved from https://www.mei.edu/publications/indias-look-west-policy-middle-east-under-modi#_edn21

Cowshish, Amit (2017), India-Israel Defence Trade: Issues and Challenges, *Strategic Analysis*, 41 (4), pp. 401-412.

Erlanger, Steven (July 28, 2019), Iran links British seizure of oil tanker to ailing nuclear deal, *The New York Times*. Retrieved from https://www.nytimes.com/2019/07/28/world/europe/iran-tanker-britain-nuclear.html

Ganguly, Sumit (2017), Has Modi truly changed India's foreign policy?, *The Washington Quarterly*, 40 (2), pp. 131-143.

Gaurav, Kunal (October 18, 2021), India, Israel agree on mutual recognition of COVID-19 vaccination certificates, *Hindustan Times*. Retrieved from https://www.hindustantimes.com/india-news/india-israel-agree-on-mutual-recognition-of-covid-19-vaccination-certificates-101634553631831.html

Gharekhan, Chinmaya R. (2017), India-Israel: Retrospective and Prospective, *Strategic Analysis*, 41 (4), pp. 314-324.

Hafezi, Parisa (December 6, 2021), UAE security official pays rare visit to Iran to discuss ties, regional issues, *Reuters*. Retrieved from https://www.reuters.com/world/middle-east/uae-security-official-iran-discuss-ties-regional-issues-state-media-2021-12-06/

Haidar, Suhasini (October 19, 2021), India, Israel, UAE, USA decide to launch quadrilateral economic forum, *The Hindu*. Retrieved from https://www.thehindu.com/news/national/jaishankar-takes-part-in-new-quadrilateral-with-israel-uae-and-us/article37064989.ece

Haidar, Suhasini (July 5, 2017), India, Israel to set up $ 40 mn research fund, *The Hindu*. Retrieved from https://www.thehindu.com/news/national/india-israel-to-set-up-40-mn-research-fund/article19217107.ece

Harkov, Lahav (October 20, 2021b), Modi invites Bennett to India on official visit, *The Jerusalem Post*. Retrieved from https://www.jpost.com/israel-news/india-israel/modi-invites-bennett-to-india-on-official-visit-682594

Harkov, Lahav (May 4, 2021a), Israel sends COVID-19 aid to India, *The Jerusalem Post*. Retrieved from https://www.jpost.com/israel-news/israel-sends-covid-19-aid-to-india-667159

Hebbar, Nistula (March 24, 2020), PM Modi announces 21-day lockdown as COVID-19 toll touches 12, *The Hindu*. Retrieved from https://www.thehindu.com/news/national/pm-announces-21-day-lockdown-as-covid-19-toll-touches-10/article31156691.ece

Hindustan Times (January 29, 2022), 30-years of India-Israel friendship: PM Modi says 'time to set new goals' to take forward ties, *Hindustan Times*. Retrieved from https://www.hindustantimes.com/india-news/30years-of-india-israel-friendship-pm-modi-says-time-to-set-new-goals-to-take-forward-ties-101643471480594.html

India Today (July 6, 2017), Narendra Modi, Benjamin Netanyahu's 3-day Israel bromance: In picture, *India Today*. Retrieved from https://www.indiatoday.in/india/story/narendra-modi-benjamin-netanyahu-moshe-holtzberg-olga-beach-haifa-26-11-mumbai-1022838-2017-07-06

Jeffay, Nathan (April 28, 2021), Oxygen to India: Israeli group dispatching medical aid to COVID-stricken country, *The Times of Israel*. Retrieved from https://www.timesofisrael.com/oxygen-to-india-israeli-ngo-dispatching-medical-aid-to-covid-stricken-country/

Jeffay, Nathan (August 5, 2020), Determined to build COVID tests of future, Israel collects 20,000 swabs in India, *The Times of Israel*. Retrieved from https://www.timesofisrael.com/determined-to-build-covid-tests-of-future-israel-collects-20000-swabs-in-india/

Kaura, Vinay (2019), Indo-Israel relations in the Modi era: A transformative shift, *Israel Affairs*, 25 (2), pp. 217-233.

Kaura, Vinay (2017), The Modi Government's Policy on Israel: The rhetoric and reality of de-hyphenation, *Strategic Assessment*, 19 (4), pp. 79-91.

Keinon, Herb (November 15, 2021), The widening and deepening of Israel-India ties – analysis, *The Jerusalem Post*. Retrieved from https://www.jpost.com/israel-news/the-widening-and-deepening-of-israel-india-ties-analysis-685069

Keinon, Herb (November 26, 2019), To India's Modi, Netanyahu remains a 'dear friend', *The Jerusalem Post*. Retrieved from https://www.jpost.com/israel-news/to-indias-modi-netanyahu-remains-a-dear-friend-609095

Keinon, Herb (January 18, 2016), Indian FM in Jerusalem: Ties with Israel of 'highest importance' to India, *The Jerusalem Post*. Retrieved from https://www.jpost.com/israel-news/politics-and-diplomacy/indian-fm-in-jerusalem-ties-with-israel-of-highest-importance-to-india-441956

Keinon, Herb (May 31, 2015), In first, Indian PM Modi to visit Israel, *The Jerusalem Post*. Retrieved from https://www.jpost.com/israel-news/politics-and-diplomacy/in-first-indian-pm-modi-to-visit-israel-404649

Khalid, Saif (July 4, 2017), Narendra Modi in Israel to meet 'friend' Netanyahu, *Al Jazeera*.

Retrieved from https://www.aljazeera.com/features/2017/7/4/narendra-modi-in-israel-to-meet-friend-netanyahu

Kumar, Sunil (2017), Indo-Israeli relations: A quest for great-power status since 1991, *Jewish Political Studies Review*, 28 (3/4), pp. 38-45.

Kumaraswamy, Polur R. (January 26, 2022), Israel à la Modi, *Tablet Magazine*. Retrieved from *https://www.tabletmag.com/sections/israel-middle-east/articles/israel-a-la-modi*

Kumaraswamy, Polur R. (2018), Reading Modi's visit to Israel, *India Quarterly*, 74 (1), pp. 1-16.

Kumaraswamy, Polur R. (May 18, 2017), Modi Redefines India's Palestine Policy, *IDSA Issue Brief*. Retrieved from https://www.idsa.in/system/files/issuebrief/ib_modi-redefines-india-palestine-policy_prkumarswamy.pdf

Kumaraswamy, Polur R. (2015), Israel: A maturing relationship. In: David M. Malone, C. Raja Mohan and Srinath Raghavan (eds.), *The Oxford Handbook of Indian Foreign Policy* (pp. 539-551), Oxford: Oxford University Press.

Kumaraswamy, Polur R. (2010), *India's Israel Policy*, New York: Columbia University Press.

Laskar, Rezaul H. (December 17, 2020), Will provide whatever 'friend' India needs to defend itself: Israel ambassador Ron Malka, *Hindustan Times*. Retrieved from https://www.hindustantimes.com/india-news/will-provide-whatever-friend-india-needs-to-defend-itself-israel-ambassador-ron-malka/story-89hqXs9wFFR02CmA7D6CCN.html

Lis, Jonathan (October 20, 2021), Modi invites Bennett for first official India visit, *Haarets*. Retrieved from https://www.haaretz.com/israel-news/modi-invites-bennett-for-first-official-india-visit-1.10311178

Malka, Ron (September 17, 2020), What the Israel-UAE-Bahrain accord means for India and the world, *The Hindustan Times*. Retrieved from https://www.hindustantimes.com/analysis/what-the-israel-uae-bahrain-accord-means-for-india-and-the-world/story-SHrfuRXQbkhaYGbc16ZcKJ.html

Ningthoujam, Alvite (October 22, 2021b), India-Israel Ties: New Opportunities in the Middle East, *The Diplomat*. Retrieved from https://thediplomat.com/2021/10/india-israel-ties-new-opportunities-in-the-middle-east/

Ningthoujam, Alvite (August 11, 2021a), India-Israel relations: Building energy ties, *South Asian Voices*. Retrieved from https://southasianvoices.org/india-israel-relations-building-energy-ties/

Ningthoujam, Alvite (April 20, 2020), India's COVID-19 cooperation with the Middle East, *The Diplomat*. Retrieved from https://thediplomat.com/2020/04/indias-covid-19-cooperation-with-the-middle-east/

Pant, Harsh V. (January 23, 2018), India-Israel ties gather momentum, *The Diplomat*. Retrieved from https://thediplomat.com/2018/01/india-israel-ties-gather-momentum/

Pant, Harsh V. (November 26, 2016), An India-Israel entente, *The Diplomat*. Retrieved from https://thediplomat.com/2016/11/an-india-israel-entente/

Pate, Tanti (2020), Re-(Modi)flying India's Israel policy: An exploration of practical geopolitical reasoning through re-representation of 'India', 'Israel' and 'West Asia' Post-2014, *Journal of Asia Security and International Affairs*, 7 (1). pp. 7-35.

Pillalamarrim Akhilesh (November 8, 2014), Israel 'ready and willing' to share technology with India, *The Diplomat*. Retrieved from https://thediplomat.com/2014/11/israel-ready-and-willing-to-share-technology-with-india/

PTI (November 3, 2021), 'Come and join my party', Israeli PM Naftali Bennett tells PM Modi, *The Wire*. Retrieved from https://thewire.in/diplomacy/come-and-join-my-party-israeli-pm-naftali-bennett-tells-pm-modi

PTI (November 27, 2020b), Israel, India partners in quest for future with low carbon, pollution levels: Netanyahu, *The Hindu*. Retrieved from https://www.thehindu.com/news/international/israel-india-partners-in-quest-for-future-with-low-carbon-pollution-levels-netanyahu/article33190364.ece

PTI (October 6, 2020a), PM Modi discusses expanding cooperation between India and Israel with Netanyahu, *The Hindu*. Retrieved from https://www.thehindu.com/news/national/pm-modi-discusses-expanding-cooperation-between-india-and-israel-with-netanyahu/article32777714.ece

Prasad, Manavendra and Kumar, Manish (January 5, 2022), India-Israel ties: New opportunities, *Deccan Herald*. Retrieved from https://www.deccanherald.com/opinion/in-perspective/india-israel-ties-new-opportunities-1068334.html

Puthan Purayil, Muhsin (2020), Shifting trajectory in India-Israel relations under Modi, *Israel Affairs*, 26 (3), pp. 471-483.

Quamar, Md. Muddassir (November 22, 2021b), Israel-UAE bonhomie and the changing dynamics in the Middle East, *Financial Times*. Retrieved from https://www.financialexpress.com/world-news/israel-uae-bonhomie-and-the-changing-dynamics-in-the-middle-east/2373745/

Quamar, Md. Muddassir (November 22, 2021a), India's Opportunity in the Middle East, *IDSA Comment*. Retrieved from https://www.idsa.in/idsacomments/indias-opportunity-in-the-middle-east-mmquamar-221121#footnote2_jxxzkol

Quamar, Md. Muddassir (2020), Changing regional geopolitics and the foundations of a rapprochement between Arab Gulf and Israel, *Global Affairs*, 6 (4-5). pp. 593-608.

Quamar, Md. Muddassir (December 3, 2016), India and Israel: Growing warmth in bilateral ties, *Indian Defence Review*. Retrieved from http://www.indiandefencereview.com/india-and-israel-growing-warmth-in-bilateral-ties/

Rajagopalan, Rajeswari P. (October 22, 2021), A quad for the Middle East?, *The Diplomat*. Retrieved from https://thediplomat.com/2021/10/a-quad-for-the-middle-east/

Rajiv, Samuel S.C. (2012), The delicate balance: Israel and India's Foreign Policy Practice, *Strategic Analysis*, 36 (1), pp. 128-144.

Ramesh, Akhil and Ruttner, Shenhav (August 1, 2019), Will the Bibi-Modi bromance deliver?, *The Jerusalem Post*. Retrieved from https://www.jpost.com/opinion/will-the-bibi-modi-bromance-deliver-597448

Rasgon, Adam (February 8, 2018), Modi to become first Indian PM to visit West Bank, *The Jerusalem Post*. Retrieved from https://www.jpost.com/arab-israeli-conflict/modi-to-become-first-indian-pm-to-visit-west-bank-542079

Reuters (August 31, 2021), 'War is over': US completes withdrawal of forces from Afghanistan, *India Today*. Retrieved from https://www.indiatoday.in/top-stories/story/us-completes-withdrawal-of-forces-from-afghanistan-1847307-2021-08-31

Roy, Pradipta (2019), Benjamin Netanyahu's state visit to India, *Israel Affairs*, 25 (5), pp. 788-802.

Roy Chaudhury, Dipanjan (December 10, 2021), India, Israel can jointly lead world in innovation: President Herzog, *The Economic Times*. Retrieved from https://economictimes.indiatimes.com/news/india/india-israel-can-jointly-lead-world-in-innovation-president-herzog/articleshow/88209832.cms?from=mdr

Roy Chaudhury, Dipanjan (February 20, 2015), Make in India: Israeli Defence Minister

Moshe Ya'alon meets PM Narendra Modi, promises technological support. *Economic Times*. Retrieved from https://economictimes.indiatimes.com/news/politics-and-nation/make-in-india-israeli-defence-minister-moshe-yaalon-meets-pm-narendra-modi-promises-technological-support/articleshow/46306787.cms?from=mdr

Sibal, Sidhant (October 18, 2021), Israel to join India based International Solar Alliance, *WION*. Retrieved from https://www.wionews.com/india-news/israel-to-join-india-based-international-solar-alliance-421685

Singh, Swaran (February 11, 2022b), Quads and triangles: Is USA losing grip on its alliances?, *Asian Times*. Retrieved from https://asiatimes.com/2022/02/quads-and-triangles-is-us-losing-grip-on-its-alliances/

Singh, Swaran (January 29, 2022a), India's evolving ties with Israel can be game changer for Mideast, *Asia Times*. Retrieved from https://asiatimes.com/2022/01/indias-evolving-ties-with-israel-can-be-game-changer-for-mideast/

Srikumar, Madhulika (July 10, 2017), India and Israel's cyber security partnership could be a potential game changer, *The Wire*. Retrieved from https://thewire.in/diplomacy/india-israel-cyber-security-partnership

The Indian Express (January 30, 2022), No better time to take India-Israel ties forward: PM Modi, *The Indian Express*. Retrieved from https://indianexpress.com/article/india/pm-narendra-modi-india-israel-relation-7747658/

The Indian Express (July 6, 2017), Modi in Israel: All that happened during PM's historic trip, *The Indian Express*. Retrieved from https://indianexpress.com/article/india/pm-narendra-modi-in-israel-benjamin-netanyahu-reuven-rivlin-all-that-you-should-know-about-this-historic-trip-4739085/

The Jerusalem Post (January 9, 2018), India and Israel, *The Jerusalem Post*. Retrieved from https://www.jpost.com/Opinion/India-and-Israel-533299

The Times of Israel (March 13, 2020), PM said to ask India to lift export bans on masks, pharmaceuticals, *The Times of Israel*. Retrieved from https://www.timesofisrael.com/pm-said-to-ask-india-to-lift-export-bans-on-masks-pharmaceuticals/

Wootliff, Raoul (June 13, 2021), Bennett sworn in as prime minister, unseating Netanyahu after 12 years in power, *The Times of Israel*. Retrieved from https://www.timesofisrael.com/bennett-sworn-in-as-prime-minister-unseating-netanyahu-after-12-years-in-power/

Wootliff, Raoul (October 12, 2015), Indian president declares support for Palestinians ahead of Israel trip, *The Times of Israel*. Retrieved from https://www.timesofisrael.com/indian-president-declares-support-for-palestinians-ahead-of-israel-trip/

Zeeshan, Mohamed (November 4, 2021), There's a New Quad in Town: India, Israel, USA, UAE, *The Diplomat*. Retrieved from https://thediplomat.com/2021/11/theres-a-new-quad-in-town/

13

Turkey's Asia: A New Initiative with Special Reference to India

Dr. Duygu Çağla Bayram and Prof. Dr. Hüseyin Bagci

ABSTRACT

Turkey's foreign policy has been Western-centred since its inception in 1923, as the founding fathers believed that focusing primarily on the Western alignment could advance the country's prosperity as well as foster the country's global posture on a solid basis. However, in parallel to the global evolution where Asia becomes the world's centre of gravity, Turkey, as bridging Europe and Asia, or the West and the East, now intends to strengthen the latter pillar of the bridge in which it has relatively remained weak through its Asia Anew Initiative. By the same token, the Indo-Turkish bilateral relations that deserves to go much further than today holds great prospects on the horizon.

Key Words: *Turkey, Turkish Foreign Policy, Asia Anew Initiative, South Asia, India, Indo-Turkish Relations.*

Introduction

Neither Turkey nor India controls the same territorial and cultural boundaries from centuries ago. Turkey too has lost large territory it once had under Ottoman rule, yet, the modern republic managed to have normal and equal relations with all countries on the basis of mutual respect. However, Turkey's founding policymakers have aspired to establish the country's foreign policy as a part of Western civilisation, which has always led them to prioritise the country's Western relations over its Eastern or Asian counterparts, which have also led to occur in time the case of the Western dependency in Turkish foreign policy. On the other hand, the structural changes on the balance of power at the global level, which had evolved in favour of China, Russia and India, as well as the yawning gap between Turkey and its Western allies and Turkey's primary security threats, which have intensely begun to come from its Western Asian immediate neighbourhood, have brought to light the need for renewing the country's Asia activism and expanding its strategic interest as far as the region. Yet, one needs to take a careful approach to view this as it does not constitute an axis shift in Turkish foreign policy. In this respect, one should consider Turkey, rather, intends to solidify its unique role as a conduit between the West and the East by recovering its neglected Asian side of Turkish identity. This goal also constitutes the basis of the Asia Anew Initiative, which was launched in late 2019, that includes the main elements as fostering economic and trade relations, enhancing political dialogue and strengthening cultural ties. Having said that, Turkey, which is the westernmost Asian and the easternmost European, intends to maintain its role as the Asian in the West and the European in the East by continuing to participate in the European integration process as well as protecting its key position in the NATO on one side, and also by reinventing its strong connection with Asia through the Asia Anew Initiative.

Additionally, amid the fluid West Asian security environment, Turkey's regional involvement has begun to be viewed almost as the country's inevitable destiny. Turkey has emerged as the only West Asian country where, since the establishment of the Republic, the secular democratic institutionalisation is well setup and fair elections have bridged the gap between the streets and State. Most of the countries in West Asia found it difficult to respond to the Arab uprisings. In the new West Asia emerging after the Syrian crisis, where there will be needed strong non-Western support, amid the uncertain policies of Western countries, Turkey could not have stayed idle while the crisis was dragging on; in just the same way as South Asia in relation to the war-torn Afghanistan in which Turkey was able to be adversely affected due to mostly a possible wave of refugees as well as a possible rise of terror threats or terrorist groups over Afghanistan. Speaking of which, it is also worth mentioning that, as is known, Turkey, which provides extraordinary humanitarian aid to millions of refugees, is a transit country for refugees trying to reach Western destinations, that is, it is in a suitable position for irregular migrant flows.

Speaking on humanitarian issues, meanwhile, is also seen as the country's moral responsibility as a "compassionate power", which means one of the manifestations of the "humanitarian nature" of Turkish foreign policy that should not be mistaken as ideologically vying for a Caliphate. By the same token, it may be recalled India had been vocal against African and Asian colonialism in the 1940s, and even today, does not hesitate when it comes to speaking for the Palestinians. As the leader of the Organisation of Islamic Cooperation (OIC), Turkey too speaks for the Palestine issue in West Asia and the Rohingya crisis in Southeast Asia. As for the Kashmir conflict in South Asia, it should also be recalled that Turkey has mediated in history between India and Pakistan and supported the dialogue that developed between the two until 2006. Turkey is aware that the only these two mentioned countries are together able to find a resolution for the Kashmir dispute and only this settlement will bring prosperity to South Asia. Moreover, Turkey knows very well that it cannot afford an "either India or Pakistan" policy. Besides, Turkey never saw its close relations with Pakistan as well as India affecting each other ever. The Indo-Turkish relationship, therefore, should not be a prisoner of external issues, that means India and Turkey should look directly at each other in their bilateral relations, as this relation is also a standalone relation.

The changing geopolitics of the region and the world has brought more opportunities for Turkey and India, as two emerging economies, to cooperate on many regional and global issues. Accordingly, increased need of diversification of connectivity, development, economic and defence cooperation at regional and global levels can bring Turkey and India together, which are facing some security threats on the one hand and, on the other hand, improving their own defence industries, and respectively an emerging energy hub-transit country and a shining example of a rapidly rising economy. Besides, there is a palpable curiosity and interest in Turkish society about Asia in general and in particular over India. While Turkish public and academia are increasingly keen on understanding and engaging in the region, the private sector strives further to benefit from the commercial and financial opportunities the region presents. In this vein, while India will likely be able to find its place in Turkey's Asia Anew Initiative, likewise Turkey is likely to be able to find its place in India's Indo-Pacific vision in general or in particular, what Indian Prime Minister Narendra Modi calls the "Look West" policy. There are, as an example, promising opportunities between the two for more cooperation in the private sector, through investment. Indeed, there is a noteworthy degree of interest among the Turkish firms in India's "Make in India" strategy as well as "Smart Cities Mission". There is, as another example, significant potential for further cooperation and collaboration in key areas from commerce to science and on common challenges from climate change to terrorism. Furthermore, as a concrete example, there are many overlapping interests on the issue of war-torn Afghanistan ranging from development to security.

Indeed, both countries are aware that keeping a diversified worldview is the only way in today's competitive world. Moreover, there is a convergence of views on several issues. Particularly, both countries strive to become self-sufficient in defence, science, and technology. In the Palestinian context, both Turkey and India are sensitive to the Palestine case and firmly support the two-state solution, while recognising the state of Israel. In the Afghanistan context, as stated before, both countries, which have made an immense contribution for years, desire Afghanistan's security, stability, and development. Besides, Turkey, which voices at every turn the motto of "the world is bigger than five" coined by President Recep Tayyip Erdoğan, has been supportive of India's call for reform and expansion of the United Nations Security Council (UNSC) in order for it to be fit for today's purposes. Turkey also supported Bangladesh's demand for OIC reform, which involves observer status for India, home to the world's second largest Muslim population. Further, Turkey has earlier been supportive of India's participation at the Nuclear Suppliers Group (NSG) and previously had supported India's membership in the Missile Technology Control Regime (MCTR).

If India has the leadership of the Non-Aligned Movement (NAM) and is a "net security provider" in the Indian Ocean, Turkey is a significant NATO member, and the single Muslim-majority member of the alliance. Both India and Turkey, on the other hand, have successfully diversified their international relations beyond the NAM and the NATO. Even if committing itself to traditional Non-Alignment, India has also been extending its regional and global engagement within the scope of its innovative political and strategic moves such as Look/Act East, Look West, and SAGAR. In doing so, India reflects a kind of "Conjunctural Non-Alignment" (CNA) posture in today's world, a posture that was coined by one of co-authors of this article, Dr. Bayram. With regard to Turkey, Turkish foreign policy has successfully transformed itself from West-centric to multidimensional and proactive. As Turkey's Ambassador to India, Firat Sunel, states "Both countries are rising stars in their respective regions with their growing economies and increasing role in the international arena", adding that "they share fundamental common values such as democracy, rule of law and liberal economies".[1] Accordingly, both Turkey and India have been redefining their regional and global engagements. The third-party prism through which both countries have long seen one another, however, has prevented them from fully appreciating the growing strategic salience of each other. Both countries today should elevate their partnerships in all fields. The enterprising, multidimensional and proactive Turkish foreign policy and the budding partnership with India raise the prospects of Turkey's Asia Anew Initiative in general and in particular Turkey's South Asia outreach and the bright future in the Indo-Turkish ties.

The Asia Anew Initiative

Turkey, which links the two continents, Asia and Europe, and is a bridge between the East and the West, has close and deep historical ties in Asia. However, Turkey's policies, since its foundation, have almost been formulated as status quoist and reactive that focuses on its close Western relations. On the other hand, Turkey has recently begun to show greater interest in regions hitherto neglected thanks to its foreign policy posture that has undergone a multidimensional and proactive transformation. To this end, Asia signifies a major area of interest that Turkey heads towards.

Since August 2019, Turkey has been following a policy named Asia Anew Initiative that mainly aims at enhancing interstate relations, expanding private sector trade, improving academic cooperation and boosting interaction between societies. The Asia Anew Initiative was officially unveiled on August 5, 2019, by Foreign Minister Mevlüt Çavusoglu at the 11th Turkish Ambassadors' Conference. As Çavusoglu pointed out, "Turkey had profound, historical and lasting ties with Asia and that in the 21st century, Asia was again becoming the centre of gravity in the world", emphasising the Asia Anew Initiative "would position Turkey in the right place in the Asian age".[2] As many countries act with the awareness of a rising Asian era in the 21st century, Turkey too is aware that the power of economy is heading from the West to the East and Asia has started to emerge as the centre of power. Çavusoğlu stated that "The 19th and 20th centuries were the centuries of Europe and America, respectively. Today, all the data suggests that the 21st century will be the century of Asia".[3] Hence, through the Asia Anew Initiative, involving the country's booming economic tools and innovative defence industry as well as its capability of soft power, Turkey, on one side, is eyeing to deepen and diversify its current ties with the Asian countries and on the other side, to build new ones. Even if Turkey has mostly had a Western identity as being a NATO member and having close ties with Europe, it also has an Eastern identity that was neglected in Turkish foreign policy, and Turkey believes its existing Eastern identity will help to deepen its political and economic relations with the Asian countries.

Recently, Turkey's Asia engagement has incrementally fostered with its innovative footprints such opening new embassies in Myanmar (2012), Sri Lanka (2013), Cambodia (2013), Brunei (2013) and Laos (2017), and becoming a dialogue partner of the Shanghai Cooperation Organization (SCO) in 2013 and in the same year establishing an informal partnership called MIKTA with Mexico, Indonesia, the Korean Republic, and Australia to support global governance, and becoming a member of the Asia Cooperation Dialogue (ACD) in 2013 in which it also assumed the chairmanship for 2019-2021, and also after acceding to the Treaty of Amity and Cooperation in 2010, becoming a sectoral dialogue partner of the Association of Southeast Asian Nations (ASEAN) in 2017, the Association that Turkey regards as the key organisation in the region. Furthermore, the Turkish Cooperation and Coordination Agency (TIKA) has increased the number of its development projects and strengthened its presence by opening offices in Yangon, Myanmar, in 2013 and Manila, the Philippines, in 2015; the Turkish Red Crescent (Türk Kızılay) also opened an office in Yangon in 2019. Besides, Turkey has elevated its relations to strategic partnership with six Asian countries—China (2010), Indonesia (2011), South Korea (2012), Japan (2013), Malaysia (2014) and Singapore (2014).[4] Meanwhile, it should be given here that the Asian countries that need to hedge to avoid being squeezed between China and the USA are in need of diversifying their partners. This, hence, means that they will provide, or have already provided, a favourable condition for Turkey's Asia engagement.

Turkey's Asia engagement intends to enhance its economic relations with Asian countries and increase its trade ties across the region as well as seek to diversify the country's diplomatic ties. In other words, Turkey primarily aims to capitalise on Asia that looms on the horizon as a new centre for global production and trade. Since 2010, the Turkish Ministry of Trade has biennially been designating target countries around the world in the context of intensifying its bilateral economic and trade relations, a designation where the private sector has been encouraged with additional public incentives to develop commercial relations with these states and where India has been included in all these lists of target countries identified in each biennial period. As of the 2020-21 term, among the 17 designated countries, India, China, Japan, South Korea, and Malaysia are from Asia.[5] Moreover, Turkey has signed Free Trade Agreements (FTAs) with South Korea, Malaysia, and Singapore that came into force in 2013, 2015, and 2017, respectively.[6] Meanwhile, through the Asia Anew Initiative, the share of Asia to Turkey's Foreign Direct Investment (FDI) has been noticeably on the rise. However, in its Asian trade relations, Turkey has persistently a trade deficit. As of 2020, for example, China was the biggest import partner for Turkey with 23 billion dollars that makes 11 per cent of Turkey's trade volume while being only the 15th biggest export partner with 2.87 billion dollars that makes 1.7 per cent. India, on the other hand, was the 13th biggest import partner with 4.83 billion dollars that makes 2.4 per cent while being the 44th biggest export partner with 890 million dollars that makes 0.53 per cent.[7] Thus, here comes the importance of the Asia Anew Initiative that essentially constitutes a political measure for the trade imbalance in Turkey's bilateral economic relations by encouraging the Turkish private sector to increase exports.

On the other hand, some favourable foreign policy moves such China's One Belt, One Road or the Belt and Road Initiative (OBOR or BRI) and Japan's Free and Open Indo-Pacific vision (FOIP) present some opportunities for Turkey to further its Asian engagement. As one of the most important countries as the Middle Corridor of China's global development plan, the BRI, Turkey has already improved its bilateral ties with that country, mostly within the framework of Chinese energy and infrastructure investments, notwithstanding some concerns about the BRI. When it comes to the infrastructure projects in Turkey, Japanese and South Korean investments have been increasing as well as Chinese. For example, the Eurasia Tunnel connecting Asia and Europe beneath the Bosporus Strait was constructed by Korean and Turkish firms, while the 1915 Çanakkale Bridge scheduled to open in 2023 is being built by a consortium of South Korean companies. The Türksat 4-A satellite that was manufactured by a Japanese firm together with Turkish engineers trained in Japan provides a good illustration of Japanese contribution to an infrastructure of space technologies in Turkey. The Marmaray tunnel linking Asia to Europe underneath the Bosporus Strait built by a Japanese-Turkish consortium is another good example, which brought Japanese finance as well as Japanese technology and know-how to Turkey.[8] In addition, Turkish start-ups benefit to utilise the Singaporean experience in smart cities development via accessing Singapore's tech ecosystem.[9] By the same token, some most prominent Turkish companies have also been investing in Asian countries such as India, Thailand, and Vietnam. Additionally, Indonesia's relocation plan of its capital from Jakarta to East Kalimantan provides another good opportunity for Turkish construction firms involved in moving Kazakhstan's capital from Almaty to Astana, the willingness to engage in the process is on the table by both countries.[10] A Comprehensive Economic Partnership Agreement, meanwhile, is in deliberation between Turkey and Indonesia as of July 2018, the two countries that are also eager to increase their bilateral trade from nearly 1.5 billion dollars per year to 10 billion dollars by 2023 in sectors ranging from defence to construction.[11] Negotiations for signing an FTA are also underway between Turkey and Thailand, whose bilateral trade is around 1.5 billion dollars per year.[12]

Turkey's South Asia Outreach

Even though the outputs of the Asia Anew Initiative can be mostly begun to be seen over ASEAN and RCEP countries, where Southeast and East Asia stand out as key regions, in fact, South Asia merits an extensive assessment. Besides, Turkey has a strong will to further develop its relations and cooperation with friendly South Asian countries.[13] Turkey's slowly but surely expanding engagement in South Asia covers diverse areas from trade and investment to defence and culture. In recent years, Turkey has not only been increasing its trade volume in the region, but has been also further deepening its presence and influence through its innovative defence industry, government support private sector investments, and effective soft power instruments. While Turkey's major two South Asian trading partners are India and Bangladesh, the main two of the South Asian nations that have placed a special focus on the Turkish defence industry are Bangladesh and Pakistan. Also, Turkey pays special attention to Afghanistan, where it has comprehensively been contributing to the country's reconstruction and modernisation as well as peace, stability and development efforts in many ways from health and education to infrastructure and security for a long time.

Given the social and cultural ties pumped through soft power assets, thanks to the soft power of Turkish TV series, Turkey is gaining huge popularity in the South Asian nations, as well as in nearly every corner of the world. Many Turkish dramas such as Diriliş: Ertuğrul (Resurrection: Ertuğrul), Magnificent Century Sultan Suleiman (Muhteşem Yüzyıl), and Payitaht Abdülhamid have been airing on South Asian TV channels. Moreover, the flourishing interest and promising social, cultural and academic interactions between Turkey and the South Asian people have been growing thanks to Turkey's expanding diplomatic and media networks and Turkey's Presidency for Turks Abroad and Related Communities (YTB) scholarships as well as Turkish foreign aid such as humanitarian and development aid. Besides, Turkish innovations in science, technology, business, and defence have also been attracting the South Asian countries.

In view of country-focused developments, Turkey's interactions have grown mostly with Bangladesh, Pakistan and India, which are the key South Asian countries due to their booming economies and strategic importance; yet the relationships with these countries, especially with India, have not reached the desirable level, unfortunately. With its sustainable development efforts, thanks to its booming economy and young population, Bangladesh is one of the key partners of Turkey's Asia Anew Initiative. The last decade has witnessed the bilateral relations between Turkey and Bangladesh dramatically gathering momentum with several high-level visits and signed agreements. Bangladesh seeks to increase economic cooperation and attract more FDI from Turkey, as well as enhance defence ties and boost cultural bonds. After India, Bangladesh is Turkey's second-biggest trade partner in South Asia with a total trade volume of 1 billion dollars and the two countries have been in talks on a Preferential Trade Agreement (PTA) to expand the economic partnership.[14] Moreover, Bangladesh, which has become the fourth-largest arms buyer from Turkey, is a critical market for the Turkish defence industry. In addition to supplying Otokar-Cobra Light Armoured Vehicles (LAVs) to Bangladesh, Turkey delivered the first batch of the TRG-300 Kaplan missile system with a range of 300 kilometres (186 miles) in June 2021, produced by one of Turkey's defence giants, Roketsan.[15] Turkey also provides military training to members of the Bangladesh Armed Forces. Furthermore, Turkey is seeking to expand its footprint in Bangladesh by taking part to participate in a variety of infrastructure and construction tenders.[16] Besides, Turkey has been giving all-round support to Bangladesh on the Rohingya refugee crisis since 2017, while it maintains its dialogue with Myanmar in order to contribute to a lasting solution of the crisis.[17] As a reflection of the importance Turkey attaches to relations with Bangladesh, the newly built Turkish Embassy compound was inaugurated in December 2020, while Turkey is also planning to build a hospital of international standards in Bangladesh in the near future.[18]

Alongside Bangladesh, the Turkish defence industry has seen considerable attention from Pakistan, a considerable attention that has injected new impetus into the bilateral relations of Turkey and Pakistan over recent years. Yet, both countries have already been enjoying a relationship that is deeply rooted in historical ties over 70 years. Over recent years, thanks to the burgeoning defence ties between the two nations, Turkey has become Pakistan's second-largest arms supplier after China, modestly easing its dependence on the USA and China. One of the largest defence deals between the two nations has been the acquisition of four MILGEM Ada-class corvettes for the Pakistan Navy, which will also involve technology transfer. According to this multibillion deal that was signed in 2018, the first pair of the corvettes will be built by 2023 and the remaining pair by 2024; while two will be built in Turkey, the other two will be built in Pakistan. The MILGEM (Milli Gemi, National Ship) is a Turkish branded project initiated in 2000. Under the MILGEM project, the four Ada-class corvettes (the TCG Heybeliada F-511 in 2011, the TCG Büyükada F-512 in 2013, the TCG Burgazada F-513 in 2018, and the TCG Kınalıada F-514 in 2019) have joined the Turkish Navy, while the first of the four I-class frigates, the Istanbul Frigate, is under construction and is planned to be delivered to the Navy in 2023.[19] Meanwhile, it merits mentioning here that Turkey is one of the 10 countries that can build, design and maintain warships using its national capabilities.

Coming back to the defence relations with the two, the second of the largest defence deals, which was signed in 2018, has been the sale of 1.5 billion dollars worth 30 T-129 Advanced Attack and Tactical Reconnaissance (ATAK) helicopters to Pakistan, which were manufactured by one of Turkey's leading defence firms, the Turkish Aerospace Industries (TAI). TAI has also opened an office in Pakistan's National Science and Technology Park in 2019. Also, Turkey has helped maintain Pakistan's fleet of F-16 fighter aircraft and upgrading three Pakistani submarines. Furthermore, Pakistani military officers have been training in the scope of

Turkey's annual armed forces training exchange programs, since 2000. Meanwhile, Turkey gifted 34 T-37 training aircraft (with spare parts) to Pakistan in 2015.[20]

In considering these improvements in defence relations, even if an FTA is not yet in force and the bilateral trade volume stands at less than 1 billion dollars, there is a strong expectation that the amount will increase in the short run. Moreover, in line with the Strategic Economic Framework and action plan agreed on by the two countries in the last year, Pakistan's connectivity and development plans, covering a wide area from agriculture and industry to science and technology, will pave the way for Turkish projects in infrastructure, construction, energy and technology transfer, while adding impetus to the bilateral trade volume that aims to surpass 1 billion dollars in the near term, and 5 billion dollars by 2023.[21] Meanwhile, Turkey was added to Pakistan's visa-free travel list in line with the country's new tourism policy in 2019, which offers further opportunities for Turkish social and business mobility.[22]

With regard to one of the tiny Himalayan kingdoms in South Asia, Bhutan, even though Turkey recognised Bhutan long ago, diplomatic relations between the two countries were established in 2012. Over the past decade, the bilateral trade volume between the two countries was recorded at approximately 1.5 to 2.5 million dollars. Turkey donated 100 thousand dollars to the country, which was affected by Cyclone Aila in 2009 and contributed 50 thousand dollars for the country's development efforts in 2015; besides, in accordance with the needs of the country, it donated a full-fledged ambulance last year. Moreover, Turkey contributed to the modernisation of the informatics infrastructure of the Bhutanese Ministry of Foreign Affairs in 2016.[23] Meanwhile, Turkey has annually been extending an invitation for a young Bhutanese diplomat to participate in the "International Junior Diplomats Training Program" of the Diplomacy Academy of the Turkish Foreign Ministry since 2011.[24]

In the same vein, Turkey extended assistance to another small Himalayan Kingdom, Nepal, during the transitional period following natural disasters and ten-year-long armed conflicts. In this framework, Turkey conveyed 50 thousand dollars worth of humanitarian assistance for flood victims in 2009 and provided over 97 thousand dollars for the construction of a dormitory for female students of the Kathmandu University. Further, Turkey delivered humanitarian assistance and took part in search-and-rescue operations after the earthquakes that struck

Nepal twice in 2015, and provided 2 million dollars of development assistance. The bilateral trade volume between the two countries has ranged from averaging around 60 to 80 million dollars in the last decade.[25] Additionally, the Turkish government has been providing a few scholarships for Nepalese junior diplomats. Although the tourism interactions are limited with Nepal, thanks to the beginning of direct flights operated by Turkish Airlines as of 2013, in line with the Air Service Agreement signed in 2010, there is still a promising growth option for people-to-people and business contacts between the two countries.[26]

In Lieu of Conclusion: Onward to the Bright Future of Indo-Turkish Ties

The world is going through significant geopolitical changes where Asia has already become a dynamic powerhouse. In view of the fact that the centre of world politics is shifting towards Asia, Turkey, as well as many other countries, has revised its policies in line with its strategy of forging closer ties with the Asian countries. With its Asia Anew Initiative that was launched in order to consolidate its unifying position between Asia and Europe, Turkey intends to breathe new life into its deep-rooted historical and cultural bonds of thousands of years with the Asian nations. On the other hand, Turkey has been facing some heavy risks in its West Asian immediate surroundings (on all its borders indeed) due to the broadening Syrian civil war, and is deeply concerned with the refugee flows coming from war-torn Afghanistan. Furthermore, Turkey's Western relations have recently been extremely erratic, where Turkey has been feeling that Europe and the USA have been ignoring Turkish claims and at times somewhat abandoned by the West during its adversities. As a natural consequence of these fluid global and regional geopolitical scenario, the importance of diversifying relations has surfaced and Asia (among others) has emerged as a desirable destination, which is suitable not just for balancing the Turkish foreign policy approach but also for providing many more new options for its multidimensional and proactive foreign policy goals involving extension of its strategic, economic, military, political, diplomatic, and cultural ties.

When it comes to Turkey's relationship with India, it is worth borrowing this statement from the Turkish Ministry of Foreign Affairs: "Turkey considers India as a friendly country taking firm steps forward to be a global power with its growing economy, huge market, military power, outstanding knowledge in space technology and informatics, rich human resources and deep-rooted historical and cultural heritage".[27] It may not be an exaggeration to say that this friendship between the two nations is an unavoidable fact. When going down the centuries, based on the traces of the Turkish-origin Babur (Mughal) Empire, it can easily be seen that the two nations share historical and cultural bonds that date back deep into history. When coming back to recent history, it should be indicated that the Indian support to the Turkish Liberation War, which later inspired India in its independence struggle, still occupies a special place in the Turkish mind. Furthermore, the Turkish Liberation War and Turkey's founding father, Mustafa Kemal Atatürk, left such a deep impression on India's pacifist independence leader, Mahatma Gandhi, that he said that "I was believing God was an Englishman until Mustafa Kemal Atatürk has defeated them". It is widely believed that India's massive movement to support Turkey that was led by Gandhi was the single mark of inter-faith harmony or of the complete unity of Hindus and Muslims in South Asia. Moreover, India's iconic poet-philosopher and the first non-European Nobel Laureate, Rabindranath Tagore, was also deeply inspired by the success of Turkey in establishing a modern state and the reconstruction of the Turkish nation and notably by Atatürk for whom he said that "Kemal set us an example of a resurgent Asia.... He carried out a crusade against the tyranny of superstition", adding that "for a progressive Asia, we should look towards Turkey". Today, the 41 books on Turkish literature and culture contributed by Atatürk on Tagore's request for the library in Visva Bharati University founded by Tagore are still in this library with a plaque saying they are a gift of love from Turkey.[28] Another impressive illustration of the Indo-Turkish emotional bond is that a central avenue in Delhi is named after Mustafa Kemal Atatürk, while one of the central avenues in Ankara is named after Mahatma Gandhi, and another after Rabindranath Tagore, in which his bust is placed as well.

As Turkey's Ambassador to India, Fırat Sunel, notes, "India and Turkey have a long history of close ties and there are many commonalities based on history and culture", drawing attention that "Turkey has a very special association with India".[29] Admittedly, Sufism and Mevlana Jalaluddin Rumi are the two more glowing examples in the context of the enrichment of Indo-Turkish links. Moreover, the shared historical and cultural links of the two nations can be further exemplified by their soft power, which exerts a reciprocal influence that grows in a short while on one another.

Within this scope, Turkish TV serials are very popular in India and likewise Indian series and Bollywood are popular in Turkey so much that the Turkish TV channel "Channel 7" (Kanal 7) broadcasts mostly Indian dramas, while Indian cinema films are watched frequently on TRT. Furthermore, Turkish cuisine has been gaining popularity in India and the famous Turkish dessert, Baklava that has recently filled most of Indian shops is a good illustration in this context. One more example that illustrates the mutual soft power connections between India and Turkey is that the Indian Embassy in Ankara runs yoga courses in the embassy premises and organises regular events regarding the International Day of Yoga, Mahatma Gandhi Lectures, the Festival of India in Turkey, India by the Bosporus, and Tagore Festival, and so on.

Besides the soft power, the flourishing tourism and trade links have injected new momentum into the bilateral relations of Turkey and India. In regard to bilateral tourism interactions, Turkey has hosted about 2.5 lakh (250 thousand) Indian tourists recently and one of the Turkish goals is to increase it to 10 lakh (1 million) by 2023. Apart from being a destination for Indian weddings, Turkey is becoming a preferable destination for Bollywood shoots, India's MICE events, and the FIT India Movement. When it comes to bilateral economic ties, Turkish President Erdoğan's latest visit to India with about a 150-member strong business delegation on 30 April-1 May 2017 as the first stop on his itinerary that included visits to Russia, China and the USA, contributed to the revival of bilateral trade. As of 2020, Turkey's trade with India has reached about 8 billion dollars, despite the corona virus pandemic; 20 billion dollars is targeted by 2023, something that shows the future direction of both countries. Ironically, even as the bilateral trade has been gaining momentum recently, there is no FTA or/and a Comprehensive Economic Partnership between the two countries yet. Meanwhile, India is one of the over 150 countries that has received aid from Turkey acting with the understanding of "a friend in need is a friend indeed" for the fight against the corona virus pandemic, with the boxes that bore the words of Rumi "There is hope after despair and many suns after darkness".

To conclude, given this broad multifaceted backdrop of Indo-Turkish ties, the two countries' nearly century-old relationship, even beyond the bond of a century, is yet to live up to its full potential. Historical and cultural bonds pumped through soft power tools are strongly able to help the enhancement of relations between the two states in every fields. Within the scope of the Asia Anew Initiative, Turkey attaches strategic importance to India particularly in line with its growing economy, space, science and technology transfer, where India has made significant leaps recently. Even if the relations between Turkey and India have soured occasionally, when Turkey looks at India, it does not see challenges; instead it sees common history, friendship and vast opportunity to further advance its ties. Once both India and Turkey do not allow their opposing views on certain issues to hold hostage the further development of bilateral relations, they will likely be poised for a much more productive relationship in almost every field. Indeed, Turkey and India have many opportunities to significantly improve their bilateral cooperation, if both countries take sincere and concrete steps to this end. Affirming the future horizons of cooperation in all fields hinges not only on allowing political misreading or misunderstandings. Once the two countries realise this, there is no other reason not to have better relations. Amid some natural differences of opinion, bilateral ties can only succeed to reach a bright future if both countries manage to walk a fine line with these differences. As India's Ambassador to Turkey, Sanjay Panda, points out, "It is high time that we put aside external issues that distract us from our larger goals. It is time now to recognise this big picture and bring about a qualitative transformation in our bilateral engagement. It is only then that India and Turkey can realise their full potential as natural partners in the 21st century".[30]

ENDNOTES

1. Sidhant Sibal, "Turkish Envoy Firat Sunel Bats for Furthering Ankara-Delhi Ties; Calls It a Fundamental Goal", *WION*, 3 September 2021, (Retrieved on 23 October 2021 from https://www.wionews.com/india-news/turkish-envoy-firat-sunel-bats-for-furthering-ankara-delhi-ties-calls-it-a-fundamental-goal-410543); Also see Nayanima Basu, "India, Turkey Don't Need 'Reset', Partners Can Have Opposing View on Issues: Turkish Envoy", *The Print*, 28 July 2021, (retrieved on 23 October 2021 from https://theprint.in/diplomacy/india-turkey-dont-need-reset-partners-can-have-opposing-view-on-issues-new-turkish-envoy/704199/).
2. "Opening Speech of Foreign Minister Mevlüt Çavusoglu at Asia Anew Workshop", *Republic of Turkey Ministry of Foreign Affairs*, 26 December 2019, (Retrieved on 11 October 2021 from https://www.mfa.gov.tr/sayin-bakanimizin-yeniden-asya-calistayi-hitabi-26-12-19.en.mfa).
3. "Time to Make New Breakthroughs in Asia", *Daily Sabah*, 18 January 2021, (Retrieved on 11 October 2021 from https://www.dailysabah.com/business/economy/time-to-make-new-breakthroughs-in-asia-turkeys-trade-minister-says).
4. "Turkey's Relations with The Asia-Pacific Region", *Republic of Turkey Ministry of*

Foreign Affairs, (Retrieved on 11 October 2021 from https://www.mfa.gov.tr/turkeys-relations-with-east-asia-and-the-pacific.en.mfa).

5. "Hedef ve Öncelikli Ülkeler (Target and Priority Countries)", *Republic of Turkey Ministry of Trade,* (Retrieved on 13 October 2021 from https://www.ticaret.gov.tr/ihracat/pazara-giris/hedef-ve-oncelikli-ulkeler).
6. "Free Trade Agreements", *Republic of Turkey Ministry of Trade,* (Retrieved on 13 October 2021 from https://www.trade.gov.tr/free-trade-agreements).
7. "Turkey Balance of Trade", *Trading Economics,* (Retrieved on 13 October 2021 from https://tradingeconomics.com/turkey/balance-of-trade).
8. For Further Reading, See Altay Atlı, "The Political Economy of Turkey's Relations with the Asia-Pacific", in *Turkey's Political Economy in the 21st Century,* Emel Parlar Dal (ed.), London: Palgrave Macmillan, 2020, pp. 271-296.
9. Ayman Falak Medina, "Turkey to Forge Closer Ties with ASEAN and Asia", *ASEAN Briefing,* 28 January 2021, (Retrieved on 16 October 2021 from https://www.aseanbriefing.com/news/turkey-to-forge-closer-ties-with-asean-and-asia/)
10. "Turkish Contractors Ready to Build Indonesia's New Capital", *Daily Sabah,* 24 June 2020, (Retrieved on 16 October 2021 from https://www.dailysabah.com/business/economy/turkish-contractors-ready-to-build-indonesias-new-capital)
11. Pizaro Gozali Idrus, "Turkey, Indonesia to Enhance Trade, Defence Cooperation", *Anadolu Agency,* 22 December 2020, (Retrieved on 16 October 2021 from https://www.aa.com.tr/en/asia-pacific/turkey-indonesia-to-enhance-trade-defense-cooperation/2085034).
12. "Turkey-Thailand Economic and Trade Relations", *Republic of Turkey Ministry of Foreign Affairs* (Retrieved on 17 October 2021 from https://www.mfa.gov.tr/turkey_s-commercial-and-economic-relations-with-thailand.en.mfa).
13. "Turkey's Relations with South Asian Countries", *Republic of Turkey Ministry of Foreign Affairs* (Retrieved on 18 October 2021 from https://www.mfa.gov.tr/turkey_s-relations-with-south-asian-countries.en.mfa).
14. "Turkey-Bangladesh Economic and Trade Relations", *Republic of Turkey Ministry of Foreign Affairs* (Retrieved on 18 October 2021 from https://www.mfa.gov.tr/turkey_bangladesh-economic-and-trade-relations.en.mfa).
15. SM Najmus Sakib, "Bangladesh Stepping Up Defence Ties with Turkey", *Anadolu Agency,* 21 June 2021 (Retrieved on 18 October 2021 from https://www.aa.com.tr/en/asia-pacific/bangladesh-stepping-up-defense-ties-with-turkey/2280868).
16. Sorvar Alam, "Turkish President's Visit to Bangladesh Will Boost Ties", *Anadolu Agency,* 4 February 2021 (Retrieved on 18 October 2021 from https://www.aa.com.tr/en/asia-pacific/-turkish-president-s-visit-to-bangladesh-will-boost-ties-/2133757).
17. "Relations between Turkey and Myanmar", *Republic of Turkey Ministry of Foreign Affairs* (Retrieved on 18 October 2021 from https://www.mfa.gov.tr/relations-between-turkey-and-myanmar.en.mfa).
18. "Turkey Opens New Embassy Compound in Dhaka, Pledges Increased Cooperation with Bangladesh", *Daily Sabah,* 23 December 2020 (Retrieved on 18 October 2021 from https://www.dailysabah.com/politics/diplomacy/turkey-opens-new-embassy-compound-in-dhaka-pledges-increased-cooperation-with-bangladesh).
19. For further details, See STM, "MILGEM Project" (https://www.stm.com.tr/en/our-solutions/naval-engineering/milgem-project).
20. Mateen Haider, "Turkey to Provide 34 T-37 Aircraft to Pakistan Free of Cost", *Dawn,*

28 October 2015 (Retrieved on 19 October 2021 from https://www.dawn.com/news/1215960).

21. "FTA, Greater Engagement to Add Impetus to Turkey-Pakistan Ties", *Daily Sabah,* 23 July 2021 (Retrieved on 19 October 2021 from https://www.dailysabah.com/business/economy/fta-greater-engagement-to-add-impetus-to-turkey-pakistan-ties).
22. Islamuddin Sajid, "Pakistan Adds Turkey to Visa-Free Travel List", *Anadolu Agency,* 12 March 2019 (Retrieved on 19 October from https://www.aa.com.tr/en/asia-pacific/pakistan-adds-turkey-to-visa-free-travel-list/1416282).
23. "Turkey-Bhutan Relations", *Republic of Turkey Ministry of Foreign Affairs* (Retrieved on 20 October 2021 from https://www.mfa.gov.tr/bhutan-economical.en.mfa).
24. "Bilateral Relations: Turkey", *Royal Government of Bhutan Ministry of Foreign Affairs* (Retrieved on 20 October 2021 from https://www.mfa.gov.bt/?page_id=8824).
25. "Turkey-Nepal Political, Economic and Trade Relations", *Republic of Turkey Ministry of Foreign Affairs* (Retrieved on 20 October 2021 from https://www.mfa.gov.tr/sub.en.mfa?0a8757c8-8cf7-4c12-8375-632e6c18b72d).
26. "Nepal-Turkey Relations", *Government of Nepal Ministry of Foreign Affairs* (Retrieved on 20 October 2021 from https://mofa.gov.np/nepal-turkey-relations/).
27. See "Turkey-India Political Relations", *Republic of Turkey Ministry of Foreign Affairs* (Retrieved on 21 October 2021 from https://www.mfa.gov.tr/turkey-india-relations.en.mfa).
28. See "PM's Remarks at the Naming of Rabindranath Tagore Avenue", *Government of India Press Information Bureau Prime Minister's Office Archive,* 18 September 2003 (Retrieved on 22 October 2021 from https://archive.pib.gov.in/archive/releases98/lyr2003/rsep2003/18092003/r1809200310.html); Also see Can Erözden, "Iconic Indian Poet Commemorated in Turkey", *Anadolu Agency* (Retrieved on 22 October 2021 from https://www.aa.com.tr/en/asia-pacific/iconic-indian-poet-commemorated-in-turkey/1473757).
29. Prashant Nayak, "Turkey Has a Very Special Association with India", *Travel Trade Journal,* vol. 11, issue 11, September 2021, pp. 8-9 (Retrieved on 23 October 2021 from https://online.fliphtml5.com/opbnh/marj/#p=1).
30. "Turkey-India Relations Need 'Qualitative Change': Envoy", *Anadolu Agency,* 26 January 2021 (Retrieved on 23 October 2021 from https://www.aa.com.tr/en/turkey/turkey-india-relations-need-qualitative-change-envoy/2122867).

14

Security Dynamic in West Asia and Defence Cooperation with India

Lt Gen Rakesh Sharma

Introduction

India has had deep historic relations with West Asia, with the Indus Valley civilization having trade links with the Dilmun civilisation of modern Bahrain. The discovery of Indus Valley-type seals, pottery and other implements of around 2000 BCE in the Arabian Gulf and Oman Peninsula connect with Indus civilization in multiple ways. In the 3rd century BCE, Egypt's Ptolemy II and the Mauryan emperors, Chandragupta Maurya and Asoka, had exchanged ambassadors. The Arabs brought Islam to India in Kerala and Sind as early as the 7th century BC. Farsi was the official language of the Mughal court and India's official language until 1835.

India had an expansive role in the First World War, in which Indian soldiers fought in the Middle East (latter-day West Asia). In fact, West Asia was the most important theatre of war for India during the Great War. Four of the six expeditionary forces India provided for the war effort were sent into action in West Asia. *Indian soldiers played a key role in British campaigns in Europe and West Asia during World War I.* Indian infantry and cavalry played an important role in protecting the Suez Canal in Egypt, and later in the battle for Palestine. Indian cavalry played a crucial role in gaining control of the city of Haifa. Indian mountain batteries and infantry units also played an important role in the ill-fated Gallipoli campaign. The most significant campaign of the war for Indian troops took place in Mesopotamia (modern-day Iraq), where over 500,000 Indians served. In recent history in the 20th century, the Indian rupee was the legal tender in the UAE, Bahrain, Kuwait, Oman, and Qatar up to 1957. Gwadar, on Pakistan's Makran coast, was in Oman's possession until 1958. Post-independence India had established diplomatic relations with different Middle Eastern states.

Post-Independence, Indian links with West Asia can be sub-divided into two periods prior to and after 1991—that is the disintegration of the USSR, end of the Cold War and opening up of the Indian economy. India's post-Independence historic links with relations with West Asia had been affected by Arab and Iranian support for Pakistan. India supported Egypt during the Suez crisis and consequent the 1967 war with Israel. India has a close relationship with Iraq under Saddam Hussein, and undertook a large number of projects in Iraq and provided military training to the Iraqi air force. Iraq was India's leading oil supplier. India had always supported the Palestinian cause with and denunciation of Israel's policies. The 1979 Soviet occupation of Afghanistan and the consequent events led to the emergence of a special relationship between Pakistan and Saudi Arabia, which included stationing of Pakistani troops in Saudi Arabia and the funding of Pakistani arms acquisitions and its emerging nuclear weapons program. The Organization of Islamic Cooperation (OIC) did not however allow India to participate after the inaugural session due to Pakistan's pressures. In fact, the OIC and its Contact Group adopted, at Pakistani instigation, strongly worded anti-India recommendations, resolutions and statements regularly on Kashmir and on the supposed plight of Indian Muslims.

The end of the Cold War was followed by the strong upward transition of the Indian economy. In time, Indian-West Asian political, strategic, and economic relations became being primarily shaped by India's policy responses to evolving geopolitical ground realities internationally and in the region. There is hence an underlying importance of strategy in the relationship between India and West Asia.

The central theme of this chapter is to delve into the strategic relationship between India and West Asia and the steadily increasing defence cooperation. The enunciation of a nation's short and long-term security strategies is inevitably based on appraisal of the prevailing and perspective geo-strategic environment. It can be argued that in addition to domestic politics, bureaucratic politics, organizational inertia, group think, psychological barriers and learning the wrong lessons from history—failure of security strategies is also due to inappropriate assessment of the environment.[1] The greatest challenge of our times is to be able to make correct and timely assessments of the changes taking place and the nature and extent of challenges and opportunities they present.[2] West Asia is an all-important region in India's security calculus.

Broad Ambit of India-West Asia Relationship

India's economic, commercial and security interests in West Asia encompass an expanding and vast array of areas including trade, investment, energy security, migrant workers and Diaspora, counter-terrorism and maritime security. The security considerations on West Asia can largely be considered in three distinct and most significant parameters. First and foremost is the importance of West Asia for energy security. India is dependent on imports for 80 per cent of its oil needs, of which roughly 55 per cent oil and 85 per cent of its natural gas requirements is sourced from the Persian Gulf region. It is also apparent that with the growth of the Indian economy, the energy requirements are bound to increase.

Energy security has remained a key ingredient of India's interest in West Asia. Saudi Arabia was India's top supplier of crude oil (20 per cent) until 2015. For all the diversification of bilateral trade between India and the Gulf states, the backbone of investments between them has been the hydrocarbon sector. Bilateral trade with the GCC countries reached $ 150 billion in 2016, with the UAE and Saudi Arabia accounting for $ 60 billion and $ 39 billion, respectively. For 2019-20, India's hydrocarbon trade with the Gulf region was worth $ 62 billion, more than 36 per cent of the total hydrocarbon trade—underscoring the critical significance of energy security that forms the fundamental matrix of relations between the two.[3] India's oil trade with the GCC—at over $ 135 billion, up from $ 5.5 billion in 2001—is a clear indication of New Delhi's principal consideration of the Middle East as a reliable source of energy. The common perception that the oil and natural gas trade is the only determinant of India's foreign policy towards the West Asian nations is, however, shortsighted.

Second is the all-important issue of the Indian Diaspora, which plays an important role in India's policy towards West Asia. A Diaspora of about 9 million gives India a creditable soft power advantage in its relationship with the West Asian states. The Diaspora hence becomes the bottom line to this relationship, earning remittances of around $ 40 billion annually. The Indian Diaspora has not always been an integral part of India's foreign, economic and security policy. The significant pull factors are primarily vast employment opportunities ranging from workers for the oil fields to skilled engineers. With the rapid development of the Middle East riding on the booming oil industry, migration from India to countries like Saudi Arabia, Qatar, the UAE, and Oman has been to work in varied fields like banking, information & technology, business, and the like.[4] The existence of a huge Indian community in Saudi Arabia and its contribution to the economy has been a catalyst for the Saudi Arabian Government to improve ties with India.

Indian expatriates have constituted a substantial, if not dominant, share of the regional labour market. The Diaspora also has considerable influence on the bilateral relations between the India and various West Asian countries, and the region as a whole. The large Indian Diaspora lays an immense responsibility on the Indian Government. In 1990, consequent to the occupation of Kuwait by Iraq, the immediate concern was the fate of the Indians in Kuwait and Iraq. A massive operation was undertaken for almost two months that managed to airlift over 170,000 Indians from Kuwait by air and sea. On receiving reports of shortages of food in Kuwait and Iraq, India sent 9,775 tonnes of essential food supplies. Four thousand seven hundred seventy three tonnes of these food items were distributed among Indian nationals.[5] India also carried out major evacuation operations from a war-like zone of Israel-Lebanon in 2006, bringing back home around 2,300 people, including some from Sri Lanka and Nepal. Similarly, consequent to the COVID-19 pandemic in 2020, another major air and sea evacuation was undertaken from West Asia, in which over 300,000 migrant Indians had registered. This will remain a major security challenge in perpetuity.

Third, the "Look West" policy assumed significance and focussed attention in India's policy approach with Prime Minister Modi's remarks at the 'Make in India' conference in New Delhi on 26 September, 2014, *"For a long time Look East policy is under discussion. I would like to talk about Link West"*. Thenceforth, Indian policy and diplomatic outreach has put the region into a policy priority and the "Look West" policy became a bright spot on Indian policy pursuit and a multi-layered engagement began. The most remarkable outcome of the "Look West" policy and dense diplomatic outreach of Prime Minister Modi in the region has been the perception of the Organisation of Islamic Countries (OIC), the 57-member organization of the Muslim world. The OIC summit invitation to India and participation of the External Affairs Minister of India, Smt. Sushma Swaraj in Abu Dhabi, is the most successful outcome of the Indian "Look West" policy in the region as Pakistan has failed to influence the forum against India. Pakistan failed again to make the OIC condemn the Indian government's revoking the special status of Jammu and Kashmir under Article 370.[6]

As a whole, India has tried to maintain cordial relations with most of the West Asian nations and has attempted to maintain a certain level of neutrality in the region, although, in recent times there has been greater interaction between India and the Middle East in terms of political and strategic alliances.

Defence Cooperation

Defence cooperation is part and parcel of foreign policy goals in furtherance of Indian national interests. The foreign policy of India seeks to promote an environment of peace and stability in the region and in the world to ensure India's accelerated socio-economic development and safeguard national security. Geographically, the Persian Gulf and West Asia are India's extended neighbourhood, and hence its extraordinary importance. As argued above, it is the source for India's ever-expanding needs of energy. It is also huge markets for Indian goods, services, and skilled manpower.

In the keynote address on 18 February 2008, on 'Defence Cooperation as a Tool for Enhancing National Interests', at New Delhi, the Defence Minister had defined Defence Cooperation as *"any arrangement between two or more nations where their armed forces work together to achieve mutual aims and objectives"*. Defence cooperation has a vast ambit; it aims at sharing operational and doctrinal expertise, joint operations and military training to enhance capabilities. It also aims at investment in defence manufacturing and production, sales of weapons and military technologies, and easing defence equipment acquisition and procurement. In time, friendly countries move towards intelligence sharing as part of defence cooperation. At the national level, it is extended to all the three services—army, navy and air force—to enhance domain awareness of partner countries.

In some matters, the Pakistan factor and its influence in the OIC had loomed large in India's growing strategic interest and interaction with West Asia. Previously, the West Asian nations were undertaking a balancing act while dealing with India and Pakistan. It is apparent with the changing times that India is no longer seen through the Pakistani prism by the West Asian nations. This is most evident in the favourable response for India as against Pakistan especially with regard to the Kashmir issue, Pulwama attack, India's abrogation of Article 370 and 35A and the invitation to India to the OIC meeting in 2019. All these incidents clearly reflect India's growing popularity in the West Asian region.

The intent to cooperate in the defence sector with West Asia took birth in 2001 when India signed an agreement with Iran. Post-2014, the move got an intensive fillip with India's introduction of 'Link West' and 'Act West' policies. Since then, India's relations with West Asian nations has seen a transformational change from India being a benign power and from mere transactional interactions to a pragmatic strategic partner with inclusion of non-traditional aspects, wherein, defence and security cooperation are most notable components.

India-West Asia Strategic Dialogues and Interactions

Strategic dialogues are an overworked phrase, though designed to have regular high level comprehensive and forward looking exchanges on a wide range of issues. These may and may not transcend to strategic relationships or partnerships, but do bring about mutual understanding of respective positions, and hence strengthen international order, peace and stability. West Asia gives India access to the oil and natural gas resources but also a larger influence on global geopolitical structures. The westward trend in India's foreign policy has not only bolstered its relations with the region but has also strengthened its stand on Kashmir by gaining the support of major Gulf countries on the issue. This shift in relationship is the creation of a wide gamut of unfolding events bilaterally, regionally and internationally. India's growing economic standing and strategic autonomy has made her a responsible and reliable nation. This India's renewed position is acknowledged by West Asian nations and is leading to expansion of relations.

Though India's defence-related interactions with the Middle East date back to 1971, when Israel supplied mortars and ammunition to India during its war with Pakistan, formal memorandums of understanding

(MoUs) on defence cooperation, with the region, were only signed since 2001 (with Iran). Gradually, New Delhi signed agreements on defence and security cooperation with five other major countries in the region, such as the UAE (2003), Qatar (2008), Saudi Arabia (2014), Oman (2016) and Jordan (2018).[7] Contextually, hence, defence relationships stand elevated to credible levels, adding on to strategic partnerships that include economy and trade, expatriates and energy.

India's defence dialogues have yet to mature with West Asian nations. According to SIPRI Factsheet 2021, around 13 per cent of arms imported by India come from Israel, the third-largest arms provider to India. India's relations with Israel had however existed with India's support to Palestine. On 24 August 1994, India and Israel had signed a unique secrecy agreement. While the exact details encompassing the agreement are classified, a $ 3 million joint science and technology fund was set up to facilitate R&D collaboration.

PM Narender Modi's visit to Israel in July 2017 (the first by an Indian PM) is what truly sparked the development of strong political ties, and both the countries used this rare occasion to raise the status of bilateral relations to that of a "strategic partnership". What had led to further expansion of the overall ties was the reciprocal visit of his Israeli counterpart, Benjamin Netanyahu, to India in January 2018. For India and Israel that had kept their defence dealings shrouded in secrecy for a prolonged period, the mentioned visits reflected the importance accorded by both sides to promoting bilateral ties, with defence cooperation one of the mainstays.[8] The intensification of defence cooperation is signified by existing collaboration programs, involving Israeli technology in the field of missiles, air defence systems, unmanned aerial vehicles (UAVs), and more.

Initially, since the 2000s, the Indo-Gulf military-security cooperation has been mainly confined to joint military exercises, naval ship visits and training of military personnel. However, gradually formalised mechanisms, such as the Delhi Declaration and the Riyadh Declaration, were signed in 2006 and 2010 respectively, between India and Saudi Arabia. The Indian Ocean Naval Symposium-IONS was established in 2008, in which all the Gulf countries are members, and several bilateral institutional agreements added vigour to defence and military-security cooperation. 'Link West' has facilitated enhancing the strategic component to the relations through regular high level visits to and from the countries with both ministerial and military-to-military interaction, joint military training, national security council level talks, signing of MoUs and agreements on counter-piracy, counter-terrorism and counter-extremism, maritime security, intelligence sharing, prisoner repatriation, etc. India has since then initiated staff talks, that is, Army, Air Force, Navy and Ministry of Defence (MoD) interactions with Israel (2005 all Services, 2002 Defence Secretary level), Oman (2019 Army, 2017 Navy, 2007 Air Force; 2006 Defence Secretary level), Qatar (2010 Joint Secretary level), Saudi Arabia (2020 Army, 2012 Joint Secretary level), UAE (2020 Army, 2007 Navy; 2003 Joint Secretary level).[9]

The transition in Indian-Saudi Arabia Strategic Relations is most significant. For the first time, an MoU on Indo-Saudi defence cooperation was signed during the visit of the then Crown Prince and Defence Minister (current king), Salman bin Abdulaziz Al-Saud, to India in February 2014 that emphasised expertise, training and defence industry cooperation. The India-Saudi Arabia Joint Committee on Defence Cooperation (JCDC) enables both sides to conduct regular meetings (4th round held in January 2019 in Riyadh) and identify areas of mutual interest and cooperation. India and Saudi Arabia have begun to explore the possibilities of initiating joint-production programmes into their defence partnerships. Progress is likely with the signing of the MoU between the Saudi General Authority of Military Industries and India's Department of Defence Production, Ministry of Defence, concerning collaboration in military acquisition, industries, research, development and technology. Taking the ties to newer heights, India and Saudi Arabia agreed in February 2019 to constitute a Comprehensive Security Dialogue at the National Security Adviser (NSA) level and set up a Joint Working Group on Counter-Terrorism. Conduct of regular NSA-level security dialogues would enable both sides to explore new areas of cooperation in the security realm. The visit of General M.M. Naravane, the Chief of Army Staff of India, to Saudi Arabia's National Defence University is noteworthy.

By upgrading the bilateral ties to Comprehensive Strategic Partnership during PM Modi's visit to the UAE in February 2015, the military-security dimension of India-UAE cooperation has gained momentum. Cooperation in the field of counter-terrorism/radicalisation/extremism, maritime security, intelligence sharing, military exercises, manufacture of defence items, Strategic Security Dialogues, capacity building, cyber security, anti-money laundering, drug trafficking, trans-national crimes, extradition arrangements as well as police training have become some of the patterns of the evolving security cooperation. The renewal of an agreement on defence cooperation in 2014 provided a general framework for strengthening ties in these specific areas. India has similar arrangements with other major Gulf nations, prominent among them being Qatar and Oman.

The joint statement released after Iranian President Hassan Rouhani's visit to India in February 2018, acknowledged the growing interaction between the two countries' National Security Councils. It was also agreed to enhance regular and institutionalised consultations on matters concerning terrorism, security and related issues such as organised crime, money laundering, drug trafficking and cyber crime.

Military/Naval Interactions and Military Exercises

The region's significance is also established by the fact that of the six major global choke points, four lie in West Asia. The Straits of Hormuz and Gulf of Aden are critical choke points for the energy trade, flow of workforce, and capital and consumer goods. Given the significance and importance of these choke points, they are vulnerable to maritime challenges such as sea piracy, trafficking, smuggling and terrorism. The Indian Navy has expanded its operations in the Western Indian Ocean, the Gulf of Aden and the Persian Gulf. According to the Ministry of Defence Annual Reports (2013-2019), the Indian Navy has a major maritime role to play in the Gulf because of its multidimensional capabilities and active presence in the region. These multidimensional capabilities include Maritime Domain Awareness.

The conduct of joint military exercises is now regular. In May 2016, the air forces conducted Desert Eagle II bilateral air combat exercise at Al Dhafra airbase at Abu Dhabi.[10] Similarly, maritime security and training have become important areas of cooperation involving the two navies. In February 2020, Indian and UAE maritime agencies carried out joint exercises as part of a goodwill visit of Indian Coast Guard Ship ICGS *Samudra Paheredar* (specialised in marine pollution control), and the exercise included "Marine Pollution Response, Maritime Search and Rescue and Maritime Law enforcement". In March 2018, two Indian Navy ships—INS *Gomati* and INS *Kolkata*—held the first bilateral exercise codenamed 'Gulf Star 1', off the coast of Abu Dhabi.[11] India-UAE Navy bilateral exercise 'Gulf Star' off the UAE was held in March 2018. These activities are crucial from the standpoint of advancing the shared maritime security objectives of both the countries in the Gulf and the Indian Ocean Region. Coordination on terrorism response activities have been initiated by conducting joint military-military training programs, such as the one held by India and Oman in 2017.

Joint Defence Production and Trade

Defence cooperation and exercises become all the more important as not only there is going to be a huge competition in the Gulf defence market post the normalisation of relations with Israel but, additionally, India's two adversaries, China and Pakistan, are already investing increasingly in the Gulf. Notably, 50 per cent of arms and ammunition from Pakistan's Ordnance Factory are exported to Gulf Cooperation Council countries since long. While it is obvious that the region is not going to immediately replace its age old reliable partners in the field to accommodate India, there is, however, an impetus provided recently by the Indian Government to expand exports of a vast range of defence products that can be supplied to the region at competitive prices and with better quality.

To make defence cooperation between India and West Asia a success, continued interactions are in the Indian interest, given that China is already pitching strongly with the West Asian nations. There are clear signs that China is going to invest heavily in the region. Therefore, India needs to further its interactions with the region with growing engagements in the defence field which will not only help in elevating its indigenous industries but will also cater to the region's diversification drive and Vision 2030.

Within the framework of the *Make in India* initiative, there is the likelihood of Indo-Emirati joint-production of defence platforms in India. The prospects appear to be promising with the launch of the UAE-based EDGE, a company that is set to reposition the country as a "notable global player in advanced technology. In all likelihood, Indian defence firms will forge a partnership with EDGE, exploring opportunities in the development of advanced defence products, which would be beneficial to both countries. Indicating an initial progress in potential Indo-Emirati arms trade, India's Ordnance Factory Board (OFB) signed a deal worth $ 45.75 million with the UAE (in August 2019) to supply around 50,000 artillery shells used with Bofors guns. Oman is the first geo-strategically located GCC country with which India has signed an MoU on defence cooperation in 2005. Presently, both countries have established robust defence cooperation not only in the maritime domain but also in the training of several Omani cadets and military officials in Indian military institutions.[12]

Military-security cooperation comprising arms trade as well as technology transfer and licensed production emerged as an important dimension of the Indo-Israeli strategic relationship. Importantly, from 2014 onwards, Israel's share in India's defence market began to increase significantly. For instance, during the period 2015-2019, India's arms imports from Israel increased by 175 per cent, making the latter New Delhi's second largest supplier of major arms.[13]

Transnational Linkages to Terrorism

Commonly shared threat perceptions from non-state actors, including the Al Qaeda, remnants of outfits like the Islamic State of Iraq and Syria (ISIS) and its tentacles in South Asia, the phenomenon of violent extremism and radicalisation, cross-border terrorism, terror financing, money laundering, etc., are some attributing factors for bringing closer the capitals of the West Asian nations and India in the recent period. Undoubtedly, cooperation in the military-security sphere forms the backbone of the growing strategic partnership.[14] This fillip has significantly contributed to the augmentation of military-security ties with West Asia. There is predominant focus on counter-terrorism, money laundering, cyber security, organised crime, human trafficking and anti-piracy.

The deepening of India-Gulf Arab relations manifested itself in various declarations and Memoranda of Understanding on trade, defence and investments, extended to the realm of security, that is, counter-terrorism. This is significant as the rise of the Islamic State as well as Al-Qaeda in the Indian Subcontinent (AQIS) towards the end of 2014 had led to apprehension of involvement of Indian nationals abroad. These anxieties have been belied as the Indian people's involvement has been insignificant, though the larger population has been at the risk of radicalization. The Gulf has been used as a haven by organizations such as the Student Islamic Movement of India (SIMI) and Indian Mujahideen (IM) even longer than AQ and IS.[15] Thus, many communication networks have been developed by Indian terrorists in the Gulf, which is also home to a large number of

Pakistanis. Due to the large migrant population in the UAE, frequent travels of terrorist group members between India and Pakistan and the Gulf nations has not been viewed with much suspicion. Over the years, such individuals have leveraged the economic opportunities in the Gulf nations to raise funds and/or conduct businesses to later finance operations and exchange information.

There are three focal points of counter-terrorism cooperation between India and its Gulf partners—terror financing, persons of interest, and travel routes. A significant amount money transferred from the Gulf to India is channelled through the informal *hawala or unregulated trust-based* system. Its unregulated nature also makes it attractive for criminals, money launderers, and terrorists. The Indian Mujahideen (IM) chief financer, Abdul Wahid Sidibappa, has used the *hawala* system as a financial pipeline from the UAE to India.[16] The Lashkar-e-Taiba had channelled money via the Gulf to orchestrate the 26/11 Mumbai attack.[17] There are also charities reportedly transferring funds though varied formal and informal methods. Combating terror financing mandates close cooperation between GCC countries and India.

A large number of Indians travel to the Gulf nations either to work, or as stopover destinations, making it difficult for intelligence agencies to detect suspicious persons. It is vital for immigration authorities in the respective countries to cooperate and share information of interest. Methods of such cooperation should also include development of common databases and joint training for authorities in dealing with suspicious persons. These operations would also encourage the formation of networks between various security officials from the respective nations boosting counter-terrorism efforts.[18]

India has also been concerned by the fact that the Gulf nations are used as sanctuaries by various individuals wanted by the country. Chief among these individuals is Dawood Ibrahim, mastermind of the 1993 Mumbai attacks. Dawood is based in Pakistan, though he has significant property and other financial assets in the UAE.[19] To disable and apprehend these criminal masterminds that operate from the Gulf nations, and operate nefariously in India, better cooperation is mandated.

China-Pakistan Factors in India-West Asia Defence Relationship

There are two major factors relating to India and West Asia having even better defence relationship. China, under the Belt and Road Initiative, has made intensive inroads into West Asia. The China-Central Asia-West Asia Economic Corridor is one such grandiose plan. West Asia is considered as one of the most critical regions for China as it lies at the crossroads of three important continents—Europe, Africa and Asia. Along with them the Mediterranean Sea, the Red Sea, the Arabian Sea, the Caspian Sea, and the Black Sea converge. More than half of the imports of China's crude oil originate from West Asia. Saudi Arabia is viewed as one of the most important trading partners with China, with the export of Saudi oil and petrochemicals primarily. The UAE lies on the Strait of Hormuz through which the majority of China's oil imports transit. Iran is another very important state that China has wanted to have cordial relations with an aim of expanding its energy supplies. China already has strategic partnerships with Saudi Arabia, the UAE, Iran, Egypt, and Israel. China has deep pockets but little soft power, while India has historic and cultural relations that must be made to compensate for the BRI.

Pakistan and the Gulf countries have long shared a bond, which was initially premised on religion and strategic ties, and has grown to include economic relations. The military relationship includes training and security cooperation, while economic relations are largely tied to the Pakistani migrant worker community that has a significant presence in the region. The military relationship includes training and security cooperation. Pakistan's army chief, General Qamar Javed Bajwa's two-day visit to Qatar in January 2021, was showcased as a routine visit, after a tense year in Pakistan-Gulf relations, suggesting that Pakistan's role in the Gulf's security architecture is diminishing.[20] Even the OIC did not accept Pakistan's request to convene a foreign ministers' meeting to discuss the issue of the abrogation of Articles 370/35A of the Indian Constitution, as they related to Jammu and Kashmir. Saudi Arabia and the UAE, which once stood with Pakistan on Kashmir, did not criticise India's move. The UAE honoured Indian Prime Minister Narendra Modi with a prestigious award soon after the decision was announced, and Saudi Arabia invited him to a glittering investment forum in Riyadh. Both countries have developed closer economic and security ties with India in recent years.

Conclusion

In sum, India has initiated strategic dialogues/interactions and defence cooperation with a large number of West Asian nations over the past two decades, most of them in the last seven years. Much success is evident in these strategic partnerships. In the long term economy, trade, energy and expatriates or the Indian Diaspora will remain very significant in the relationships between India and West Asian nations. Hence, the region will remain strategically very important for India. In the intra West Asian nations' conflicts, India has correctly maintained neutrality. Working along these parallel tracks, India and its Gulf partners should coordinate responses as well as iron out nuances in the respective extradition treaties or develop them in cases where they do not already exist.

India and the Gulf Cooperation Council have taken the primary steps for countering terrorism. The transnational terrorist linkages between India and West Asia have had adverse impacts on the stability of both the regions. There are numerous avenues through which India and the Gulf nations should expand their counter-terrorism and criminal organisation cooperation. India is augmenting its cyber capabilities to disrupt terrorist attacks, and employing these capabilities to prevent extremism and radicalization. Such expertise can well be shared with the West Asian nations by joint cyber training and conduct of deradicalisation workshops. The terrorism threat is unlikely to substantially diminish any time soon. There is also a grave need to enhance collaboration to defeat the activities of the Islamic States and degrade the Al-Qaeda. There is also ample opportunity to foster such cooperation, given the wellspring of mutual trust and strong economic ties that India and its Gulf partners have forged over the years.[21] In the same context, there is also a need to act against the *Hawala networks*, as these unregulated fund transfer networks have been widely used by terrorist outfits.

ENDNOTES

1. Tang Shiping, A Systemic Theory of the Security Environment, *The Journal of Strategic Studies*, vol 27, no 1, March 2004, p. 1.
2. Jasjit Singh, 'A Security Strategy for the 21st Century', in AVM Kapil Kak, (ed.), *Comprehensive Security for an Emerging India*, Centre for Air Power Studies, New Delhi, 2010, p. 1.
3. India's rapid strides in boosting Gulf energy security, India Inc Ltd, accessed at https://indiaincgroup.com/indias-rapid-strides-in-boosting-gulf-energy-security/amp/

4. Swapneel Biswas, Indian Diaspora in the Middle East, *The Kootneti*, 18 June 2020, accessed at https:/thekootneeti.in/2020/06/18/indian-diaspora-in-the-middle-east/
5. Seenivasan, T.P., Before Vande Bharat, India Airlifted 1.7 lakh expats when Iraq annexed Kuwait in 1990, On *Manorama*, 16 May 2020, accessed at https://www.onmanorama.com/news/global-indian/2020/05/16/vande-bharat-airlift-kuwait-iraq-india-1990.
6. Khushnam, P.N., India's "Look West" policy in the Middle East, *The Diplomatist*, 28 August 2020, accessed at https://diplomatist.com/2020/08/28/indias-look-west-policy-in-the-middle-east/
7. Manjari Singh, India and West Asia–Elevation in Relations through Defence Cooperation, *SP Guide Publications*, New Delhi, 47th issue, 2020-21, p. 59
8. Alvite Ningthoujam, The Military-security Dimension of India-West Asia Strategic Partnerships, Forum for Integrated National Security, 18 January 2021, accessed at https://finsindia.org/journal/the-military-security-dimension-of-india-west-asia-strategic-partnerships/#sdendnote1sym
9. Alvite Ningthoujam, The Military-security Dimension of India-West Asia Strategic Partnerships, Forum for Integrated National Security, 18 January 2021, accessed at https://finsindia.org/journal/the-military-security-dimension-of-india-west-asia-strategic-partnerships/#sdendnote1sym
10. Rajat Pandit, "India hold air combat exercise with UAE," *The Times of India*, 27 May 2016, accessed at https://timesofindia.indiatimes.com/india/India-holds-air-combat-exercise-with-UAE/articleshow/52468271.cms
11. Two Indian ships take part in UAE-India naval exercise, *Gulf News*, 18 March 2018, https://gulfnews.com/uae/two-indian-ships-take-part-in-uae-india-naval-exercise-1.2190342
12. Alvite Ningthoujam, The Military-security Dimension of India-West Asia Strategic Partnerships, Forum for Integrated National Security, 18 January 2021, accessed at https://finsindia.org/journal/the-military-security-dimension-of-india-west-asia-strategic-partnerships/#sdendnote1sym
13. Alvite Ningthoujam, The Military-security Dimension of India-West Asia Strategic Partnerships, Forum for Integrated National Security, 18 Jan 2021, accessed at https://finsindia.org/journal/the-military-security-dimension-of-india-west-asia-strategic-partnerships/#sdendnote1sym
14. Alvite Ningthoujam, The Military-security Dimension of India-West Asia Strategic Partnerships, Forum for Integrated National Security, 18 Jan 2021, accessed at https://finsindia.org/journal/the-military-security-dimension-of-india-west-asia-strategic-partnerships/#sdendnote1sym
15. Viswavnathan Balasubraminayan, "Indian Mujahideen: The Face of 'New Terrorism' in India?" *Geopolitical Monitor*, October 4, 2013, accessed at https://www.geopoliticalmonitor.com/indian-mujahideen-the-face-of-new-t....
16. Rahul Tripathi, 'IM terrorist Abdul Wahid Siddibapa may have facilitated jailed Yasin Bhatkal's travel in 2005: Officials,' *Economic Times*, March 24, 2016, accessed at https://economictimes.indiatimes.com/articleshow/52410945.cms?utm_source=contentofinterest&utm_medium=text&utm_campaign=cppst
17. Animesh Roul, 'Lashkar-e-Taiba's Financial Network Targets India from the Gulf States,' *Jamestown Foundation*, July 2, 2009, accessed December 17, 2017, https://jamestown.org/program/lashkar-e-taibas-financial-network-target....

18. Alvite Ningthoujam, The Military-security Dimension of India-West Asia Strategic Partnerships, Forum for Integrated National Security, 18 Jan 2021, accessed at https://finsindia.org/journal/the-military-security-dimension-of-india-west-asia-strategic-partnerships/#sdendnote1sym
19. Indrani Basu, 'Reports of UAE Government Seizing Dawood Property are Baseless: Intelligence Sources,' *Huffington Post* January 6, 2017, accessed December 06,2017, http://www.huffingtonpost.in/2017/01/06/reports-of-uae-government-seizi
20. Arhama Siddiqa, 'Why Pakistan's influence in the Gulf is waning', Middle East Eye, 5 March 2021, accessed at https://www.middleeasteye.net/opinion/pakistan-india-gulf-influence-waning-why
21. Mohammed Sinan Siyech, Indo-Gulf Counterterrorism Cooperation, MEI@75, Washington DC, 21 December 2017, accessed at https://www.mei.edu/publications/india-gulf-counterterrorism-cooperation

15

Maritime Security Challenges in West Asia and India's Options

Vice Admiral Satish Soni (Retd.)

ABSTRACT

Sectarian divisions, ethnic conflicts and geopolitical competition amongst regional and extra-regional powers has made West Asia one of the most volatile and conflict-ridden regions of the world. West Asia remains on the boil even as the big power rivalry shifts to the Indo-Pacific. An impending dilution of US military presence could trigger a power struggle amongst aspiring powers. Turkey, Iran, Russia, China, India, and the European countries amongst others, are jostling for influence to deepen existing partnerships with the littorals. Non-traditional challenges, economic dependencies and 'Grey zone' warfare are the new-age challenges to the global arteries for energy and other resources. India's dependence on Gulf crude and the presence of more than seven million Diaspora in the region makes the area significant with regard to our national maritime interests. It may no longer be in India's interests to remain a mere bystander to the developments in our extended neighbourhood. It may be time for India to 'Act West'.

Introduction

The last two decades in West Asia have been punctuated by the US invasion of Iraq in 2003, violent crackdowns of the Arab Spring uprisings of 2011, intractable civil wars in Syria and Yemen, and a hasty withdrawal of the US-led forces in neighbouring Afghanistan in August 2021. The onset of the corona virus pandemic in 2020 and the consequent slowdown of the world economy caused a crash of oil prices, dealing a major economic shock to the oil-rich states. Geo-political tensions remain and a 'No war-No peace' situation prevails with occasional fraying of tempers vented at sea. The Indian Navy plays an important role as the primary manifestation of our national maritime power by positioning itself as the 'Preferred Security Partner' for enhancing maritime cooperation in the region. How is the scenario unfolding and what are our options in the maritime landscape?

Maritime Geography

Geographically, the waters of West Asia are of immense importance for connectivity of an increasingly complex globalized world. As the only passage between the Black Sea and the Mediterranean, the Bosporus Strait is a major sea access route for the Black Sea riparian states, viz., Bulgaria, Romania, Russia, Georgia, and Ukraine besides Turkey. The 105-nm long Suez Canal records a transit of 12 per cent of the total world trade. The Canal's importance was underscored during the grounding of the 400-metre-long vessel 'Ever Given' on 23 March 2021, thereby blocking the movement of 400 other merchant ships. Lloyd's List estimated that the Suez Canal blockage cost around $ 9.6 billion USD per day. Bab-el-Mandeb, a 17-nm wide stretch of water, represents an economic and political region subject to violence, famine, piracy, and the effects of the global pandemic. The conflict in Yemen, which has caused the world's worst humanitarian crisis, is centred on the strategically important port of Al-Hudaydah, which is under the control of the Houthis who occasionally target merchant marine in the Red Sea. The Strait of Hormuz, connecting the Persian Gulf to the Gulf of Oman and Arabian Sea, has no maritime detour, rendering it a critical choke point and a singular point of vulnerability for much of the energy resources emanating from there. 20 per cent of the world's LNG, and 90 per cent of the Gulf's oil exports, i.e., 17 mn barrels of oil accounting for 30 per cent of the total oil traded in the world, transit through this Strait. On an average, 20 big oil tankers sail through this waterway every day. *Any closure of this Strait would severely affect the energy security of many nations, including India.*

East Mediterranean

In the East Mediterranean, we are witnessing a resurgence of the historical antagonism between Turkey and Greece. Cyprus has been a major bone

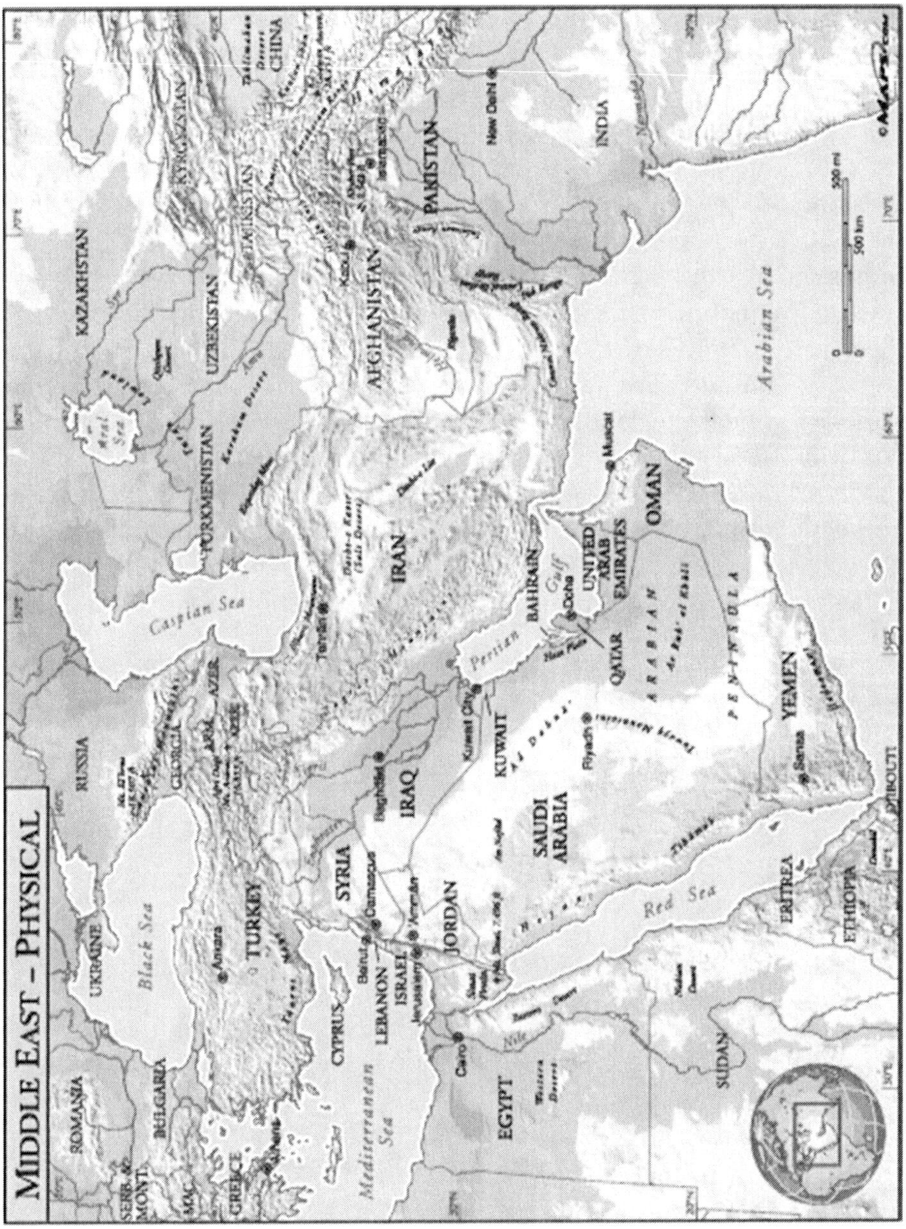
MIDDLE EAST – PHYSICAL
RUSSIA
KAZAKHSTAN
UZBEKISTAN
TURKMENISTAN
KYRGYZSTAN
TAJIKISTAN
CHINA
AFGHANISTAN
PAKISTAN
INDIA
IRAN
IRAQ
SYRIA
TURKEY
GEORGIA
AZER.
ARMENIA
UKRAINE
ROMANIA
BULGARIA
GREECE
CYPRUS
LEBANON
ISRAEL
JORDAN
KUWAIT
BAHRAIN
QATAR
UNITED ARAB EMIRATES
OMAN
SAUDI ARABIA
YEMEN
EGYPT
SUDAN
ERITREA
ETHIOPIA
DJIBOUTI
Black Sea
Caspian Sea
Aral Sea
Mediterranean Sea
Red Sea
Persian Gulf
Arabian Sea
ARABIAN PENINSULA
Karakum Desert
Kabul
Tehran
Baghdad
Kuwait City
Riyadh
Doha
Muscat
Sanaa
Damascus
Beirut
Amman
Jerusalem
Cairo
Ankara
New Delhi
Nile
Tigris
Euphrates

of contention between the two countries for long, but in recent times, a desire to dominate the maritime zones and ownership over the energy resources has further deteriorated relations amongst them. While the length of the Greek and Turkish coastlines bordering the Aegean Sea are somewhat similar, most of the Aegean islands close to the Turkish coast belong to Greece, whose close proximity to Turkey prohibits it from extending any of its maritime zones beyond a few nautical miles off its coastline. Turkey feels that it is a prisoner of geography and has not ratified the United Nations Convention on the Law of the Seas (UNCLOS), as provisions of article 121 of UNCLOS specify that maritime zones of islands (except uninhabited rocks) are determined by the same principles as for the other coastal territories. Turkey does not accept any increase of the territorial waters beyond six nautical miles in the Aegean Sea. There is no Turkish national legislation on the Exclusive Economic Zone (EEZ) or the continental shelf. No Turkish EEZ proclamation exists for the Mediterranean Sea; however, it has signed an agreement in 2011 with the Turkish Republic of Northern Cyprus to delimit their continental shelves. An emerging controversy is with regard to the planned USD 7 billion, 1,900-km Eastern Mediterranean oil and gas pipeline project connecting

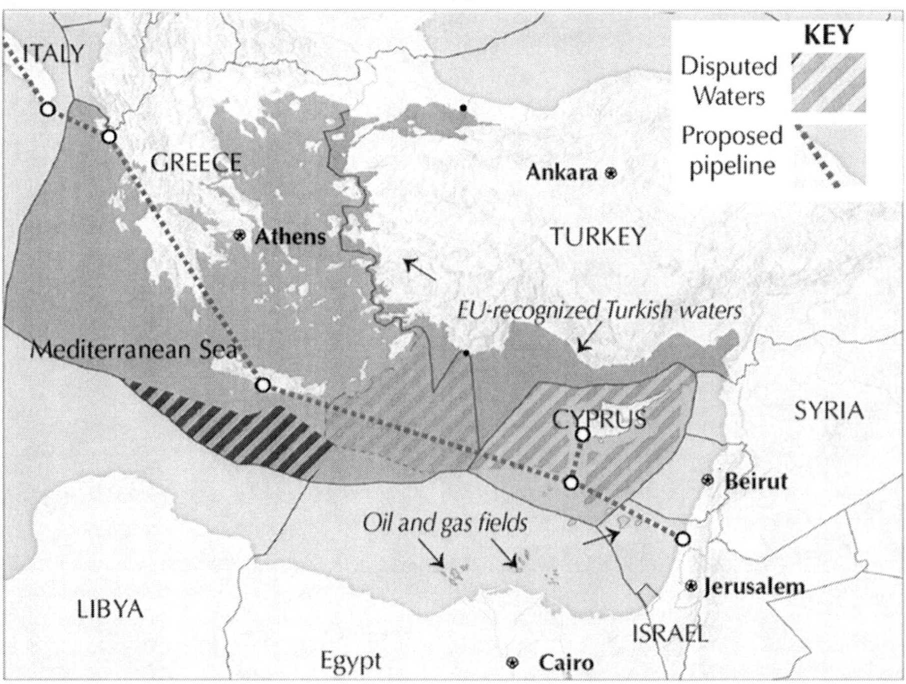

Israel to the European continent via Cyprus and Crete. The proposed pipeline was approved by Cypriot, Greek and Italian governments in 2015 but a 2019 Turkey-Libya deal to demarcate EEZs puts much of its 1,300 km sea leg in disputed waters. The pipeline project continues to progress for now but Turkey's muscle flexing could become an obstruction in the future.

Turkey's Oceanic Thrust

Turkey's strategic reorientation is changing fast and echoes with 'Mavi Vatan', the Blueland doctrine, a term first coined by Rear Admiral Cem Gürdeniz of the Turkish Navy. The doctrine focuses on Turkey's growing maritime claims based on its interpretation of the maritime zones and promotes a strategy to protect, safeguard, and develop maritime rights and national interests.

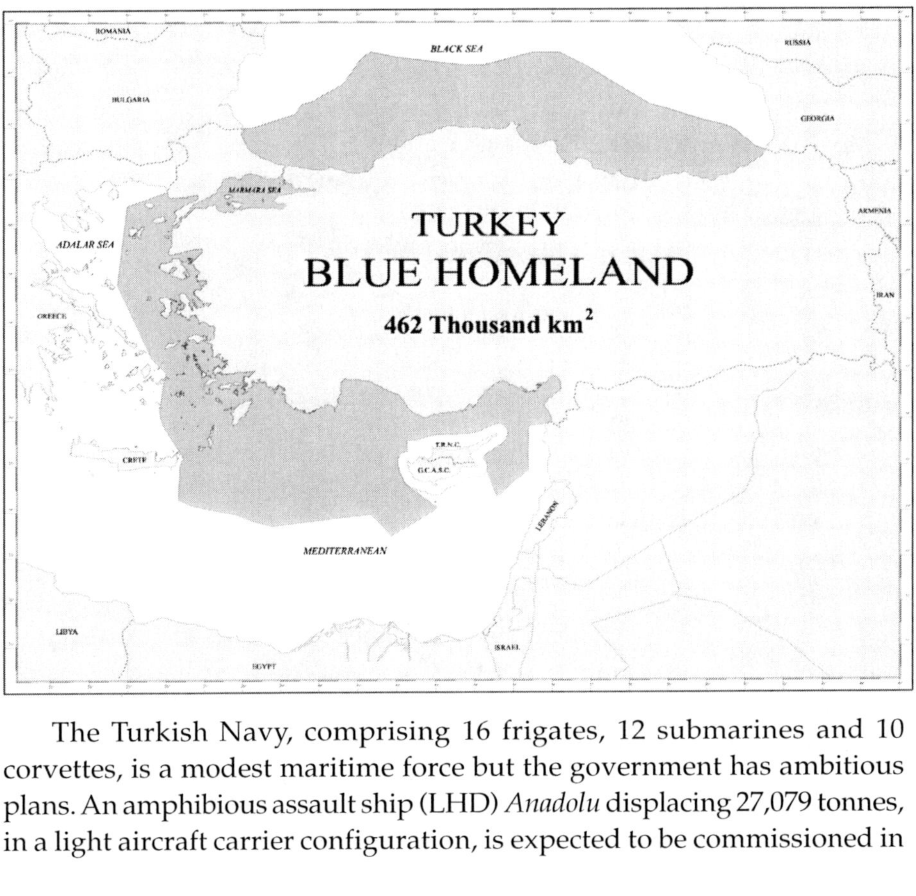

The Turkish Navy, comprising 16 frigates, 12 submarines and 10 corvettes, is a modest maritime force but the government has ambitious plans. An amphibious assault ship (LHD) *Anadolu* displacing 27,079 tonnes, in a light aircraft carrier configuration, is expected to be commissioned in

2022 and there are perspective plans that focus on indigenous development of big modern state-of-the-art ships including frigates, destroyers and an aircraft carrier.

Turkey's aggressive maritime posturing is dragging extra-regional players into the region. During a recent Greece-Turkey flare up, France, Greece's traditional ally, despatched two warships and two maritime strike aircraft as a show of solidarity with Athens. The annual bilateral naval drill "Noble Dina", between Israel and Greece held in March 2021, included France and Cyprus for the first time. According to reports published by *Tass* on September 9, 2021, the Russian Navy for the first time increased the number of its type-636 diesel-electric submarines in the Mediterranean Sea to five. Notwithstanding the resistance to its maritime assertions, Turkey intends to proceed with drilling in the area defined by the Memorandum of Understanding between Turkey and Libya but not accepted by others. India could widen its strategic outreach in this region to balance a strident Turkey-Pakistan nexus. In recent times, India has deepened its strategic ties with France and the United Arab Emirates (UAE); both these countries would like to resist the growing Turkish quest for regional dominance. The Abraham Accords, widely seen as making a breakthrough in relations between Israel and moderate Arab states, could bring India closer to the growing political consensus between the UAE, Greece, France, Israel and hopefully Egypt. *The recent coming together of the 'Quartet' comprising the USA, India, the UAE and Israel could herald a more definitive role for us.*

Persian Gulf

During the past four decades, the region has experienced a revolution (Iran, 1978-79) and three major wars, viz., Iran-Iraq (1980-88), Persian Gulf (1990-91), Iraq (2003-11) and an ongoing civil war in Yemen. US commitment seems to be on the wane as it is no longer as dependent on Gulf crude whereas more Gulf oil (80%) has started to flow to China (19%), India (16%), Japan (15%) and South Korea (13%). The Iranian Navy is once again seeking dominance of the Gulf. A new naval base, the 'Martyr Seyed Majid Rahbar' has been built near the entrance to the Strait, adding to the new ports of Bandar-e-Jask and Chabahar. There are unconfirmed reports about talks between archrivals Saudi Arabia and Iran; a breakthrough could bring about a tectonic shift in security dynamics in these waters. *We may be witnessing the dawn of a new "Great Game" in the Persian Gulf!*

Naval Engagement by Extra Regional Navies in the Persian Gulf

US Dominance to Strategic Fatigue

US core interests in the Gulf comprise maintaining a favourable balance of power; preventing the spread of weapons of mass destruction; anti-terrorism and securing freedom of navigation in international waters. The US Navy's Fifth Fleet based in Manama, Bahrain, is home to over 7,000 American military personnel. The Commander, US Naval Forces Central Command (NAVCENT) is the naval component commander for US Central

Command responsible for combat operations in the Middle East. From major exercises to day-to-day operations, NAVCENT plays a major role in maintaining stability and deterring aggression in the region. These forces normally comprise an aircraft carrier battle group, an amphibious ready group, surface combatants, submarines, maritime patrol and reconnaissance aircraft and logistics ships. The forward headquarters of the US military's Central Command is at Qatar's sprawling Al Udeid Air Base, home to up to 13,000 American troops. The USA also has 5,000 military personnel in the UAE, many at Abu Dhabi's Al Dhafra Air Base, where American drones and advanced F-35 jetfighters are stationed. Iraq hosts another 5,000 troops and 13,000 American troops are stationed with the US Army Central's forward headquarters located in Kuwait. In addition, the US Navy has basing facilities and visiting rights to the many ports in the region. Units of the US Africa Command are stationed in Seychelles and Djibouti. The USA is also spearheading international Naval Task Forces 150 and 152 operating in the Gulf, and Task Force 151 in the Horn of Africa. Over the years, the USA has displayed increasing hesitation and strategic fatigue in the region. Successive US administrations have been asking allies and partners to contribute more to their own and regional security. *Post US withdrawal from Afghanistan in August 2021, a reduction of 'boots on the ground' has started to be discussed. The decreasing US appetite for underwriting security in the region may well have unintended consequences. It is yet uncertain how this security vacuum will be filled.*

France: A Committed Player

French commitment to the Persian Gulf is a subset of its larger Indo-Pacific strategy. France has concluded defence agreements with the United Arab Emirates, Qatar and Kuwait, in addition to a long-standing and trusted relationship with Djibouti. The French initiated the European Maritime Awareness mission in the Strait of Hormuz (EMASOH) to protect European economic interests and prevent conflicts in the world's busiest shipping waterway. Naval ships from NATO countries for anti-piracy duties and the European Union Naval Force (EURO-NAVFOR) in support of the 'World Food Programme' missions are deployed off Somalia. France also maintains its own naval bases in Abu Dhabi and Djibouti, under the operational control of the French Joint Forces Commander in the Indian Ocean (ALINDIEN). Additional French naval forces and Air Force aircraft are deployed in the Gulf as the security situation demands. The French Navy contributes a naval ship on permanent deployment within the multilateral framework of the Combined Maritime Forces. *However, in a nuanced approach to appease Iran, the French have distanced themselves from the USA-led naval responses in the Persian Gulf. The recent 'slight' perceived by the French over the AUKUS deal could also galvanise future French efforts to emerge as an independent and a credible maritime stabiliser in the region.*

United Kingdom: A Resurgence

Britain's naval base HMS Jufair, established in 1935 in Mina Salman, Bahrain, was formally closed in 1971 with the entire facility being taken over by the USA. Britain has however maintained a regular naval deployment. 'The Armilla Patrol' from 1980 to 2011 has been replaced by the ongoing 'Operation Kipion'. In December 2014, the British and Bahraini governments announced that the Royal Navy would re-establish a permanent naval base and construction for the new HMS Jufair began in November 2015. The Naval Support Facility was officially opened in April 2018 and hosts a Type 23 Frigate, four mine counter-measure vessels and one Bay-class landing ship dock. In 2016, the British and Omani governments concluded an agreement for the development of a British naval facility at the Duqm Port complex, which includes a dry dock capability for submarines, and the Queen Elizabeth-class of aircraft carriers. In addition to the new British bases in Bahrain and Oman, the headquarters of the Royal Air Force No. 83 Expeditionary Air Group is located at the Qatari Al Udeid Air Base along with US and Qatari Air Force units. Complemented by the RAF base in Akrotiri, Cyprus, Britain has a substantial capability to stage air operations in the Middle East. *Deployment of two Royal Navy patrol ships on 2 September 2021 on a five-year deployment to the Indo-Pacific and the announcement of the AUKUS security construct is an indication that we are likely to see more of the Royal Navy in this region.*

Russia: Aspiring to Take a Lead

Currently, Russia possesses just one naval base in West Asia, i.e., Tartus in Syria. In early December 2020, Russia concluded a deal for establishing a Russian naval logistics base on the coast of the Red Sea in Sudan, which would facilitate repairs and replenishment of supplies for visiting Russian men-of-war. Russian naval presence is to be limited to four Russian naval ships and 300 personnel. Speaking at the UN Security Council high-level debate on maritime security on 8 August 2021, President Putin stated that as a leading maritime power, Russia is doing much to preserve maritime security in the Persian Gulf and would be interested in building on productive cooperation with the Indian Ocean Rim Association and the Indian Ocean Commission. *As reiterated by Foreign Minister Sergey Lavrov on July 2, 2021, Russia is 'working on an updated concept for security in the Persian Gulf region, and will present it soon'.*

Pakistan: The Omnipresent Mercenary

Pakistani armed forces have punched way above their weight in maintaining an overseas military presence in the Middle East. Its Islamic credentials allow Pakistan to remain engaged as a significant player, despite her meagre resources. Pakistan signed defence protocols during the 1970s with several Arab countries including Saudi Arabia, Libya, Jordan, Iraq, Oman, the United Arab Emirates and Kuwait, under which it has maintained military contingents, provided technical assistance and imparted professional training to their defence forces. The peak numbers have averaged up to 50,000 to 60,000 with the largest representation of about 20,000 deployed in Saudi Arabia. With the first five Chiefs of Air Staff of the UAE Air Force being from Pakistan, the UAEAF at one point was dubbed to have been "an extension of the Pakistan Air Force". Pakistani defence personnel have actively participated in operations too. Pakistan Air Force pilots flew Royal Saudi Air Force aircraft in 1969 to repel South Yemeni incursions and deployed troops in Saudi Arabia for "security duties" in the wake of the 1979 Iranian Revolution. Pakistan was a member of the coalition forces against the 1990 invasion of Kuwait and its personnel took part in UN mine-hunting operations in Kuwait. Other participations during conflicts include the Six-Day War, Operation 'Black September' in Jordan and the freeing of the Grand Mosque. The traditional active engagement of the Pakistani Navy in the security matrix of the Persian Gulf has continued. Since 2004, the Pakistan Navy has contributed a ship to the Coalition Maritime Campaign Plan (CMCP), the maritime component of Operation 'Enduring Freedom'. One hundred ship deployments have been claimed with senior Pakistan naval officers commanding the Combined Task Forces over 15 times. *The recent withdrawal of the USA from Afghanistan has also positioned Pakistan as the de-facto influencer in the region.*

China-Naval Engagement to Safeguard Economic Interdependence

Beijing is poised to expand its political influence in the Gulf, where its concept of centralised economic development, non-interference in governance, indifference to human rights concerns, and lack of historical baggage make it an attractive choice for partnership. This is especially true for many West Asian nations who are otherwise viewed less than favourably by the Western Liberal democracies and are asked to prove their political and social credentials before being delivered assistance or a favoured status. China's economic interdependence with the region has been increasing steadily. In 1996, China imported USD 1.2 billion worth of oil from the Persian Gulf. By 2019, it had increased to USD 106.5 billion accounting for 40 per cent of its oil imports. During the 2000–2019 period, combined imports from China among Gulf Cooperation Council members rose by 267 per cent, from roughly USD 24 billion to USD 87 billion. Over the last 15 years, China has invested roughly USD 101 billion in the six GCC states, which accounted for almost 42 per cent of China's total investments in the region. In March 2021, Iran and China signed an estimated USD 400-bn 25-year agreement on economic and security cooperation. The *PLA (Navy)'s current naval engagement with the region comprises a Naval Task Group for Anti-Piracy patrols in the Gulf of Aden and an increasing number of port visits and joint naval exercises. Presently, it does not have the capability to replace the USA as the guarantor of regional maritime security. However, its quest for 'Strategic strong points' overseas, as articulated in a White Paper published in 2019, is likely to lead them to the Persian Gulf. A beginning has been made in Gwadar and Djibouti. China has demonstrated no hesitation in using economic threats to leverage political compliances and the Persian Gulf is unlikely to be any different.*

Turkey: The new Ottomans

Geographically and strategically, Turkey has been at the crossroads of European and West Asian security issues. Turkey has deftly straddled its continuing NATO membership with the now-growing appetite to be seen as the representative of the Islamic world. Its access to Western technology makes it a sought-after partner by nations who otherwise would be denied the same. Turkey's naval influence in the Persian Gulf is fledgling but noticeable. In December 2014, Turkey concluded an agreement with Qatar for forward deployment of Turkish forces and establishment of the USD 39 million Tariq bin Ziyad base, intended to house 3,000 personnel from

Turkey's naval, air and special operations forces. In September 2019, the Qatar-Turkey Combined Joint Force Command was expanded to include stationing of 5,000 Turkish military personnel. On September 30, 2017, Turkey inaugurated a USD 50 million military training facility for Somalian forces in Mogadishu, where the Turkish Navy will be able to position its assets, thereby complementing its presence in the Persian Gulf. *Saudi Arabia, the UAE and Iran view Turkey as an emerging rival, complicating an already complex maritime security environment.*

Maritime Disputes in the Persian Gulf

The term 'Persian Gulf' has been contested by the Arab States since the 1960s, coinciding with the rise of pan-Arabism and Arab nationalism. Until 1971, British-led forces arbitrated local disputes in the Gulf countries. After their withdrawal, old territorial claims and suppressed tribal animosities resurfaced but most of them have subsided with time. Iran's claim to Bahrain was settled through a 1970 UN-sponsored plebiscite. Iraq's claim to Kuwait was decided by a war. The dispute between Qatar and Bahrain over the Hawar Islands and other areas was resolved by the International Court of Justice on 16 March 2001. A boundary agreement between Oman and the UAE has reportedly been signed in 2003, including the disputed Musandam Peninsula and Al Madhah exclave. Delimitation of the Shatt al-Arab River, a point of contention inherited by Iran and Iraq, was also resolved at the end of the 1980-88 war, when both sides agreed to treat the Algiers Accord signed on 13 June 1975 as binding. However, the islands of Abu Musa, the Greater and Lesser Tunbs straddling the sea lane of the Persian Gulf at the mouth of Hormuz, remain a source of friction between the UAE and Iran with both countries claiming sovereignty over them. Whilst the islands have been under Iranian control after the withdrawal of the British forces in 1971, the UAE argues that the islands were under the jurisdiction of the Qasimi sheikhs, whose rights were inherited by the UAE. The UAE has attempted to bring the dispute before the International Court of Justice (ICJ), but Iran has consistently refused mediation or arbitration. Bilateral negotiations in 1992 failed. Both the UAE and the GCC have not contemplated a military solution because Iranian fortifications make it difficult to invade the islands. *Even after nearly 50 years, the debate over the ownership of the Abu Musa and the Tunb islands rages with claims and counter-claims resonating as recent as in end September 2021 during the UN Security Council meet.*

Abu Musa and the Tunbs

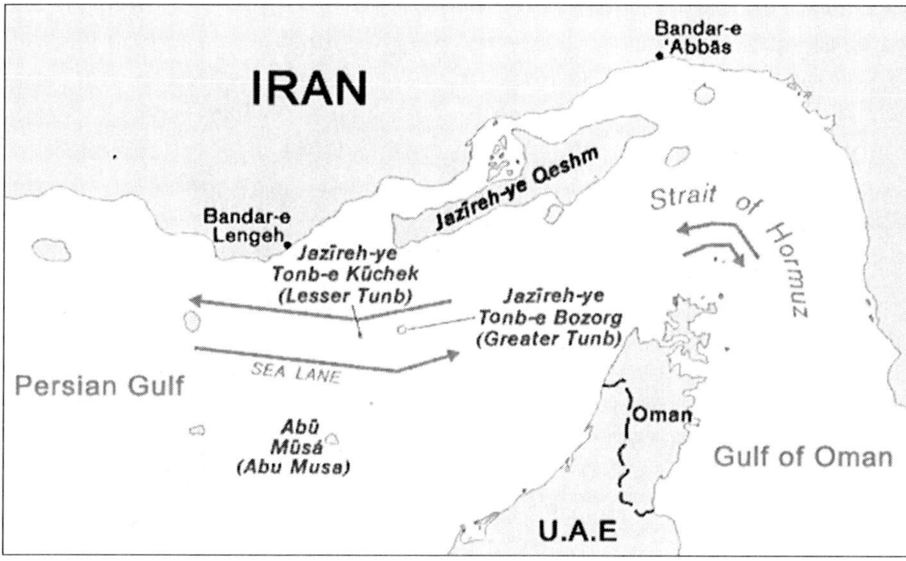

Emerging Threats to Maritime Security

Big Power Naval Rivalry

Whilst the Pacific and Atlantic oceans were contested fiercely during the two World Wars, the Indian Ocean has not seen the same level of contestation. Acceptance of the Indo-Pacific concept could be an indication that it may no longer remain isolated and is now poised to become the centre of geo-political, geo-strategic and geo-economic rivalry. Over 70 warships of extra regional navies are always present in the North Indian Ocean, ostensibly for combating piracy and protecting their own perceived national maritime interests. Regional navies are seeking sophisticated hardware and developing partnerships for securing their Exclusive Economic Zones to harness the dividends of the Blue Economy. The USA, France and Britain have given shape to their Indo-Pacific strategies and increased their commitments. The Germans and the Dutch have followed suit. The European Commission has also articulated their Indo Pacific Strategy in September 2021. The PLA Navy's aggressive posturing in the South China Sea is being followed up by increasing their naval presence in the Indian Ocean. By 2030, the PLA (N) could be in a fairly good position to deploy and sustain a major naval contingent in the Indian Ocean Region comprising a Carrier Battle Group including modern destroyers and frigates. The Chinese are simultaneously expending substantial energy on undermining their rivals through highly sophisticated hybrid warfare operations comprising the use of naval, paramilitary, space and cyber forces. USA-Iran confrontations in 2018-2020 and Iran-Israel face-offs during 2020-21 were very serious but did not cross the threshold. Notwithstanding the restraints, 'Big power rivalry' is imminent. *A congested Persian Gulf could witness unexpected encounters between rival men-of-war wherein a rush of adrenalin has the propensity to spiral spirited nationalistic displays into avoidable unintended embarrassing situations. Regardless of the differences at the political high table, all navies should establish linkages for mitigating the risk of any unforeseen incident, and lay the basis for negotiating an 'Incidents at Sea' or 'Code of Conduct' agreement. India could consider taking the lead in facilitating such discussions.*

Non-Traditional Maritime Security Challenges

Non-traditional challenges do not care much for borders and affect a larger cross-section of mankind across contrasting economic and political strata. Small littoral nations are realizing that Climate Change, Humanitarian Assistance Disaster Relief, Loss of bio-diversity of the oceans, Illegal, Unreported and Unregulated (IUU) fishing, Human and Drug Trafficking, etc., impact the well-being of their people. An apt example lies in the breakout of piracy off Somalia in the Gulf of Aden. The root cause lay in the lack of maritime governance, which resulted in exploitation of the Somali waters by advanced nations. The impoverished Somalis retaliated and piracy was born. During 2008-12, USD 400 mn was paid to Somali pirates in ransom for 178 successful hijackings in 645 attempts. After spending USD 7 to 9 bn a year, ironically by the countries who directly or indirectly gained from Somali exploitation, piracy has been brought under control but not before underscoring the lesson that lack of maritime governance affects the rich and poor alike. The *littorals are realising the enormous impact of these challenges and seek permanency in defining collaborative response mechanisms, which are not only predominately organic but wherein they role play as equals.*

Grey Zone Warfare

Military strategists are beginning to discern the limitations to the use of hard power. Grey zone warfare is the new buzzword. States are beginning to use military or paramilitary means in disputed areas as means of coercion and strategic intimidation. Provocations tend to remain below the threshold of conflict and cause uncertainty in escalation management. *Grey zone activities have spread into all domains, including maritime space, presenting disparate challenges in the Persian Gulf.*

Trade Warfare

Tensions between Iran and Israel have resulted in Iranian and Israeli-flagged merchant vessels being targeted with limpet mines, drones and rockets. At least seven such incidents have been reported since February 2021 in these waters. In July 2019, a muscular Tit for Tat in the Persian Gulf—British tanker *Stena Impero*/Strait of Gibraltar and IIranian tanker *Adrian Darya* -1—highlighted the complexity of 'Trade Warfare' as the crew, cargo, owners and the flag of a merchant ship could well have different nationalities. On 30 July 2021, one Romanian and one British citizen died during an attack on M/T Mercer Street, the Liberian flagged Japanese tanker managed by Zodiac Maritime. The ship was being run by a London-based company owned by Israeli tycoon Eyal Ofer. Volatility in the Sea Lines of Communication has resulted in M/s Lloyd's and the International Underwriting Association (IUA) notifying a large swath of the area as 'High Risk', which has resulted in an almost ten-fold increase in marine insurance. *Trade warfare in the region may or may not throttle the economy of a targeted country but would certainly have an impact on the stability of the entire region. Whilst belligerent states have managed to keep the attacks and counter-attacks below a threshold, a strategic miscalculation could endanger international shipping including India's maritime trade.*

Unmanned Combat

The drone attacks against the state-owned oil producer, Saudi Aramco, in September 2019 first drew the attention of the world to the threat posed by this capability. Autonomous unmanned combat vehicles that can operate in the air, on the surface and under the surface are of great interest to all navies because of their ability to remain on the task for extended periods of time and extend combat operations into the adversary's anti access/area denial zone. Zephyr T, being developed by Airbus Defence and Space, is being designed to fly for months and act like a surveillance platform similar to a satellite, while offering the flexibility of an Unmanned Aerial Vehicle (UAV). Advancement in technologies would facilitate incorporating a greater degree of autonomy and 'Artificial Intelligence' in UAVs for combat/surveillance; developing swarm drones and manned or unmanned systems for surface and sub-surface tasks. The market for unmanned combat vehicles is getting to be dominated by Chinese UAVs. They are becoming more advanced than their reverse-engineered predecessors of US and Israeli origins. China will readily export this technology with few qualms over the manner in which it will ultimately be operated. The *proliferation of this low-cost niche capability is an emerging challenge on account of its force multiplier effect.*

Maritime Militias

China's maritime militia comprising fishing boats have played a significant role in a number of naval campaigns and coercive incidents in the South China Sea. These fishing boats displacing nearly 800 tonnes, ostensibly carry out fishing but are used for gathering intelligence or simply obstructing the passage of naval ships. *An opaque Maritime Domain Awareness in the Indian Ocean and poorly executed endeavours to regulate IUU fishing has encouraged the Chinese to expand their use to the Indian Ocean Region. The congested waters of the Persian Gulf would be no exception as the PLA (N) starts to operate from Gwadar and Djibouti.*

Threat to Undersea Cables

The Internet is more physical than many believe. Ninety-eight per cent of all international voice, data, video, and Internet traffic is carried through the 750,000 miles of fibre optic submarine cables. They are not only the backbone of the international telecommunications system but are absolutely fundamental to our financial system. The cables are most vulnerable to covert attacks as they make landfall in the landing stations that are operated by private companies and therefore liable to lapses in security. Data flowing through these cables can also be spied upon and some of major hubs such as Alexandria may be easier to infiltrate. Mauritania in 2018 and Tonga in 2019 have been victims of Internet outages on account of accidental severing of cables. In 2013, Egypt arrested three scuba divers attempting to cut submarine cables. A cable severed in 2008 by a ship attempting to anchor in bad weather off the Egyptian coast left 75 million people worldwide without access to the Internet. *The fibre optic cable could become a coveted target for state and non-state actors alike. Nowhere is the risk greater than in West Asia, where the density of these cables is the highest and security mechanisms the weakest.*

International Maritime Cooperation

Whilst we have a plethora of challenges, countries and their security agencies are working hard to provide maritime security to their people. Formal cooperative mechanisms include the Indian Ocean Rim Association (IORA-1997), Indian Ocean Naval Symposium (IONS-2008), Gulf Cooperation Council (GCC-1981), Arab League (1945), Djibouti Code of Conduct (2009), European Union's MASE (Maritime Security) and CRIMARIO (Critical Maritime Routes Indian Ocean) maritime security initiatives for the South and Eastern Indian Ocean, the Indian Ocean Commission (IOC), etc. The International Maritime Security Construct (IMSC) formed on 16 September 2019 in Bahrain, by the United Kingdom, Australia, Albania, Saudi Arabia, Bahrain, Lithuania, the United Arab Emirates, and the USA, is a consortium of countries contributing to 'Operation Sentinel' for maintaining order and security in the Persian Gulf, Gulf of Oman, Gulf of Aden and the Red Sea. Belgium, Denmark, France, Germany, Greece, Italy, The Netherlands and Portugal navies contribute as constituents of the European Maritime Surveillance Mission in the Strait of Hormuz (EMASOH). Indian contributions have been most visible in nurturing IORA and IONS. *India could play a more active role in coordinating an organic response to improve maritime governance and address specific requirements of the littorals for combating myriad challenges.*

India's Naval Engagement with West Asian Countries

Defence analysts of West Asia assess India as a benign actor that avoids participation in security issues. This is true to some extent. We have basic-level naval cooperation with all West Asian countries. Our warships visit almost all ports in the Persian Gulf and have increased their show of presence in the Mediterranean. Some of our retired officers and sailors have been involved in training naval personnel of West Asian countries. With Oman, the level of naval cooperation is a bit advanced, in that we train their personnel in our training establishments, hold a biennial joint naval exercise and have logistics facilities at their port in Duqm. An MOU on exchange of White Shipping data was concluded between the two countries on 27 September 2021. The Indian Navy has also initiated joint bilateral naval exercises with Qatar, the UAE, Iran and Saudi Arabia and proposed the UAE's inclusion in the bilateral annual naval exercise between India and France. INS *Tabar*, whilst on deployment in the Mediterranean Sea in mid-2021 participated in bilateral naval exercises with the Egyptian, Moroccan, Algerian and Italian navies for the first time. Hydrography is an important area of naval cooperation as West Asian naval capabilities in this specialisation are either limited or non-existent. After the breakup of the Soviet Union, our technical naval cooperation with Israel has increased exponentially and it has become the 'Go To' county for state-of-the-art weapons and electronic systems, e.g., Barak SAMs and UAVs. *India needs to leverage its maritime industrial complex and the Navy for deeper involvement than the current, somewhat cosmetic engagement.*

Security of India's Oil Imports

Sixty-three per cent of India's crude oil imports are sourced from Persian Gulf countries—very high figures for an energy deficient nation, which in the foreseeable future is likely to remain dependant on imports to meet its crude requirements. Whilst alternative sources of crude are available in South America and Africa, the revenue for shipping from a source farther away could be as much as ten times higher. In recent years, India has diversified its sources of energy imports and 67 non-Persian Gulf countries have been identified as possible alternative suppliers to mitigate India's 'Hormuz Dilemma'. Solutions to 'Energy security' also lie in our ability to build adequate strategic reserves and divert oil imports through overland routes. *Till then, securing the maritime routes of energy from the Gulf countries remains a challenge, aggravated by an increasing Chinese influence along the Makran coast in Pakistan and Iran.*

Recommendations: Options for India

In conclusion, India can no longer remain reticent and must seek a role for itself in the fast-changing geo-political landscape of West Asia. Articulation of an intent and developing reliable partnerships has never been more important. We must develop responses to the emerging challenges of grey zone warfare and evolve cooperative responses to non-traditional challenges. Some recommendations for consideration are:

- As India gains recognition as an economic and military power with an ability to influence events in the maritime landscape, it may be prudent to formally articulate an Indian perspective on Maritime Security of West Asia and the role it seeks to play. Orchestrating sub-regional groupings could be considered—France, Greece, Israel, Egypt and India for the East Mediterranean;

Qatar, Bahrain and India for the Northern Gulf and the UAE, Oman and India for the Southern Gulf.

- India must consider an increase in defence allocations and revision of *inter se* priorities with an aim to strengthen capabilities at sea. The Indian Navy has around 130-odd ships and submarines. The timeline to reach the 200-ship mark has been revised from 2027 to 2050. Given that in the preceding five years, fewer ships have been commissioned than those retired, it seems unlikely that we would be able to meet the revised milepost. We must build a strong Navy and early.
- India must orchestrate a home-grown order to improve maritime governance at sea. The IORA must expand its membership to include all eligible littorals (Saudi Arabia and many others are not members). The IONS needs to be empowered and not be a mere adjunct needing governmental oversight at every step. An all-pervasive 'Code of Conduct' could be considered for discussion to allay apprehensions of smaller navies.
- Maritime Domain Awareness is the *sine qua non* for addressing non-traditional challenges such as Illegal Fishing, Human Trafficking, Piracy, Maintenance of Marine Ecosystems, etc. Conclusion of more 'White Shipping Agreements' with countries and offering them representation at our International Fusion Centre in Gurugram would facilitate confidence building.
- With 847 troops, India is the fourth largest constituent of the 10,000 strong United Nations Interim Force in Lebanon (UNIFIL). The inclusion of an Indian naval ship has however remained conspicuously absent. Reportedly, the Indian Navy has expressed its readiness to participate in the maritime element of UNIFIL. It would be in our interests to extend our outreach into the East Mediterranean and the presence of a naval ship in UNIFIL could mark a beginning.
- Whilst India has consistently contributed towards anti-piracy and maritime security operations in the Gulf of Aden, it has chosen to stay away from contributing to the US-led Combined Maritime Forces (CMF) comprising naval ships from 34 countries. As a dominant regional power, India must be a prominent contributor to all maritime security constructs in the region. The Indian Navy could join the Combined Maritime Task Forces and the French/European Union-led initiatives for maritime security in West Asia.

- Countries of West Asia look up to India for ameliorating their maritime industrial base and building indigenous ship-building ecosystems. This would help in weaning smaller navies away from dependencies on extra-regional powers for their hardware requirements.
- Our initiatives for developing marine infrastructure in the neighbourhood have fallen well short of what the Chinese have been able to achieve. We need to be able to walk the talk. 'Sagarmala', India's flagship programme for promoting port-led development could be extended to our immediate neighbourhood. Facilitating developments of the ports of Fujairah and Basra, amongst others, could be examined.
- The Indian Navy has a formidable reputation as a professional force with modern training infrastructure. The enhancement of naval cooperation with West Asian navies must form an important constituent of our strategic outreach. We need to progress beyond cosmetic initiatives to embedded commitments.

16

India's West Asia Connect: Way Forward

Amb. Anil Trigunayat

West Asia is the most critical extended neighbourhood for India. It is a natural extension of India's security perimeter. Therefore, any development in the region has a direct and immediate impact on India's wellbeing in the narrowest to broadest possible dimension of this civilizational relationship. Somehow in India's foreign policy establishment, the engagement or lack of it was ascribed to the Islamic factor and consequent closeness of most countries with archrival Pakistan. Instead of following a Venn diagram matrix, for decades, India tried the mutually exclusive approach, which despite extensive dependencies, remained a buyer-seller or a mere transactional relationship. India was seen as a poor country with a blue collar labelled labour providing a reservoir especially since the 1970s until recently. That has changed in recent years as professionals and entrepreneurs are proving their mark and heading organizations and enterprises in these countries. Moreover, the last decade has also witnessed a significant change in India's interactive and strategically expansive approach that has led to greater high-level interactions as well as conscious policies and efforts to exploit the full potential of the bilateral engagement through a real strategic partnership.

It had become essential as the regional hotspots and geopolitical and geo-economic and geo-religious competition and contestations increased. A general perception of the USA's fading footprints and consequent growth in the strategic presence of China and Russia in the region to try to fill that vacated landscape is gaining ground as the nervous regional powers had become used to the US security umbrella for far too long. Therefore, it is imperative that the Indian engagement moves in a focused and much higher orbit of bilateral and regional collaboration in order to maintain security and stability so that her hard-won strategic interests are not threatened in the short term and are further strengthened in the medium term. It has become quite visible as the Middle Eastern states, especially the Gulf countries including Iran, are bracing for the new uncertain post-pandemic and possibly post-US localitis era where the geo-political landscape is changing rather fast. That too fraught with uncertainty.

Apart from a bilateral matrix, India ought to carve out a niche for itself also in the regional and sub-regional context as there are some nascent efforts within the region to reduce tensions among themselves and evolve a home-grown Gulf security architecture while dependency levels on external powers are being assessed and ascertained. Major regional powers like Saudi Arabia, the UAE, Qatar and Turkey, apart from Iran, have been working to exploit their influence in the Horn of Africa, the Red Sea and the western Indian Ocean choke points. Therefore, from India's Indo-Pacific perspective also, the eastern Indian Ocean and the Horn of Africa are strategically important for its maritime security that would require scouting for strategic partnerships and sharing of assets as it has done with France, the USA, and Oman and could possibly do with the UAE in Socotra in Yemen or Somaliland and elsewhere. As China flexes its muscles in the region through its BRI initiatives and tries to fill the security gap, possibly in concert with Russia, New Delhi will be required to step up the game to secure her strategic and security objectives. It will also have to play a regional and sub-regional role as it has done recently with the establishment of a new economic QUAD with the UAE, the USA, and Israel that should not limit its choices but enable an expanded menu within the region and beyond.

Disruption and Disputes in the Region

Since the Arab Spring of 2010, the Middle East has been in a downward flux and the present-day conundrum has the potential to destabilise the region, which can have a devastating impact on India, which is a close strategic neighbour. While this situation may have been externally induced and exacerbated with the 2003 misadventure by the USA in Iraq or, for that matter, against the backdrop of the so-called Arab Spring, the NATO bombing of Libya and extended conflict in Syria, the Arab countries have also given wind to their deep-seated intra-Arab and Shia-Sunni conflicts. The quest for religious leadership and the race for one-upmanship and superiority in varying regional landscapes like Syria, Yemen, Libya, and Lebanon, through militarisation of their foreign policies, is leading to further destabilisation and unpredictability that could have disastrous ramifications for the countries themselves in this " Mutually Assured Destruction" syndrome.

While the Arab Spring in the last decade has witnessed a qualitative change broadly through the overthrow of well-entrenched regimes and the Gulf monarchies, despite the rifts and inherent contradictions, installed the younger and impatient leaders in decisive leadership positions, be it Saudi Arabia, Qatar or the UAE and even Bahrain, Oman and Kuwait. No wonder major economies of the Gulf Cooperation Council (GCC) and West Asia that went for an internecine Qatar blockade and turmoil since June 2017 until January 2021 when Crown Prince Mohammad bin Salman (MBS) realised the futility of it all and enabled the rapprochement at the Al Ula Summit even if the UAE was not seemingly keen on it though it has begun to follow a 'Zero Problem' policy. The problems were compounded by the then US Administration and its one-time President Trump who directly or indirectly nudged the Saudis and other allies into reversing the Obama outreach to Iran and casting doubts on the viability and veracity of the famous agreement the JCPOA reached with the P5+1. Eventually, he abandoned it in 2018 bringing the region to near war-like situations more than once through his 'maximum pressure and severe sanctions ' regime against Iran. Peace remains under threat. Saudi-Iran-USA-Israel vitriolic was further accentuated and their direct and proxy wars in Yemen and Syria can conflagrate further. The GCC and Iran are also heavily armed as the major suppliers and vacillating benefactors like the USA make hay while petro dollars flush the treasury. Saudi Arabia is, as such, heavily armed and perched in a delicate balance with an unwinnable Yemen war on its hands. Riyadh remained the largest importer of US weapon systems.

According to SIPRI, over 33 per cent of global arms exports were destined to the West Asian region.

The regional institutions are under stress despite the efforts being made by the GCC and Arab League as well as the OIC (Organisation of Islamic Cooperation) to salvage the situation. Qatar walked out of the OPEC. The GCC was nearly on the verge of irrelevance and disintegration due to the simmering conflict between Qatar and the Saudi/UAE-led combine with Bahrain and Egypt toeing the line. In the process, Turkey and Iran have expanded their influence and stood up for Doha and Palestine. Kuwaiti and Omani efforts to patch up took nearly four years to succeed as Doha continued to project itself as a viable interlocutor for the USA and other major powers in the context of Afghanistan. No wonder it has been conferred with a non-NATO ally status by the Biden Administration as Sheikh Tamim was invited to the White House in February 2022 to ensure gas supplies to Europe should Russia invade Ukraine. Saudi Arabia and the UAE entered into an unprecedented strategic partnership and security agreement despite their own foreign policy contours and competing objectives given the Biden Administration's equanimous interdiction and 'back to basics approach' including return to the Iran Nuclear Deal (JCPOA) that has gone into eight rounds; eventually the Iranians have agreed to have direct talks with the Americans within the Vienna Talks format as the USA lifted some sanctions. Hope for resumption of the JCPOA emboldened the thinking that it would eventually be good for stabilising the region at least in the short term even though Tel Aviv is likely to remain cautious and overtly critical of it.

Various conflicts in the region have the potential to further expand the footprints of diverse extremist and terrorist groups which is ironic as almost all nations are voicing hoarse their credentials for the fight against terrorism. The ISIS (Daesh) and al-Qaeda appear to be back in the saddle as the hotspots are the preferred incubators for the radicalization, recruitment, and training of terrorists by the social media-savvy ISIS and its centripetal localised entities across geographies.

The Trump Administration's somewhat ad hoc and unconventional Twiplomacy and junking of the multilateral agreements, arrived at after great difficulty and prolonged negotiations, especially relating to Iran or, for that matter, declaring Jerusalem as the capital of Israel or announcing Golan Heights to be part of Israel or suzerainty of Morocco over the Western Sahara have done lasting damage in the Middle East. Big power rivalry in the region adds fuel to fire and has been lamented upon in the wake of the USA, the UK and France air strikes pitched against Moscow and Tehran in Syria, which UNSG Antonio Gutteres termed dire. " The situation in the Middle East is in such chaos that it has become a threat to international peace and security. New equations and alliances are emerging with Turkey and Iran becoming bigger players in the Gulf spat and Shia-Sunni divide. And today, Syria represents most serious dimension of that threat". Combined with other arenas of distrust among the major powers, Cold War 2.0 is threatening to heat up.

At the same time, Israel's seemingly advanced engagement with some GCC countries, especially with Oman, Saudi Arabia, and the UAE and Bahrain in pursuance to the US-initiative led to the game changing Abraham Accords. While in the UNGA, all ME countries made noises and voted against the USA declaring Jerusalem as the capital of Israel they have begun to ruminate over the possibility of a "one state solution" as was mentioned by UAE Minister Anwar Gargash in New Delhi who appeared ready to persuade the Palestinians. Even Saudi Crown Prince Mohammed bin Salman acknowledged the right of Israel to exist that was in departure to their policies until now and since it appeared rather radical, King Salman did try to tamper it somewhat reiterating at the Arab Summit at Riyadh to appease the popular sentiment. But it is a fact of changing ground dynamics and it will not be easy for the Palestinian leadership to ward it off for too long given the current state of affairs and thaw between major Arab countries and the Jewish state. Of course popular discontent among the Palestinians, support from the Arab streets and Intifada will be hard to manage. Given the change in Israeli composite leadership, with the departure of Netanyahu, perhaps some *modus vivendi* and gradual redressal of Palestinian grievances might follow even if it is a long shot, since the Palestinians are also a divided lot and Arab fatigue with the cause is pretty evident.

Currently, as the JCPOA talks go on and the perception of US disengagement and its emergence as a major oil and gas producer and competitor rises, the regional rivals are beginning to find a *modus vivendi*. Saudi Arabia is talking to Iran via Iraq and now directly as three Saudi diplomats returned to their mission to OIC in Riyadh. Diplomatic exchanges might be restored; the UAE is normalising and expanding its interactions with Tehran too as the new hardliner Ebrahim Raisi government has taken over and can be more predictable being closer to the Spiritual Leader. The Emirati NSA visited Tehran and invited Raisi to visit Abu Dhabi; Iran is trying to persuade the Houthis to come to the table and end the conflict with Saudi Arabia; Turkey is reaching out to its arch rivals, Saudi Arabia, the UAE and Egypt, and looking to re-engage and reduce the trust deficit; the UAE and Bahrain and Oman reaching out to President Assad of Syria bodes well for regional peace and stability. Efforts are being made to calm tensions and move the transition forward in hotspots like Libya as well as to mitigate the Saudi-Lebanon spat over the Yemen war and the Morocco-Algeria diplomatic disruption over western Sahara.

But for countries like India that wish to maintain the symmetry of benign cooperation with almost all countries, some potential challenges are inherent should things go out of hand. Equanimity for us in the regional and bilateral context will be confronted by hard choices especially as India has defence agreements with some of the conflicting parties in the region. This would include playing a much bigger role in the intra-regional affairs as an honest interlocutor which, interestingly is also sought by the countries in the region. Meanwhile, India continues to enjoy the affection of the region due to its huge economic potential and benign foreign policy outreach and interests. However, we need to continue to work on finding the right balance that will serve our national and strategic interests better. As India grows in stature and ambition and follows a policy of a clearly articulated objective assessment, it will be able to achieve the requisite credibility to be an honest arbiter of peace and productive engagement.

Deficit in High Level Engagement

Most West Asian nations, especially the Gulf countries, are barely few hours away from Indian shores. But for decades after Mrs. Indira Gandhi in the 1980s, no Indian leader visited any of them until 2008-10 when PM Manmohan Singh was persuaded to visit Oman, Qatar, and Saudi Arabia. In, 2014, after PM Modi took over, the Arab governments were apprehensive that India might adopt a more pro-Israeli policy under the new government at the expense of traditional relations with them and the Palestinian cause itself might suffer. Besides, the longstanding personal friendship and bonhomie between PM Modi and former PM Netanyahu made them wary. This was soon dispelled. PM Modi understood the exceptional importance of relations with the Middle East as a whole that included Israel. Hence, a rounded and balanced relationship followed. PM Modi converted the "Look West" policy to "Link and ACT West " through his very first visit to the UAE followed by Qatar and Saudi Arabia as well as to Iran (August 2015 to June 2016) in the first two years and to Israel in 2017 to celebrate the 25th anniversary of diplomatic relations. He also became the first Indian Prime Minister to visit Tel Aviv and Ramallah via Jordan under the new de-hyphenated policy as it continued to adhere to its principled position on the two-State solution and direct dialogue between Palestine and Israel that was again reiterated during the 4th Israel-Gaza war when India was in the UNSC. Several leaders from the region visited India. In an unusual gesture, the Crown Prince of the UAE was the chief guest on our Republic Day. In fact, PM Modi was scheduled to visit the UAE (4th time) for the Dubai Expo 2020 and Kuwait for the first-ever visit by an Indian PM in the beginning of 2022 but that had to be postponed due to the pandemic. Moreover, as a unique and special gesture, PM Modi was conferred with their highest national honours during his visits which is a testament to the importance these countries attach to India.

On January 29, 2022, India and Israel celebrated their 30th anniversary of establishment of diplomatic relations with a pledge to 'set new goals' as PM Modi put it in his congratulatory video message. In an unusual joint Oped 'Namaste Shalom To Friendship' Indian External Affairs Minister Dr. S. Jaishankar and Yair Lapid, the Israeli Foreign Minister, described the two countries as 'We are an ideal duo' and even though 4,000 km apart they are cooperating in various fields including water management, agriculture, innovation and security through knowledge sharing projects with a vision for the future. Referring to the Abraham Accords of 2020, they said 'the new relationships in the region are already bearing economic fruit and heralding strategic change in the Middle East whose ripples are reaching India. This past year, we harnessed those new relationships into a new quadrilateral group with India, Israel, the UAE and the USA coming together to execute joint projects'.

India has in fact de-hyphenated its relationships with several countries—Saudi Arabia, Iran, Israel including Palestine—which is now being appreciated by many of them since it is advocating resolution of problems through dialogue and deliberations and is ready to assist where it can. It did not favour external interventions in Iraq, Libya or in Syria and Yemen. Speaking at the Westminster, UK, it was perhaps the first time that India's recent independent foreign policy was expounded in no uncertain terms by Prime Minister Narendra Modi in his "Bharat ki Baat Sabke Saath". Apart from speaking about the decisive surgical strikes against terrorists across the western border, the PM wondered, "What prevented Indian Prime Ministers from going to Israel. Yes, I will go to Israel and I will even go to Palestine. I will further cooperate with Saudi Arabia and for the energy needs of India I will also engage with Iran." The fact that he specifically chose to refer to West Asia clearly underlines the importance India attaches to our relations with the region but with a fine-tuned de-hyphenation and strategic autonomy.

Dividends and Outcomes

For years, our relations were held hostage by the shadow of their relationship with Pakistan and the Islamic connect. Even that has changed. Both Saudi Arabia and the UAE and others have recognised Islamabad's hand-in-glove approach with globally denounced and sanctioned terrorist groups. This was evident during their reaction to India's abrogation of Art 370 in J&K and action with regard to the Uri and Pulwama terror attacks and retaliatory Balakot strikes. It was a significant diplomatic achievement. Besides, the UAE Foreign Minister invited his Indian counterpart, the Late Mrs. Sushma Swaraj, to address the OIC (Organisation of Islamic Cooperation) meet much to the chagrin and objection of the Pakistani Foreign Minister who considered it their home turf. Clearly, their bilateral relationship and engagement has been calibrated in view of exposed realities. But, India may need to work on its 'Islamic card and credentials' and, as suggested by several Muslim countries including Saudi Arabia and the UAE, should consider closer engagement with the OIC or even full membership in order to call the Pak bluff from within since most of the member-countries tell India not to pay heed to the statements issued at the insistence of Islamabad.

Our close friendship and concerted engagement has begun to yield tangible results in several areas of our strategic interests in a rather short time as enunciated in the Joint Statement of August 2015 during PM Modi's visit to the UAE, the first by an Indian PM in a quarter century, " Recognising that India is emerging as the new frontier of investment opportunities, especially with the new initiatives by the Government to facilitate trade and investment, encourage the investment institutions of the UAE to raise their investments in India, including through the establishment of the UAE-India Infrastructure Investment Fund, with the aim of reaching a target of USD 75 billion to support investment in India's plans for rapid expansion of next generation infrastructure". The UAE is among India's top three trade partners and has the most engaging relationship in the region. Likewise, Riyadh has committed $ 100 bn investments across sectors.

Exceptional collaboration in security and intelligence matters with an unusual emphasis on counter-terrorism cooperation was the hallmark of the declarations post various visits that clearly targeted the cross-border and havens of terrorism, especially in Pakistan, that was a warning to Islamabad since hitherto under the Islamic cloak Pakistan was able to garner Arab support as its age old benefactors. This was no longer available or at least was qualified which is a stellar achievement. The joint statement with the UAE was an exceptional document as it forbade Pakistan to use UAE territory for anti-India activities which had hitherto been the case as the fugitive terrorist Dawood and his D Company and several others had taken refuge in the UAE and shuttling between Pakistan and the UAE while carrying out anti-India activities. In fact several accused Indian origin terrorists were extradited to India. Most recent case was that of a close aide of Dawood, the notorious Farouq Takla, which is clearly an indication of the respect and resolve to genuinely address mutual concerns.

Dependence on Energy Security

West Asia, especially the Gulf countries and their stability, are critical to India's energy security as it depends for two-thirds of its hydrocarbon requirements on the region and despite a greater emphasis on renewable energy its dependence on oil and gas for next three-four decades is for India's fast economic growth cycle as it embarks on renewables. Hence, the importance of oil supplies will remain while diversification of sources continues.

During various high-level interactions, several MoUs were signed relating to railways, energy sector, financial services, and manpower. But for the first time, an MoU between an Indian consortium (OVL, BPRL & IOCL) and Abu Dhabi National Oil Company (ADNOC) was signed that allows the acquisition of 10 per cent participating interest amounting to $ 600 million in Abu Dhabi's offshore Lower Zakum concession for 40 years—a highly significant development that was not conceivable until recently as hitherto we only had a buyer-seller relationship with the UAE. Similarly, strategic storage of oil reserves and establishment of refineries are in the pipeline. Even at the OPEC, Crown Prince Salman reportedly took care of India's interests and provided heavier discounts in the wake of the USA-Iran war of nerves and sanctions.

Diaspora Dividend

In the West Asian region, the nine million Indians have become an integral part of the exceptional development and progress, especially of the oil-rich Gulf economies. They comprise high-quality professionals, bankers, entrepreneurs, medical professionals including nurses and paramedic staff, and blue-collar workers. Their enterprise, loyalty, and discipline are admired and respected by their local hosts. They have helped the Indian economy through foreign exchange remittances and most of it stays back in the country unlike from some other regions which are market-driven deposits. They have been remitting over US$ 40-50 bn annually from the Gulf region and India gets the highest remittances worldwide. However, the general downturn in the Gulf economies and low crude oil prices could have an impact on employment and remittances in recent years even though the 2021 figures are encouraging at a total of $ 87 bn. With the COVID-19 pandemic combined with low crude prices, the economies were expected to contract by 25-30 per cent and major projects might be deferred or a complete restructuring of their economic model might ensue in a changed global order. This obviously will have an adverse effect on the employability of expatriate workforce in these countries. The World Bank estimated that in view of the deadly corona virus pandemic, remittances to India are likely to drop by 23 per cent from US$ 83 bn (2019) to US$ 64 bn this year. It will be largely due to a fall in the wages of migrant workers. Retrenchments and repatriation in large numbers may follow which will have its socio-economic consequences on several sending states. In addition, those industrialists and entrepreneurs who set up shop abroad might find it difficult to salvage their balance sheets without a huge injection of capital and state support. This vicious cycle will have its own dynamics that is difficult to exactly define and predict at this stage but countries have to prepare for rehabilitation, re-training, and re-employment of their surplus returning citizens. Fortunately, the remittances during 2021 were pegged at $ 87 bn and oil producers are enjoying the highest price boom in the last seven years as major economies bounce back from the COVID impact.

Defence and Security

For decades, the Pakistan factor dissuaded us from developing strategic ties with the region and only a buyer-seller relationship ensued. It was a flawed policy and Pakistan benefitted by default. It had a singular objective of demonising India. We got baited and the void remained and the narrative strengthened. Now a change is perceptible, especially with the GCC countries in addition to Iran and Israel. These are also being calibrated in the context of the Indo-Pacific and even the Mediterranean where India is weighing its options with Greece and Cyprus along with the UAE, Israel, and Saudi Arabia.

After decades of routine transactional interaction, India's relations with the region have moved into a real strategic orbit since 2008 with an institutional matrix especially in strategic security, cyber security, counter-terrorism and defence collaboration which should be carried forward and intensified further. The Abraham Accords have provided a greater opportunity for collaboration in intelligence and technology as well as health care, space and nuclear energy since most oil-rich countries are moving towards renewables and reforms in their economic structures. Military exercises and defence exchanges have become more frequent with regional powers in pluri-lateral formats. The Indian Chief of Army Staff, Gen Naravane, had visited Saudi Arabia and the UAE for the first time.

(Two preceding chapters by Vice Admiral Satish Soni and Lt. General Rakesh Sharma specifically deal with this dimension)

Diversification is the Key

The Indian trajectory is on the rise in the Gulf. COVID assistance and cooperation are of immense significance for both sides as are the post COVID collaboration in newer areas including IT, Fintech, AI, Quantum Technology, Space, Sustainable Technology, and Renewables and Healthcare, apart from trade and routine investments for which institutional frameworks have been assiduously worked out in the recent past.

Indian companies should also invest in critical projects in the region to ensure long-term supplies of oil, gas, fertilisers, and other minerals as they scout for opportunities in the reconstruction efforts of the conflict zone countries which are hoping to settle down. This could be possible in concert with the PPP model along with willing partners from the region who will have a natural advantage and access. Third country and continental partnerships could be explored, especially in the agricultural and ICT sectors in Africa.

Developing Stakes

The developments in the West Asian region need to be seen as a subset of developments in the Indo-Pacific region as a new Great Game is emerging for the control of Eurasia. The rise of China is a shared concern for both India and the USA. India should attempt to tap and harness the opportunities emerging from the US Administration. While India is unhappy with the US sanctions, it has complied with them. It should, therefore, look for dividends from the USA for complying with the US sanctions as it keeps its 'Strategy Autonomy' principle intact.

India's approach to West Asia is deeply interlinked with the larger political objectives in Africa and Central Asia. These inter-connections are crucial for India, hence it should focus on sub-regional cooperation that could include select Central Asian, African and West Asian states sharing common objectives to achieve tangible goals in multiple arenas.

Social dimension through educational initiatives and people-to-people contacts would need framing of policy objectives through an in-depth understanding of societies in West Asian states. It is interesting that an Abu Dhabi or a Bahrain provides land or maintains Hindu temples and Saudi Arabia encourages the study of the *Ramayana* and the *Mahabharata* in their schools as Yoga becomes increasingly popular across the region and the world.

Sub-regional grouping with France, Greece, Israel, and Egypt could be highly effective for India to expand its maritime presence in the Eastern Mediterranean region. India's sub-grouping with Qatar and Bahrain and its participation in the US-led Combined Maritime Forces (CMF) and collaboration with the UAE in Socotra Islands could help it to entrench its presence in the naval sphere. India should identify the areas it could collaborate with in Russia's growing military and economic endeavours in the region. Major risk of militarisation in the Eastern Mediterranean Sea, Indian Ocean, Persian Gulf, and Arabian Sea is that any unintended encounters causing an accidental clash could spark off a major conflict. India through its strong maritime connections in the region could play a key role in de-escalating tensions.

Moreover, due to the geo-political and geo-economic contestations like the Sino-US Cold War 2.0 and the USA continuing to consider Russia as its strategic rival, one could witness the emergence of a new informal alliance with China, Russia, Iran, Pakistan Turkey, and Afghanistan, with

Qatar on the periphery (CRIPTAQ) countering the US-led Abraham Accords and Sunni national alliance structure. Of course, it will depend on how rabid the rivalry becomes as there are many moving parts. For the time being, a welcome change is the efforts for rapprochement and reconciliation among key adversaries.

Direction and Decisions–Key is being Proactive and not Reactive

- The Palestinian issue will continue to occupy front stage unless real CBMs are introduced and accepted and reciprocated by all stakeholders. India has always stood up for the Palestinian cause while enhancing its strategic ties with Israel. It may have to devise some *modus operandi* to be proactive in helping the sides to revert to dialogue and eventual resolution or *modus vivendi* in concert with the original Quartet and the regional powers that are now so much more accommodative of the Jewish state.
- Although, with lesser dependence on the ME energy supplies and greater focus on China in the Indo-Pacific, the USA is perceived to be backing out of the region as an arbiter of security. However, it is doubtful as the region is far too important to be abdicated without adequate balancing mechanisms. In all likelihood, the USA will continue to protect its defence deals and markets as the Saudis and other GCC countries are their biggest importers of arms and advanced equipment. In addition, huge Sovereign Wealth investments in the USA from these countries are very crucial. Geo-Strategic importance and Israeli security and the interests of its European and Asian partners like Japan and South Korea as well as counter-terrorism and anti-piracy efforts, including Afghanistan, are also equally important for the Americans. Even as it slows down, New Delhi gets a window of opportunity to try to be a reliable and trustworthy security partner and interlocutor and work closely with the USA, France, Japan and other European countries where necessary.
- Emergence of Turkey as a major player in the Gulf and in the Levant—Syria, Iraq and Libya, the Mediterranean and in Nagorno Karabakh by militarising and dronising its diplomacy—has become a game changer. Despite being a NATO member, it has taken several unilateral decisions for achieving Islamist leadership and Ottomanic ambitions.

From India's perspective, it is a key challenge and its influence with the Islamic Umma and extremist groups needs to be factored. So-called charitable activities in India from the region will have to be monitored to curtail any radicalisation activities. Politically, on Kashmir as well as in the OIC and UN, etc., we need to monitor overt references to alleged persecution of Muslims in India at the behest of Pakistan. However, if Ankara is able to recalibrate its outlook and approach towards New Delhi, beyond the prism of Islamabad, both sides have much to gain. Every effort should be made to garner that opportunity. A frank dialogue is necessary at the highest decision-making level to make them see reason.

- Russia has gained significantly in the Middle East, especially in Syria, Egypt, Algeria, and Libya and, to a greater extent, with Saudi Arabia and the UAE while having closer ties with other Arab countries. Its special relationship with Iran continues. It will try to fill the leadership gap in the region and may even collaborate with China. However, Moscow also seeks stability in the region and we could leverage our special and privileged partnership with them and goodwill in the region, even if it becomes issue-based.
- China is the biggest challenge for India in the region as, in the last decade or so, it has expanded its economic and defence and security outreach within the BRI context and is a major player. Its Digital and Health Silk Roads as well as forays in securing ports and hydrocarbon supplies from Iran to Israel speak for themselves. So far, it has been under the threshold not to provoke US security concerns and, in fact, benefited from it but the increased Sino-US rivalry will eventually play out in the region. Both Russia and China have used the region for their vaccines and technological embedding by entering into key AI-driven collaborations.
- The Middle East, especially the GCC, is crucial for India's trade, transit, energy security, and Diaspora welfare. Hence, it is essential that in the current uncertain scenario when even an unintended act could trigger a military confrontation and subsequent chaos, India, as a major stakeholder, should begin to reach out to all concerned to prevent war lest it be seen as passive, unreliable, irrelevant, and unwilling to take risks. At present India may not have the means to mediate in the regional issues despite tremendous goodwill; however, it may be necessary for an emerging regional and global power to eventually

get involved in reconciliation efforts with a like-minded and trusted group of countries. Trilateral cooperation should be envisaged as a means of alleviating some of the problems associated with India's lack of capacity and inability to deliver. Proactive engagement is essential.

- India should be able to work with regional powers for ensuring maritime security. The issue of freedom of navigation and SLOCs is vital in the Gulf for India's energy security and other interests. Informal coalitions with countries like Russia, Qatar, Turkey, Oman, and Iran on one side, and the USA, Israel, Saudi and the UAE on the other, could provide the exit ramps. Iran has to be part of the solution.
- More consistent regional engagement is necessary as global geographies from the Indo-Pacific to Eurasia undergo a transformation. While strengthening bilateral ties is important and New Delhi has had great success in that regard, the regional configuration as a whole should be prioritised.
- Perhaps a credible Special Envoy or several of them conversant with the region or countries could be appointed to conduct the outreach. However, they need to be provided resources, clear direction, and a reasonable tenure to avoid the implicit pitfalls.
- In order to keep the channels open at all times, it will be useful to have Track 1.5 or 2 dialogues with the GCC and Arab League and bilaterally with the participation of experts from various think tanks and experts. A standing group, supported fully by the Government, could be instituted to examine and broaden the access and contours of pressure points and opportunities at any given time.
- As crude oil and gas are essential for its economic progress, in the medium term India needs to ensure long-term uninterrupted supplies at a reasonable cost from alternative sources. It may be useful to explore a Buyers' Cartel with China, Japan, and South Korea and some others which could provide the requisite negotiating leverage. Since unilateralism is on the rise, India could consider creating some companies in the PPP mode that could work on bilateral exchange formats, i.e., Rupee-Rial, Rupee-Rouble or Rupee-Yuan while exploring options under the BRICS or other financial institutions which are not dependent on SWIFT or Bretton Woods Financial mechanisms.
- With over eight million Indians in the region, any spiralling conflict will pose an unprecedented challenge for the Government and so it

has to be ready for any eventuality at all times. While standard contingency plans are in place and may be scrambled at a short notice, it might be useful to institute a standing group of former ambassadors, defence attaches and intelligence officers who have experience in conflict zones and were instrumental in evacuations, etc.. and have retained their contacts in the region. The hope is that we will not have to cross that bridge but a boat should be ready to sail.

- Several countries, especially Saudi Arabia, Qatar, Turkey and Iran are actively involved in Tablighi or Islamic extremist groups. Their envoys and governments are in the loop. Bilateral or regional dialogue mechanisms to address such issues and aberrations should be formed to flag the issue and seek mitigation measures. The Israelis run their own ops in India essentially to cater to their own requirements but in the defence market competition they are spreading quite deep like the Russians, French and the Americans, in that order. Hence a closer watch is needed.
- Jordan, in terms of intel, is one of the best in the region and has excellent connections with Mossad and CIA as well as other Gulf agencies. Dy NSA-level mechanisms and the Aqaba Dialogue must be followed intensely. King Abdullah II wants closer relations with India, especially in security and counter-terrorism and is dead against Takfiris philosophies. He is impatient against terrorism. Coming from the lineage of Prophet Mohammed, he is a voice of reason and authority as indicated in his 'Amman Message' and discussions with PM Modi. Israel and Jordan have a very close intelligence and security partnership despite political challenges pertaining to Palestine. It provides a good channel.
- We could deploy assets and focus on the UAE, Israel, Saudi Arabia, Qatar, Iran, Oman, Egypt and Sudan as they like India and Indians and expect India to play a larger regional role and try becoming a security provider as well as trusted interlocutor. If we do not have the gumption for it, we might remain peripheral buyers of their resources rather than strategic collaborators and confidantes. We should also use our Diaspora for outreach with the right constituency.
- The NSA/Dy NSA/Agency-to-Agency-level cooperation must be intensified and all intelligence needs to be looked at in a comprehensive manner including economic, technological, defence,

cyber, space, healthcare, and education, to name a few. We need to saddle up in our defence and intelligence cooperation with the region to avert any major issues that might adversely impact our strategic advantages. In fact, we need to learn to securitise our 'Look West' policy beyond pursuing softer options from Vande Bharat to Vaccine diplomacy in the region to play a significant role where India actually counts, and the region looks up to her.

- Knowledge of language, culture and traditions are extremely important for cultivating assets and goodwill for P2P diplomacy in the region. Interpersonal relations and trust at all levels is key to befriend the people and leadership. It should also take advantage of India's cultural assets which could be used as soft power. Collaborations in the cultural spheres, including cinema, could provide a boost to India's engagement with the region.

- Commercial intelligence and techno-diplomacy are as necessary as the political or military; hence, special tools and training are necessary. Perhaps the skill sets of diplomats like those from IIT, medicine and engineering could be collated and developed into an internal techno savvy diplomatic corps since the 21st century is the technological century. While AI will rule, Humint will drive it. Bureaucratisation of intelligence and diplomacy has to be assiduously avoided. The asset base has to be expanded across geographies.

- For counter-terrorism, actionable intel is difficult but analysis, objectives and motives are equally important, timely dissemination and action more so. In today's age, monitoring social media and open communication platforms have been very successfully used by the ISIS and others in the past, hence a big challenge will be to keep track.

- In a changing regional scenario and possible calming of hotspots, it is essential to position Indian industry and enterprise through a proactive alignment of approaches, action and activity. The allocation of intent and resources needs to be planned for countries going into reconstruction like Libya, Iraq and Syria. As we have excellent relations with several countries in the region like the UAE, Bahrain, Saudi Arabia and Jordan we could work through them in post conflict reconstruction. In Libya, a more focussed approach would be needed so that we are not late in coming yet again. To begin with, it could engage in capacity-building exercises for training civil servants, and supply vaccines, health care, impart knowledge on the electoral process and parliamentary procedures and infrastructure development.

- We must have regional cooperative mechanisms as well with corresponding counterparts. A good beginning with the West Asian Quartet has been made. Regional frameworks have proliferated into a rich, overlapping global patchwork with a variety of political, security, and economic arrangements. Some are soft and do not go beyond occasional conferences; others have reached full institutionalization, with permanent secretariats, political bodies, and sectoral institutions. Most countries are members of several such frameworks, reflecting the complex webs of state interests in today's world. Regional frameworks have become a necessary element of the decentralizing global order.
- Build a team of eminent personalities comprising security experts and diplomats that could engage in informal engagement to set the priorities and address its interests to the West Asian states. There is also a need for general expertise and creation of specialists with in-depth knowledge of the region who could be appointed in the External Affairs Ministry and research think-tanks. On a multilateral level, India-West Asia summits could be organised to deepen engagement and it could participate in multi-lateral peace initiatives and offer its expertise in conflict resolution.
- An India-West Asia Strategic Forum with participation of key stakeholders and think tanks on both sides must be established that will go a long way in understanding and exchanging the strategies for the way forward.

In conclusion, it is time to reassess and reinforce our diplomatic capabilities commensurate to emerging crises in this volatile region and examine what will be the central premises of our West Asia policy, and whether, merely balancing the three poles (Arab, Iran and Israel) and equanimity would serve the purpose or an enhanced regional role would enable it to craft positive outcomes in the region. We have lost enough time on the excuse of a Pakistan syndrome; now the China syndrome need not replace it. Although we are beginning to develop an 'Extended Neighbourhood' Policy, it would be prudent to develop an 'Asia First' holistic policy with emphasis on strategic subsets for focussed demarche.

Contributors' Credentials

James M. Dorsey is an award-winning journalist and scholar. He is a senior fellow at the Middle East Institute of the National University of Singapore and an adjunct senior fellow at the S. Rajaratnam School of International Studies.

With over 25 years of regional expertise, **Dr. N. Janardhan** analyses and unravels the evolving multi-dimensional partnerships between the countries of the Gulf and Asia. As Senior Research Fellow at the Anwar Gargash Diplomatic Academy, Abu Dhabi, he also offers diplomats PGD and MA courses on Gulf and Asian foreign policies. The latest of his four academic publications is *The Arab Gulf's Pivot to Asia: From Transactional to Strategic Partnerships* (ed., Gerlach, 2020). With a PhD from Jawaharlal Nehru University, New Delhi, Dr. Janardhan is also Managing Assistant Editor of the *Journal of Arabian Studies* (Routledge).

Professor P.R. Kumaraswamy teaches contemporary Middle East in Jawaharlal Nehru University, New Delhi, and is the Honorary Director of Middle East Institute, New Delhi (www.mei.org.in).

Dr. Waiel S.H. Awwad, South Asia based Senior foreign journalist since 1979. Travelled extensively in most of South and South East Asian countries, interviewed many Asian leaders. Graduated from Delhi University, MBBS, PDA, studied post-graduation in journalism and underwent a number of programs in international law and human rights, diplomatic correspondents and video journalism from Delhi, London and Dubai. Dr Wael Awwad, an investigative correspondent, extensively covered wars in Sri Lanka, Kashmir, Afghanistan, West Asia, and the Gulf Region. He survived many attempts on his life during the coverage of wars in Jaffna, Kargil, Afghanistan and, lastly, as an embedded journalist with US troops, when he was ambushed in Iraq in 2003, captured and kept captive for 10 days and escaped execution with his team. Worked as South Asia Bureau Chief of Al Arabiya TV Channel-Dubai Media City, MBC-London, MBCFM Radio. Had a special program, Dateline South Asia in Arabic, the first of its kind with Asian News International (ANI). He is a radio correspondent and analyst for Kuwait, Oman and Damascus radio. Many of his writings have been published in English and Arabic in major newspapers and magazines. He has interviewed many world leaders from Asia and the Arab world.

Kingshuk Chatterjee is a Professor in the Department of History, Calcutta University, and an adjunct faculty at the Institute of Foreign Policy Studies, Calcutta University. He has also served as Deputy Director, Centre for Pakistan and West Asian Studies, Calcutta University. He has previously served as a Founding Professor in the Department of History, School of Humanities and Social Sciences at Shiv Nadar University and as Fellow at the Maulana Abul Kalam Azad Institute of Asian Studies. He was a Fulbright Scholar-in-Residence at the United States Naval Academy in Annapolis, Maryland. Chatterjee's area of expertise is in Middle Eastern politics and he specialises in Political Islam in the Modern World. He is the author of *Ali Shari'ati and the Shaping of Political Islam in Iran* and *A Split in the Middle: the Making of the Political Centre in Iran* (1987-2004). He is also the editor of titles like *India and the Middle East: Problems and Prospects; Pakistan and Afghanistan: the (In)Security Factor in India's Neighbourhood; and Arab Spring: Significance of the New Arab Awakening; The Dilemma of Popular Sovereignty in the Middle East: Power from or to the People?*.

Dr. Michael Barak is a senior researcher at the Institute for Counter-terrorism where he serves as the head of the Global Jihad & Palestinian terrorism desks (ICT). He is a lecturer at the Lauder School of Government Diplomacy and Strategy in the Reichman University (IDC). He is also a senior researcher at the Moshe Dayan Centre for Middle Eastern and African Studies (MDC) at Tel Aviv University. He has written several books.

H.E. Dr. Jawad Anani obtained a PhD Degree in Economics from the University of Georgia, USA. Since then, he has held several high positions in the Jordanian government including Deputy Prime Minister, several Ministerial and Deputy Minister Posts; Chief of the Royal Court, President of the Royal Scientific Society and Senate Member. Dr. Anani is well known for championing and leading privatization in Jordan and personally supervised the privatization of Royal Jordanian Airlines, Telecom and the cement factory. His contributions in the private sector include the establishment of three companies, running a consultancy firm and driving the governance in both public and private sectors in Jordan. He chaired the boards of many public institutions and was appointed as a member in another lately, Chairman for Lafarge Cement Jordan. Dr. Anani is a frequent contributor to various media outlets in English and Arabic with more than seventy scientific research papers and a number of books. Dr. Anani currently is a distinguished Professor at Talal Abu Ghazaleh University College for Innovation since May 2019. Dr. Anani is appointed as the Chairman of the Board of Trustees, Al Balaqa Applied University as of 9.8.2021.

Prof. Dr. Sahar A.M. Al-Majali, Professor of Political History, Princess Alia University College, Al-Balqa' Applied University, Jordan,

Nina Slama is a Guest Lecturer and Teaching Assistant at the Interdisciplinary Centre (IDC) Herzliya. She holds a M.A. in International Relations from Bar-Ilan University (BIU). Her thesis focuses on "Foreign Policy Turning Points: India's Israel Policy 1948-2018". She also holds a B.A. in Government, Diplomacy and Strategy, and a Certificate in European Studies from IDC Herzliya. Her areas of interest are international relations, India's politics and foreign policy, India-Israel relations, Israel's foreign policy, and the European Union. She is fluent in English, French and Hebrew.

Dr. Duygu Çağla Bayram is an India researcher based in Ankara, Turkey. She has a PhD in International Relations since December 2020 and is the author of a book titled *"New Course in Turbulent Waters: The Indo-Pacific Narrative and India"* which was published in Turkish in July 2021. Her academic interests focus on Indian politics and the Indo-Pacific region. She can be reached at caglabayramm@hotmail.com and she tweets @drcagla_

Prof. Dr. Hüseyin Bağci, teaches at Department of International Relations, Middle East Technical University, Ankara, Turkey.

Lt Gen (Dr.) Rakesh Sharma was commissioned in the Gorkha Rifles in 1977, and had a career in the Army spanning forty years. He has had extensive operational experience in Jammu and Kashmir, the North-East and on the western borders. The officer had trained the Botswana Army for three years in Africa, and attended the National War College at Abuja, Nigeria. Lt Gen Rakesh Sharma attended the NDC at New Delhi. He was Research Fellow at IDSA and has done PhD in Defence Studies. General Rakesh Sharma commanded the Fire and Fury Corps in Ladakh, facing both Pakistan and China. The General was the Adjutant General responsible for the Human Resource Management of the Indian Army. He is a regular participant in seminars, lectures in various institutions, and regularly writes for newspapers, military journals and contributes chapters to edited books. He is currently on the Executive Council of the Institute for Defence Studies and Analyses (IDSA) and Global Counter Terrorism Council (GCTC) and Distinguished Fellow with Vivekananda International Foundation (VIF) and Centre for Land Warfare Studies (CLAWS).

Vice Admiral Satish Soni retired from the Indian Navy on 29 February 2016 after 40 years of service. During the last ten years of his career, he held the appointments of Flag Officer Commanding in Chief Eastern Naval Command, Flag Officer Commanding in Chief Southern Naval Command, Deputy Chief of Naval Staff, Commandant National Defence Academy, Chief of Staff Eastern Naval Command, Flag Officer Commanding Eastern Fleet and Assistant Chief of Naval Staff (Human Resource Development). Post retirement he has been writing, travelling, participating in seminars and discussions. He is a member of the Governing Council and a Distinguished Fellow of the United Service Institution of India, Delhi. He is also a life trustee of the Dayal Singh Trust and mentors schools and colleges of the Trust.

K.P. Vijayalakshmi is a Fulbrighter, Salzburg Seminar Fellow and Professor of US Studies at the Centre for Canadian, US and Latin American Studies, School of International Studies, JNU, New Delhi and Honorary Adjunct Visiting faculty at the International Strategic Studies Programme (ISSP,) National Institute of Advanced Studies (NIAS), Indian Institute of Science Campus, Bangalore. She is Executive Council member at the MP-IDSA New Delhi. Her research interests include: Role of US in 21st Century, US Domestic Politics, Congress and Elections, US, Asia and Emerging Geopolitics, Indo-US relations, Rise of China, Prospects of Scientific Cooperation, Decision making in US -India Foreign and Strategic policy, National Security, Democracies and Gender. Recent works include: *Synergising Global Strategic Objectives to Policy: Indo-US Strategic Partnership* and *Biden Administration and Indo Pacific Axis, What to expect from Biden's walk back to JCPOA with Iran?*

Dr. Omair Anas teaches International Relations at Ankara Yildirim Beyazit University. He is an expert faculty for Gulf Affairs at ORSAM. Omair Anas holds M.Phil and PhD from India's Jawaharlal Nehru University in West Asian Studies. Prior to joining Ankara Yildirim Beyazit University in 2018, he was a research fellow at the Indian Council of World Affairs in New Delhi spring 2015-2018. He was Visiting Scholar at Freie University Berlin, Germany in 2012-2013. He specializes and teaches Non-Western International Relations, Middle East-Asia Relations, Religion and Politics and Arab Media And Culture. He is edited a volume *Turkey's Asia Relations* (Palgrave 2022). He has publsihed several papers and chapters on India-West Asia relations, and Arab Media Studies. He has published commentaries on Middle Eastern affairs in prominent media outlets including in *Middle East Eye*, *Daily Sabah*, *First Post*, *Indian Express*, Observer Research Foundation, Indian Council of World Affairs, and Al Jazeera Studies Center.

Amb Anil Trigunayat has been a professional Indian Diplomat for over three decades serving India's national interests across continents from Asia to Africa to Europe and Americas including Russia and USA . Prior to his superannuation in 2016 he served as India's Ambassador to Jordan, Libya and Malta. He is a regular commentator on foreign affairs and a prolific writer. Currently apart from his association with various Think Tanks, Strategy Groups and Chambers of Commerce & Industries in India and abroad, he is a Distinguished Fellow with prestigious Vivekananda International Foundation; heading their West Asia Experts Group. His key areas of interest include West Asia, Africa, and Russia. He is a Peace Ambassador with Unity Earth, Australia as well as a Rotarian serving the society to the extent possible.

*

Index

*